ALCOHOL PROBLEMS
AND ALCOHOLISM

ALCOHOL PROBLEMS AND ALCOHOLISM

A Comprehensive Survey

James E. Royce

SEATTLE UNIVERSITY

THE FREE PRESS
A Division of Macmillan Publishing Co., Inc.
NEW YORK

Collier Macmillan Publishers
LONDON

The Free Press
A Division of Macmillan Publishing Co., Inc.
866 Third Avenue, New York, N.Y. 10022

Collier Macmillan Canada, Ltd.

Library of Congress Catalog Card Number: 81-67421

Printed in the United States of America

printing number
                    10

Library of Congress Cataloging in Publication Data

Royce, James E.
    Alcohol problems and alcoholism.

    Bibliography: p.
    Includes index.
    1. Alcoholism.   I. Title.
HV5035.R9   362.2'92   81-67421
ISBN 0-02-927540-7   AACR2

To the many, many alcoholics—
recovered, recovering, and still suffering—
from whom I have learned so much

Contents

Preface

A VAST AMOUNT of literature exists on the use of alcohol and on alcoholism. Contributions come from a multitude of disciplines, from professionals and from laymen, from objective researchers and from fiery proselytizers. The scientific literature contains many reports on single facets of alcohol-related conditions; there are also many excellent collections of such papers, all by different authors with only minimal editorial efforts to integrate them. And semipopular writings form a large additional body of literature. There does not seem to be any general survey of the whole field that is suitable as a college textbook or any integrated formulation by a single author that provides the general reader with an overall, balanced understanding. This book is an attempt to fill that double need.

This book will also attempt to provide a general perspective on alcohol use. A few examples of the problems in doing so will suffice. Alcohol use is involved in many more problems than alcoholism. In recent years excessive use of alcohol is more often than not combined with the use of other drugs. Theories of the causes of alcoholism are varied and contradictory, treatments and the goals of treatment are controversial, prevention is still more of a hope than a reality. Vested interests, which range from the alcohol beverage industry to those who would restore prohibition, try to influence what is thought and done. Research continually uncovers new facts. Amid such a clamor of voices, there is a need for a dispassionate survey and evaluation.

It would be more than naive to imagine this will be easy. Not only is the subject matter broad, complex, and changing, but emotions play a large part in shaping attitudes. Bitter memories of prohibition, lingering moralistic do-goodism. libertarian resentment of any infringement on one's freedom to drink, alarm at the tragic death toll from alcohol-related accidents and the medical complications of alcoholism, the perennial popularity of drinking songs—all attest to the wide divergence of values placed on the use, excessive or otherwise, of alcoholic beverages. The joys of wine have been praised by poet and psalmist for thousands of years, yet we all feel uncomfortable when passing the skid-road derelict lying in a drunken stupor.

The field of alcoholism is full of controversy. Although one of man's oldest problems, anything like a scientific or professional approach to it is relatively recent. The result is that everybody and nobody is an expert.

On the one hand there is vast ignorance as to causes, nature, cure, and prevention, even among the most knowledgeable, so nobody's an expert. On the other hand it's like the weather: Everybody has an opinion, and many are quite willing to be dogmatic about it. Being a young field, it is largely pioneer territory to which many different and opposing factions are laying claim, with the inevitably resulting jealousies and rivalries. Since all are supposed to be concerned with helping the sick alcoholic, one could paraphrase Winston Churchill thus: "Never have so many fought each other so bitterly in a common cause."

The concept of alcoholism as a disease is looked upon as progress by one group and escape by another. How do we reconcile the disease concept with that of moral responsibility? How do we implement the new Uniform Alcoholism and Intoxication Treatment Act without making our detoxification units just a more expensive medical version of the old revolving-door drunk tank? How are we to discourage premature drinking among youth without putting a premium on drinking as a sign of maturity? These and a dozen other questions challenge our collective wisdom. But at least we must start with as clear a picture as possible.

One of the most exciting developments has been the recognition by professionals that standard academic courses have not given them expertise in this specialized field, and likewise by recovered alcoholics that the experience of recovery is not enough: special training and professionally supervised experience is necessary to prepare either to perform effectively in what is being called the "new profession" of alcoholism workers. This book is intended for both groups, and is based on experience in working with both.

Why a book on alcohol rather than on counseling or treating alcoholics? Because there is nothing more important than knowing what alcoholism is—except perhaps knowing what it is *not*. In a national survey of recovered alcoholics who were asked what elements were most helpful in the therapy process, in spite of the fact that they were all college graduates, they ranked as the most important element in their recovery "learning about alcoholism" (Fichter, 1977a, p. 460).*

Thirty years ago Dr. Selden Bacon of the Yale Center for Alcohol Studies reviewed the extant materials in alcohol education and found errors in 98 percent of them. Although that situation has since improved, both professionals and recovered alcoholics come to the field with preconceived ideas that prove to be incorrect or incomplete. Much is known about counseling, but the lack seems to be a real understanding of the nature of alcoholism. As former president of two national psychological associations, the author can say without being an outsider that this is true of

---

*For easy reading, only a brief identification of sources is in the text. Full identification will be found in the General Bibliography. If there is more than one book or article by the same author published during the same year, they are listed as 1977a, 1977b, etc.

most psychotherapists. But today there is a fair consensus among alcohol specialists on the essential points. Granted, there is still much we do not know; this book will focus on what we do know. Available knowledge is not being used; as the farmer retorted to the pushy book salesman, "Mister, I don't farm right now half as well as I know."

The plan of the book is fairly obvious from the Table of Contents. Part I deals with alcohol and its effects, Part II with alcoholism in its various ramifications, and an attempt at understanding the nature of alcoholism by exploring its complex causality. Part III is on primary and secondary prevention, and Part IV deals with treatment and rehabilitation.

The author's interest in the field began in 1942, through discussions with Father Ed Dowling, S.J., a close friend of Dr. Bob and Bill W., the cofounders of Alcoholics Anonymous. This led to some thirty years of counseling alcoholics and their spouses. He is now senior professor of psychology at Seattle University, where he began his "Symposium on Alcoholism" in the winter of 1949 50, probably the oldest college course on alcoholism in the country to be offered as part of the regular undergraduate curriculum during the school year. He is still teaching it as the basic course in the Alcohol Studies Program of which he is the director. He is neither a recovered alcoholic nor a prohibitionist, but a teacher with no treatment to sell and no special cause to plead. Always interdisciplinary in approach, the symposium has, over the years, gained a reputation for broad balance, representing all viewpoints. The hope is that this book can make a real contribution in clarifying concepts and balancing attitudes toward our nation's number-one public health problem.

JAMES E. ROYCE, S.J.

Acknowledgements

Joan K. Jackson, Ph. D., has provided invaluable service as collaborator, contributing to every aspect of the book and especially the bibliographical. James W. Smith, M.D., and Nola Moore, M.D., are foremost among the many physicians to whom I am indebted. Of the many others, space permits that I mention only Jean Keeffe of Seattle University. The book's shortcomings are to be attributed to the author.

Thanks are due to the following for permission to quote from copyrighted materials:

A.A. World Services, Inc.
Al-Anon Family Group Headquarters, Inc.
Annals of Internal Medicine
American Journal of Psychiatry
National Council on Alcoholism, Inc.
Quarterly Journal of Studies on Alcohol

PART I

Alcohol

CHAPTER 1

Introduction

IN MOST MINDS the word *alcoholic* conjures up an image of a skid-road bum. (Incidentally, *Skid Road* is the original term, named for Yesler Way in Seattle, where logs were skidded down to Yesler's mill; *skid row* is a later version by analogy with Cannery Row.) Yet only about 3 percent of alcoholics are on skid road. Many do not think of alcohol as a drug at all, only as the social beverage it is to most people who use it. Most do not realize the immense problems related to alcohol, of which alcoholism is only one. Hence this book is not just about alcoholism.

These and other facts about alcohol are distorted by our emotionally charged attitudes toward drinking, drunkenness, and alcoholism. These attitudes are the result of many factors: family situation, sociocultural experience, biological differences, prohibition, differing religious beliefs, and political, economic, and personal feelings unique to each individual. Obvious as they may seem, we must spell out some distinctions that are ignored in most arguments on the subject.

Drinking. Abstinence from alcohol is the opposite of drinking. Technically anyone who drinks alcoholic beverages, however rarely and moderately, is a drinker. About 71 percent of Americans over eighteen drink at least occasionally; most are neither drunkards nor alcoholics. In fact, one estimate is that 7 percent of drinkers consume 40 percent of our

3

beverage alcohol, another that 10 percent of drinkers consume 60 percent, whereas many of those technically classed as drinkers have only a New Year's toast or the like. Less than half of American "drinkers" use alcohol more than once a month.

Drunkenness.   Temperance is the opposite of drunkenness. As indicated above, most drinkers do not get drunk. In Chapter 3 we shall see how the prohibitionists created untold confusion by assuming that everyone who drinks is a drunkard. On the other hand, anybody can get drunk on a given occasion; they might not even be a drinker in the usual sense of the term. To the naive guest at a wedding reception or the person honored at a retirement banquet, the champagne seems much like ginger ale; a subsequent arrest for driving while intoxicated (DWI) is not presumptive of a drinking problem or alcoholism. However, intoxication even by nonalcoholics is a major source of both civil and criminal problems: battered spouses and children, rape, fights, homicides, unwanted pregnancies, poor health, suicides, lawsuits, family disruptions, job loss, and a major share of accidents—not only traffic but also home, boat, small plane, and industrial. The degree of intoxication need not be that required to be legally drunk, as we shall see in Chapter 5.

Alcoholism.   This is the state of a person whose excessive use of alcohol creates serious life problems. An alcoholic may never get drunk, as in the Delta type (maintenance drinker) common in France and described in Chapter 6. They may not even drink, as in the case of the million or so recovered alcoholics who still identify themselves as such (Chapter 10). Alcoholics may be young or old, male or female, black or white, banker or bum, genius or mentally retarded.

Alcoholics

What kinds of people are alcoholics? A large body of research data has accumulated on this subject, and there have been intensive educational efforts to make these facts known to the public. Yet the old stereotypes persist and must be dealt with before any meaningful discussion of alcoholism can occur.

Skid Road?   It is essential to eradicate right now the stereotype of the alcoholic as a skid-road, old, male, weak-willed, inferior derelict. If 3 percent of alcoholics are on skid road, the other 97 percent of American alcoholics have jobs, homes and families. About 45 percent of alcoholics are in professional and managerial positions, 25 percent are white collar workers, and 30 percent are manual laborers. Over half have attended college; only 13 percent have not finished high school. No suggestion of skid road there. Physicians, brokers, attorneys, judges, dentists, and clergymen all have a high incidence of alcohol problems.

Instead of being inferior, the intelligence of alcoholics is slightly above that of comparable groups; for example, compared with other employees in their company. Alcoholics also appear to be superior in talent and sensitivity. Hence it is not mere emotional loyalty that prompts a spouse or foreman to assert that their alcoholic is "the finest" when not drinking. This is important, because both alcoholic and spouse tend to deny the problem by saying that the person is too intelligent to be an alcoholic.

FIGURE 1. Facts about alcoholics

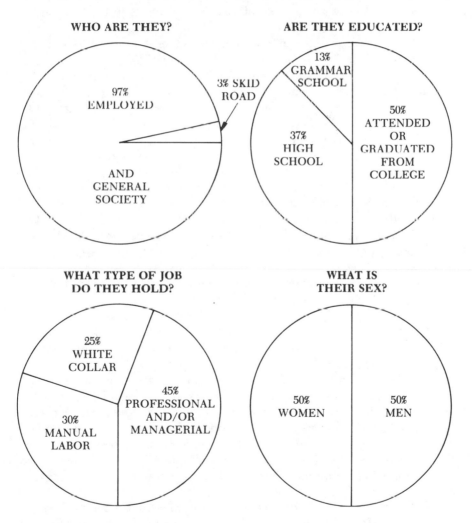

Weak Will? Anyone with experience in the field can testify that when a alcoholic needs a drink there is no one on earth with a stronger will: They will get a drink come hell, high water, or prohibition. The notion of weak-willed, moral depravity rather than a compulsive disorder stems from the days before the disease concept of alcoholism was accepted, as it is now by the World Health Organization and important national professional associations.

Mentally Ill? The notion that a typical alcoholic is a person who drinks to escape from some inner conflict is a complex question that is addressed in Chapters 9 and 10. Suffice it to say here that research now shows that about 80 percent of alcoholics began drinking for the same reasons as anybody else: custom, sociability, relaxation, or just to feel good.

Male? The ratio of men to women alcoholics is often still reported as four or five to one. This is probably due to the double standard in our society regarding women and drunkenness. Women alcoholics are often better able to hide their drinking at home (though in the business world they may be more exposed than men), and, in any case, are not as likely to be counted by the fact gatherers. Even when they die of alcoholism, the diagnosis is written as a total liver failure or something else like it, because the doctor is a gentleman and it's not ladylike to be an alcoholic. Hence the statistics are questionable. If the truth were known, the ratio of male to female alcoholics in this country is probably fifty-fifty, an opinion shared by such national authorities as M. Block, L. Cloud, R.G. Bell, R. Fox, M. Mann, M. Nellis, and M. Chafetz (see Homiller, 1977, p. 6). For this reason, the pronoun "they" will usually be used in this book when referring to alcoholics even when the singular would be gramatically more correct, since English just does not have a suitable pronoun for the clumsy he/she or her/his. An occasional lapse is not to be taken as sexist, but simply as due to the inadequacy of our language.

Old? One does not have to drink heavily for thirty or forty years in order to develop alcoholism. About 700,000 American teenagers have serious alcohol problems. There are full-blown alcoholics who are ten or eleven years old. A visitor at open AA meetings will frequently hear, "I was an alcoholic at the time I took my first drink." Although this evidence is subjective, it is in accord with the percentages reported in the scientific literature, which range from 10 or 15 percent up to one estimate that 60 percent of alcoholics are such from the onset of drinking. The average age in AA as well as of the clients in treatment centers has steadily decreased as recognition of the problem becomes more acceptable.

Polydrug. Lastly, we must correct the idea that alcoholics misuse only alcohol. It used to be that alcoholics might switch from beer to hard liquor and eventually to cheap fortified wine, but an alcoholic stayed with alcohol. And an addict might move from barbiturates to morphine to heroin, but was not an alcoholic. This former picture is true today only of some older male alcoholics. Especially among women and youth, mixing alcohol with other drugs is most common and constitutes what is called the polydrug scene. One is skeptical in the biological and social sciences of universal statements, but we hear now of studies where 100 percent of the young people are involved with at least two drugs (alcohol and marijuana), and many with a third. Alcoholism workers often assert they have not seen a "pure" alcoholic in several years. It must be noted that prescription drugs like barbiturates (sleeping pills), tranquilizers, and amphetamines (speed), are more of a problem than street drugs like heroin, marijuana, cocaine, and Phencyclidine (PCP, "angel dust"), although these latter cause serious trouble. The point is that both prescription and street drugs are now combined with alcohol, with devastating results due to what we shall describe as potentiation or synergism.

Alcohol as a Drug

We reject the phrase "alcohol and drugs" because this implies that alcohol is not a drug, and insist on "alcohol and *other* drugs." But is alcohol really a drug? In every sense of the word. Alcohol can produce all the classic signs of addiction: changes in tolerance (the ability to function with higher levels of blood alcohol affecting the brain), cellular adaptation or tissue change, and withdrawal. Chemically very similar to ether and chloroform, alcohol is a sedative, a hypnotic, a tranquilizer, a narcotic, and sometimes a hallucinogenic. For centuries it was our only anesthetic, although for practical reasons a very poor one. If it were not dangerously addictive, it would be hailed as the world's greatest tranquilizer. It is most like the barbiturates, except for three important differences:

1. *Stimulant or depressant?* Alcohol is perhaps the only common drug that gives a lift or stimulates before acting as a sedative or depressant. Some of this is only pseudostimulation resulting from the depression of inhibitory centers in the brain. But the initial effect of alcohol on tissue is to irritate or agitate or stimulate, as well as to provide quick caloric energy. Some research evidence indicates that this is more true for alcoholics than for others, perhaps right from the beginning of their drinking career; and it is this initial stimulation that many beginning alcoholics seem to look for rather than the later sedative effect. (See Chapter 5.)

2. *Selective addiction.* The reason why alcohol is often not thought of as a drug is because in contrast to other drugs it becomes addictive to only one in a dozen of its users. Most people drink moderately all their lives, with perhaps an occasional drunk. Why only some drinkers become addicted to alcohol is not known for certain; we shall examine this question

when we treat of causality. The fact that alcohol seems safe for most people makes it harder to accept that it is a dangerous drug for a minority of nine or ten million, making alcohol by far the biggest problem drug in America. The important thing here is that people differ in their reaction to alcohol.

3. *Socially acceptable.* One is tempted to call alcoholism a respectable addiction. Millions of people casually invite friends in for a drink who would be horrified at hearing "Come over tonight and we'll shoot a little heroin, or drop a few barbs." Even when there is misuse, we pass it off lightly or with minor embarrassment and a remark that everybody has a few too many once in a while. How often do we think of drunkenness as a drug overdose? Serving drinks is a mark of hospitality, and failure to do so smacks of puritanical prohibition. As a result of these attitudes, even when a friend is in serious trouble with alcohol there is a tendency to minimize or excuse the behavior rather than face the issue of debilitating and even terminal illness.

Definition of Alcoholism

There are nearly as many definitions of alcoholism as there are those who write or lecture on the subject. Justice Benjamin Cardozo once said, " 'peril lurks in definitions' is an ancient maxim of law." If you appointed a committee of ten people to the task of formulating the definition of an elephant, you would find them three months later still unable to agree on an acceptable wording, even though all of them knew perfectly well at the start what an elephant is. Alcoholism is certainly more controversial.

Why bother to define? There are many reasons. The alcoholism worker must have a definition that will stand up in court under cross-examination, whether alcoholism is being used as a defense or as grounds for involuntary commitment. The counselor must be able to proffer a definition that will induce the client to accept treatment, and be neither so loose nor so rigid that clients can say in their denial, "That doesn't apply to me!" (In this vein, an alcoholic is said to define alcoholism as a disease that *others* get.) If insurance companies are going to pay health benefits for treatment, they are going to demand a strict definition of the object of their dollars. Physicians need solid criteria for making a diagnosis. Some of the fallacies occurring in the controversy about conditioning alcoholics to drink socially stem from dubious definitions of who is an alcoholic. Industrial alcoholism programs need to be precise in order to protect the rights of both labor and management. Defining alcoholism as a disease has moved it from the criminal justice system and the drunk tank to the health care system and treatment centers, and is crucial to any prevention campaign.

Problems in Definition

A good definition must be coterminous with whatever is being defined. A definition of alcoholism as "a horrible disease that affects the whole person" is unacceptable, because it is so broad it can apply to cancer or schizophrenia. Conversely, to define alcoholism in terms of one type of alcoholic is likewise unsatisfactory, because it misses many other types of alcoholics. Alcoholics cannot be defined as those who get drunk every time they drink, nor as those with a prolonged history of drinking, nor as those who crave alcohol, nor as those with any other single symptom.

A common fallacy is to define alcoholism by the amount or beverage consumed. "He only drinks beer" ignores the fact that the same alcohol is present in the most expensive liquor and in the cheapest beer or wine. At Shadel Hospital for alcoholics in Seattle, where the clientele is largely from levels well above what is considered a beer income, 15 percent of the patients have never drunk anything but beer. People in Australia, New Zealand, and other countries with an incidence of alcoholism as high as that in America, drink beer as their primary source of alcohol. Yet our laws and our advertising still imply a difference.

The amount of alcohol drunk and the frequency of drinking (quantity/frequency index) is also a misleading way to define alcoholism. Because of individual differences some alcoholics might actually drink less than some nonalcoholics. More important than how much one drinks is the question of *how* one drinks; that is, whether one just enjoys alcohol or *uses* it: what alcohol does for the person, both in the immediate and in the long term. Average consumption per week or month means nothing. An Italian might spread out fourteen ounces of absolute alcohol per week over fourteen meals with lots of spaghetti and not be alcoholic, while an American alcoholic might consume the same amount of absolute alcohol in the form of a quart of 86 proof whiskey each Saturday night with total intoxication. Moreover, alcoholics either lie about the amount they drink, or just don't remember.

A current vogue in some circles is to define an alcoholic as one who cannot predict what will happen after one drink. But one can think of many alcoholics who can predict exactly what will happen: They'll get drunk! Or, in the case of the maintenance type alcoholic, they may predict with certainty that they will not get drunk, but will continue to drink. In either case, one is an alcoholic while not fitting that definition.

Some define alcoholism by one criterion set out by the World Health Organization (Seeley, 1959), or by Mark Keller (1960), which talks of drinking alcoholic beverages in excess of customary dietary usage or social use of the community. This confuses average and normal, a common fallacy discussed in *Personality and Mental Health* (Royce, 1964, pp. 48–57). In a "dry" southern town one beer on a hot day would exceed custom, but that is hardly alcoholism. In a northern village where every adult male gets drunk every weekend, the mere fact that this is customary usage does not preclude the presence of alcoholism. Of course, the above-mentioned definitions go on to include our notion of interference with health or other normal functioning. Disease or dysfunction is a departure from that, regardless of custom or social usage.

The "grand old man" of the scientific study of alcoholism, Dr. E. M. Jellinek, once defined alcoholism as any use of alcoholic beverages that causes any damage to the individual or society (1960, p. 35). This is obviously too broad, for one could hardly be classified as alcoholic because one turned an ankle as a result of the only drink one ever took in his life. I recall Mark Keller (whom we will meet in Chapter 3) saying in 1969 that Jellinek meant this as a joke; at any rate, it forces us to get more scientific.

A Working Definition

We define alcoholism as *a chronic illness or disorder characterized by some loss of control over drinking, with habituation or addiction to the drug alcohol, or causing interference in any major life function: for example, health, job, family, friends or the law.*

a) *Some loss of control* is involved, but it need not be total. Most alcoholics can take one or two drinks under certain circumstances without getting drunk, but this does not prove they are not alcoholic. Sooner or later they are in trouble again. Total loss of control is usually seen only in late-stage, deteriorated alcoholics. Loss of *consistent* control is sufficient for diagnosis.

The loss can be over *how much* they drink, or over *when* they drink, or both. One may not get drunk, but drinking more than one intends or drinking at inappropriate times would indicate alcoholism.

b) *Dependence or need* can be either psychological or physiological. *Habituation* (discussed in Chapters 5 and 10) is psychological dependence or need. As the poster slogan says, "If you have to drink to be social, that's not social drinking." Discomfort if deprived of alcohol and inability to quit on one's own even if desired are symptoms, even if no physical need is apparent. *Addiction* is physiological (physical) dependence or need, with its familiar signs of increased tolerance initially, cellular adaption, and withdrawal symptoms. One physically needs a drink to function.

The tendency in America is to focus on addiction, and to dismiss habituation as "only" psychological need. Yet in every respect except the physical dangers of withdrawal, psychological dependence can be more devastating (Hazelden, 1974). To appreciate this one has only to look at the way compulsive gambling can destroy a family.

c) *Interference with normal functioning.* The interference must be notable or habitual, to avoid the case of the turned ankle from one drink. This criterion has been summed up as "when alcohol means more to a person than the problems it causes." This is the least subjective criterion and closest to an operational or behavioral definition, and can be quantified for research purposes. Anybody can be arrested for drunk driving once, for example, but three DWI's in the same year suggest alcoholism. Likewise if drinking is involved in more than one fight where there is serious injury or a lethal weapon is used.

This portion complements the earlier parts of the definition, because the fact that one continues to drink after he has been told his health or marriage or job is endangered would indicate a sick dependence and some loss of control; otherwise why continue?

Let us round out our definition by noting three common errors in diagnosis:

a) Joe can drink anybody under the table. He is not safe, but rather in serious danger. Increased tolerance, the ability to function with higher than average amounts of alcohol in the bloodstream, is the first sign of physical addiction.

b) Cutting down or quitting drink for a period of time (going on the water wagon) is not proof that one has it under control. Most do not realize that this is a classic symptom of alcoholism. The true social drinker does not need to play these games of control.

c) The assertion, "I can take it or leave it alone," especially when made often or with vehemence, is usually indicative of denial and betrays the alcoholic. The social drinker doesn't feel compelled to say such things. This subtle self-deception is so characteristic that we have long defined an alcoholic as "one who says I can quit any time I want to."

For practical use in identifying alcoholics and problem drinkers during an initial interview or after apprehension on a drunk-driving charge, several tests have been developed which are easily administered and scored. The best known are the Michigan Alcoholism Screening Test or MAST (Selzer, 1971; Favazza, 1974) and the Mortimer-Filkins Test or HSRI test (Jacobson, 1976a, 1976b) which is perhaps the most thoroughly researched. W. R. Miller (1976) reviews some 200 attempts to make alcoholism scales. More medically oriented are the definition and criteria developed by the National Council on Alcoholism, which appear as an Appendix to this chapter.

Primary versus Secondary Alcoholism

Unfortunately, the terms primary and secondary have acquired ambiguous and even contrary or reversed meanings in the alcohol literature. In this book we shall use *primary* when the alcoholism is the basic pathology, regardless of cause, and *secondary* to refer to alcoholism as a symptom of some other disorder. In many cases "the symptom has become the disease," and the alcoholism must first be treated before psychotherapy for other conditions is even possible. Remove the alcohol, and you will find anything: normal people, neurotics, sociopaths, mentally retarded, psychotics. Any psychopathology may then be either the cause of the alcoholism or the effect of the alcoholic drinking on the brain.

Alcoholic versus Problem Drinker

Scientific researchers like W. Madsen, D. Cahalan, and S. Bacon rightly insist that to gather meaningful and comparable data one must have an operational, quantifiable definition that guarantees consistency as to which cases are counted as alcoholics and which are not.

But clinicians and field workers often find it advantageous to ignore such precision and not allow themselves to get trapped into games of labeling or arguments about whether a client is or is not an alcoholic. Even research-oriented scholars are willing to use the terms *alcoholic* and *problem drinker* synonymously (Selzer, 1971; Schuckit, 1976a, p. 28), and say that it is a mistake to focus on whether a person is alcoholic rather than on what problems a person has with alcohol (E.M. Pattison, 1967, p. 127). A survey of the literature indicates a general tendency to use the term *alcoholic* when loss of control and dependence are stressed, and *problem drinker* when the emphasis is on interference with normal life functions. Some use *problem drinker* to express psychological dependence, and *alcoholic* when there is physical dependence. There is no standard or sacrosanct terminology here. One could argue the pros and cons of dropping the term *alcoholic* entirely:

Con. In view of the great progress that has been made in the last few decades to eliminate the social stigma attached to alcoholism, it would seem a strategic mistake to reverse the trend. Dropping the term would cause the alcoholism movement, after having espoused the term, to lose face before the medical profession, the courts, and the insurance companies. There would be a loss in continuity of research. It might feed the denial system of some alcoholics, encouraging them to delude themselves into attempts at social drinking. A major loss would be the sense of identity that a million people feel within the fellowship of Alcoholics Anonymous.

Pro. Yet dropping the term would have its advantages. In spite of progress, alcoholism is still odious in the minds of many. Some wish to name it Jellinek's disease, as we now call leprosy Hansen's disease. The stereotype of the skid-road derelict or the "fallen woman" prostitute and the suggestion of insanity still cling to the word, making early detection more difficult and fostering a defeatism or sense of hopelessness not warranted by current success rates in rehabilitation.

For alcoholics in the denial stage the term raises their defenses, and many an initial interview goes smoother if there is no attempt to hang the label "alcoholic" on a new client but just calmly explore together whether drink is causing some problems. If the client later wishes to label himself, perhaps in an A.A. meeting, the victory was well worth the tactic. (A.A. members working in the field too often take for granted the ease with which such words are used among them now, and forget how defensive they were in the denial phase.)

Dropping the term might make it easier to sell a program to industry, and lessen the denial or defensiveness of the spouse and family by making them less self-conscious. Alcohol education would be easier and more positive, with less scare tactics centered around alcoholism. Traffic problems and court referrals might be handled more easily if alcoholism were brought into the picture under a different name.

The change might even stimulate a fresh, innovative approach to research. Alcoholism is not a single disease entity like TB or malaria, and cross-cultural differences further confuse the issue. The Jellinek formula puts too much emphasis on cirrhosis of the liver. Data might be more objectively gathered from emergency hospitals and police stations if not contaminated by subjective perceptions of alcoholism, as in the Wolf and Chafetz (1965) study where the physician missed the diagnosis half the time if the patient was well-dressed and not unkempt. Last and perhaps most important, the connotations of the term *alcoholic* prevent many women from being properly diagnosed, which not only yields misleading statistics but keep these women from getting the help they need.

What to do? As in many aspects of this field, there is no clear answer. Alternate terms such as *substance abuse* suggest choice rather than compulsion, and like *chemical dependency* they seem to detract from the fact that alcohol is our biggest drug problem. Willoughby (1979) presents a strong case for dropping *alcoholic* in favor of *alcohol troubled person* (ATP) and although the term is clumsy his reasoning is sound. *Problem drinking behavior* is more acceptable to many workers and might be the best answer (Krimmel, 1971, pp. 15–17). But if alcohol is interfering with any major life area then you have a problem and you'd better do something about it, whether you call it alcoholism or problem drinking or mashed potatoes.

Sources

Full identification of sources given here or referred to in the chapter will be found in the General Bibliography. What is given here does not pretend to be exhaustive but merely to list some of the more useful and available items suggested for further reading. Listing here does not mean full agreement; the reader must decide on particular points.

Two important bibliographical resources in the United States are the Classified Abstract Archives of Alcohol Literature (CAAAL) initiated at Yale and continued by the Rutgers Center of Alcohol Studies in New Brunswick, N.J., and the bibliographical search service provided by the National Clearinghouse for Alcohol Information (NCALI) in Rockville, Md. In Canada, the Addiction Research Foundation (ARF) in Toronto has done extensive bibliograhical work.

The major scholarly journal for the field is the *Quaterly Journal of Studies on Alcoholism (Q.J.S.A.)* which in January, 1975 became a monthly *Journal of Studies on Alcohol (J.S.A.)*. It is edited at the Rutgers (formerly Yale) Center of Alcohol Studies in New Brunswick, New Jersey. In 1976 *Alcoholism: Clinical and Experimental Research* was begun by the American Medical Society on Alcoholism (AMSA) and published by the National Council on Alcoholism (NCA) in New York. There are numerous other journals and periodicals, some with broad coverage of alcohol and other drugs such as *The Journal* published monthly by the Addiction Research Foundation in Toronto, Ontario, and others with specialized focus as *Alcoholism Report* from Washington, D.C. which emphasizes Congressional activity but includes many aspects of alcoholism.

No attempt is made to list the many biographies and autobiographies of recovered alcoholics, though these are especially useful for those who are not recovered alcoholics themselves. Nor do we list the many popular and semi-popular pamphlets and books, many of them in paperback, produced especially by the publishers listed in the Appendix. We mention here a few general books. See the Sources at the end of Chapter 4 for a list of collections of scientific research materials.

Alcoholics Anonymous (book) and extensive literature of A.A. and Al-Anon.

BELL, ROBT. GORDON, *Escape from Addiction*.

CATANZARO, RONALD J., *Alcoholism: The Total Treatment Approach*.

EWING, JOHN A. and BEATRICE A. ROUSE, *Drinking: Alcohol in American Society*.

FORT, JOEL, *Alcohol: Our Biggest Drug Problem*.

GLATT, MAX M., *Alcoholism: A Social Disease*, and other works.

JELLINEK, E.M., *The Disease Concept of Alcoholism*.

JOHNSON, VERNON, *I'll Quit Tomorrow*.

KINNEY, JEAN and GWEN LEATON, *Loosening the Grip*.

MADSEN, WILLIAM., *The American Alcoholic*.

MANN, MARTY, *New Primer on Alcoholism*: and *Marty Mann Answers Your Questions about Drinking and Alcoholism*.

MAXWELL, RUTH, *The Booze Battle*.

CHRISTOPHER D. SMITHERS FOUNDATION, *Understanding Alcoholism*.

STRACHAN, J. GEORGE., *Alcoholism: Treatable Illness;* and *Practical Alcoholism Programming*.

ZIMBERG, SHELDON, JOHN WALLACE and SHEILA BLUME, *Practical Approaches to Alcoholism Psychotherapy*.

Appendix to Chapter 1: The NCA/AMSA Definition and Criteria

The American Medical Society on Alcoholism (AMSA), which is the physicians' component of the National Council on Alcoholism (NCA), published the following definition of alcoholism (NCA, 1976).

Alcoholism is a chronic, progressive and potentially fatal disease. It is characterized by: tolerance and physical dependency, pathologic organ changes or both, all of which are the direct or indirect consequences of the alcohol ingested.

1. "Chronic and progressive" means that physical, emotional and social changes that develop are cumulative and progress as the drinking continues.
2. "Tolerance" means brain adaptation to the presence of high concentrations of alcohol.
3. "Physical dependency" means that withdrawal symptoms occur from decreasing or ceasing consumption of alcohol.
4. The person with alcoholism cannot consistently predict on any drinking occasion the duration of the episode or the quantity that will be consumed.
5. Pathologic organ changes can be found in almost any organ, but most often involve the liver, brain, peripheral nervous system, and the gastrointestinal tract.
6. The drinking pattern is generally continuous but may be intermittent with periods of abstinence between drinking episodes.
7. The social, emotional, and behavioral symptoms and consequences of alcoholism result from the effect of alcohol on the function of the brain. The degree to which these symptoms and signs are considered deviant will depend upon the cultural norms of the society or the group in which the person lives.

In addition, the definition committee of AMSA/NCA recommended the following statements be forwarded for insertion in DSM III (*Diagnostic and Statistical Manual* of the American Psychiatric Association, Third Edition):

1. The term "alcoholism" be retained as a separate diagnostic category under the general heading of alcohol abuse.
2. This diagnosis be restricted to the AMSA/NCA recommended definition.
3. A second category is designated "alcohol-related behavior problems, other." This encompasses persons who experience social, economic, legal or personal problems related to alcohol use, but who do not show the symptoms of alcoholism, as described above, and whose drinking may or may not progress to alcoholism in the future.

One might regret the emphasis on late-stage, organic symptoms because many early and early-middle stage alcoholics could use it as part of their denial system. If alcoholism is a progressive illness, it should be identifiable in its early stages. Moreover, a majority of alcoholics never progress to the end stage, but remain miserably stuck in a middle phase neither progressing to obvious deterioration nor able to get out of their pathological pattern of drinking (Pattison, 1967, p. 130; Jacobson, 1976a). But the wording is probably necessary to establish credibility for the disease concept of alcoholism with the medical profession and the insurance industry, as well as for matters of law enforcement and involuntary commitment proceedings where the definition would be subject to rigorous cross-examination by opposing attorneys. An earlier NCA committee had written the following detailed list of criteria, published in 1972.

NCA Criteria for the Diagnosis of Alcoholism *

The guidelines are presented in two tracks: Track I is physiological and clinical; Track II is psychological, behavioral and attitudinal. Major criteria listed in Table 1 are conclusive evidence of alcoholism. Minor criteria in Table 2 are symptoms usually associated with, but not necessarily indicative of, alcoholism. Although there is no uniformity in the progression of the illness, since early diagnosis is important, the symptoms are separated into "early," "middle" and "late." And each symptom is assigned a diagnostic level, with 1 being the most significant and 3 the least.

Diagnosis. It is sufficient for the diagnosis of alcoholism that one or more of the major criteria of diagnostic level 1 are satisfied, or that several of the minor criteria in Tracks I and II are present: see Tables 1 and 2. If one is making the diagnosis because of major criteria in one of the tracks, there should also be a strong search for evidence in the other track. A purely mechanical selection of items is not enough; the history, physical examination, and other observations, plus laboratory evidence, must fit into a consistent whole to ensure a proper diagnosis. Minor criteria in the physical and clinical tracks alone are not sufficient, nor are minor criteria in behavioral and psychological tracks. There must be several in both Track I and Track II areas.

Alcoholism with Intermittent or Recurrent Drinking. Intermittent or recurrent drinking may represent a phase in the course of alcoholism. This pattern should be noted separately. The same criteria control the diagnosis. In some individuals there are recurring episodes of inebriation that become more frequent over a period of years until a daily drinking pattern emerges. In many individuals daily drinking increases until the individual slowly becomes aware that physiological and psychological dependence exist. At this point, periods of "going on the wagon" may occur, with a resulting intermittent or recurrent pattern of drinking. For most drinkers, there are lesser or greater periods of time when, because of circumstances or the acute effects of alcohol, drinking is not possible. This pattern is not inconsistent with other drug-dependence situations, in which interruptions of use are commonplace and have been accepted without the necessity of making a separate category for them. Even with a "steady" pattern of alcohol use, there are marked fluctuations in the blood alcohol level during each day.

Complications. Intoxication may be mild, moderate, or severe, or may lead to coma. Although alcoholics are frequently obviously intoxicated, mere intoxication

*This article, by the Criteria Committee, National Council on Alcoholism, is reprinted with permission from the *American Journal of Psychiatry*, Vol. 129, pp. 127–135, 1972, copyright American Psychiatric Association 1972, and Annals of Internal Medicine, Vol. 77, pp. 249–258, 1972, copyright Annals of Internal Medicine 1972.

is not sufficient for the diagnosis of alcoholism. Indeed, the physician should be cautious in making a diagnosis of alcohol intoxication on the basis of a staggering gait, slurred speech, other neurological signs, and an odor of alcohol on the breath. In such cases, one must be sure to rule out diabetic acidosis, hypoglycemia, uremia, impending or completed stroke, and other causes of cerebral impairment. An alcohol breath test, determination of blood alcohol level, or serum osmolality measurement may assist in making a diagnosis of alcohol intoxication. A history from the patient and from family members or friends is usually helpful but must in itself be subject to evaluation. Alcohol intoxication must be thought of with any person in coma; in addition, barbiturate and other sedative intoxication must be investigated: cross-dependence and cross-tolerance are common.

Cross-dependence (or cross-addiction) may begin iatrogenically (doctor-induced) or spontaneously with the use of any of the sedative class of drugs, barbiturates, or "minor" tranquilizers, in an attempt to control the anxiety generated by heavy alcohol use or in the mistaken impression that pharmacological control of the anxiety will stop the alcohol use. Such cross-dependence is so common that it must be investigated in any person suspected of alcoholism.

In addition, the life-style of persons who seek pharmacological "highs" is associated with heavy alcohol use along with other psychoactive chemical materials. Such persons are at risk of alcoholism, and patients being investigated for the diagnosis of alcoholism should also be evaluated for the use of these substances. Treatment programs for the use of other drugs engender a significant proportion of "instant alcoholics" who, having relinquished the other drugs, turn to alcohol and experience an unusually rapid onset of dependence.

Other Diagnoses. Reactive, secondary, or symptomatic alcohol use should be separated from primary forms of alcoholism. Alcohol as a psychoactive drug may be used for varying periods of time to mask or alleviate psychiatric or situationally induced symptoms. This may often mimic a prodromal stage of alcoholism and is difficult to differentiate from it. If the other criteria of alcoholism are not present, this diagnosis must be given. A clear relationship between the psychiatric symptom or event must be present; the period of heavy alcohol use should clearly not antedate the precipitating situational event (for example, an object loss). The patient may require treatment for alcoholism, in addition to treatment for the precipitating psychiatric event; one may be able to confirm the diagnosis only in retrospect.

After a suitable evaluation, a separate psychiatric diagnosis should be made on every patient, apart from the diagnosis of alcoholism. Patients may suffer from schizophrenia, latent or overt; from manic-depressive psychosis, obsessive-compulsive neurosis, recurrent depression, anxiety neurosis, or psychopathic personality; or have no psychiatric constellation differing from normal. The diagnosis should be made after treatment for withdrawal is complete, since alcohol is anxiety-producing and can also bring out psychological mechanisms and traits that are not apparent without alcohol. In particular, the hallucinatory behavior induced by alcohol withdrawal is not to be equated with schizophrenic hallucinatory behavior.

In some individuals a small amount of alcohol will evoke violent, aberrant behavior. This *Pathological Intoxication* or "mad drunk" is an idiosyncratic response to alcohol and is separate from alcoholism. Again, some old medical literature uses the term "acute alcoholism" to refer to any severe intoxication.

TABLE 1. Major Criteria for the Diagnosis of Alcoholism

Criterion	Diagnostic Level
TRACK I. PHYSIOLOGICAL AND CLINICAL	
A. Physiological Dependency	
1. Physiological dependence as manifested by evidence of a *withdrawal syndrome** when the intake of alcohol is interrupted or decreased without substitution of other sedation.** It must be remembered that overuse of other sedative drugs can produce a similar withdrawal state, which should be differentiated from withdrawal from alcohol.	
a) Gross tremor (differentiated from other causes of tremor)	1
b) Hallucinosis (differentiated from schizophrenic hallucinations or other psychoses)	1
c) Withdrawal seizures (differentiated from epilepsy and other seizure disorders)	1
d) Delirium tremens. Usually starts between the first and third day after withdrawal and minimally includes tremors, disorientation, and hallucinations.*	1
2. Evidence of *tolerance* to the effects of alcohol. (There may be a decrease in previously high levels of tolerance late in the course.) Although the degree of tolerance to alcohol in no way matches the degree of tolerance to other psychotropic drugs, the behavioral effects of a given amount of alcohol vary greatly between alcoholic and non-alcoholic subjects.	
a) A blood alcohol level of more than 150 mg/100 ml. without gross evidence of intoxication.	1
b) The consumption of one-fifth of a gallon of whiskey or an equivalent amount of wine or beer daily, for a period of two or more consecutive days, by a 180-lb. individual.***	1
3. Alcoholic "blackout" periods. (Differential diagnosis from purely psychological fugue states and psychomotor seizures.)	2
B. Clinical Major Alcohol-Associated illnesses. Alcoholism can be assumed to exist if major alcohol-associated illnesses develop in a person who drinks regularly. In such individuals, evidence of physiological and psychological dependence should be searched for:	
Fatty degeneration in absence of other known cause	2
Alcoholic hepatitis	1
Laennec's cirrhosis	2
Pancreatitis in the absence of cholelithiasis	2
Chronic gastritis	3
Hematological disorders:	
Anemia: hypochromic, normocytic, macrocytic, hemolytic with stomatocytosis, low folic acid	3

Clotting disorders: prothrombin elevation, thrombocytopenia	3
Wernicke-Korsakoff syndrome	2
Alcoholic cerebellar degeneration	1
Cerebral degeneration in absence of Alzheimer's disease or arteriosclerosis	2
Central pontine myelinolysis ⎫ diagnosis	2
⎬ only possible postmortem	
Marchiafava-Bignami's disease ⎭	2
Peripheral neuropathy (see also beriberi)	2
Toxic amblyopia	3
Alcoholic myopathy	2
Alcoholic cardiomyopathy	2
Beriberi	3
Pellagra	3

TRACK II. BEHAVIORAL, PSYCHOLOGICAL, AND ATTITUDINAL

All chronic conditions of psychological dependence occur in dynamic equilibrium with intrapsychic and interpersonal consequences. In alcoholism, similarly, there are varied effects on character and family. Like other chronic relapsing diseases, alcoholism produces vocational, social, and physical impairments. Therefore, the implications of these disruptions must be evaluated and related to the individual and his pattern of alcoholism. the following behavior patterns show psychological dependence on alcohol in alcoholism:

1. Drinking despite strong medical contraindication known to patient   1

2. Drinking despite strong, identified, social contraindication (job loss for intoxication, marriage disruption because of drinking, arrest for intoxication, driving while intoxicated)   1

3. Patient's subjective complaint of loss of control of alcohol consumption   2

TABLE 2. Minor Criteria for the Diagnosis of Alcoholism

Criterion	Diagnostic Level	Criterion	Diagnostic Level
TRACK I. PHYSIOLOGICAL AND CLINICAL		3. Late:	
A. Direct Effects (ascertained by examination)		Decreased tolerance	3
1. Early:		C. Laboratory Tests	
Odor of alcohol on breath at time of medical appointment	2	1. Major—Direct	
2. Middle:		Blood alcohol level at any time of more than 300 mg/100 ml.	1
Alcoholic facies	2	Level of more than 100 mg/100 ml. in routine examination	1
Vascular engorgement of face	2	2. Major—Indirect	
Toxic amblyopia	3	Serum osmolality (reflects blood alcohol levels): every 22.4 increase over 290 m0sm/liter reflects 50 mg/100 ml. alcohol	2
Increased incidence of infections	3	3. Minor—Indirect	
Cardiac arrhythmias	3	Results of alcohol ingestion:	
Peripheral neuropathy (see also Major Criteria, Track I, B)	2	Hypoglycemia	3
3. Late:		Hypochloremic alkalosis	3
(see Major Criteria, Track I, B)	3	Low magnesium level	2
B. Indirect Effects		Lactic acid elevation	3
1. Early:		Transient uric acid elevation	3
Tachycardia	3	Potassium depletion	3
Flushed face	3	Indications of liver abnormality:	
Nocturnal diaphoresis	3	SGPT elevation	2
2. Middle:		SGOT elevation	3
Ecchymoses on lower extremities, arms, or chest	3	BSP elevation	2
Cigarette or other burns on hands or chest	3	Bilirubin elevation	2
Hyperreflexia, or if drinking heavily, hyporeflexia (permanent hyporeflexia may be a residuum of alcoholic polyneuritis)	3	Urinary urobilinogen elevation	2
		Serum A/G ration reversal	2

Blood and blood clotting:

Anemia: hypochromic, normocytic, macrocytic, hemolytic with stomatocytosis, low folic acid — 3

Clotting disorders: prothrombin elevation, thrombocytopenia — 3

ECG abnormalities

Cardiac arrhythmias; tachycardia; T waves dimpled, cloven, or spinous; atrial fibrillation; ventricular premature contractions; abnormal P waves — 2

EEG abnormalities

Decreased or increased REM sleep, depending on phase — 3

Loss of delta sleep — 3

Other reported findings — 3

Decreased immune response — 3

Decreased response to Synacthen test — 3

Chromosomal damage from alcoholism — 3

TRACK II. BEHAVIORAL PSYCHOLOGICAL AND ATTITUDINAL

A. Behavioral

1. Direct effects

Early:

Gulping drinks — 3

Surreptitious drinking — 2

Morning drinking (assess nature of peer group behavior) — 2

Middle:

Repeated conscious attempts at abstinence — 2

Late:

Blatant indiscriminate use of alcohol — 2

Skid Row or equivalent social level — 2

2. Indirect effects

Early:

Medical excuses from work for variety of reasons — 2

Shifting from one alcoholic beverage to another — 2

Preference for drinking companions, bars, and taverns — 2

Loss of interest in activities not directly associated with drinking — 2

Late:

Chooses employment that facilitates drinking — 3

Frequent automobile accidents — 3

History of family members undergoing psychiatric treatment; school and behavioral problems in children — 3

Frequent change of residence for poorly defined reasons — 3

Anxiety-relieving mechanisms, such as telephone calls inappropriate in time, distance, person, or motive (telephonitis) — 2

Outbursts of rage and suicidal gestures while drinking — 2

B. Psychological and Attitudinal

1. Direct effects

Early:

When talking freely, makes frequent reference to drinking, alcohol, people being "bombed," "stoned," etc. or admits drinking more than peer group — 2

TABLE 2. Continued

Criterion	Diagnostic Level	Criterion	Diagnostic Level
Middle:		Major family disruptions: separation, divorce, threats of divorce	3
Drinking to relieve anger, insomnia, fatigue, depression, social discomfort	2	Job loss (due to increasing interpersonal difficulties), frequent job changes, financial difficulties	3
Late:		Late:	
Psychological symptoms consistent with permanent organic brain syndrome (see also Major Criteria, Track I, B)	2	Overt expression of more regressive defense mechanisms: denial, projection, etc.	3
2. Indirect effects		Resentment, jealousy, paranoid attitudes	3
Early:		Symptoms of depression: isolation, crying, suicidal preoccupation	3
Unexplained changes in family, social, and business relationships; complaints about wife, job, and friends	3	Feelings that he is "losing his mind"	2
Spouse makes complaints about drinking behavior, reported by patient or spouse	2		

CHAPTER 2

Scope of the Alcohol Problem

"SO A FEW PEOPLE have a few too many once in a while. What's the big problem?" To paraphrase R. Fox, M.D. (NCA, 1959, pp. 1–2): Suppose a new and fatal disease were to strike with terrible force across America. Suppose it had so harmful an effect on the nervous system that ten million citizens would go insane for periods lasting from a few hours to permanently, and during these spells of insanity commit acts of so destructive a nature that the lives of whole families would be in jeopardy, with a resultant fifty million persons actually affected. Work in business, industry, and professions would be sabotaged or left undone, at a cost of nineteen billion dollars yearly. Finally, let us imagine this disease to have the peculiar property of so altering a person's judgment that he would be unable to see that he had become ill at all; actually so perverting his view that he would wish with all his might to go on being ill. This disaster would surely be treated as a national emergency, and billions of dollars and thousands of scientists would be put to work to find the cause of the disease, to treat its victims, and to prevent its spread. That dread disease is here. It is alcoholism.

In the late 1960s and early 1970s there was a big scare about drug abuse, particularly its use by youth. Yet in 1973 the National Commission on Marihuana and Drug Abuse concluded that alcohol dependence is without question the most serious drug problem in this country today. In

23

1976 a federal investigation concluded that alcohol abuse was also the major drug problem among the military. Alcohol misuse is one and a half times the problem that nicotine use is and at least forty times the problem that heroin is. The First Special Report to the United States Congress on Alcohol and Health (p.21) in 1971 pointed out that many drug experts considered alcohol abuse a more significant problem than all other forms of drug abuse combined.

So dramatic are these facts and so contrary to what Americans have believed, that it has become common for lecturers to bore their audiences with lengthy statistics about the magnitude of alcohol problems. Such statistics have not been heard in the land since preprohibition campaigns. Even reasonably well-informed people do not realize the extent to which alcohol use and misuse pervade every aspect of American life: social, economic, political, medical, legal, historical, moral, and emotional. Once you poke your nose into these issues, the problems seem to explode in your face.

Some decades ago, alcohol misuse was considered to be our fourth biggest health problem. Later, when heart attacks and strokes had been combined into a single category of cardiovascular disorders, alcohol was ranked third after this and cancer as a killer. It was called the number-one *public* health problem, which emphasizes the social complications of alcohol misuse in traffic, family, industrial, and other problems. After all, cancer rarely causes one to cross the highway center line to wipe out a carload of innocent people.

Alcohol is now being recognized as the number-one *killer* in America. We now know that a great number of deaths once attributed to accidents and to physical illnesses such as heart or liver failure, acute pancreatitis, internal hemorrhaging, and the like should really be counted as alcohol deaths. This is especially true of women. Even most of the skid-road deaths that are attributed to malnutrition and pneumonia could legitimately be said to be caused by alcoholism. Our major health expense may well be the mountain of medical bills for nonfatal injuries and illness, sometimes lifelong, caused by alcohol misuse. Half the patients in some county hospitals are alcoholics, and 15 percent in the general wards of other hospitals. The Veterans Administration alone estimates that there are three million alcoholic veterans, the largest group in VA hospitals, costing the taxpayers nearly a billion dollars a year.

Estimating is Difficult.   Lengthy treatises—to some more boring than the statistics themselves—have been written about the problems involved in trying to compile accurate figures on alcoholism, and about the fallacies involved in the figures we have gathered. Vagueness of definition and a lack of standard criteria for alcoholism are complicated by our society's emotional attitudes toward the misuse of alcohol and consequent tendencies to gloss over it. Some apparent increases in the estimates of the numbers of alcoholics are, no doubt, merely a reflection of better methods of case finding and reporting, along with the new willingness to face alcohol problems openly and without disguise, especially among women.

Estimates of the extent of alcohol abuse based on arrests and court convictions can be misleadingly low. Arresting officers will often settle for lesser charges, such as reckless driving, because there is a better chance of proving the charge in court. More severe penalties tend to predispose a jury toward acquittal. In one state (Michigan) a team of researchers followed up independently of the police on auto accidents where alcohol was a suspected factor, uncovering many facts that point to prior drinking as a cause, even though it never became a matter of police record.

Often neglected in such discussions are the figures from the National Safety Council and other sources on the role of alcohol in death and injury other than by automobile. A third of industrial and home accidents, and an unknown but high number of boat and small plane deaths and injuries, occur after drinking. Commercial pilots are rigidly monitored, but the Federal Aviation Agency (FAA) has no effective means of checking private planes. People who are used to boats and are around them all the time don't fall off and drown in the wee hours because they have been drinking milk all Saturday night. Not drunk nor an alcoholic, the man who has a few beers before climbing the ladder to paint his house may dull his sense of balance just enough to cause a broken neck, but it will not be reported as alcohol-related (see Wechsler, 1969).

One of the more frustrating results of a review of the literature is to find twenty pages of tables and figures about drinking to one page on alcoholism. Granted, drinking is a factor in alcoholism, but one would suspect that the difference in availability of statistics has more to do with ease of fact-gathering than relative importance. Rates on per capita consumption of alcohol do not necessarily reveal rates of alcoholism. Orthodox Jews, Greeks, and wine-drinking southern Italians have low rates of alcoholism (not zero, as is mistakenly thought) but relatively high rates of alcohol consumption. Some Scandinavian and other northern countries have high rates of alcoholism without overall per capita consumption of alcohol ranking equally high. High consumption rates for convention and vacation cities do not necessarily mean high alcoholism rates for the local citizens. Moreover, consumption data must be adjusted to proportion of available income (after taxes) spent on alcoholic beverages. This consumption in proportion to available income may actually decrease while total per capita consumption increases, as happened in the United States over the past several decades (Efron, 1974), giving a different picture as to the relative value placed on alcoholic beverages from that by mere amounts consumed.

A minor irritation is that statistics on rates of alcoholism among adults do not use a uniform age base. Thus some figures are based on all people over 21, others on those over 20, and some on those over 18 or even 15—

making comparisons difficult. Lastly, since research takes time to compile and this is a rapidly changing field, the latest figures are bound to be obsolete before the ink is dry.

Methods of Estimating. The best-known method of estimating the percentage of alcoholics in a given population has been the formula developed by E.M. Jellinek (Haggard and Jellinek, 1942) based on deaths from cirrhosis of the liver. Jellinek himself repudiated the formula (1959). Not all cirrhosis is due to alcoholism, and not all alcoholics develop cirrhosis. In addition, there are problems of reporting: accurately, consistently from state to state, and even honestly. Autopsies are performed in only a small fraction of total deaths. Although the formula takes this into account, its reliability is questionable on sampling grounds alone if only 5 percent of liver cirrhosis is reported, as one pathologist in a large hospital estimates. In general the formula tended to estimate only late-stage, organically deteriorated alcoholics. Keller (1975b) describes the history and difficulties of the Jellinek formula, arguing for restriction of the term *alcoholic* to those with physical addiction. The formula reads

$$A = \left(\frac{P \cdot D}{K}\right) R$$

A = the number of alcoholics alive in a given year

P = the percentage of liver cirrhosis deaths attributable to alcoholism, a presumed constant which Jellinek originally calculated at 51.5% for males and 17.7% for females, but revised to 62.8% and 21.6% respectively

D = the number of reported deaths from liver cirrhosis in a given year; use only the federal vital statistics, for uniformity

K = the percentage of all alcoholics with medical complications who die of cirrhosis of the liver, which Jellinek calculated by multiplying 9% of alcoholics with liver cirrhosis by 7.71% who had died from it, equals .00694, presumed a constant

R = the ratio of all alcoholics to those alcoholics with medical complications, originally estimated at 4 but revised to 5.3 by Jellinek

As noted above, the Jellinek formula tended to underestimate the number of alcoholics. Other methods that yield low figures are those based on deaths reported as due to alcoholism, and those based on data from treatment or medical centers. Such statistics indicate only those alcoholics who contact some agency where they are officially diagnosed as alcoholics, thereby losing those who are not so diagnosed for a variety of reasons, and those who do not come to the attention of these agencies.

Polling practitioners such as physicians, social workers and clergymen regarding prevalence of alcoholism in their clientele may not be very reliable, but it is useful to uncover those who do not get counted in data from agencies explicitly designated as serving alcoholics. Criminal justice system and per capita consumption data have been mentioned; in spite of difficulties, they can indicate prevalence, increases, and group differences.

Sociological surveys of drinking practices and alcohol problems, using methods like those of D. Cahalan and his associates, are perhaps the most realistic approach. These combine consumption data with evidence that alcohol is interfering with life functions, according to quantifiable criteria. The Marden method uses demographic data and established risk factors to estimate "drinkers with problems." W. Schmidt, J. de Lint, and S. Ledermann use annual per capita consumption of alcohol. Community surveys, especially longitudinal studies that follow a group over a long period of time, are the most expensive but the best source of data when properly designed and administered. Even here, getting a representative cross section for one's sample and standardizing criteria for comparison with other groups present nearly insurmountable problems, while adequate follow-up may require dogged (and expensive) detective work.

These sociological survey methods tend to yield figures notably higher than Jellineklike approaches; for example, ten million instead of five million. But the larger figure includes those classed as problem drinkers as well as alcoholics. In the light of the last section of Chapter 1, this seems preferable and a truer picture of the real number of early and middle-stage alcoholics, those whose dependence on alcohol is causing life problems, although they may not have yet progressed to overt physical addiction.

Some Facts about Alcohol Problems

With all the above cautions in mind, we will summarize the literature to substantiate our assertion that alcohol is a large factor in American life and a major cause of problems. For reasons given, very few statistics here are more than estimates; but the expertise of social scientists is such that they are on guard against pitfalls and skilled in acquiring the most accurate data possible. It is better to lean toward the conservative side, lest we lose credibility. We must resist the temptation to inflate figures in order to impress either the public or legislators, though this becomes a crucial issue when funds are being allotted. Youngsters especially may not believe us on anything if they catch us in even one exaggerated statement.

Number of Alcoholics

Keller and others, using a modified Jellinek formula, estimated 5.5 million true alcoholics in the United States in 1972, but increases since 1945 suggest that the figure can be extrapolated to about 6.8 million for 1982.

Even these authors estimate that the total, including problem drinkers, runs between 9 and 10.5 million.

Using our working definition given in Chapter 1, but applying it conservatively, one can use as a rule of thumb that alcoholics constitute 4 percent of the general population, or 8.8 million Americans. In an adult population where at least three-fourths are drinkers (as in some large companies), about 6 percent of the total group are probably alcoholic. In groups where nearly all are drinkers, as in certain professions or types of work, the alcoholism rate may run about 8 percent or one in twelve.

These percentages vary markedly by locality and ethnic background, so the chances of developing alcoholism if you drink are not always 8 percent or one in twelve. They may be 1 percent for some and 90 percent for others. These are averages, which can be very misleading when applied to individuals, just as the concept of average temperature is meaningless if we talk about a man with his head in the refrigerator and his feet in the stove.

The rate of alcoholism seems to be higher in urban than in rural areas, and perhaps highest in wealthy suburban and ghetto areas. The opinion that it is equally high among men and women has been stated; an added reason for disagreeing with the higher ratio of men is that these figures are usually based on the Jellinek formula, which may be a very poor indicator of middle-stage female alcoholism.

Among Americans, Eskimos and then other Native Americans seem to rank highest, followed by blacks, Irish, Poles, and those of Scandinavian origin. But again generalizations are unwarranted, since upper-class blacks may have less per capita alcoholism than whites at the same socioeconomic level but worse rates at the lowest poverty level. Catholics and "liberal" Protestants have higher rates of both use and heavy use than do "conservative" Protestants. Although alcoholism among Jews is much higher than previously thought, they still have the lowest rate of alcoholism in spite of a high rate of use.

The military constitutes a distinct subculture, with high rates of alcohol problems among members and dependents. Boredom, loneliness, low prices, and the "machismo" image of the fighting man are all accentuated by pressure to drink in social gatherings of both servicemen and their wives. Starting in 1974 there has been a major change in this situation, with the U.S. Navy and then the other branches making an excellent effort to reverse these attitudes.

Comparisons between countries in per capita incidence of alcoholism suffer to an even larger extent from all the research difficulties presented earlier in this chapter. Methods, samples, and survey objectives differ so widely that one despairs of any valid rankings. France tops all lists, followed, usually in varied order, by the United States, Chile, England-Wales, Ireland, some Scandinavian countries, Canada, and Australia.

The Irish in America have a higher incidence than the Irish in Ireland. Russia and Poland have very high rates, but it is difficult to get accurate figures from behind the iron curtain. There has been a sharp rise in alcoholism in Japan in the last decade or so. It is a mistake to lump all of Italy together; rates among wine-drinking southern Italians have traditionally been reported as low, whereas industrialized northern Italy shows high rates now. China has over 800 million people scattered over a vast area; to generalize about the Chinese seems vapid, as there must be wide differences in their use and reaction to alcohol.

France's high rate contrasts with, or perhaps is betrayed by, its former denial of a nationwide alcoholism problem. Partly because the wine industry is the major national industry, and partly because of myths about wine contributing to virility and the workingman's stamina, the French have been very tardy in admitting the extent of their alcoholism problems. It may have been that in earlier times a man could tolerate a twelve-to-fourteen-hour workday better if he anesthetized himself to his unpleasant condition with alcohol. What we know now about the effects of alcohol on both performance and health refute any other value claimed. France has the highest rate of cirrhosis of the liver in the world, including that for youngsters. This parallels the report that 18 percent of them are drunk before age thirteen and only 13 percent of them say their first drink was part of a family meal (Sadoun, 1965). France had a 12.23 percent decline in alcohol consumption between 1960 and 1970, and a 19.6 percent reduction in excessive alcohol use over the same period (de Lint, 1975, pp. 4, 9). These changes are undoubtedly due to changes in *attitude*, a word we shall stress in our next chapter.

Other Victims, Other Problems

If each alcoholic affects the lives of four or five others—spouse, children, employer, employee, innocent victim of accident, or other—then our 8.8 million alcoholics have an impact on 35 to 43 million others for a total of about 50 million citizens.

How are they affected? Alcohol causes more than alcoholism. Numerous reports (for example, Rada, 1975) indicate that about 67 percent of child beating cases, 40 percent of forcible rape cases, and 51 percent of felonies are alcohol related. (One convict warned me that the figures on crime may be suspect, remarking, "The smart ones stay sober when they pull a job, we alcoholics get caught." Also, convicts need to blame something for their predicament. Again, some nonalcoholics may join AA in prison just to enhance their chances of early parole.)

Studies show that in 69 percent of beatings, 72 percent of stabbings, and in 64 percent of homicides, either the attacker or the victim or both had been drinking. Some 38 percent of suicides are alcohol-related; alcohol accentuates depression and makes one 14.7 times more likely to commit suicide, or 58 times according to one report (James, 1966). As high as 45 percent of our social welfare aid in categories like Aid to Dependent Children and 60 percent of "mental cruelty" divorce cases have been estimated as associated with excessive drinking, which is the primary complaint in one third of all broken marriages.

Traffic.   Automobile accidents in the United States kill more people each year than the total of 46,483 American soldiers killed in the entire dozen years of the Vietnam war. Including the drinking pedestrian, alcohol is involved in about 52 percent of these fatalities. Alcohol-related traffic deaths peaked at about 28,000 Americans per year. (Why no protest parades about that?) Short of death, the cost from traffic accidents in broken bones, permanent disabilities, hospital bills, and auto repairs is staggering: hard to estimate, but in the billions of dollars. Not all of these drinking drivers are alcoholics; some of them were not even drunk.

Polydrug.   We must keep in mind that all the above figures are drawn from sources of data concerned just with alcohol. In addition, the National Institute on Drug Abuse (NIDA) in 1976 reported that the combination of alcohol with other drugs topped the drugs of abuse listed by their Drug Abuse Warning Network (DAWN).

Cost.   Money may not be the most important value, but it is a useful measure to help grasp the size of alcohol problems. We complain about the high cost of life's necessities, yet we Americans spent $43.8 billion in 1979, or $120 million a day, on taxable alcoholic beverages, plus an untold amount on bootleg liquor (about 24 million gallons in 1972) and home brew. In 1977 the National Institute on Alcohol Abuse and Alcoholism (NIAAA) estimated that we spend another $42.75 billion to pick up the pieces: $12.7 billion in health care, $5.14 billion in motor vehicle accident losses, $.43 billion in fire losses, $2.86 billion in losses caused by violent crime, about $2 billion in social programs responding to the problems created by alcoholism, and $19.64 billion in loss to business and industry.

About 29.2 percent of our liquor bill goes to federal and local taxes, over ten billion dollars a year. Obviously this is not enough to pay for the loss, even if all alcohol tax went into programs instead of only one-twentieth or less, as now happens. Yet treatment and rehabilitation could turn a large number of alcoholics from tax liabilities into tax payers; one Seattle treatment center claims that the recovered alcoholics it returned to society as wage earners paid over $100,000 in taxes in one year. A cost/benefit study by NIAAA in 1976 shows that for every dollar spent in treatment there would be three dollars in benefits returned to the nation. In some states a public welfare recipient gets more from the state if he continues drinking than is paid to a rehabilitation center if he tries to stop. Families seem to get less help than the alcoholics.

The Immeasurables. We cannot measure in dollars the value of lost human lives, wrecked families, deteriorated personalities, and human misery. We cannot even know the impact of all this deep inside a spouse or child. Statistics ignore individuals: Even one alcoholic in your family is one too many. We talk of "victimless crimes" but here we are all victims, and especially the alcoholic.

This also answers the question, "Is it any of your business if I drink?" If you pay taxes and insurance premiums, it is indeed your business. As the number-one public health problem, alcohol misuse adds enormously to the cost of living for all of us. In addition, the life of everyone who gets into a car is threatened by drinking drivers. Alcohol impinges on almost every aspect of our lives.

Sources

In addition to the references cited in the chapter that are identified in the General Bibliography, the following are a small sample of the pertinent literature.

AGERIOU, M., "The Jellinek Estimation Formula Revisited," *Quarterly Journal of Studies on Alcohol (QJSA)*, 1974, 35:1053–1057.

BERRY, RALPH E. and JAMES P. BOLAND, *The Economic Cost of Alcohol Abuse.*

CAHALAN, DON, I.H. CISSIN and H.M. CROSSLEY, *American Drinking Practices: A National Study of Drinking Behavior and Attitudes.* Rutgers, Monograph No. 6.

COAKLEY, JUDY F. and SANDIE JOHNSON, *Alcohol Abuse and Alcoholism in the United States: Selected Recent Prevalence Estimates*, NIAAA, Washington, D.C., March 27, 1978.

DELINT, J., and W. SCHMIDT, "The Epidemiology of Alcoholism," In: Y. Israel and J. Mardones (eds.), *Biological Basis of Alcoholism*, pp. 423–442.

EDWARDS, G., "Epidemiology Applied to Alcoholism: A Review and Examination of Purposes," *QJSA*, 1973, 34:28–56.

HABERMAN, PAUL W. and MICHAEL M. BADEN, *Alcohol, Other Drugs and Violent Death.*

KELLER, MARK, "The Definition of Alcoholism," *QJSA*, 1960, 21:125–134.

KELLER, M. "Problems of Epidemiology in Alcohol Problems," *JSA*, 1975, 36:1442–1451.

KELLER, M. and C. GURIOLI, *Statistics on Consumption of Alcohol and on Alcoholism, 1976 Edition*, Journal of Studies on Alcohol, Rutgers, 1976.

MILLER, GARY and NEIL AGNEW, "The Ledermann Model of Alcohol Consumption," *QJSA*, 1974, 35:877–898.

SCHMIDT, W.G. and J. DE LINT, "Estimating the Prevalence of Alcoholism from Alcohol Consumption and Mortality Data," *QJSA*, 1970, 31:957–964.

SCHMIDT, W.G. and R.E. POPHAM, "Heavy Alcohol Consumption and Physical Health Problems: A Review of the Epidemiological Evidence," *Drug and Alcohol Dependence*, 1975–1976, 1:27–50.

CHAPTER 3

Sociocultural Aspects

IF ALCOHOL IS a chemical substance introduced into a living organism, one might well ask why we should consider social, cultural, and historical factors instead of just the biochemistry and pharmacology of alcohol. The reasons are many.

Obviously there would be no alcoholism if there were no drinking of alcoholic beverages. Since most drinkers do not become alcoholics, this can not be the sole or sufficient cause of alcoholism. But drinking is a necessary and important cause, and drinking is largely a matter of social custom, determined greatly by attitudes prevalent in the culture. Attitudes and customs develop over time and because of certain events and conditions, so history is an important factor in understanding both drinking customs and social attitudes toward drinking, drunkenness, and alcoholism.

Attitudes are especially important because alcoholics usually come from a background of confused and ambivalent attitudes about drinking. This was the conclusion of research done decades ago by Ullman (1953), and is confirmed by the stories of alcoholics heard at AA meetings and elsewhere. Jackson and Connor (1953b) found that alcoholics come from homes where the two parents tended to disagree quite markedly in their attitudes toward the use of alcohol. Most of us cannot remember our first drink; alcoholics often do, with a smirk or a wince that suggests they were confused or even mystified at the time. Cultures that have clear-cut, consistent attitudes about drinking and do not condone drunkenness usually have low rates of alcoholism, while those that don't know what to think or how they feel about alcohol tend to have higher rates. Orthodox Jews use wine in ritual and at meals; but to be "drunk like a Gentile" (*shikker vie ein goy* in Yiddish) is an absolute disgrace. Greeks and southern Italians drink wine daily at lunch and dinner, yet drunkenness is despised. Wine with meals is simply taken for granted.

Conversely, in Paris there is more drinking outside of mealtime, more hard liquor (brandy) is consumed, far more social significance is attached to drinking, and drunkenness is more tolerated. Other societies push drinks, and might even boast about how drunk Pat was last night: "What a party! He really tied one on!" These latter cultures have higher rates of alcoholism.

We already had occasion to mention the difficulties inherent in the World Health Organization's (WHO) definition of alcoholism as drinking that exceeds the customary dietary usage of a community. Any norm based on custom rather than on the nature of alcohol and its effect on the organism is bound to be troublesome, since customs differ so widely among cultures. Moreover, guilt feelings will vary widely, depending on divergent moral values. The problems might be similar in different countries, but how they are perceived is a major factor in what is done about them. Because custom is largely a social phenomenon, we cannot handle it by mere biochemical research nor by passing laws.

But, you say, alcohol is alcohol. True, but people are different. In counseling alcoholics one cannot ignore the attitudes both client and therapist bring to the situation from their own backgrounds. A black or native American is less likely to be helped by one who does not understand their culture. The origins of an alcoholic's drinking problems are enmeshed in social, religious, economic, legal, and health systems that must be understood even to make a proper diagnosis. Denial and rationalizations can only be penetrated and dealt with if the counselor knows their language and social setting.

No rehabilitation effort will have lasting success if recovered alcoholics are not prepared in a very realistic and practical way to go back and live in their own environment with its specific drinking practices and values. Funding for treatment depends on understanding the impact of alcoholism on all our lives as a public health problem rather than as a difference of moral opinion. And no prevention campaign has a chance of success if it is conceived in a vacuum that ignores the attitudes of society, especially a society where both use and misuse of alcohol are accepted by custom and even reinforced by peer pressure.

Because America has been the melting pot for a mixture of peoples from different racial and national origins, with peculiar histories of use

and misuse of alcohol, we probably have the most confused and ambivalent attitudes toward alcohol of any nation in the world. No wonder we
have problems. The "drys" think it is a sin to have even one drink, while
the civil libertarians will defend one's right to drink oneself to death. Rehabilitation experts in several parts of the country asked people whether
they would rather be blind, crippled, etc. and found that alcoholism
ranked as "most undesirable" among twenty-one handicaps listed. Witness the emotional reactions to recent Federal disability regulations that
protect alcoholics from discrimination.

Drinking alcohol is considered sophisticated and a mark of hospitality,
even among people who look down on those addicted to other drugs.
Youngsters are not impressed when parents view with alarm their marijuana use while holding a double martini. Contrast our picture of the
skid-road bum with the "gentleman of distinction" liquor advertisements:
Is alcohol a mark of moral depravity or of mature refinement? Is it an ap-
petizer? We know that alcoholics are notoriously undernourished. Is it a
sign of manliness, or weakness? If it proves one a tough he-man, why does
the salesman need a few belts before he goes after that big sale, or a boy
need a couple of beers before he asks that pretty girl for a dance? Is alcohol "the root of all evils" or is it "good for what ails you"? Is whiskey good
for a cold and brandy for shock, or are the American Medical Association
and the Red Cross correct in rejecting all medical uses of alcohol, especially in an emergency? We boast about somebody flying high at a party,
yet despise him in the gutter. Even our jokes betray a certain uneasiness
and mixed attitudes about drinking. More on this later; suffice it to say
that we cannot ignore cultural attitudes and history.

History of Alcohol

Alcohol is the product of a natural process called fermentation, the action
of yeast upon sugar. It can be made from almost any fruit or grain, and
was probably discovered accidentally by primitive man when he tasted
some rotting fruit just as birds sometimes exhibit inebriation from eating
overripe berries. Archaeology indicates that these natural products have
been a part of human life since before recorded history. Certainly there is
evidence from the very earliest writings: a brewery in 3700 B.C., a temperance tract in ancient Egypt, prohibition in Mesopotamia and among the
ancient Greeks, Noah passed out from too much wine, ancient Chinese
proverbs about beer and its abuse. The Code of Hammurabi, circa 1900
B.C., punished only two crimes by burning to death: incest and alcohol
abuse.

Beer and wine are the result of fermentation. Beer and ale are ordinarily made from malted grain flavored with hops, and contain usually

about 4 percent (rarely more than 8 percent) alcohol. Wines are either dry (table) wines or sweet (dessert) wines. Either may be red or white. Dry wines contain 12 to 14 percent alcohol, while sweet wines contain 18 to 20 percent and are made by adding alcohol before all the sugar has been fermented.

Spirits or hard liquor (Scotch, bourbon and rye whiskey, gin, vodka, rum, brandy) are the result of distillation, a method of concentrating the alcohol by evaporating it and then condensing the vapor. This yields a beverage of 40 percent to 50 percent alcohol (80 to 100 proof). The Chinese may have invented the distillation process before 2000 B.C., and the Arabs, from whom our word *alcohol* comes, had improved it by 1700 B.C. It was known in India before 1000 B.C. and is mentioned by Aristotle and Pliny. About A.D. 1000 the Italians began to make brandy (*grappa*) out of wine, but distilled liquor did not become common in western Europe until about A.D. 1500, when gin became popular in England and brandy in France—each country then calling the other "the land of the drunkards."

Alcohol has been made by almost every people, and from almost anything. Mead was fermented from honey in Britain long before the Romans came. Laplanders fermented reindeer milk into *pima*, and the Japanese use their rice to make beer, wine (*sake*), and liquor. In Abyssinia there was a strong beer called *bouza* from which the word *booze* may have originated. Tartar tribesmen made an intoxicating drink from the milk of mares and camels. Magellan found Filipino natives drinking fermented sap of the coconut palm. Mexicans make *pulque* from the fermented juice of the maquey cactus.

Columbus found the Caribbean Indians drinking beer from fermented maize, and the Incas of Peru were making wine and beer before the arrival of Pizarro. But there was no distillation in this hemisphere before the white man came, and except for the areas mentioned, and especially in the northern and northwestern areas of North America, the native Americans seem to have had no contact with alcohol. We shall return to this fact when we discuss causality.

What is more important than its widespread use are the attitudes people develop toward alcohol. Once it has become part of a culture, it seems never to be eradicated. China is said by one author to have tried prohibition seventeen times, and another says forty-one times. England went through prohibition six times. Russia, Finland, and Iceland have all tried prohibition and repealed it. Mohammed strictly prohibited alcohol among his followers, perhaps because the date wine they made was very strong. But reports from predominantly Mohammedan countries indicate a certain amount of alcohol consumption, some of it in unusual forms such as shaving lotion, and other psychoactive drugs are not unknown. One tribe of Mohammendans gave us our English word *assassin*: They were known as *hashashin* because they killed Christians with some enthusiasm while under the influence of hashish, the active ingredient in marijuana. The Hindus and some other sects also prohibit alcohol.

Among some South Pacific island peoples there was an absolute taboo against alcohol; we can surmise that the motivation included fear of getting lost at sea, as when they migrated to Hawaii with no modern navigational aids. Even small amounts of alcohol can dull one's sense of direction, as many a lost hiker or hunter has learned. *Kava* (*'awa* in Hawaii) is a nonalcoholic intoxicating beverage made from the pounded root of the pepper tree throughout Polynesia and in some parts of Melanesia and Micronesia. *Sakau* on the islands of Ponape and Fiji is similar, and both are harder to make than alcohol. The tragic fact is that the *kava* culture, which was a highly disciplined, ritualized use important in their society, was destroyed when the white man brought liquor and chaos to the islands. Among primitives, the use of alcohol seems to have been in the control of the group, not of the individual. In some tribes, the women took away all the knives and clubs before drinking began. Conversely, the Chinese are regarded as never getting hostile from drink: they got a characteristic flush, perhaps a bit boisterous, and sleepy. As the eleven-minute WHO film *To Your Health* says, "Alcohol means many things to many people."

Coming back to our Western Judeo-Christian tradition, we note that although drunkenness is condemned in both Old and New Testaments, nowhere in the Bible is total abstinence mandated. Drinking is often mentioned; the wines of Israel are praised. In medieval European monasteries the Benedictines developed Benedictine, and the Carthusians made Chartreuse. Wine making became a fine art. Drunkenness was a sin, but church leaders were not total abstainers: popes and cardinals drank, as did Luther, Calvin, Knox, and even Wesley, founder of the Methodists.

Although beer and wine contain the same intoxicating ethanol as distilled spirits, it seems that misuse and prohibitionistic reactions to it intensified when hard liquor became more widespread in Europe after about A.D. 1500. The proliferation of gin mills in England led to ineffectual attempts at prohibition by both Charles I and James I. The first restriction was usually attempted through an excessive tax, whose purpose was not revenue but control. History is full of ironies, and what we see here is a series of cyclic events redolent of our own more recent history: Abuse led to high tax and eventual prohibition, which occasioned graft and corruption, which led to repeal, followed by abuse and then prohibition again. Another shameful and vicious circle was a triangle: Rum made in New England or England was traded in Africa for slaves, who were traded in Jamaica for molasses, which was brought north and made into rum. One irony was the discovery in 1525 of the "miracle drug" laudanum, a mixture of opium and alcohol. (Before we laugh at the British, face this: We in America hailed heroin as a "cure" for soldiers who had been addicted to morphine in the Civil War.)

In 1606 England shifted public drunkenness from ecclesiastical to civil law: instead of just a sin it became a crime. Since the high sheriff was busy pursuing felons, the town constable became involved with "handling drunks" as one of his major functions. Public inebriates evolved into "problem people" and were looked upon as a different kind of people, human derelicts whose souls might be saved if they could be converted in a slum mission, but of no use to humanity.

In sharp contrast to all this was the fact that alcohol had become an accepted part of most societies. Contrary to our stereotypes, it seems that in ancient times it was the rich who were the drunkards; the poor and slaves were allowed to drink only at festivals. Drinking has always been a part of the ritualistic ceremonies of almost all civilized peoples. Men pledged their loyalty and sealed a contract in wine. Eventually this mode of pledge was integrated into celebration of betrothals, marriages, births, baptisms, and wakes at death. Red wine was (erroneously) thought of as analogous to blood, and spirits were called *aquavit*, water of life. The effects of alcohol added zest to social entertaining and relief from stress and boredom. Wine or beer became a part of the meal in most European countries. Since alcohol can be made anywhere and out of almost anything, it has pervaded every stratum of life. Even in prison, where it is forbidden, convicts not only obtain it in a variety of forms (48-ounce bottles of Listerine disappear very fast in some prisons) but they hoard raisins and prunes (hence "pruno") and ferment them into wine, and even fashion ingenious distilling apparatus to manufacture moonshine behind the walls.

Can alcohol be eliminated? Symbolic of the problem is the action of one prison warden who heard that the inmates were fermenting apples and oranges into wine, so he substituted prunes! But the United States engaged for a century in a gigantic and less amusing attempt, to which we must now turn.

Alcohol in America

1620–1725—No Fuss.   In the early American colonies the use of beer and wine with meals was simply transported across the Atlantic as a way of life, with no special significance. Drunkenness was not tolerated, but even the Puritans drank. More beer than water was brought over on the *Mayflower.* Beer was served in the dining hall at Harvard, and at dinner in the Protestant seminaries.

1725–1825—Excessive and Harmful Drinking.   In the previous century 90 percent of the beverage alcohol consumed in America was in the form of beer, 5 percent as wine, and 5 percent as spirits or hard liquor. During this second century a dramatic shift occurred: 90 percent of the alcohol was consumed as distilled spirits, with only 5 percent as beer and 5 percent as wine. The reasons were varied. The harsh climate of the eastern seaboard was not conducive to viniculture. The British taxed French wine heavily. Beer was bulky to transport in an era before railroads and highway truckers. A barrel of whiskey contained as much ethanol as a wagonload of beer. (Ironically, bourbon whiskey was invented by a Kentucky Baptist minister.) Whiskey became so negotiable that it was used for money when the Continental currency failed in 1780. A 1791 excise tax on it so encroached upon the lives of Pennsylvania farmers that George Washington had to send troops to quell the Whiskey Rebellion.

This shift toward hard liquor meant a major increase in intemperate drinking. Another factor was a total ignorance of addiction, at least as applied to alcohol. American doctor Benjamin Rush, in 1785, and British doctor Thomas Trotter, in 1804, had both recognized the danger of alcohol addiction, but they were not heard because of lack of good mass communication media and widespread illiteracy—to say nothing of popular denial. Thomas Jefferson, as third president, observed that "one-third of the people in these United States are killing themselves with whiskey." No doubt the lack of social controls in this free and rapidly expanding frontier country made excess much easier than in a structured society.

Added to these is a most important fact: Excessive drinking was not only tolerated but admired. Drunkenness, if you will pardon the whimsy, was looked upon in much the same terms as adultery: It was immoral, but it was manly and it was fun. The image of the pioneer frontiersman as a hard-fighting, hard-drinking tough guy became the paragon of manliness. This persists to the present day, with obvious implications for prevention strategies.

A similar American attitude that persists from this period is that serving and even insisting on drinks is a mark of hospitality. Before jet travel, it was indeed a warming welcome when one came in off the road or trail —tired, wet, cold, and aching. From this developed a further and insidious feeling: If one did not push drinks, one was liable to be thought of as inhospitable or downright stingy. No American wants to be thought of as either of these.

Later, another twist added to these pro-drinking attitudes: a backlash to the total abstinence movement. It is only partly in jest that I speculate as to how many Catholics may have drunk themselves into alcoholism trying to prove they were not Methodists or Baptists . . . but this does lead to our next period, the prelude to Prohibition.

1825–1919—Temperance to Abstinence. As early as 1789, in Litchfield, Connecticut, there began to stir a movement to oppose this widespread intemperance. It grew out of a genuine concern for the future of the young nation whose democratic form of government depended on the people keeping their wits intact. But even more, it bespoke the Calvinist, Puritan theology common in the colonies, especially in the Presbyterian and Congregationalist Churches of New England. The Calvinist clergyman Lyman Beecher (1775–1863) spearheaded the movement, beginning in 1812, with a strong stand for temperance that did not oppose wine and beer but only spirits. By 1825, however, he began advocating total abstinence from all alcoholic beverages. The Temperance Society had become an Abstinence Society by 1836. It lost half its members, but not its momentum. The Good Templars, the Anti-Saloon League, the National Prohibition Party and other groups were formed, especially the Women's Christian Temperance Union (WCTU), in 1874, which completely distorted the issue because the T did not stand for temperance but for abstinence, creating confusion in the American mind to this day.

Over these decades of increasingly strident propaganda, the focus shifted from the *abuse* of alcohol or the person misusing it to the substance itself: Alcohol became "demon rum" and was to be extirpated from the country. Only the Washingtonian Movement, and later the Salvation Army, showed concern for the *person* affected. To most he was a moral reprobate, a depraved person of weak will who could "reform" if only he willed it. To avoid any such connotations we now never say "reformed alcoholic" but prefer "recovered," which affirms that the person is not bad, but rather recovering from a chronic illness. (This terminology has been accepted by the Associated Press/United Press International *Style Book*.) Likewise, to avoid criminal implications we say "relapsed" and not "recidivist."

It is hard for us today to grasp how profoundly this controversy pervaded every facet of American life for a century. Prohibition of alcohol by law became a major issue in every political campaign. Maine, in 1851, was the first state to pass the law. By 1863, thirteen states had voted in prohibition, but all except Maine had repealed it. In spite of this, by December of 1917, 95 percent of the land in the United States and two-thirds of its population were legally dry. The legend of Carry Nation smashing saloon windows with a hatchet seems exaggerated to us, but it typifies the intense zeal of the prohibitionists and seems to be historical fact, though there is now some question as to her sanity.

The emotional bitterness was matched by conceptual confusion. People failed to distinguish between use and abuse. Temperance was confused with total abstinence, so many a moderate drinker who abhorred drunkenness found himself unwittingly in the camp of its defenders. The two factions polarized the positions and created artificial dichotomies we are still trying to live down. Unfortunately, the Lutherans, Episcopalians, Greek Orthodox, Roman Catholics, and Jews who advocated temperance

were accused of condoning drunkenness because they did not support total abstinence. In the 1928 presidential campaign of Al Smith the slur was
cast combining "rum, Rome, and rebellion" because he was a Catholic
and advocated repeal of prohibition. Religious and political party affiliation were so intertwined with the prohibition issue, and feelings ran so
high, that it became a rule of polite society not to allow them in conversation.

1920–1933—Prohibition.   The total abstinence or so-called temperance movement culminated in the passage of the eighteenth Amendment to the U.S. Constitution on January 16, 1920, and its implementation by the Volstead Act on October 20 of that year. It prohibited the
manufacture, sale, or transportation of any intoxicating beverage, except
for medicinal or sacramental purposes. Thus began a massive struggle between a whole people and its law enforcement authorities, the effects of
which not only echo in our language (speakeasy, hijack, bootlegger) but
affect our attitudes toward law and authority to this day.

It is often said that Prohibition did not fail; it was never tried. In the
sense that it never had the whole-hearted support of the people, that is
true. At the height of Prohibition, for example, speakeasies in New York
City known to the police totaled 32,000. "Knock twice and ask for Joe"
and "Benny sent me" became household phrases. Bathtub gin and rotgut
whiskey were more than phrases, and if you could get hold of a bottle of
good Canadian rye you were the prince of your neighborhood block. Real
Scotch became "the real McCoy" because Captain Billy McCoy had a fast
ship that was able to outrun the U.S. Revenue Service boats charged with
enforcing the law. A sad twist is that the rumrunners and those who drank
were the heroes, and the U.S. federal agents (revenuers) were the bad
guys. It is usually admitted that more women drank in bars than ever before, since going to a speakeasy or night club became the smart thing to
do. Adolescents were subject to no different laws than anyone else, and
often were not only the customers but the bootleggers, as this author can
attest from living through it.

It is true that statistics show a drop in per capita consumption, but the
above facts make one wonder how accurate they could be. The law-abid-
ing citizens who did decrease their drinking were probably those less
prone to alcohol problems regardless. People who really need a drink can
always get it, and Prohibition days were no exception. Drinking out of defiance or surreptitiously is more open to abuse than relaxed, uncomplicated
drinking—if for no other reason than the need to finish the bottle and dispose of the evidence. In 1933, about 10,000 full-blown alcoholics were
admitted to hospitals in New York City (Keller, 1975a). In Chapter 11 we
present a current trend favoring moderate controls as a means of prevention.

1934—Repeal.   Pressures for repeal resulted in a redefinition of intoxicating beverage to allow beer with 3.2 percent alcohol in 1933, and finally on December 6, 1934 the Twenty-first Amendment repealed the Eighteenth and the "noble experiment" came to an end. Many factors contributed to repeal. The Great Depression led many to hope that restoring the alcoholic beverage industry would stimulate the economy by providing jobs in agriculture and viniculture, manufacture, transportation, and sales. Needless to say the industry concurred, and pressed for repeal. Some women's groups opposed the WCTU. Poor enforcement and widespread corruption were another incentive: A "godfather" or big-city boss like Al Capone considered law authorities simply pawns who could be bought for a price. But probably the crucial factor was the infringement on the personal freedom of people whose culture had sanctioned normal use of alcohol for centuries. Imagine the revolt if tomorrow's morning paper announced that coffee is now forbidden!

The confusion and warped attitudes engendered by this long and bitter struggle have not disappeared. National prohibition is dead, but the movement is still with us under different names. The fifty states have varied and even conflicting laws; for example, in one state food must be served in the same place as liquor, while in an adjoining state not one but two walls must separate food from liquor. A few counties in local-option states are legally dry. Attitudes toward law and authority still suffer as an aftermath. Drinking and drunkenness are still equated by some, with moralistic implications contrary to the concept of alcoholism as a disease.

An illustration that should discourage any simpleminded thinking is the percentage of drinkers in supposedly "dry" denominations: 61 percent of Methodists and 48 percent of Baptists drink (Mulford, 1964), 53 percent of some Fundamentalist sects, and a percentage of Mormons that can only be guessed at from the alcohol tax revenue in Utah and other evidence. Now the serious complication is that Mulford and others report a higher than average rate of alcoholics and problem drinkers among these dry group members who drink. It is not certain whether the reason is guilt or lack of consistent drinking norms or something else, but the fact seems clear.

Per capita consumption of alcohol in the United States has increased, but the percentage of available income spent on alcohol has decreased. There is a tendency away from the 90 percent of alcohol consumed as spirits in the last century to about 40 percent now, with 45 percent as beer and 15 percent as wine. In some Pacific Coast states the proportion consumed as wine is higher. Since this is largely table wine consumed with meals, it is probably a mark of moderation and not necessarily an increase in the cheap fortified wine of the skid-road "wino" who, in any case, comprises only 3 percent of the alcoholic population. However, we must not forget that there are true alcoholics who have never drunk anything but beer or dry wine.

TABLE 3.   Percentage of Beverage Alcohol Consumed in United States

	BEER	WINE	SPIRITS
1630	90%	5%	5%
1825	5%	5%	90%
1970	50%	10%	40%
1973	46%	12%	42%
1978*	45%	15%	40%

*Estimates

1935–Present.   Since repeal, a new vision of the problem of excessive drinking has been slowly evolving. Whereas Rush and Trotter had stressed drunkenness, the concept of alcoholism as an illness began to be discussed in the late nineteenth century in both Europe and America, notably in the *Journal of Inebriety*, founded in this country in 1876, and in the *British Journal of Inebriety*, begun in 1892 (now the *British Journal of Addiction*). The American Journal of Inebriety folded after thirty-eight years, and its ideas were never widely popular, even with the medical profession. Various attempts at treatment were tried, the best known of which was the Keeley cure.

In 1935, Dr. Bob and Bill W., two "hopeless" alcoholics, discovered they could stay sober by helping others and following a program of twelve steps, which they extracted from their experience: The fellowship of Alcoholics Anonymous was born. They were careful to avoid affiliation with anything that smacked of Prohibition, focusing on the person rather than on the substance, alcohol. Not espousing any particular theory, in general the fellowship tended to think of alcoholism as an illness instead of a sin. They avoided moralizing and opened the way for renewed interest in the disease concept of alcoholism.

Coincidentally in the same year, 1935, Charles Shadel founded the Shadel Hospital in Seattle, which was to become the first member of the American Hospital Association devoted exclusively to the treatment of alcoholism. He used an aversion conditioning technique quite different from the approach of AA, but they had in common a focus on alcoholic drinking as the primary problem and on stopping it as the first line of attack. Both looked upon alcoholism as a pathology in its own right rather than merely the symptom of some other problem.

Also in 1935, again quite independently of the above events, Mark Keller and Norman Jolliffe, at Bellevue Hospital in New York, embarked upon a major research project to explore alcoholism. Through a series of events they involved Dr. Howard Haggard of Yale and E. M. Jellinek, a biometrician doing research on schizophrenia, and in 1940 founded the multidisciplinary Yale Center of Alcohol Studies under Jellinek and the *Quarterly Journal of Studies on Alcohol* (QJSA) under Keller. In 1962 both were moved to Rutgers, the State University of New Jersey, and in 1975 the *Quarterly Journal* became a monthly (*JSA*). Meanwhile, a landmark date was the publication in 1960 of Jellinek's book, *The Disease Concept of Alcoholism*.

The World Health Organization had acknowledged alcoholism as a medical problem in 1951, and by 1956 the American Medical Association had declared alcoholism an illness. The next year the American Hospital Association accepted it as an illness treatable in general hospitals. The disease concept of alcoholism is in a 1965 statement by the American Psychiatric Association, and in a joint statement on September 16, 1969 from the American Bar Association and the American Medical Association.

The Scandinavian countries (Sweden, Norway, Denmark, Finland) had been among the first to acknowledge alcoholism as a serious national problem and to initiate scientific research. Switzerland, Canada, and England got involved early, and by 1968 the Twenty-eighth International Congress on Alcoholism in Washington, D.C., attracted over two thousand persons—the largest group up to that date ever assembled on alcoholism. Significant at that meeting was the granting of the first Jellinek Memorial award to the young Swiss biochemist Jean-Pierre von Wartburg for his work on biological, including genetic, factors. Antabuse (disulfiram, see chapter 14) was discovered in Europe in 1947, and in 1949 Dr. Ruth Fox went to Copenhagen to study its use and brought it back to the United States.

Except for AA, the above has largely been the story of professionals. What of the general public? In April 1944, Fox had introduced to Jellinek a talented and articulate recovered alcoholic: Mrs. Marty Mann. Within a year she had founded the National Council on Alcoholism (NCA), a volunteer group dedicated to eradicating the stigma of alcoholism and educating the general public to its ultimate conquest through treatment and prevention. Like Alcoholics Anonymous, the council avoided the prohibition issue, and concentrated on alcohol misuse and the problems arising therefrom. NCA now has many local affiliate councils scattered throughout the fifty states, and a State Volunteer Alcoholism Associations (SVAA) office. Highly important is the development by NCA of the National Nurses Society on Alcoholism (NNSA); the American Medical Society on Alcoholism (AMSA); its labor-management division; more recently its offices on education and prevention, minorities, and women; and the Research Society on Alcoholism (RSA). In 1961 began the Association of Labor-Management Administrators and Consultants on Alcoholism (ALMACA). Other national organizations have now sprung up, too numerous to mention and too fluid in their changes of name and mergers to keep current. Thus the 1957 North American Association of Alcoholism Programs (NAAAP) became, in 1972, the Alcohol and Drug Problems Association (ADPA).

Many states had meanwhile developed alcoholism programs, usually as part of their public health department or (later) of their social welfare department. But Senator Tydings of Maryland could state that "the prob-

lem of alcoholism had been sadly neglected by the federal government"
(*Congressional Record*, June 7, 1967, S7846) and it was not until 1970
that Senator Harold Hughes, who had been elected governor when the
people of Iowa knew he was a recovered alcoholic, was able to facilitate
passage of the Comprehensive Alcohol Abuse and Alcoholism Prevention,
Treatment and Rehabilitation Act (PL 91–616). The Hughes Act established the National Institute on Alcohol Abuse and Alcoholism (NIAAA);
authorized financial assistance to states, communities, organizations, institutions, and individuals; funded research, education and training, and
a variety of treatment and rehabilitation programs; withdrew federal
funds from hospitals that refused to treat alcoholics; and require a comprehensive program for military and civilian federal employees with alcoholism.

Have Public Attitudes Changed?   Very slowly. Ignorance, apathy,
and downright hostility still pervade all levels, from the medical and
other top professions down to the local tavern. Alcoholism in 1976 still got
only 90 cents per victim in private support, in contrast to $197.52 per vic-
tim for muscular dystrophy, $180 per victim for hemophilia, $171.62 per
victim for cystic fibrosis, and $87.37 per victim for cancer. At least this is
better than the 40 cents per victim alcoholism received in 1967.

Progress is being made. In 1974 the Internal Revenue Service ruled
that not only is treatment for alcoholism a deductible medical expense,
but even transportation to and from an Alcoholics Anonymous meeting or
clubhouse could qualify. Some states have passed laws that all group medical insurance policies must include coverage for alcoholism treatment.
Every year prominent persons fight the stigma of alcoholism by coming
out in the open with a declaration of their recovery as no more of a disgrace than any other illness. Along with this, and more important for prevention, is the first glimmer of a change in our attitudes about pushing
drinks and tolerating drunkennesss, spurred in part by recent court decisions that people can be held liable for damages inflicted by a customer or
guest to whom they served drinks. Another important development has
been the model Uniform Alcoholism and Intoxication Treatment Act
(commonly referred to as the Uniform Act), which has now been enacted
by more than half the states, making the alcoholic not a criminal but a
sick person.

Sources

History

The history of alcohol use and abuse has been dealt with effectively by Mark Keller in several articles. Two in particular can be recommended, "Problems with Al-

cohol: An Historical Perspective," (1976a) and "Alcohol in Health and Disease: Some Historical Perspectives," (1966). Bacon, in an article entitled "Concepts," (1976) has looked at the history from a somewhat different perspective; he has surveyed the ways of looking at alcohol and alcoholism in the past and the relationship of these points of view to the kinds of actions people have taken. Part I of Ewing and Rouse's *Drinking: Alcohol in American Society*, and Chapter 3 of Fort's *Alcohol: Our Biggest Drug Problem*, also give surveys of the history of drinking, as does Fleming's *Alcohol: The Delightful Poison*. Daniel J. Anderson's *A History of Our Confused Attitudes Toward Beverage Alcohol* is a Hazelden pamphlet (see Appendix).

Sociocultural Aspects

The literature that deals with the history of alcohol and alcoholism cannot avoid dealing also with the ways in which culture and society affect drinking behavior. Bacon's "Concepts," cited above, is particularly important in making such relationships explicit. Everett, Waddell, and Heath's *Cross-Cultural Approaches to the Study of Alcohol: An Interdisciplinary Perspective* is, to date, the best single presentation of sociocultural aspects and their implications. One of the authors, Heath, has also written an article entitled, "Anthropological Perspectives on Alcohol: An Historical Review" (1976), which covers some of the same material. Mac Marshall has edited an excellent collection of both general and specific articles entitled *Beliefs, Behaviors, and Alcoholic Beverages: A Cross-Cultural Survey* (1979).

Older but still valuable sources include: Craig MacAndrew, *Drunken Comportment*; David Pittman and Charles R. Snyder, *Society, Culture and Drinking Patterns*; J.B. Roebuck and R. Kessler, *The Etiology of Alcoholism*; Ebbe Hoff, *Alcoholism: The Hidden Addiction*; and William Madsen, *The American Alcoholic*. In addition there are many studies that focus on a specific cultural upbringing pattern of drinking and the likelihood of becoming an alcoholic: for example, C.R. Snyder, *Alcohol and the Jews: A Cultural Study of Drinking and Sobriety*, and articles such as those by Bacon (1973), Keller (1970), and Negrete (1973).

Most of the sources for Chapter 7 of this book also deal with the effect on drinking behavior of having been raised within a particular group. The references we have given all contain extensive bibliographies. In addition, The National Clearinghouse for Alcohol Information (NCALI—see Appendix) has published several lists of references on sociocultural aspects of alcohol use and alcoholism.

Prohibition

Prohibition had far-reaching and profound effects on our society, only one of which was its importance in shaping our attitudes toward the use of alcohol and toward those who used it. Because of its importance in this respect, an attempt was made to pick out from the voluminous literature on the subject a sampling of the books that have been written about the temperance movement and Prohibition itself. It should be noted that all the historical references cited above also deal with these subjects.

ASBURY, HERBERT, *The Great Illusion: An Informal History of Prohibition*, 1950.

BARKER, JOHN M., *The Saloon Problem and Social Reform*, 1970.

BILLINGS, JOHN S. et. al., *The Liquor Problem*, 1903.

CHERRINGTON, ERNEST, *The Evolution of Prohibition in the United States of America*, 1920.

CHIDSEY, D.B., *On and Off the Wagon: A Sober Analysis of the Temperance Movement from the Pilgrims through Prohibition*, 1969.

CLARK, NORMAN H., *Deliver Us from Evil: An Interpretation of American Prohibition*, 1976.

COFFEY, THOMAS M., *The Long Thirst: Prohibition in America*, 1975.

FURNAS, J.C., *The Life and Times of the Late Demon Run*, 1965.

GUSFIELD, JOSEPH R., *Symbolic Crusade: Status Politics and the American Temperance Movement*, 1963.

HOFSTADTER, R., *The Age of Reform: From Bryan to F.D.R.*, 1960.

JOHNSTON, HENRY ALAN, *What Rights Are Left*, 1930.

KOBLER, J., *Ardent Spirits: The Rise and Fall of Prohibition*, 1973.

LEE, H., *How Dry We Were: Prohibition Revisited*, 1963.

MERTZ, CHARLES, *The Dry Decade*, 1931.

ODEGARD, PETER H., *Pressure Politics: The Story of the Anti-Saloon League*, 1966.

SINCLAIR, ANDREW, *Prohibition: The Era of Excess*, 1962.

SORENSEN, ANDREW A., *Alcoholic Priests: A Sociological Study*, Chapter 1, 1976.

TAYLOR, R.L., *Vessel of Wrath: The Life and Times of Carry Nation*, 1066.

UDELL, GILMAN G., *Liquor Laws*, 1968.

See also the articles by Houghland, Whealon, and Winkler in the General Bibliography.

CHAPTER 4

Alcohol and the Body

So far we have delineated what we are talking about and the extent of the problems. At this point a psychologist might be expected to launch into an analysis of why the alcoholic drinks. Indeed we shall; but a good psychologist starts with the fact that man is an organism—one indeed distinguished from other animals by powers of thought and choice—and alcohol is a chemical introduced into that living organism. The physiology of addiction is essential to any understanding of alcoholism. Before that, the physiology of alcohol itself is basic to all aspects of drinking behavior.

A large portion of the myths and misinformation still heard in the local tavern and even in alcohol education are in this area. "I drank a fifth of whiskey that evening and was cold sober when I drove home" or "You can't get drunk on beer; just avoid the hard liquor" are typical myths contrary to the facts of biochemistry. The alcoholism counselor need not be a biochemist, but must know the basic facts in order to deal effectively with drinking behavior.

Alcohol

Alcohol is a colorless, flammable, volatile liquid with a burning taste. (It is nearly odorless, so what is smelled on the breath is more likely other components of the beverage, or acetaldehyde.) Since alcohol absorbs water readily from the atmosphere, it is practically impossible to obtain in pure form. It is an excellent solvent and is widely used in many products, such as paint and perfume. Fermentation easily takes place in a warm place when yeast, a microscopic plant either placed manually or dropped from the air where it exists naturally, acts upon crushed fruits or grains that contain sugar or starches readily convertible into sugar. Tiny amounts of alcohol are produced naturally within the human body by certain enzyme systems, and are disposed of in various ways.

Beverage alcohol is ethyl alcohol, called *ethanol* in chemistry and sometimes abbreviated as ETOH. The formula is usually written C_2H_5OH, but can be written C_2H_6O or CH_3CH_2OH as well. It is the same alcohol found in all intoxicating beverages, from the most expensive Scotch or liqueur to the cheapest wine or beer. The main difference is not chemical but physical: the sheer volume of fluid which is taken in along with the ethanol. It is true that there are minor chemical differences due to other substances in the drink, especially in wine. But the major ingredient besides water is ethanol.

Congeners. The other substances in alcoholic beverages are called congeners, a term sometimes restricted to other alcohols and sometimes applied to many small-molecule compounds that may be present, depending on the fermented materials and the sanitary conditions of the process. All alcohols are intoxicating. Ethanol (two-carbon alcohol) is much less toxic than the others because the body breaks it down into harmless substances, carbon dioxide and water. Methyl (wood) alcohol, or methanol, breaks down into formic acid and formaldehyde, which has a special affinity for the optic nerve and may cause blindness. Methyl (one-carbon), propyl (three-carbon), butyl (four-carbon) and amyl (five-carbon, fusel oil) alcohols occur in trace amounts in many drinks. Although ethanol is the major intoxicant, other alcohols are present in real-life drinking, which make it different from the ethanol experiments in a laboratory—a fact that some researchers forget.

Proof is an old way of expressing alcohol concentration, from the days when "proof" of a whiskey used in barter was to mix it with a bit of gunpowder and see if it burned. Proof is twice the percent; a 100-proof liquor is 50 percent ethanol (in Canada and Britain 100 proof is 57 percent) and 86-proof whiskey is 43 percent ethanol. Wine and beer are usually expressed in straight percentages of alcohol, as described at the beginning of Chapter 3.

Ingestion

We have already noted that amount consumed is less a criterion of alcoholism than is how it affects one's behavior, dependency and control. We speak here simply of drinking. "A drink" is not a scientific term. Consumption rates are usually reduced to quantities of absolute alcohol, since this is the important factor rather than volume of beverage. The following are some common drinks with nearly equivalent amounts of alcohol (about 12.5 grams):

One 12-ounce bottle of 4 % beer . . . . 0.48 oz. ETOH
A 3½-ounce glass of dry 13 % wine. . . . . 0.45 oz. ETOH
A 2½-ounce glass of sweet 18 % wine . . . . 0.45 oz. ETOH
One ounce of 86-proof liquor . . . . 0.43 oz. ETOH

Rate of Ingestion.   In addition to the amount of ethanol ingested, the length of time over which consumption takes place is important. Sipping at the rate of one small drink an hour may allow the liver to prevent the blood level of alcohol from rising notably. A dare to "chug-a-lug" a pint of 100-proof whiskey at once killed a thirteen-year-old boy in our city.

So much for drinking. How does intoxication or drunkenness occur?

Absorption

Alcohol is one of the few substances, along with water and salts, that does not go through the usual digestive process even when taken into the digestive organs. Rather, it is absorbed directly and unchanged into the blood through the lining of the mouth and esophagus in tiny amounts, more through the stomach, and 70 to 80 percent through the upper or small intestine. Within two or three minutes after ingestion the alcohol begins to be circulated throughout the body, including the brain. This shows the importance of that first drink, which the recovered alcoholic seeks to avoid, since it almost immediately affects one's ability to judge or control whether one should have a second drink.

Blood Level

The result of absorption is blood alcohol level (BAL), or blood alcohol content (BAC). Think of pouring so many ounces of alcohol into so many pints of blood and measuring the strength or percentage of the resultant solution. This depends on many factors, so it is foolish to judge blood level, and therefore degree of intoxication, solely by the amount one drinks. Because Mary had three drinks and is so drunk, we cannot conclude that Jane is equally drunk with the same three drinks.

Body Size.   Even two people drinking the same amount over the same time will achieve different levels of blood alcohol. The larger person has more pints of blood into which the alcohol is diluted, so a 250-pound man will have a lower BAC than a 100-pound boy drinking the same amount. In addition, two people of the same weight will have slightly different blood levels, depending on the proportion of body weight that is fat as opposed to bone and muscle; since alcohol does not dissolve in fat, this results in a higher concentration in the blood. But why do two people of equal weight and build, drinking equal amounts in the same time, still have different blood alcohol levels?

Rate of Absorption   A major reason is the rate at which the alcohol is absorbed through the lining of the digestive tract into the bloodstream. This in turn depends on many factors, varying so widely between individuals, and between different occasions for the same individual, that comparisons are useless and misleading. These factors include the following:

1. Strength, or percentage of alcohol in the beverage. Beer contains so much more water that it is absorbed more slowly than stronger drinks. But too high a concentration of alcohol seems to sear the mucosa and retard absorption. The most rapid rate is, by no coincidence, that of the martini (35 to 40 percent).
2. Other chemicals in the drink, especially in beer and wine.
3. Carbonation, either natural, as in champagne, or added, as in a Scotch-and-soda highball. The tiny bubbles speed absorption by opening the pyloric valve into the small intestine, where absorption is more rapid, and they may also facilitate penetration of the gastrointestinal walls.
4. The amount and kind of food in the stomach. If the alcohol is soaked up with large amounts of food, especially fatty food, it will not be absorbed as quickly as in an empty stomach.
5. The condition of the tissues of stomach and bowel linings, whether healthy or not. Important here also is the pylorus, or pyloric valve, which opens to empty the contents of the stomach into the small intestine where absorption is more rapid than from the stomach. The pylorus may go into spasm and cause the person to vomit, or open suddenly and "dump" the alcohol quickly into the rapidly absorbing intestine.
6. Nervous or emotional state. Fear, anger, stress, and fatigue can influence the conditions of the stomach and bowel, usually speeding the process of absorption but sometimes slowing it. These states may also reduce tolerance in the central nervous system.
7. Altitude can also make a difference, as mountain climbers and aviators know. Rarified air means less oxygen for the brain, which alcohol further diminishes.
8. Individual differences in body chemistry and drinking history. No two people are exactly alike biochemically, nor have they had the same life experiences with alcohol. Each body reacts differently, so

again no comparisons are justified even if all the above conditions were equal—which is most unlikely.

Metabolism and Excretion

All the alcohol absorbed into the bloodstream is pumped by the heart to every part and tissue of the body, with effects on both short-term behavior and long-range health. Both of these we shall examine shortly. Intoxication results when the alcohol being circulated through the brain reaches a level that interferes with the normal functioning of nerve cells. The precise mechanism is still in dispute, although research is making it better understood than formerly.

What determines blood alcohol level? The rate of ingestion and absorption into the bloodstream varies with a dozen factors, as we have seen. In contrast, the rate at which it leaves the blood is fixed. Nothing can hasten the process, practically speaking. So the difference between the rate of absorption and the rate at which alcohol is gotten rid of gives us the residual blood alcohol level. If one takes in more alcohol than the body can dispose of, alcohol blood level rises. Only time will lower it after ingestion ceases.

Metabolism

Most of the alcohol (90 to 95 percent, depending on the BAC) is eliminated by being *metabolized* (oxidized, changed, detoxified, burned, broken down) into other substances, which are eventually eliminated from the body in the usual ways. Most of this metabolic activity takes place in the liver. Since it happens at a fixed rate, only part of the alcohol being pumped through the liver is metabolized at a time, while the rest continues to circulate. Chemically, the process of metabolism is as follows:

$$\text{Ethanol} + \text{Oxygen} \rightarrow \text{Acetaldehyde} \rightarrow \text{Acetate} \dashrightarrow \text{Carbon Dioxide} + \text{Water}$$
$$(C_2H_5OH) \quad (O_2) \quad (C_2H_4O) \quad (C_2H_4O_2) \quad (CO_2) \quad (H_2O)$$

which simply says that ethanol is oxidized first into acetaldehyde, which breaks down into some acetate, a salt or ester of acetic acid, and eventually into carbon dioxide and water.

All this metabolism is controlled by enzymes (biological catalysts which facilitate the process). Thus ethanol is broken down into acetaldehyde by alcohol dehydrogenase (ADH), and acetaldehyde is broken down to acetate by aldehyde dehydrogenase (ALDH). Both processes involve other enzymes, and also the coenzyme NAD (nicotinamide adenine dinucleotide), and its reduced form NADH. The reader need not understand all the chemistry involved, but should recognize the role of enzymes and know they are important for research.

The liver has at least one alternate metabolic pathway for the elimination of alcohol. It is the MEOS (microsomal ethanol oxidizing system). Research suggests that there may be important differences between the MEOS of alcoholics and nonalcoholics. Another difference may be a greater use of the enzyme catalase instead of ADH.

The enzyme action at the acetaldehyde stage can be blocked by the drug Antabuse (disulfiram, tetraethylthiuramdisulfide), preventing the acetaldehyde from breaking down further. If alcohol is taken while the drug is in the system, this blocking causes a buildup that results in acute acetaldehyde poisoning, or "Antabuse reaction." We shall discuss this under treatment, and only note the process here.

Rate of Metabolism.   Overestimating how fast liver burns up alcohol can send dangerously impaired drivers out on the highway. Ranging from less than 1/3 ounce to about 1/2 ounce, it is usually stated as 1/3 ounce per hour. Although a highly tolerant liver might burn up to a maximum of 12.5 grams or .535 ounce, Becker (1974, p. 13) says that a "normal" liver can metabolize about 7 grams (0.3 ounce) of ethanol per hour.

Seven grams is about the amount of ethanol in 3/4 ounce of 86-proof whiskey (= 0.32 ounce ETOH). Unfortunately, some writer carelessly transcribed this to 3/4 ounce of *alcohol* instead of 3/4 ounce of *whiskey*, and the error was copied from one book to another, including some otherwise standard works. Thus "one drink an hour" can be very misleading. No human liver can metabolize 3/4 ounce of alcohol in an hour. The 1/3 ounce, which is the most the average liver can handle, is less than the 0.43 to 0.48 ounces ETOH contained in the common drinks we listed under Ingestion. It is the amount contained in 8.8 ounces of beer, 2.6 ounces of dry wine, or 2/3 ounce of 100-proof liquor.

The rate at which the liver metabolizes alcohol may differ slightly between individuals, depending on the size and health of the liver. It may differ very slightly with the kind of alcoholic beverage. But by and large the rate is fixed by nature, except that chronic use can increase it somewhat. Research is still trying to discover a way of speeding up the process, and every party-goer would like to be able to eliminate the toxic effects once the party is over. Exercise, oxygen, cold showers, and black coffee are among the means tried, to no avail. If you give a gallon of black coffee to a drunk, you do not get a sober person but only an alert drunk. Fructose, or pure fruit sugar, was claimed by some to accelerate metabolism of alcohol. Besides being impractical, later research showed that it has harmful side effects such as depletion of ATP in the liver and lactic acidosis (Levy, 1977; Iber, 1977).

There is a faster metabolism rate at higher blood levels, but obviously to raise the alcohol level in order to speed the metabolism rate is to get nowhere fast. And stimulating a drunk with coffee may send him out on the highway instead of letting him sleep it off.

Excretion

Some 5 to 10 percent of the alcohol circulating is passed out of the bloodstream unmetabolized in the breath, perspiration, and urine. The amount varies slightly with higher BAC, but this is irrelevant because regardless of how much comes out this way, it is in a fixed ratio to the blood alcohol, for example, 1:2100 in the case of alveolar air from deep in the lungs. Since this alcohol is unchanged, the Breathalyzer or other device is measuring true blood alcohol, not some product of metabolism. It is thus a fair measure of intoxication, in spite of differences in amount consumed or rate of absorption. It tells the concentration of alcohol affecting the brain at the moment, regardless of how it got there. We shall see that two factors that can complicate this picture are individual differences in tolerance and whether the blood alcohol level is rising or falling.

Hangover

The sobering-up process is dependent primarily on the ability of the liver to burn up the alcohol in the blood, so there is little one can do except wait for that to happen. The morning-after misery we call hangover has been the subject of many myths, both as to cause and cure. The headache, nausea, and fatigue have been ascribed to such causes as drinking more than one type of beverage in an evening, but is simply the result of drinking too much alcohol in any form. Hangover can be prevented only by not drinking, or by drinking very slowly, with food in the stomach and under relaxed social conditions.

Hangover is an unpleasant experience, but rarely dangerous. No satisfactory treatment is known. The numerous folk remedies—tomato juice, raw egg, hot sauce, and so on—have no scientific validity. Coffee may help, but can harm a stomach already irritated by alcohol. Aspirin can be quite harmful to the stomach lining. None of these remedies speed up the sobering-up process; they merely relieve some of the uncomfortable symptoms.

Medical treatment of withdrawal in chronic alcoholism is an entirely different and more serious matter, to be dealt with later. Meanwhile, the search for amethyst or magic pill goes on: a pill one can take before the party so as to enjoy alcohol without suffering its harmful effects, a pill to sober up quickly afterward, a pill so the recovered alcoholic can drink socially, and a pill for instant cure of the hangover. All of these seem founded only in man's hope, and contrary to what we know of the biochemistry. In any case, they betray a questionable value assigned to alcohol.

Alcohol and Health: Long-range Effects

We shall conclude this chapter with a brief overview of the long-range effects of alcohol on health, postponing for the next chapter our consideration of its short-term effects on behavior.

Nutrition

Some quibble about whether alcohol should be classed as a food. Certainly it is a poor one. But since it can supply up to 70 percent of the body's caloric needs and is a ready source of energy, it meets a common meaning of the term *food*. Pure alcohol yields 7.1 calories per gram or over 200 calories to the ounce. Wine and especially beer have some additional calories from the content of the original material that survives fermentation. Alcohol serves as a substitute source of energy, which allows the body to store other foods as fat, so it is fattening in an indirect but positive way.

Alcohol is the classic example of "empty calories" because it contains no vitamins, minerals, or proteins. Even the small amount of vitamins and trace minerals in wine and beer cannot redeem its poor nutritional value. Moreover, alcohol interferes with the body's ability to utilize the vitamins and other nutrients in what foods are eaten. Hence, even fat alcoholics are usually suffering from some degree of malnutrition, especially avitaminosis (lack of vitamins). The "wine sores" on the skin of skidroad alcoholics, due to the substitution of cheap wine for a balanced diet, can occur in wealthy alcoholics also.

Alcohol: A Direct Cause

The truth of the preceding paragraph makes it tempting to blame malnutrition for all physical pathology in alcoholics, and even alcoholism itself. This is simplistic, and the answer is not to place multivitamin pills in all bars—if for no other reason than that alcohol interferes with their assimilation.

In 1938 an article appeared claiming that the so-called wet brain was an unscientific scare story spread by the Women's Christian Temperance

Union to promote prohibition, and that alcohol itself did not cause damage to the brain, liver, and other organs. This was repeated for the next two decades even in the scientific literature, until research by J. Beard and D. Knott in Memphis, Charles Lieber in New York, and others at outstanding medical research centers began to show that along with avitaminosis and other nutritional factors, alcohol itself can cause, both directly and indirectly, organic damage in well-nourished experimental animals and human beings. C. B. Courville's 1955 book *The Effects of Alcohol on the Nervous System of Man* has been superseded by more recent works by Ernest Noble, James Rankin, A. E. Bennett, H. Kalant, Yedy Israel, Frank Seixas, and a host of scientists, making the conclusion irrefutable. Lieber (1976), perhaps the world's leading authority on alcohol and the liver, is quite clear that adequate diet does not prevent alcohol from doing widespread damage in the body. Of special interest is the research of James W. Smith and others, showing lowered intelligence and brain damage in alcoholics with middle to upper socioeconomic backgrounds to be equal to that in impoverished and presumably less well-nourished alcoholics.

Research is only now uncovering the specific mechanisms whereby alcohol causes physical damage, and much remains to be discovered. Although alcohol in high doses is a depressant in its ultimate effect, its initial effect on tissue is to irritate. For example, its role as a possible carcinogen in the upper digestive tract may be partly due to its property as an irritant.

We can only briefly enumerate the principal organic pathologies and refer the reader to more detailed medical treatises. But it should be kept in mind that the following does not apply only to alcoholics, and much of it not even to drunkenness. Even moderate social drinking can produce many of the phenomena to be presented here, to a lesser degree of course.

Liver

Although the action of alcohol on the brain produces the most common and serious behavioral consequences, the liver is the site of most illness and mortality among alcoholics. An enlarged, fatty liver is the first stage, due to accumulation of excess fat. This is reversible, and disappears with cessation of alcohol intake. However, Lieber says that some deaths may be due to just fatty liver. If fatty infiltration continues, necrosis, or death, of hepatic (liver) cells, irritation, and swelling that causes blockage, result in inflammation of the liver called alcoholic hepatitis. This is not to be confused with infectious hepatitis or serum hepatitis, all of them having jaundice as a symptom. Although there is a high mortality rate, alcoholic hepatitis may still be reversible. But the next stage is not: cirrhosis. This is scar tissue in the liver, fibrous hard material, which like any scar is non-functional and will never be normal again. Cirrhosis is a major cause of death among alcoholics.

In assessing liver damage we must distinguish anatomy (structure) from physiology (function). Nature tends to compensate, so tests of liver function will sometimes send up word, "Everything going fine down here, doc" when up to 70 percent of liver cells may be sick. But 80 percent damage could mean death. An old alcoholic with "just one more drunk left" might be in between the 70 and the 80 percent, though his friends don't know the exact explanation of his death after a binge. An alcoholic living on the 10 percent margin could die if the doctor allows drinking to be resumed when liver function tests are normal. Even the SGPT test shows *rate* of liver cell necrosis, not *extent*. Snipping a bit of tissue in a biopsy may tell a different story, as in the experiment on a group of British medical students who drank only up to 0.1 percent (legal) BAC every night for two weeks. A biopsy on every one of them showed structural change.

The liver is the body's chemical laboratory, with an incredible array of functions. It manufactures bile, glycogen, albumin, globulin, prothrombin, and other substances for fighting infection, blood clotting (hence alcoholics show more bruises and bleeding), and general health. In vulnerable persons, drinking can trigger a painful gouty arthritis due to excessive uric acid. The liver controls the levels of cholesterol, fatty acids, and triglycerides, which harm both liver and cardiovascular system.

Since alcohol interferes with the proper conversion of sugar, it is obviously hard on diabetics. High blood sugar (hyperglycemia) and low blood sugar (hypoglycemia) can both be due to a sick liver. We must distinguish hepatic, or alcoholic, hypoglycemia from true hypoglycemia, which is relatively rare. Hypoglycemia is *not* a cause of alcoholism, but a complication for which the worst remedy is a candy bar. This shoots blood sugar up, exciting the pancreas to secrete more insulin and thus dropping blood sugar even lower, as well as stressing the pancreas. What is needed is a balanced, low-carbohydrate, high-protein diet that levels off the blood sugar and prevents these gross fluctuations. (However, hypoglycemia in an unconscious alcoholic patient may cause brain damage from low glucose levels; here intravenous glucose is indicated and can do no harm.)

Another major function of the liver is that it *detoxifies* many substances in the blood, from alcohol and other psychoactive drugs to excess female hormones in the male. A sick liver fails to eliminate the residue of dead red blood cells, with resulting yellow color in skin and whites of the eyes so characteristic of liver disease. The liver is thus an important part of the body's defenses.

Because a damaged liver makes less globulin and is otherwise less efficient, heavy drinkers are less able to throw off colds and infections. Tuberculosis has been practically wiped out in America, except among vagrant alcoholics whose systems do not readily handle the TB bacillus we are all exposed to, or whose life style is conducive to reactivating a latent case while others stay cured. Alcohol seems to exacerbate skin diseases like psoriasis and acne rosacea, which often mitigate when drinking stops.

Is alcohol good for a cold? It may make you feel the discomfort less, but it impedes the body's ability to fight off viruses and bacteria. Alcohol also interferes with the effectiveness of most medicines, including antibiotics and antihistamines. "I drink lots of alcohol and that kills the bugs" not only contradicts the above two statements but also contains another fallacy. A solution of alcohol strong enough to be antibiotic is a hundred times stronger than the lethal dose of blood alcohol: It would kill you long before it killed anything else. "Red wine kills viruses" was a May 1977 front-page headline; but careful reading of the story revealed that grape juice was even more effective, as the active ingredient was some agent in the red skin of the grape and not the alcohol that characterizes wine.

Cardiovascular System

Before discussing the heart and blood, we must point to a major impact of liver disease on blood circulation. Almost all blood circulating through the digestive tract passes through the liver on its way back to the heart; both hepatic inflammation and cirrhosis cause obstruction of this flow, with resulting back pressure in the portal vein. From this may develop varicose swelling in abdominal veins, internal bleeding, hemorrhoids (piles), and esophageal varices. These latter are swollen veins at the base of the esophagus, just above the stomach, due to this back pressure. With high acidity and lowered clotting power to increase the danger, rupture of an esophageal varix is an extremely high mortality risk and is often precipitated by the alcoholic's vomiting or "dry heaves."

Heart.   Richard J. Bing of Huntington Memorial Hospital introduced the 1978 AMSA panel of specialists on alcoholic cardiomyopathy by stating that research has shown both that alcohol causes direct damage to the heart and the biochemical explanation of how it does so. Once in question, there is now no doubt that in addition to fatty infiltration, alcohol causes heart damage even when malnutrition or lipids are not a factor. Likewise, that even moderate amounts of alcohol can stress the myocardium, or heart muscle. Even one drink has been shown to diminish myocardial contractility (Schuckit, 1978a, p. 77). High blood pressure often drops to normal when drinking stops. Binge drinking followed by strenuous exercise can be fatal even in young people. The work of Pennington and Knisely (1973) on blood sludging has not been accepted by all authorities in the field, but there is enough other evidence to yield a consensus that alcohol, and especially prolonged heavy drinking, is a significant cause of congestive heart failure, enlarged heart, elevated diastolic blood pressure, peripheral edema (swelling), and myocarditis (Burch, 1971; Smith, 1977b).

An old myth perpetuated by many physicians prescribed wine as beneficial to the heart, especially in the elderly. But as early as 1965 an AMA committee reported that although alcohol dilates arterioles in the skin, it has no beneficial effect on the coronary arteries (see Webb, 1965). More recently, some researchers claimed that moderate drinkers live longer than total abstainers or heavy drinkers. As every freshman in statistics knows, correlation does not mean causality. Probably there is a population sampling fallacy here: It is not necessarily true that moderate drinkers live longer because they drink, but because the personality and life style of total abstainers may make them more prone to heart attack than moderate drinkers. In any case, the one drink a day associated with longevity is quite foreign to the problem drinkers who would love to use this to bolster their rationalizations. Habit-forming and open to self-prescription, alcohol is too easily abused for the physician to encourage its use. In fact, the same AMA committee reported that there is no acceptable use of alcohol as a medication—even for snake bite. And we do know that life expectancy for alcoholics is twelve to sixteen years shorter than for nonalcoholics. Recent claims of "good cholesterol" from alcohol mitigate the picture only slightly.

Blood. "Red wine builds red blood" is another myth that modern science has disproven. The hematopoietic (blood-building) system is slowed down by alcohol, decreasing the production of red blood cells primarily, but also platelets and white cells. This interferes with clotting, fighting infection, and, in extreme cases, with the supply of oxygen to the brain.

Brain and Nervous System

The brain is by far the most important organ through which alcohol affects behavior. Nerve action requires energy from oxidizing glucose, with the aid of coenzyme Adenosine Tri-Phosphate (ATP). Alcohol interferes with the supply of oxygen to the brain, decreasing the use of oxygen by the brain cells as much as 30 percent at 0.3 percent BAC, and 60 to 80 percent at 0.5 percent BAC. Even at blood levels of 0.1 percent to 0.2 percent, alcohol diminishes notably the ATP action.

In addition, alcohol interferes with the production and functioning of a host of substances in the brain whose role and even existence research is still discovering, going by such names as endorphins, enkephalins, biogenic amines, neuro-hormones, neuro-transmitters, catecholamines, etc. and including serotonin, dopamine, salsolinol, acetylcholine, and norepinephrine. Some of these are opiatelike substances naturally produced in the brain, which may be the key to the process of addiction.

The results of all this interference may be divided into three phases: *immediate* effects on behavior and mental functioning due to alcohol being present in the blood; *temporary* effects after alcohol has been eliminated; and *permanent* brain damage. The first will be treated in the next chapter.

Temporary.   The second phase includes withdrawal phenomena, rebound effects like interference with sleep patterns, which may last some days or weeks, and residual toxicity in the brain, which may last long after blood alcohol has reached zero. Some are speaking now of "90 day detox" for this latter reason, and there is a rule of thumb allowing one month for every year of drinking, which is not scientifically accurate but has some foundation in fact. Injured brain cells may take up to two years to return to normal. Electroencephalographic changes last for six months to a year after sobriety (Seixas, 1977, p. 64). Alcohol diminishes the body's defenses against auditory nerve damage due to loud sound, which may explain why the morning after brings pain from sudden noises. Drinking bouts often leave the person anxious and depressed, which is ironic in view of the fact that many people drink in a futile attempt to combat anxiety and depression.

Sleep disturbances may be due in part to nature's compensating for the depressing effect of alcohol by sending up extra volleys of nerve impulses through the reticular activating system (RAS), which continue after the alcohol has worn off. Thus it is a common experience to have alcohol make one drowsy in the evening, but to wake up earlier than usual as this compensation occurs. Other causes of insomnia can be the action of alcohol on biogenic amines like serotonin and norepinephrine, drug withdrawal, and the clinical depression that is often a concomitant of alcoholism (Smith, 1977a, pp. 123–125).

Blackouts are losses of memory, not to be confused with passing out. Anybody who drinks enough alcohol may become unconscious, but in a blackout people remain conscious and may continue with conversation or activities, only to discover later that they cannot remember parts or all of what went on. The period of amnesia may cover a few minutes or hours, a lost weekend, or much more. It can range from mere fuzziness as to where one parked the car to forgetting serious matters. The person may be astonished later when confronted with such tangible evidence as signed traffic citations, receipts, or checks. These reminders and therapeutic means of recall do not restore memory of the events, because rather than inability to recall there seems to be failure of memory-storage processes in the brain. It is usually associated with a rising BAC (Goodwin, 1977), possibly due to oxygen deprivation. Blackouts are not to be confused with fainting (syncope) or with seizure states.

Hallucinations may be visual, auditory, or mixed. This author has never known an alcoholic who saw pink elephants, but imaginary dogs and cats running in and out of the room, little red bugs crawling all over the body, and imaginary voices are common. The old distinction that ascribed visual hallucinations to alcohol and auditory ones to schizophrenia or other psychosis seems invalid (Becker, 1974, p. 40). More important is the distinction between alcoholic hallucinosis and delirium tremens.

Hallucinosis in the first thirty-six hours of withdrawal may involve mild disorientation in time, but generally the patient is not disoriented, memory is fairly good, sensorium remains clear (patient is fairly alert and may be easily startled), and the patient may be able to converse intelligently with insight into the fact that he is hallucinating. It may appear in the history only if the patient is asked about nightmares and vivid daydreams, and is not serious.

Delirium tremens (DTs) is a most severe withdrawal state, with a high mortality rate from cardiovascular collapse if not well handled. It usually peaks after about three days of abstinence, but can occur several days thereafter. It is marked by severe tremors, agitation and fast pulse, anxiety, paranoia, and profound disorientation with no insight. Profuse sweating, hypothermia, fever, diarrhea, vomiting, and short breath may also accompany the delirium. The distinction must be carefully made and emergency medication given.

Seizures, convulsions of the grand mal (epileptic) type, rarely occur during delirium tremens. These "rum fits" tend to occur during the first forty-eight hours of withdrawal after prolonged heavy drinking, but may occur later, especially in polydrug users. They are usually not dangerous, but can be. Alcoholic seizures are presumed not to be a symptom of epilepsy if clearly related to withdrawal and if neurological signs are normal. Alcohol does lower the seizure threshold in borderline epileptics, and a history of this should be investigated. *Status epilepticus* occurs in 3 percent of alcohol withdrawal seizures, with no agreement as to specific cause. It is a continuous series of seizures without regaining consciousness, and is very serious.

Peripheral neuropathy usually begins with pain in the calf muscles, tingling or burning sensations or numbness in the feet and lower extremities, and eventually in the hands and arms. It weakens muscles, producing a drop-foot gait; poor balance may lead to walking with legs spread. It can be due to many causes, but is often found in malnourished alcoholics. Symptoms disappear with abstinence from alcohol, a good diet, and B vitamins. Antabuse is not recommended for these alcoholics.

Permanent Brain Damage. The third phase is interwoven with the normal loss of brain cells we all suffer, estimated over a lifetime at about 10 percent of the billions we are born with, which results in little, if any, loss of function because nature can compensate to some extent by developing shunt, or alternate, pathways. It has long been known that alcoholics have permanent brain damage. Dead nerve cells (gray matter) never regenerate, so such damage is irreversible. The electron microscope has revealed details of cell damage, and gross brain shrinkage is observed in postmortem examinations, by pneumoencephalogram (Xray of skull after replacing cerebrospinal fluid with air), by computerized brain scan, by changes in brain-wave patterns as measured on the electroencephalogram (EEG), and by psychological tests of mental function designed to measure brain damage. One medical school professor is reported to have refused to accept cadavers of transients picked up by police because the brains were so deteriorated as not to be representative of the human brain he wanted his pupils to study.

It was once thought that malnutrition, and specifically avitaminosis, caused all this. It is now conceded that alcohol itself also causes brain damage (Seixas, 1973) although the precise mechanisms are still being researched. Noble points out that young brains are particularly vulnerable, so this is not a mere matter of aging. Actually, a lot of damage explained away as just aging is due to alcohol. Sludging, decrease in brain protein synthesis (Carlen, 1978), interference with RNA, damage to nerve cell membranes, fluid pressure leading to atrophy, and other mechanisms may play a part in alcohol brain damage. Magnesium loss is a big factor in brain malfunction, according to Dr. Gustava Steindelenberg of the Karolinska Institute in Sweden. The Wernicke-Korsakoff syndrome is known to be due in great part to vitamin B_1 deficiency, but Maurice Victor and others have shown that at least cerebellar degeneration is due to alcohol rather than just to avitaminosis; studies by Tewari and Noble seem to point to this in the cerebral regions also. Needless to say, the numerous head injuries sustained by alcoholics no doubt contribute to the total picture of cerebral deficit.

The Wernicke-Korsakoff syndrome (Victor, 1972; Smith, 1977a) is a result of brain damage. Symptoms of Wernicke's disease are first confusion and excitement, then double vision from palsy of the third or sixth cranial nerve, then sleepiness and stupor, with perhaps hypothermia. Korsakoff's psychosis is often found in patients clearing from the Wernicke syndrome. Peripheral neuropathy is common. There is illogic, hallucinosis, disorientation, and severe memory deficit for recent events. This memory loss coupled with poor judgment of appropriateness or plausibility leads some patients to make up improbable stories: confabulation. Others confabulate stories far beyond the need to fill a memory gap. Not all exhibit confabulation, but all have severe lack of verbal recall, and

emotional disturbances resembling psychosis. The symptom is often reversible with thiamine treatment in the Wernicke phase, but in the Korsakoff
phase often shows only partial and poor recovery rates. The symptoms occur in other patients, but are most common in chronic, undernourished
alcoholics. See Chapter III of *Alcohol and Health*, the Fourth Special Report to Congress by NIAAA, 1981.

Other Systems

Genitourinary Tract.   Does alcohol enhance sex? There are many
myths that associate drinking with virility. Yet long ago Shakespeare
(*Macbeth*, Act II, Scene 3) noted that drink both provokes and unpro-
vokes lechery: "It provokes the desire, but it takes away the performance." In spite of the fact that drink lowers inhibitions and may remove
romantic desires from the control of good judgment, alcoholics are known
to be poor sex performers. We now know the reasons (Van Thiel, 1975,
1976; Smith, Lemere, and Dunn, 1974): a) Alcohol causes inflammation
of the prostate gland (prostatitis), which interferes with erection and cli-
max; b) it causes sedation and eventual atrophy of the testicles, causing
decreased sperm output and lower male hormones in the blood (Gordon,
1976); c) a toxic liver may produce up to five times the amount of liver enzyme that normally breaks down testosterone; d) lastly, the adrenal
glands in both men and women secrete both male and female hormones
into the bloodstream, but in men a healthy liver detoxifies the female hormones. In an alcoholic man the adrenals may be putting out more female
hormones than his sick liver can detoxify, with a resultant buildup that
causes feminine characteristics, such as enlarged breasts and more hair
(which may explain the lower rate of baldness some claim for alcoholics).
In women, sexual drive can also be decreased by alcohol, and alcoholic
women seem to have a higher incidence of menstrual irregularities
(Schuckit, 1971).

Digestive System.   Alcohol irritates the lining of the gastrointestinal organs, especially the stomach, and complicates the problem of acidity. The result is gastritis and heartburn, and eventually ulcers. Hemorrhage from a perforated ulcer, or just seepage through the stomach lining,
can be massive. We have already mentioned death from ruptured esophageal varices. Death can also occur from choking on one's own vomit (as-
piration).

Sudduth has theorized (1977) that drinking causes enterotoxemia (in-
flamed stomach and bowels) and more alcohol then sedates the irritation
from these bacterial neurotoxins. This may provide a physiological explanation for the vicious circle of alcohol addiction. He also points out that

(along with malnutrition) alcohol causes liver damage via endotoxins from gasterointestinal bacteria rather than directly, as carbon tetrachloride does; the evidence is that this cannot happen in a germ-free animal where enterotoxemia is impossible.

The pancreas is a major organ of the body, because of its secretion of digestive enzymes and insulin, which converts blood sugar. Alcohol causes inflammation, or pancreatitis, and pancreatic cirrhosis, sometimes resulting in alcoholic or pseudo-diabetes. Acute pancreatitis is extremely painful and has a high mortality rate. But after an attack subsides pain may not occur, which does not mean that the damage is gone.

Electrolytes and Fluid Balance.   Many of the ions important for body functioning are dissipated or lost because of the action of alcohol on the kidneys. Magnesium, phosphate, calcium, and potassium levels are among those that can be affected. In addition, when blood level is rising, alcohol inhibits the antidiuretic hormone from the pituitary gland in the brain, causing frequent urination and flushing out of body electrolytes. This action reverses as blood alcohol goes down, causing retention of body fluids and bloating. Not all alcoholics admitted to the hospital are dehydrated; the thirst may be from the drying effect of alcohol and from breathing through the mouth while unconscious, but mostly it is due to a shift of water from inside the body cells. Hence routine intravenous feeding of fluids is not indicated, but only after true dehydration is diagnosed and overhydration is ruled out. J. Beard and D. Knott have written extensively on this (for example, Knott, 1967; Beard, 1968).

Other Disorders

In addition to fractures and other injuries, the disorders associated with excessive use of alcohol range from dermatitis to weakening of body muscles (myopathy and myositis), from subdural hematoma to necrosis of the femoral head requiring surgical replacement. One surgeon reports that every male patient over fifty on whom he has performed this operation was a heavy drinker.

Hypothermia, or loss of body heat, is an important effect of alcohol. We talk of feeling a glow, but actually the warmth felt in the face and extremities is because heat is being dissipated at an abnormal rate. Many deaths of hunters and hikers listed as due to exposure are really due to rapid loss of body heat because they were drinking. Patients in detoxification units must be kept warm to prevent death from hypothermia. Although Lieber and others have challenged the notion that alcohol precipitates shock through adrenal failure, its use in emergencies is prohibited by the Red Cross *Manual* for good reasons. To explode another myth, the St.

Bernard dogs who rescued people in the Swiss Alps had cold tea and not brandy in the keg tied around their necks. Brandy would interfere with the dog's sense of smell.

Cancer. "Alcohol is indisputably involved in the causation of cancer. . ." according to the HEW-NIAAA *Third Special Report to Congress on Alcohol and Health* (1978, pp. 47–51). An impressive amount of evidence suggests that it may be at least a contributing factor or part cause in many cases (Whelan, 1978; Tuyns, 1978). The high incidence of cancer in the mouth, esophagus, and stomach among those who drink hard liquor points to its irritant quality before it gets diluted in the bloodstream. It also seems to be carcinogenic in lower concentrations in all parts of the body and especially in the pancreas and liver. Tobacco complicates the issue, and the two may be mutually reinforcing.

Fetal Alcohol Syndrome

In ancient Carthage and Sparta there was a custom that newlyweds drink no wine, lest a defective child be born. Aristotle said there was good reason. In 1748 a British physician noted that when gin became cheap more mothers gave birth to babies that were physically defective or mentally retarded. Similar observations were made by Liverpool physician William C. Sullivan in 1899 and 1900, and in a 1923 British scientific journal by A.L. McElroy. During the long and bitter fight over Prohibition, these facts were brushed aside as WCTU scare tactics. Even more enlightened alcohol publications in the 1940s through the 1960s repudiated them. In 1968 Lemoine made the observation in France. Controlled studies began to be made elsewhere. Medical reports confirmed that the fetus does indeed take in alcohol through the placenta from the mother's blood. Infants are born intoxicated, and show distinct signs of withdrawal (much of what was called colic may have been just this). But more permanent and irreversible damage to the newborn child was identified in 1973 with a fairly consistent pattern of symptoms now known as the *fetal alcohol syndrome* (FAS).

Babies whose mothers were known to be imbibing alcohol during pregnancy are statistically more likely to exhibit some or all of the following symptoms: short length and underweight, which do not catch up to normal later; small head, small brains, and mental deficiency; heart defects, poor coordination, abnormal creases on the palms; joint and limb irregularities, such as hip dislocation and odd fingers or toes; hyperactivity later in childhood. But along with the irreversible mental retardation and underweight, the most characteristic sign is the peculiar face: short palpebral fissures (narrow eye socket), epicanthal folds (skin over the inner corner of the eye), low nasal bridge with short upturned nose, narrow upper lip giving the mouth a fishlike shape, and often a receding chin, protruding forehead, and deformed ears. Winsome, "elfinlike" children of this description are often mentally retarded, says Ann Streissguth (1976, 1978).

After some healthy scientific skepticism, it is now recognized that maternal blood alcohol is the specific cause. Many animal studies show these results with good controls: no smoking, no other drugs, no nutritional deficiency. But wide studies on human mothers also controlled for these variables, including socio-economic and other environmental factors, nutrition, and smoking. Many alcoholic mothers do smoke heavily, and nicotine may combine with alcohol here. But FAS still occurs in the progeny of drinking mothers who do not smoke.

This is not heredity, but intra-uterine environment. It seems most likely to occur in the first trimester of gestation, especially if binge drinking produces high levels of blood alcohol at a crucial point in the development of the infant's central nervous system. But since the nervous system is by no means fully developed by the end of three months, and since there is some evidence that even moderate blood levels can produce defects, mothers are well advised not to drink at all during pregnancy. Other psychoactive drugs should also be avoided. The catch is that most women only learn they are pregnant after missing a menstrual period, by which time they may be six weeks along. It is wise to avoid alcohol if they are planning to have a baby, or at least limit themselves to one drink maximum (not average) a day so that blood alcohol never rises notably.

Sources

The literature on the effects of alcohol on the body is prodigious. General treatment of the subject is given in Gross, "Psychobiological Contributions to the Alcohol Dependence Syndrome: A Selective Review of Recent Research," which appeared in *Alcohol-Related Disabilities*, a World Health Organization publication, in 1971; and in such books as *Alcohol as a Drug: A Curriculum of Pharmacology, Neurology and Toxicology*, by Charles Becker and others; and in the four special reports to the United States Congress by the Department of Health, Education, and Welfare and NIAAA entitled *Alcohol and Health*. Chapters or sections of general texts also provide overviews, for example, Part II of Estes and Heinemann. In addition, there are numerous collections of research articles, some of which are listed below, which deal in great detail with specific aspects of the physiological effects of alcohol on the body and with the methodology of investigating them, and which provide extensive bibliographies at the end of each chapter. For up-to-date information on the effect of alcohol on a particular bodily system, it is well to consult the medical specialty journals. Some other useful sources:

Alcohol and Nutrition, NIAAA Research Monograph No. 2, 1979.

Begleiter, Henri (ed.), *Biological Effects of Alcohol*.

Bourne, Peter and Ruth Fox (eds.), *Alcoholism: Progress in Research and Treatment* (especially chapters 4, 5, 6 and 15).

Cole, Jonathan O. (ed.), *Clinical Research in Alcoholism.*

Edwards, G., Milton M. Gross, Mark Keller, J. Moser, and R. Room (eds.), *Alcohol-Related Disabilities* (especially the article by Gross mentioned above).

Estes, Nada and M. Edith Heinemann (eds.), *Alcoholism: Development, Consequences, and Interventions.*

Forsander, O. and K. Eriksson (eds.), *Biological Aspects of Alcohol Consumption.*

Gibbins, R.J. (ed.), *Research Advances in Alcohol and Drug Problems*, Y. Israel (ed.), vol 4; Oriana Kalant (ed.), vol. 5.

Gross, Milton M. (ed.), *Alcohol Intoxication and Withdrawal: Experimental Studies I, II.*

Israel, Y. and J. Mardones (eds.), *Biological Basis of Alcoholism.*

Kissin, B. and H. Begleiter (eds.), *Biology of Alcoholism*, 5 vols., several of which go well beyond biology.

Lowenfels, A.B., The Alcoholic Patient in Surgery.

Majchrowicz, E. and E.P. Noble (eds.), *Biochemistry and Pharmacology of Ethanol.*

Mello, N.K. and J.H. Mendelson (eds.), *Recent Advances in Studies of Alcoholism: An Interdisciplinary Symposium.*

Mendelson, J.H. and N.K. Mello (eds.), *Diagnosis and Treatment of Alcoholism.*

Noble, Ernest P. (ed.), *Biochemical Pharmacology of Alcohol.*

Roach, Mary K., and William M. McIsaac (eds.), *Biological Aspects of Alcohol.*

Schuckit, Marc A. (ed.), "Alcoholism: A Symposium with CME Credit Quiz," *Postgraduate Medicine*, December 1978, 64(6):76–158.

Seixas, Frank A. (ed.), *Currents in Alcoholism*, 6 vols. He also edited *Work in Progress in Alcoholism: Annals of the New York Academy of Sciences*, yearly since 1970.

Seixas, Frank A., K. Williams and S. Eggleston (eds.), "Medical Consequences of Alcoholism," *Work in Progress in Alcoholism: Annals of the New York Academy of Sciences.*

Sudduth, William, "The Role of Bacteria and Enterotoxemia in Physical Addiction to Alcohol," *Journal of the International Academy of Preventive Medicine*, 1977, 4(2):23–46.

Wallgren, H. and H. Barry (eds.), *Actions of Alcohol*, 2 vols.

Fetal Alcohol Syndrome

It is worthwhile to provide a special bibliography on the fetal alcoholism syndrome as, for the most part, it is not yet covered in collections of articles such as those cited above. Jones and his colleagues published their observations on the fetal alcohol syndrome in *Lancet* in 1973 and so piqued the interest of clinicians and researchers that publications on the subject have been proliferating since then. A good popular presentation can be found in a booklet, *Just So It's Healthy* by Lucy B. Robe, and a good bibliography of the literature up to 1977 is included. Other bibliographies have been issued by NCA and NIAAA. The latter is contained in Blane and Hewitt, *Alcohol and Youth. An Analysis of the Literature, 1960–1975* (Appendix I). David Smith's chapter, "Fetal Alcohol Syndrome: A Tragic and Preventable Disorder," in Estes and Heinemann, is an excellent summary of the findings to that date. More recent is "The Fetal Alcohol Syndrome: A Review of the World Literature" by S. K. Clarren and D. W. Smith, *New England Journal of Medicine*, 1978, 298:1063–1067. The recent burst of interest in the effects on the offspring of maternal drinking is part of a long history of observation and concern. Warner and Rosett trace this history in their article "The Effects of Drinking on Offspring: An Historical Survey of the American and British Literature." See also El-Guebaly (1977).

CHAPTER 5

Alcohol and Behavior; Driving

WE HAVE ALREADY SEEN the effect of alcohol on the health and functioning of many body organs. We now turn to how alcohol affects behavior, and especially when driving a motor vehicle because of its large place in American life and the high death and accident rates it engenders. If Ralph Nader were as concerned about safe drivers as about safe cars, there would be far fewer deaths on our highways.

We have seen that if ingestion and absorption of alcoholic beverages is faster than the rate at which the liver can metabolize the alcohol, blood alcohol level (BAC) rises. Until detoxified in the liver or eliminated through excretion, all the alcohol is being circulated through all organs of the body. But we shall focus on its effect on neural tissue, especially the brain, of both alcoholics and nonalcoholics.

Stimulant or Depressant?

At a cocktail party, after a few drinks the noise level goes up and the conversation is more animated. The obvious conclusion is that alcohol is a stimulant. Much of this is pseudostimulation, the result of the depressing action of alcohol on those brain centers that mediate inhibitions, judgment, and control. Knocking out the brakes is a depressant action on the braking system, but the net result might be more action by the car.

69

For years this was widely accepted as the total explanation, although Mark Keller (1966) reviewed a long history of experimentation which showed that alcohol is a stimulant before it is a depressant. It is now recognized that the first action of alcohol on neural tissue is to irritate, agitate, or stimulate. In addition, the calories present in alcohol supply quick energy—"candy is dandy, but liquor is quicker" has some biochemical basis. All this has been known for some time (Wallgren and Barry, 1970) and confirmed by more recent research, such as that of Yedy Israel on the hypermetabolic state in alcoholics (Isselbacher, 1977, p. 612). It will be relevant when we discuss the theory that all alcoholics drink to sedate inner stress from emotional conflict.

This is not simple, since some brain cells are inhibitory and some are excitatory, and alcohol may facilitate nerve transmission in some cells while depressing it in others, even though it is bathing the whole brain. The "onion" or "layers" notion of brain functions is only schematic at best; but it may well be that alcohol depresses the more delicate areas of the cerebral cortex before depressing the centers for vital functions located in the old, or lower, brain. Suffice it to say that although the long-range effect of alcohol, even on alcoholics, is to depress nerve action to the point of coma and even death, its immediate effect is to stimulate.

Important is the fact that alcoholics seem to get more of an initial lift from alcohol than nonalcoholics do (Goodwin, 1978a, p. 129). There is some evidence that this is true right from the beginning of their drinking career, but research on this latter point is difficult, since it depends on retrospective reports that are highly subjective as well as distorted by time. This initial lift is congruent with the mounting evidence that alcoholics differ physiologically from nonalcoholics from the onset of drinking. Instead of sedation (nobody hosts a social hour where barbiturates are passed around instead of cocktails), it may be that the alcoholic is looking for that "glow," or extra lift, rather than for tension reduction (Cappell, 1972; Keehn, 1970).

Another reason why the alcoholic may function better after drinking a little alcohol is that he has developed a physical dependence and now needs alcohol to bring functions up to normal. And for everyone there is the possibility that a drink may quell anxiety and allow abilities to reach maximum operation, which does not mean that alcohol actually adds to our abilities. Research has shown that artists and writers who were alcoholic produced great works in spite of being alcoholic, not because of it (see *Writer's Digest*, October 1978, pp. 25–33).

Effects on Behavior

Psychologists earn their living measuring human behaviors, and a review of the literature yields the following chart, which depicts the effects of al-

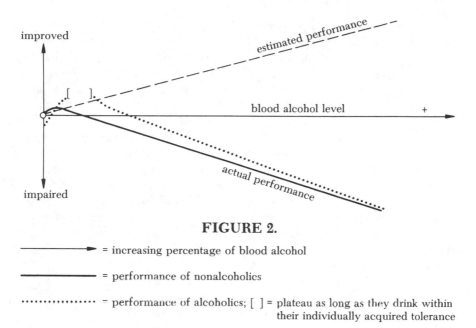

FIGURE 2.

—————▶ = increasing percentage of blood alcohol

————— = performance of nonalcoholics

················ = performance of alcoholics; [ ] = plateau as long as they drink within their individually acquired tolerance

— — — — —· = estimated performance of both groups

cohol on driving and every other measurable behavior; the horizontal line represents increased levels of BAC from zero to coma and death. What it tells us is that alcohol initially improves behavior slightly for a brief time, then decreases performance. Alcoholics with zero alcohol often start below normal, improve more than others, and continue improved for as long as they stay within their individually acquired tolerance. But as the blood level rises the quality and quantity of performance for all drops below the initial norm, a fact we have all observed as we watch a very drunk person attempt the simplest tasks and eventually pass out.

Many experiments have been done on this, often using cab or truck drivers or racing drivers, all of whom were drinkers, so they were not novices at either experience. Objective ratings according to standard criteria by driving instructors and licensing inspectors consistently showed the results charted here: performance improved only slightly and temporarily, and quickly deteriorated. Similar results are obtained when any other human task or function is measured. Visual acuity, for example, was shown experimentally to improve with BAC below 0.02 percent (which many people could hardly feel), but to decrease at blood levels above that, even within a low legal limit of 0.08 percent (Tong, 1974).

Judgment. Most important is the dotted line on the graph that depicts estimated performance as rated by the persons themselves during the same period. Because alcohol interferes with judgment centers in the brain, our ability to judge how well we are doing is impaired equally or worse than actual performance. "I always drive better after a couple of drinks" is not born out by objective ratings; we only *think* we are driving better. As the great physician Sir William Osler put it, "Alcohol does not make us do things better; it just makes us less ashamed of doing them badly." The drivers in the above experiments varied more on their estimate of their own performance, but generally were surprised at how poorly they had done—particularly those who began convinced that they could drink and drive. Interesting and sometimes amusing confirmation of this discrepancy between estimated and actual performance has been garnered in other experiments. One college professor gave an objective test to his class, then repeated it a week later after giving each a bottle of beer. Asked whether the first test was easier or harder than the second, they all insisted they had done better on the second when actually they had made 17 percent more errors. Better yet, tape record a party and play it back the next morning. In the cold gray dawn what you hear is that laughter got louder as the jokes got worse; we thought we were funnier (estimated performance up) but the quality of humor went down.

Obviously the situation is much more serious where driving is involved, since a person may insist on driving home when he is unable to judge how badly impaired he may be and consequently pose a threat to the lives of others. For this reason, otherwise excellent slogans are really not effective: "If you drink, don't drive" and the like. Much as one may accept their logic while sober, one cannot judge their applicability when most needed. Coffee at this point may increase the danger, as the person may feel alert enough to drive but blood alcohol has not gone down.

Driving.   It is said that alcohol attacks judgment before skill, and then attacks the most recently learned skill. Driving is a skill learned much later in life than walking and talking. There are many specific ways in which driving is affected by alcohol, never fully appreciated by the driver because judgment is first dulled. Reaction time is slowed an extra fraction of a second in switching from accelerator to brake. With alcohol things seem to happen too fast, and one does not plan ahead as good driving demands. Deep muscle sense, a feel for the car's position and movement, which racing drivers rely on a great deal ("driving by the seat of one's pants"), is impaired. Depth or space perception of relative position to another car is less accurate, as are estimates of relative speed. Narrowing of the visual field ("tunnel vision"), blurred or double vision, and poorer discrimination between hues and between lights of different intensities have been reported. Night vision and resistance to glare (ability to readjust after exposure to bright lights) are notably impaired.

Poor motor coordination, faulty judgment, and lowered inhibitions further complicate a most important factor: emotional mood and personality change. Under the influence of alcohol, some people become very aggressive and impatient when they get behind the wheel, careless of others' rights and much more willing to take risks. Drowsiness and shortened attention span are dangers. Another aspect is a decreased ability to react to an unfamiliar situation; many alcoholics can drive home from their favorite bar or tavern while quite inebriated as long as they know what to expect, but don't make it when something occurs that requires a new reaction.

Apparently the initial stimulation does not last long enough to enhance driving, except perhaps for a high-tolerant alcoholic—and then only at low levels for a short time. Figures that suggest fewer accidents after one drink than after none are probably sampling errors tied to general characteristics of moderate versus nondrinkers, similar to what was mentioned in connection with heart attacks in the previous chapter.

Other Behavior. The drinking situation, the drinker's mood, attitudes, and previous experience with alcohol will all contribute to his or her reactions to drinking. Alcohol has little effect on the sense of touch, but dulls sensitivity to pain. Sometimes this can result in fractures going unattended until too late to set them properly. It is a dangerous anesthetic, however, because there is too narrow a margin between the level of anesthesia and the level which could cause death. Even low doses of alcohol reduce sensitivity to taste and odors, which can mean failure to be alerted to danger. Critical or self-monitoring functions are dulled by even slight amounts of alcohol, decreasing the ability to profit from psychotherapy. In business negotiations a few drinks may lower your opponent's shrewdness, but they will not enhance your own ability to think sharply. Worse, the relaxed feeling may make you unaware of your lowered potential. Alcohol may dull one's sense of values because the drinker is too anesthetized to feel loss or emotional pain. This loss in value system is one reason why alcoholism is said to be also a spiritual illness.

Tolerance

Before we can discuss the relation between behavior and specific levels of blood alcohol, there are two important complicating factors to be noted: tolerance and potentiation.*

Tolerance here means the ability of brain cells to function in the presence of alcohol. It may be either initial or acquired. *Initial*, or innate, tol-

---

*Lack of standard terminology results in different authors using terms in different ways. Keller (1977) prefers to restrict the word *tolerance* to initial tolerance, and use *adaptation* for acquired tolerance. Biologists sometimes use the terms *adaptation* or *habituation* for acquired physical tolerance. We use *habituation* in its psychological meaning.

erance is that with which a person is born, be it high or low. It is not rate of metabolism, which may also vary initially and is often confused with tolerance in discussion of whether there are individual or racial differences. And the precise relation of either of these to alcoholism is by no means clear. Thus, poor tolerance may be a protection against alcoholism rather than making one more vulnerable.

Acquired tolerance, or tissue adaptation, means that cellular changes have occurred as a result of drinking, which make the same amount of alcohol to have less effect on the central nervous system. In other words, more alcohol is now required to get the same effect as previously. It also means that eventually when deprived of alcohol the brain does not function so well, causing symptoms of withdrawal that are alleviated (temporarily) by alcohol.

Changes in Tolerance.   It is commonly accepted that changes in tolerance are a sign of addiction. Different types of alcoholism, however, prevent us from generalizing too much here. Many alcoholics increase their initial tolerance in the early stages of their drinking, maintain this plateau through most of their alcoholic career, and eventually experience a notable drop in tolerance, perhaps below their initial level. This drop seems irreversible. This would explain why some "experienced" drinkers cannot handle even a single small drink, even after a long period of sobriety. Their tolerance level has dropped below their euphoria level; that is, they get drunk (or sick) before they get happy, as shown in the diagram. Many middle-stage alcoholics, on the other hand, typically have a high tolerance level. In this case, it is a symptom of alcoholism rather than a sign they are immune. A high BAC upon admission to treatment, with ability to still function, is thus a useful diagnostic sign.

In addition to the increase in physical tolerance, alcoholics usually develop some behavioral skills in masking the effects of alcohol: They learn not to slur their words, to walk straight, etc. In any case, alcoholics do not develop physical tolerance to the extent that those who use heroin do. Moreover, both behavior and tolerance become unpredictable when alco-

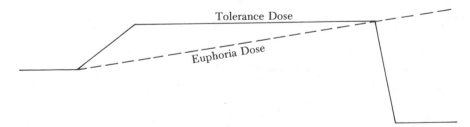

FIGURE 3.

hol is used with other drugs. For example, the high tolerance of an alcoholic can be masked by a synergistic vulnerability, which we must now examine.

Potentiation or Synergism

Since the use of alcohol in combination with other drugs is widespread, especially among women and youth, we must always be aware that cross-addiction and cross-tolerance are common. It should be routine for the intake interviewer to ask, "What other drugs have you been taking?" Most young people coming into AA have used more drugs than the older members have even heard of. With all the media attention given to the Karen Quinlan case, only rarely was it mentioned that her condition was the result of combining alcohol and Valium! A good anesthesiologist was always careful to get a drinking history, since tolerance to alcohol may mean need for a greater amount of the anesthetic for an operation and the dosage must be adjusted accordingly. Now the anesthesia must allow for a history of other drugs as well.

Conversely, if the person already has some sedative drug in the bloodstream, less will be required to achieve the effect, because of a phenomenon called potentiation or synergism. Some use synergism to refer to the additive effect of two drugs being present in the blood at the same time, and use potentiation to refer to a multiplying effect. Terminology is not standard, and we shall speak of potentiation with an emphasis on the multiplier aspect.

Hollywood Death. To "slip someone a Mickey Finn" or knockout drops in former days meant to put a barbiturate pill in his or her drink. The effect of the two was not what would be expected from the mere addition of the two, but drastically more. The two drugs potentiate each other in the system; that is, they not only add but multiply their effects. One half plus one half here does not equal a full dose, but many times that. To be more scientific, one-fifth of the lethal dose of alcohol when combined with one-twentieth of the lethal dose of a barbiturate can be a fatal dose (Seixas, 1975, p. 87). This is obviously more than simple addition, which would yield only about one-quarter of a lethal dose. Here we have the explanation of the so-called Hollywood death, or apparent suicide, which is really an accidental death due to taking sleeping pills after drinking. One may not even be drunk, but immediately upon taking the pill one may become so disoriented that he or she loses all track of what is taken, or how many.

Many Drugs

Alcohol potentiates with many drugs, including tranquilizers such as Valium and Librium, sedatives like the barbiturates and other sleeping pills, marijuana, Demerol (a common problem for doctors, nurses, dentists), opiates like morphine and heroin, and "innocent" prescription drugs such as blood thinners or the antihistamines one takes for allergies and hay fever. Even nonprescription drugs can potentiate with alcohol. The only safe rule is never to drink alcohol when one is taking any other drug. And many a recovered alcoholic has relapsed when the dentist gave Percodan, not realizing its similarity to alcohol. Amphetamines (speed, diet pills) interact in a different way, with bizarre reactions and a tendency to think one's behavior is normal because the depressant effect of alcohol is not felt. Thus begins a vicious circle of uppers and downers.

Marijuana potentiates with alcohol, but in a peculiar way. Doses of alcohol and tetrahydrocannabinol (THC, the active ingredient in marijuana), which by themselves produce no significant change in perception or behavior, have been shown experimentally in combination to cause distortions of sensory perception, time sense, and reaction time, which make driving hazardous (Franks, 1975). But the marijuana tends to delay the peak effects of the BAC, with the result that the person may leave the party not feeling very intoxicated and become a serious menace later on the highway.

Withdrawal

Polydrug abuse creates serious problems in the hospital emergency room, where the attending physicians may fear to use any medication because the patient might already have something similar in the blood. Sometimes they can only watch vital signs and hope for the best until nature detoxifies the patient. Since the liver does not eliminate all substances at the same time but tends to do selective burning whereby it metabolizes all of one substance before beginning another, in cross-addiction the result is a second withdrawal after the patient has successfully come through one withdrawal. A minimum of ten days may be necessary for the detoxification of polydrug cases. The author knows of one patient who was still toxic after 32 days, and another who required three months for complete withdrawal.

We have seen that withdrawal from alcohol, especially delirium tremens, can be very dangerous. In contrast, death from heroin withdrawal is extremely rare. Most heroin deaths (other than hepatitis from dirty needles, etc.) are probably from a synergistic "overdose" similar to the Hollywood death described above, in that they are due to the potentiating effect of combining heroin and alcohol in the bloodstream at the same time (Brecher, 1972, pp. 101–114). Prognosis in the polydrug misuser is rather unpredictable. Many are combining methadone and alcohol.

Effects of Blood Levels

The previous chapter contains a long list of factors which can cause different blood levels even from the same amount of alcohol. Add to these the individual differences in body chemistry and learned behavior, the facts of potentiation and synergism, and especially tolerance differences between individuals. And in the same individual, tolerance will vary with BAC level (Gross, 1977). Also, the same BAC level seems to affect behavior more when blood alcohol level is rising than when it is falling. The obvious conclusion is that one can hardly predict the consequences even when one knows the amount and kind of alcoholic beverage consumed, drinking time, and body weight. Yet these are usually the only factors included in popular charts or handy gadgets which purport to indicate levels of blood alcohol and whether it is safe to drive.

Taken with all these cautions, Table 4 gives a general idea of the effects of different blood levels. We use the two most common of many ways of recording blood alcohol. Although testing devices often give figures in milligrams (mg.) of alcohol per 100 cc. (ml.) of blood, the most understandable is a simple percentage. Thus a reading of 500 mg. equals 0.5 percent blood alcohol. Note that this is not 5 percent, but five-tenths of one percent—a tiny fraction of the concentration of alcohol used as an antiseptic.

TABLE 4. Some Blood Alcohol Concentrations (BAC), with Effects Not Corrected for Individual Differences (see text).

mg/100 cc.		Percentage	
500 mg	=	0.5%	Death (varies from 0.3% in young to 0.8% in alcoholics with very high tolerance)
400	=	0.4%	Coma, unconsciousness (not "blackout")
300	=	0.3%	Visibly drunk
150	=	0.15%	Old law on driving while intoxicated (DWI)
100	=	0.10%	Present law in most states
80	=	0.08%	DWI in Austria, Britain, Canada, Switzerland, Idaho
50	=	0.05%	DWI in Utah, Sweden, Norway
35	=	0.035%	All drivers on six subtests showed some impairment
30	=	0.03%	Belgium, E. Germany, Czechoslovakia
>0	>	0%	Finland: any detectable alcohol in bloodstream

Usually our judgment and self-control are affected first, at the lowest concentrations of alcohol in the blood. Moving up Table 4, sensory perception and coordinated muscular activity may be slightly impaired at a BAC as low as 0.035 percent, and notably at 0.1 percent. At 0.3 percent most people would appear quite drunk, with staggering gait and slurred speech. At about 0.4 percent, consciousness goes.

If blood alcohol reaches the 500 mg. or 0.5 percent level, brain centers controlling heart and breathing are sufficiently depressed to cause death from respiratory failure. Unless alcohol is potentiated by other drugs, this is rare for two reasons: pyloric spasm or just nausea causes the person to vomit the alcohol before all of it passes into the small intenstine for full absorption, or one passes out in coma before drinking enough to cause death. However, it can happen, as in the case of the boy who drank the pint of whiskey on a dare and did not quite reach the 0.5 percent level. Conversely, some alcoholics develop such tolerance that they can still walk at 0.7 or 0.8 percent, a level that would kill most people. But lethal dose-tolerance increase does not parallel behavioral tolerance, as in heroin; the gap narrows so that the behavioral tolerance gets dangerously close to the lethal dose, as shown in Figure 4.

Impaired Driving

All driving skills are affected to the point that formerly at 0.15 percent, now at 0.10 percent in practically all states, one is legally impaired, or under the influence, or driving while intoxicated (DWI), however the statute is worded. At 0.15 percent one is twenty-five times more liable to have an accident than with no alcohol, and at 0.10 percent one is seven

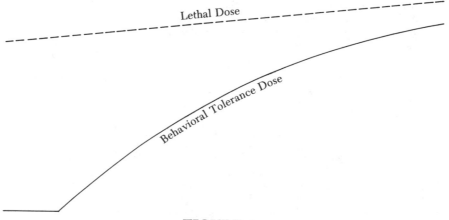

FIGURE 4.

times more likely. These are averages, skewed by the fact that alcoholics with high tolerance are better at these levels, which are therefore even more dangerous for the inexperienced or less tolerant. In a study of 6,000 people, ten percent were intoxicated at 50 mg. or 0.05 percent, and a third before they reached 100 mg. or 0.10 percent (Crancer, 1969). So one does not have to be legally drunk, much less an alcoholic, to kill somebody with an automobile. In one study, 20.6 percent of accidents occurred with a BAC below 0.05 percent in the driver.

Despite this, between 0.10 and 0.05 percent in these states there is no legal presumption either for or against impaired driving, and other evidence is used. Below 0.05 percent one is presumed legally "safe" as far as the test goes.

What Is Safe?

Are these legal limits too severe? This has been thoroughly researched in the Scandinavian countries, in England and Canada, and in many of our states using university laboratories and other facilities. The results were so impressive that long ago Britain, Canada, Austria, Switzerland, Idaho and Utah lowered the legal limit to 0.08 percent, hence the film title *Point Zero Eight*, which depicts racing drivers impaired at this level. Sweden, Norway, and Utah, among others, soon lowered it to 0.05 percent, and Belgium, East Germany, and Czechoslovakia to 0.03 percent or 30 mg. An example of the kind of evidence that led to these changes was an experiment in which experienced drivers were given alcohol and subjected to a battery of tests of driving skill; at 0.035 percent every one showed some impairment on each of the six tests (this is one-third the legal limit in most states). Such evidence caused Finland to change its law so that any measurable amount of alcohol in the blood is presumptive of being under the influence.

The Scandinavian countries have passed very severe penalties for drunk driving, such as deprivation of the driver's license for life after a second conviction (at 0.05 percent) or mandatory jail sentences, to be served on weekends if one must work. Unfortunately, in America the net effect of tougher penalties has been merely to make juries more lenient in many cases, reluctant to inflict the severer punishment. This in turn encourages the arresting officer to settle for a lesser charge, like reckless driving, because he knows there is a better chance of conviction. More constructive are deferred-prosecution laws (as in the state of Washington), which divert the suspect into community alcohol centers where drinking problems can be assessed and appropriate remedies can vary from attendance at an Alcohol Information School (AIS) to in-patient treatment for alcoholism.

How Many Drinks?

With trepidation one approaches the question, how many drinks will it take to reach a given level of blood alcohol? "A drink" can mean anything from a one-ounce jigger of 86-proof liquor to a massive highball glass containing three or more ounces of 100 proof. One friend says, "Just let mine run until it gets good and cold." Moreover, we often lie or just forget how much we have actually had. Police officers always smile at my assertion that never in the history of law enforcement has any driver had more than "two beers." Even if size and strength of drink is controlled, we have emphasized so many variable factors and individual differences that the reader should be most wary of jumping to conclusions.

Using the "drinks" given at the beginning of the previous chapter, we shall consider a drink to be one bottle of beer, three and one-half ounces of dry wine, or one ounce of 86-proof liquor—not to be confused with the amount of alcohol the liver can metabolize in an hour, which is slightly less than this but must be subtracted from the amount consumed over a given time.

Thus understood, one can estimate that a 160-pound person would need to drink, within one hour, four to five drinks to attain a BAC of 100 mg. or 0.10 percent, the legal limit in most states. A 240-pound muscle man might require up to six drinks, and a 100-pound girl only two or three. The 160-pound man would reach the legal limit in those countries which set it at 50 mg. or 0.05 percent by consuming two or three drinks; at this level one is twice as liable to have an accident as with no alcohol, and is above the 0.035 percent level in the driving experiment where all six subtests showed some impairment.

Obtaining Evidence of Drunk Driving

We saw that alcohol in the breath is in direct and fixed ratio to alcohol in the blood. It is more accessible than samples from sweat, urine, or of the blood itself, being easily obtainable by having the subject blow into a toy balloon or tube hard enough to get alveolar or deep-lung air. It was first used in 1927, and in 1938 Harger invented a portable apparatus, the Drunkometer. Many devices have since been developed, varying in cost per use, accuracy, ease of use, and portability: Breathalyzer, Intoximeter, Alcotester, Alcometer, Sober-meter, and others. Some statutes allow the suspect to obtain blood or urine tests, but not to use delaying tactics so as to allow blood alcohol level to fall meanwhile.

It must be noted that the arresting officer has other tests, used long before chemical tests of BAC were developed. These include walking a chalk line, touching the nosetip with the index finger while the eyes are closed, and other harmless exercises as well as observed erratic driving. Most impressive now is a video tape of the arrested driver's behavior, which, when played later for a jury, belies the well-dressed appearance and decorum of the defendant in court.

For these and other reasons the use of chemical tests has been upheld as admissible evidence in spite of the disparaging tactics of defense lawyers. One study verified this in courts of appeal for all states, and another study for 550 decisions in forty-four states (Donigan, 1966). The devices are always set to favor the accused, and are specific to alcohol (not reactive to onions or garlic as sometimes claimed). It is true that alcohol in the breath from mouthwash or cold medicine containing high amounts of alcohol can affect it, but this does not discredit the test if deep alveolar air is obtained. Use of the test is not a violation of secrecy, since the driver enters into no confidential relationship with the arresting officer. Blood level is a public fact, like one's fingerprint. Lastly, the implied consent law involves no violation of human rights, since the granting of a license is a privilege granted under whatever conditions the voters wish to impose and freely entered into when the driver obtained a license.

Blood alcohol tests can protect the innocent as well. If a person is observed lying unconscious with the smell of liquor on the breath, a test might show that blood alcohol is far too low to account for the coma and thus help diagnose a diabetic coma, heart attack, head injury, or any of a dozen possible causes other than alcohol. Likewise, if one is driving after a single beer and is arrested for a traffic violation by an officer who smells the beer on the breath, a test will exculpate from a drunk driving charge.

Sources

We list only a sampling of the pertinent literature.

Bennett, A.E., *Alcoholism and the Brain*.

Birnbaum, I.M. and E.S. Parker (eds.), *Alcohol and Human Memory*.

"Booze and the Writer," *Writer's Digest*, 1978, 58:25–33.

Cappell, Howard and C.P. Herman, "Alcohol and Tension Reduction," *Quarterly Journal of Studies on Alcohol*, 1972, 33:33–64.

Donigan, Robert L., *Chemical Tests and the Law*.

Eidelberg, Eduardo, "Acute Effects of Ethanol and Opiates on the Nervous System," in Gibbins, R.J., et al. (eds.), *Research Advances in Alcohol and Drug Problems*, vol. 2, pp. 147–176.

Finch, John R., *Psychiatric and Legal Aspects of Automobile Fatalities*.

Goldman, M.S. and others, "Recoverability of Sensory and Motor Functioning Following Chronic Alcohol Abuse," in Seixas, F. (ed.), *Currents in Alcoholism*, vol. 3, pp. 493–504.

HIGHWAY SAFETY RESEARCH INSTITUTE, *HIT LAB Reports*, University of Michigan, Ann Arbor, 1970 ff.

ISSELBACHER, KURT, "Metabolic and Hepatic Effects of Alcohol," *New England Journal of Medicine*, 1977, 296:612–617.

KEEHN, J.D., "Neuroticism and Extraversion: Chronic Alcoholic's Report on Effects of Drinking," *Psychological Reports*, 1970, 27:767–770.

KELLER, MARK, "A Lexicon of Disablements Related to Alcohol Consumption," in Edwards, G. et al. (eds.), *Alcohol-Related Disabilities*, pp. 23–60.

MILNER, G., *Drugs and Driving: A Survey of the Relationship of Adverse Drug Reactions, and Drug-Alcohol Interaction to Driving Safety.*

RYBACK, RALPH S., "The Continuum and Specificity of the Effects of Alcohol on Memory," *Quarterly Journal of Studies on Alcohol*, 1971, 32:995–1016.

SEIXAS, FRANK A. (ed.), "Alcoholism and the Central Nervous System." *Annals of the New York Academy of Sciences*, 1973, 215:1–389.

"Studies of Drinking and Driving," *Quarterly Journal of Studies on Alcohol*, Supplement No. 4, 1968.

TONG, J.E. et al., "Alcohol, Visual Discrimination and Heart Rate," *Quarterly Journal of Studies on Alcohol*, 1974, 35:1003–1022.

WALLGREN, H. and H. BARRY, *Actions of Alcohol*, 2 vols.

ZELHART, PAUL F. and BRYCE SCHURR, "People Who Drive while Impaired: Issues in Treating the Drinking Driver," in Estes and Heinemann (eds.), pp. 204–218.

Polydrug

The literature review by Sidney Cohen and the three articles by J.F. Carroll and T.E. Malloy are most useful. The bibliography by Polacsek was comprehensive up to 1973.

ADAMS, K.M. et al., *Polydrug Abuse: The Results of a National Collaborative Study.*

CARROLL, J.F. and T.E. MALLOY, three consecutive literature reviews and evaluations on combined use and combined treatment, in *The American Journal of Drug and Alcohol Abuse*, 1977, 4:293–362.

COHEN, SIDNEY, "The Effects of Combined Alcohol-Drug Abuse on Human Behavior: A Review of the Literature," *Drug Abuse & Alcoholism Review*, 1979, 2 (3):1–13.

COLEMAN, J.H. and W.E. EVANS, "Drug Interaction with Alcohol," *Alcohol Health and Research World*, Winter 1975–76, pp. 16–19.

CRANCER, ALFRED et al., "Comparison of the Effects of Marihuana and Alcohol on Simulated Driving Performance," *Science*, 1969, 164:851–854.

FORNEY, ROBERT and FRANCIS HUGHES, *Combined Effects of Alcohol and Other Drugs.*

FRANKS, H.M. et al., "The Interaction of Alcohol and Tetrahydrocannabinol in

Man: Effects on Psychomotor Skills Related to Driving," in Israelstam, S. and S. Lambert (eds.), *Alcohol, Drugs, and Traffic Safety*, 1975, pp. 461–466.

GUST, DODIE, *Up, Down and Sideways on Wet and Dry Booze*. CompCare pamphlet.

PIROLA,, R.C., *Drug Metabolism and Alcohol: a Survey of Alcohol-Drug Reactions—Mechanisms, Clinical Aspects, Experimental Studies*.

POLACSEK, E. (ed.), *Interaction of Alcohol and Other Drugs*.

SEIXAS, FRANK A., "Alcohol and Its Drug Interactions," *Annals of Internal Medicine*, 1975, 83:86–92.

PART II

Alcoholism

CHAPTER 6

Patterns and Progressions

THE EFFECTS OF ALCOHOL and alcohol misuse on our health, driving, social relations, and pocketbook depicted so far could apply to any of us, alcoholics or not. This chapter will address the development of alcoholism, which occurs only to some. The approach will be descriptive rather than explanatory, leaving to Chapter 9 any consideration of the causality of alcoholism. The focus here is on *what* alcoholism is, not *why*. The distinction is important, for much needless quibbling about types is really mistaking description for explanation.

Types of Alcoholics

Alcoholics differ over the whole range of human variation in physiological and psychological characteristics. No two people are exactly alike. Each alcoholic is a unique individual, so that one is tempted to settle for nine million alcoholisms for nine million alcoholics. Or as one of them put it, "each alcoholic is in a clash by himself." Alcoholism itself is not a single disease entity any more than cancer is, but a multiple illness, which amply justifies a growing trend toward use of the term *alcoholisms*.

These two facts point up the serious mistake of assuming that a "true" or "typical" alcoholic must be much like the one you know or are. The result, of course, is that the client may not be able to identify with this, and either feels left out or bolsters the denial of being an alcoholic at all. The mere fact that the counselor or older AA member can't imagine an alcoholism different than the one with which he or she is familiar does not disprove its existence. Even those who object to any mention of types often refer to different strategies of management or different patterns of control. By any name, alcoholics present a variety that cannot be ignored, while having some basic features in common.

The best-known classification is that presented by the late E.M. Jellinek in his *The Disease Concept of Alcoholism* (pages 36–41). Jellinek deliberately identified his various types of alcoholics by letters of the Greek alphabet, to avoid names that might imply theories as to cause or nature. Whether or not one accepts his scheme, it is so much a part of the literature that one must be familiar with it in order to read or converse intelligently in the field. Note that these are not stages of progression, that is, from Alpha to Beta and so on.

Jellinek Types of Alcoholisms

Alpha. This is purely *psychological* dependence on alcohol. These people have poor frustration tolerance or inability to cope with tensions. They use alcohol to boost morale, block out reality, bolster self-confidence or relieve emotional or bodily pains. They drink too much and at the wrong times, which may result in offense to others, family squabbles, absenteeism from work, and a drain on the family budget. They can be called problem drinkers, but Jellinek rejects the term here since it can include the physically dependent. There is little or no progression, and a lack of physical addiction or withdrawal symptoms (although there can be some of the nutritional deficiencies of alcoholism). Hence Jellinek was reluctant to call it an illness per se (p. 37) although he definitely says it is alcoholism (p. 41). Some call it a symptom of mental conflict, but it is a symptom that has become the disease in its own right. At least 10 to 15 percent of AA membership is of this type (p. 38). Psychotherapy can help with the conflict, but medication would only lead to dependence on more alcohol or other drugs. Alpha alcoholism may develop into Gamma alcoholism, says Jellinek, but it can also continue for thirty or forty years with no progression (p. 37).

Beta. This is characterized by *social* dependence on alcohol, without either psychological or physical dependence. The usual problems from excessive drinking arise, including nutritional deficiencies and organic damage such as cirrhosis and gastritis. These alcoholics are often seen in general hospitals, where their physical ailments are all too often treated without remedying the drinking habits that caused them. Their joining

AA is infrequent. The cause of their drinking is largely sociocultural or situational, and is common in occupations where "everybody" gets drunk every weekend. This "everybody does it" feeds denial, and, in any case, heavy social dependence should not be dismissed lightly. It is one of the major obstacles in long-term rehabilitation of chronic alcoholics. Jellinek says this Beta type is alcoholism (p. 41), and it meets the third element of our working definition because there is interference with major life functioning. Both Alpha and Beta may involve some loss of control, but this is not paramount in either type.

Gamma. This is the chronic, *progressive* type of alcoholism most commonly seen in American males. It usually begins with psychological dependence and progresses to physical dependence. There is progressive loss of control over *how much* one drinks: except in the later stages, one can usually still choose *when* to drink or not but once started there is little or no control over when to stop. There is usually an increase in tolerance, and in the middle stage it may reach a remarkable degree. There may be shakes or tremors for days after withdrawal. In the late stages withdrawal symptoms are severe, and tolerance drops irreversibly to below one's initial level so that a single drink is quite toxic. This is the classic instance in which the habitual addiction *is* the disorder. Search for reasons why these people drink is superfluous; they drink because they are alcoholic. This type is most responsive to the AA approach, but anything that will break the habit pattern can be useful: Antabuse (disulfiram), aversion conditioning, a religious conversion, or intensive in-patient treatment with a strong emphasis on understanding the nature of the illness and good physical rebuilding—any approach that attacks the pathological drinking as the primary disorder, which all of the foregoing approaches agree on.

Because members of Alcoholics Anonymous were the most available and cooperative when Jellinek did his research, the majority of his 2,000 subjects reported histories that comprised this type. He observed that Alcoholics Anonymous "naturally created the picture of alcoholism in their own image" (p. 38) and in spite of his great admiration of AA he warns sternly that we must not let this selective sampling deceive us into imagining that the Gamma is the only typical or true alcoholic.

Delta. This is often called the *maintenance* drinker: the alcoholic who has lost control over *when* he or she drinks rather than how much. Inability to abstain, rather than inability to stop once they start, is the characteristic. Unlike the Gamma type, Deltas cannot "go on the water wagon" for even a day or two; yet they seldom appear to be drunk. Are they alcoholics? Yes, they show increased tolerance and even go into severe withdrawal symptoms (delirium tremens) if deprived by accident or other circumstances, though they may have never been drunk in their lives. Social attitudes that favor regular drinking seem to play a major role. This is the commonest type of alcoholism in France and other wine-drinking countries like Chile, and perhaps among American women. The lady who sips wine all day is again an unscientific stereotype, but she is a true alcoholic although never visibly intoxicated. The author knows one retired military man who had his pension checks mailed directly to his favorite tavern, where he lived out his life without ever getting drunk—but he was never quite sober. Or one can be a member of the three-martinis-for-lunch bunch, the executive who must have alcohol to get through the day. A striking case is that of a very wealthy couple in their sixties who had used separate bedrooms for years until a mixup in hotel reservations in Bangkok occasioned their sharing the same room. For the first time one spouse discovered that the other was a Delta alcoholic who could not go for more than a few hours without a drink. Deterioration is so gradual that the Deltas do not realize that they don't feel very good most of the time; changes in the family relationships are likewise so subtle that nobody recognizes the problems. Because their drinking rarely precipitates a crisis that would bring them to AA, they are not highly visible in the fellowship. Another reason is that they cannot identify with the distressing and sometimes amusing experiences which other alcoholics recount from their drinking escapades.

Epsilon. This is the *periodic* or binge drinker, who abstains without difficulty for long periods but once started drinks heavily until passing out in a stupor. The period of abstinence may be a week, a month, or a year. It may be regular or varied in length. They differ from the Gamma type who is between drinking bouts in that they may experience no craving or struggle to maintain sobriety. They may serve liquor in their homes with no temptation to indulge. No meetings or slogans are necessary. Often the spouse knows the telltale signs that signal the approach of a binge, but once the time comes there seems nothing anybody can do to avert it.

Called *dipsomania* in Europe, periodic alcoholism is a most puzzling type about which little is known, a feeling that Jellinek shares. The dependence seems to be both psychological and physical. The loss of control is baffling. Because nature must compensate and reverse itself many times, some think that organic damage is more severe. Research on this type is obviously difficult, and understanding may not be achieved for a long time to come.

Other Classifications

Zeta. Some have added a sixth type to Jellinek's five: Zeta alcoholics, who get violent when they drink. This is akin to the old psychiatric term *pathological intoxication*.

Jellinek wrote that there are many other types of alcoholism, more than there are letters in the Greek alphabet. While agreeing that all five of Jellinek's types are alcoholism, Blythe Sprott and others have subdivided them in various ways. The refinements are no doubt founded in fact, but the counselor will usually find the above adequate. A few more classifications will be mentioned which can be useful at times.

One can distinguish alcoholics by their reaction to alcohol into friendly, belligerent, quiet, boisterous, or sullen types. Notable personality change upon drinking is a symptom of alcoholism, and the person who gets violent or vicious after a few drinks is probably headed for serious trouble over a lifetime.

Some divide alcoholics by drinking patterns: situational or occupational, social (get drunk to imitate others), willful (drink to get drunk, not from compulsion), escape (drink to forget), and symptomatic or reactive (drink to hide an underlying emotional disorder). Since these classifications get into questions of causality, they will not be pursued here. Partington (1969), Pattison (1973) and many others have found different personality types among alcoholics, which may be useful in choice of treatment but add little to our understanding of alcoholism.

Common Characteristics

More useful to our understanding is an examination of some experiences that most alcoholics have in common, in ways and degrees that, of course, will vary. Wallace (1977) has given us an excellent explanation of those experiences, which we can do no better than to summarize. His approach is especially useful because it helps us understand many things often dismissed as mere denial when they are better called confusion. No doubt the two are interwoven, but denial seems to imply some willful refusal or dishonesty. This implication mars the feeling of respect and trust between client and counselor. Wallace's approach may aid in avoiding this.

Confusion

Contrary to what he or she may have heard, the alcoholic did not get drunk each and every time, nor experience unpleasant effects on each drinking occasion. Many report periods of normal social drinking in between alcoholic binges. All have some happy memories of boisterous good times, due, in part, to retroactive falsification, whereby any human being tends to remember the pleasant and forget the unpleasant. Thirty years later they are still pursuing that pleasant "glow" they recall from early drinking experiences, and the incongruity between illusory images from the past and their present misery adds to the confusion.

Diagnosis of alcoholism is confusing enough to the objective professional, so it is no wonder that the alcoholic cannot apply to himself or herself the welter of diagnostic criteria with all the and's and or's that naturally leave open the possibility that they do not fit. Due to differences in drinking patterns and social customs, many a criterion would not be conclusive if taken by itself. This is true of a blackout, which by itself may not be as significant as when part of a total symptom picture. Lastly, the alcoholic looks out at the world and sees a lot of drinking and even drunkenness, and a lot of people in far worse shape; surely those others are the alcoholics. "If they don't admit it or go to treatment, why should I?" Thus the alcoholic shares in a lot of the same confusion that plagues the professional. It is no wonder the alcoholic does not come up with a clear-cut diagnosis.

Search for Magic. Another major part of the alcoholic's thinking is the vague, unfounded hope that if one searches hard enough and long enough, one can find a way to control and enjoy drinking. Even acceptance of the label "alcoholic" does not mean acceptance of the true nature of alcoholism in all its implications. Full participation in a good recovery program like Alcoholics Anonymous quells this subtle hope and keeps one conscious that the only sensible answer is not to drink. But the occasional resurgence of what AA calls "stinking thinking" shows that the wild possibility of this hope being realized is never quite dead.

Who Am I? Again, the alcoholic leads a sort of dual life. When sober, he is a fine, upstanding citizen, whose life and values are quite different from what comes out during the drinking and its aftermath. This is not just self-delusion; the alcoholic really is a different kind of person than what the alcoholic behavior attests to. What am I really like? What sort of person? The alcoholic not only does not know what is wrong with him, but even who he is.

Feelings

Despite great individual differences, practically all alcoholics experience remorse, guilt, shame, and self-hatred. Their self-esteem sinks very low, and often is shattered entirely. Feelings of loneliness and alienation are common. Depression and feelings of hopelessness, futility, and a sense of meaninglessness in their lives are characteristic of alcoholics. The depression is, of course, only augmented by alcohol.

Coping Devices

It is not surprising that all this leads the alcoholic to develop some rather elaborate, if subconscious, escape and defense mechanisms or coping devices. (Unlike neurotics, alcoholics do not profit from common psychotherapeutic practices of getting their feelings out in the open and certainly are not helped if given Valium or even alcohol as a way to cope. But some insight may be helpful, provided the analysis is combined with a strong emphasis on the nature of compulsive addiction itself.)

Rationalization is a broad term for much of the devious thinking the alcoholic employs. It does not mean rational thinking, but very irrational or emotional thinking. Most common is the ability to find reasons why one should really have a drink: to relax, to get some sleep, to celebrate, to avoid offending someone or just to keep them company. This is confirmed by the euphoric recall of only good effects of drinking. It seems impervious to logic when an observer notes the contradictions involved: We have a drink to relax and one to pep us up; a tall cool one in the summer and one to warm us up in the winter. Which does alcohol do? We talk about being fogged up with alcohol, and taking a drink to clear our head. We have a drink because our team won, or we lost; at a wedding, or at a funeral; because we are married, or divorced; happy, or sad. The alcoholic can always come up with a thousand reasons to take a drink, when in reality there is not one valid reason to do so. One must learn to cope with the inevitable stresses of life without resorting to alcohol. The fact that you must use a drug because you feel hot or cold, high or low, means you need it to be "normal" and that is one definition of addiction.

Projection of blame is another favorite defense mechanism. The spouse, the boss, the parents, the police, "the system"— anyone or anything except alcohol must be to blame for all the miseries of the alcoholic. The alcoholic is often skillful at drawing others into this delusional system, especially a spouse or lover who sympathizes and thus becomes an enabler, as described in Chapter 8. Or the alcoholic may subtly maneuver the other to provoke a fight, which then becomes an excuse for drinking. Other coping devices the alcoholic may indulge in include chronic failure, accident proneness, pleas for sympathy, and neurotic perfectionism.

Denial. Much of what a counselor is tempted to ascribe to denial is really honest confusion in the alcoholic's mind, as described previously. Nonetheless there is some truth in the statement that alcoholics suffer from a fatal disease whose primary symptom is denial that they are sick. Denial is rationalization, kidding ourselves. Being very much like human beings, only maybe a little more so, alcoholics are not the only ones capable of it, but they seem to excel. Certainly a high IQ is no guarantee of avoidance. Our experience, confirmed by numerous recovered alcoholics now working professionally in the field, is that the more intelligent alcoholics are, the more adept and devious they are at denial.

None of us are impartial judges in our own case. One cartoon shows a man at the bar putting his hand very kindly on his neighbor's shoulder and saying, "Better take it easy, Fred, your face is getting kinda blurred!" Fr. Ralph Pfau (Fr. John Doe) tells of nearly shaking to pieces waiting for the minute hand to hit twelve so he could drink, while assuring himself that he was not an alcoholic because he had heard that an alcoholic was one who drank before noon. In a nation where 4 percent of the population are alcoholics, Cahalan in 1969 found only 0.1 percent of those questioned characterized *themselves* as even heavy drinkers. The first twenty minutes of an intake interview is often taken up with listening to how much the client does *not* drink. Alcoholics have developed such an elaborate alibi system that they are almost incapable of recognizing the role that alcohol plays in their problems. The list is endless: I can't be an alcoholic because I'm too young; because I only drink beer; because I don't drink before 5:00 P.M.; because I am Jewish; because I am a clergyman; and, of course, "because I can quit any time I want to."

Denial by others. It is not only the alcoholic who plays these mental games. As described in the now classic booklet *Alcoholism: A Merry-Go-Round Named Denial*, by Joseph Kellerman, the family and others are drawn into this rationalization in an effort, often quite subconscious, to avoid facing the fact of alcoholism. The mother tells herself and her children that daddy is not "one of those" and fools herself that the neighbors don't know. After a binge the alcoholic may give the spouse an extravagant present or otherwise try to make up; this not only reinforces the denial of the spouse, but by accepting the favor the spouse reinforces the alcoholic's own denial. In industry the foreman covers up for the alcoholic employee, and many companies are still denying there is any problem in their ranks.

Professionals are involved in the denial system also. The physician, social worker, lawyer and clergyman all assure the spouse that their partner is too nice a person to be an alcoholic. In one study 91 percent of the clergy saw a need for alcohol programs in the nation, but only 40 percent saw a need in their own congregation. Lisansky (1974), in the *Bulletin of the American College of Physicians*, calls alcoholism "the avoided diagnosis" and points out how many physicians either miss the diagnosis or treat only the effects and not the alcoholism even if recognized. When a high mortality rate from drunk drivers was reported for a certain stretch of highway, the solution of the county council members (one wonders how many were defensive about their own drinking) was to widen the highway! As a nation we, like France, have tended to deny the magnitude of the problem. Until recently the news media tended to skip any mention of the role alcohol played in various accidents and other tragedies. Even in the helping professions some pay lip service to the disease concept of alcoholism, but persist in evasive and uncomfortable feelings about alcoholics.

Progression

Because at least the Alpha and Delta types may show no progression, the word *progressive* does not appear in our working definition of alcoholism as it does in some. The charts usually used to graph the development of the illness are based on the work of Jellinek, who admits that his sample was heavily biased toward a predominance of Gamma type alcoholics and is therefore *not* typical of all. Even when progression occurs, it does not follow a uniform pattern. The steps may be reversed in order, or some steps omitted. Symptoms progress, too; something that was minor in an early stage may appear later in a different form or to a greater degree. The symptoms have widely different meanings for different individuals or in different social contexts: "Hitting bottom" might mean finding oneself in jail or suicidal, while for another it might be burning the toast once too often.

Rate of progression varies also. It tends to be more rapid for some individuals and among certain races, probably due to a physiological predisposition. Generally it is faster for women than for men, and in very young alcoholics. Some alcoholics take thirty or forty years to reach the chronic stage. Others remain at the middle stage indefinitely. Chronological age is also less important than stage of development of the illness.

Useful Information.   With all of these pitfalls it is still useful to chart alcoholic progression as it occurs in many Americans, provided the foregoing factors are kept in mind. Figure 6 helps penetrate denial, and provides a means for the alcoholic to understand what is happening and where it will probably end. It gives the counselor a basis for assessment of the case, and gives the client something to identify with. Familiarity with the common symptoms is a necessary tool in the kit of any professional, and an important part of public education about the illness. Granted that some blindness to alcoholism symptoms is due to denial, the extent of ignorance still rampant about the signs of developing alcoholism is incredible. Attending open AA meetings, one hears constantly, "I was hooked on alcohol and didn't know it" and this has been estimated to be true of 80 percent of alcoholics. The spouse shows equal ignorance; one wife claims she didn't even know her husband drank until he came home sober one night.

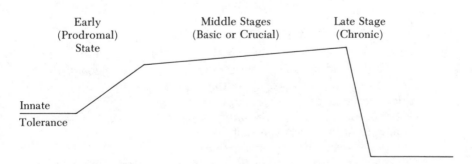

FIGURE 5.   Basic scheme of Jellinek progression chart

The Jellinek (1952) progression chart shows innate tolerance increasing during the early or prodromal stage, remaining relatively high during the middle (basic, crucial) stages, and dropping sharply at the late (chronic) stage. We give just a schematic diagram here without listing the symptoms, because they vary in position. The other most common chart, often called a dip chart, is based on the work of the British physician M.M. Glatt (1974b, pp. 334–335). While it does not show tolerance changes, it has the advantage of showing the stages of recovery also. In Figure 6 an American version is printed here which gives more detail. The same cautions apply, namely that one may skip or reverse some steps.

Early Signs

It is easy to diagnose alcoholism in the last deteriorative stages. The challenge is to recognize the early signs, so important in secondary prevention (early intervention). This is not always easy, since the symptoms vary widely and are often subtle.

Persons at High Risk of Alcoholism.   The fact that the statistical probability for certain groups to develop alcoholism is quite high should alert us. Epidemiological and sociological studies show that the following factors indicate high risk for the development of alcoholism. There is not complete agreement on the extent of risk for each factor.

- A family history of alcoholism, including parents, siblings, grandparents, uncles, and aunts.
- A history of total abstinence in the family, particularly where strong moral overtones were present and, most particularly, where the social environment of the patient has changed to associations in which drinking is encouraged or required.
- A history of alcoholism or teetotalism in the spouse or the family of the spouse.
- Coming from a broken home or home with much parental discord, particularly where the father was absent or rejecting but not punitive.
- A lack of leisure activities that do not involve drinking.
- Origin from cultural groups (for example, the Irish, native Americans, and Scandinavians) having a high incidence of alcoholism.
- Having female relatives of more than one generation who have had a high incidence of recurrent depressions.
- Heavy smoking: Heavy drinking is often associated with heavy smoking, but the reverse need not be true.
- A tendency to use other psychoactive drugs.
- Confused and inconsistent attitudes about one's own drinking, even with no conflict about drinking by others.

Prodromal Phase

Early stage alcoholism is characterized by the following symptoms.

- Increased tolerance. The person needs more to get the same effect. One feels proud of being able to hold one's liquor, never dreaming that this is a danger signal. Hangovers may be minimal or absent.
- *Using* alcohol for its effect rather than merely enjoying it. One learns early the pampering effects of alcohol and uses it for relief of tension, fatigue, disappointment, or self-consciousness. Some alcoholics get this on the first drink, and never have to make a transition from social lubricant to psychological dependence. Others undergo an unconscious learning process as reinforcement enhances the discovery.
- Preoccupation with drinking. Thus almost from the start, alcohol means a little more to the alcoholic than to others. So they begin to worry about whether there will be drinks at the party, or whether there will be enough.
- Having a few before leaving home. One begins to select companions, restaurants, and recreational activities largely according to whether alcohol will be available.
- Thinking about the next drink.
- Gulping and sneaking drinks. Always ready for the second round before everybody else, the alcoholic is looking for an effect when others are still just getting acquainted. This is gulping in a social way, but if things are slow one can volunteer to help the hostess and thus gain access to the kitchen or bar where one can sneak an extra drink. At a restaurant, they order a double.
- Excuses for drinking, as detailed earlier in this chapter under *Rationalization*.
- Personality change after a few drinks: pleasant to mean, imprudent, irrational, etc.

Middle Stage

The transition from early to middle-stage alcoholism could be marked by the time when the alcoholic stops boasting about how much they drink and begins to lie about both amount and frequency. Actually, some of this is not a lie but simple confusion or forgetting; the alcoholic cannot recall how much he or she had. Some forgetfulness may be due to repression. Some of it may be due to blackouts as described toward the end of Chapter 4.

Blackouts, in our opinion, have been exaggerated as a diagnostic sign. Other research does not confirm the importance suggested by Jellinek's

FIGURE 6. Alcohol addiction

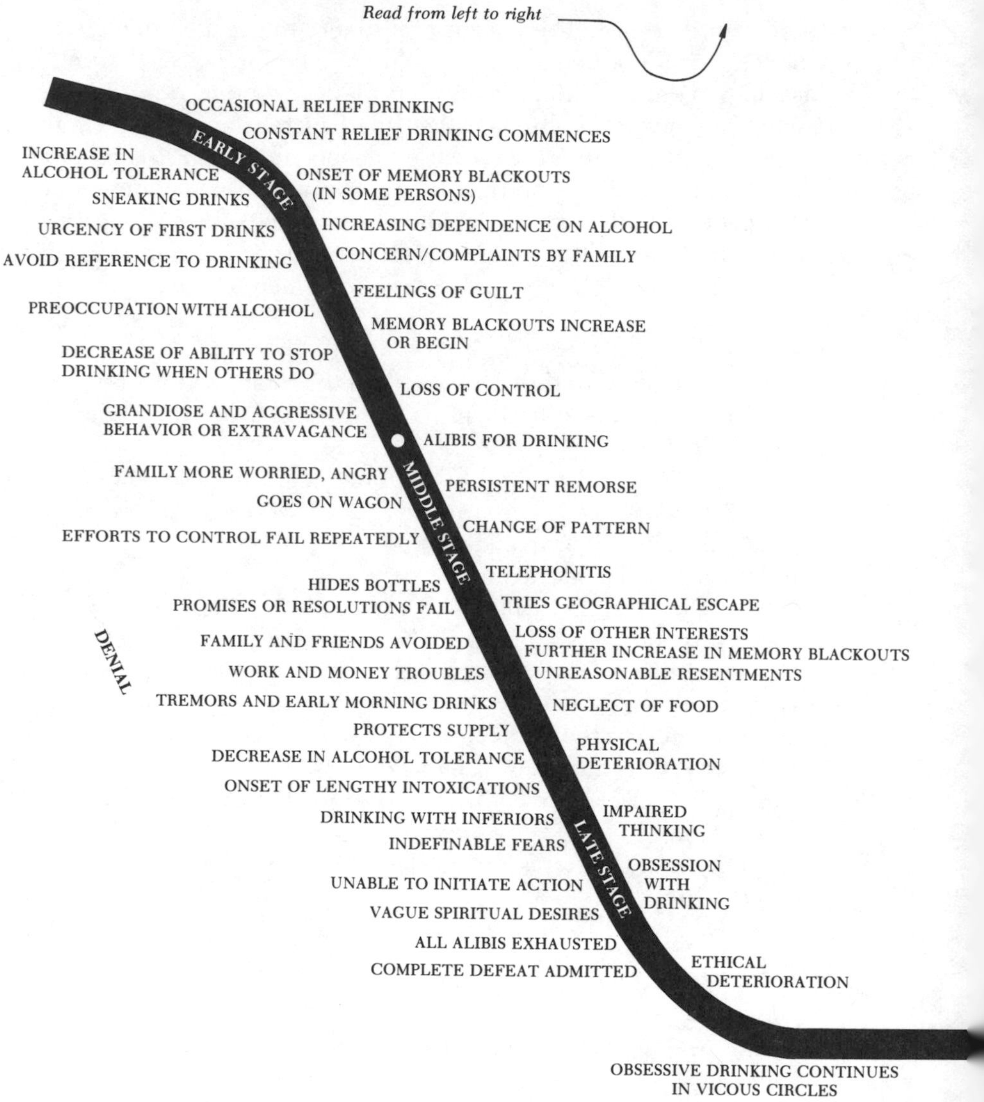

Read from left to right

OCCASIONAL RELIEF DRINKING

CONSTANT RELIEF DRINKING COMMENCES

EARLY STAGE

INCREASE IN ALCOHOL TOLERANCE

ONSET OF MEMORY BLACKOUTS (IN SOME PERSONS)

SNEAKING DRINKS

URGENCY OF FIRST DRINKS

INCREASING DEPENDENCE ON ALCOHOL

AVOID REFERENCE TO DRINKING

CONCERN/COMPLAINTS BY FAMILY

FEELINGS OF GUILT

PREOCCUPATION WITH ALCOHOL

MEMORY BLACKOUTS INCREASE OR BEGIN

DECREASE OF ABILITY TO STOP DRINKING WHEN OTHERS DO

LOSS OF CONTROL

GRANDIOSE AND AGGRESSIVE BEHAVIOR OR EXTRAVAGANCE

ALIBIS FOR DRINKING

MIDDLE STAGE

FAMILY MORE WORRIED, ANGRY

PERSISTENT REMORSE

GOES ON WAGON

CHANGE OF PATTERN

EFFORTS TO CONTROL FAIL REPEATEDLY

TELEPHONITIS

HIDES BOTTLES

TRIES GEOGRAPHICAL ESCAPE

PROMISES OR RESOLUTIONS FAIL

LOSS OF OTHER INTERESTS

DENIAL

FAMILY AND FRIENDS AVOIDED

FURTHER INCREASE IN MEMORY BLACKOUTS

WORK AND MONEY TROUBLES

UNREASONABLE RESENTMENTS

TREMORS AND EARLY MORNING DRINKS

NEGLECT OF FOOD

PROTECTS SUPPLY

DECREASE IN ALCOHOL TOLERANCE

PHYSICAL DETERIORATION

ONSET OF LENGTHY INTOXICATIONS

DRINKING WITH INFERIORS

IMPAIRED THINKING

INDEFINABLE FEARS

LATE STAGE

UNABLE TO INITIATE ACTION

OBSESSION WITH DRINKING

VAGUE SPIRITUAL DESIRES

ALL ALIBIS EXHAUSTED

COMPLETE DEFEAT ADMITTED

ETHICAL DETERIORATION

OBSESSIVE DRINKING CONTINUES IN VICOUS CIRCLES

THE ROAD TO RECOVERY

ENLIGHTENED AND INTERESTING WAY
OF LIFE OPENS UP WITH ROAD
AHEAD TO HIGHER LEVELS THAN
EVER BEFORE

FULL APPRECIATION OF
SPIRITUAL VALUES

GROUP THERAPY AND MUTUAL HELP CONTINUE

CONTENTMENT IN SOBRIETY

FIRST STEPS TOWARDS
ECONOMIC STABILITY

CONFIDENCE OF EMPLOYERS

INCREASE OF EMOTIONAL CONTROL

APPRECIATION OF REAL VALUES

FACTS FACED WITH COURAGE

REBIRTH OF IDEALS

NEW CIRCLE OF STABLE FRIENDS

REHABILITATION

NEW INTERESTS DEVELOP

ADJUSTMENTS TO FAMILY NEEDS

FAMILY AND FRIENDS
APPRECIATE EFFORTS

DESIRE TO ESCAPE GOES

REALISTIC THINKING

RETURN OF SELF-ESTEEM

REGULAR NOURISHMENT TAKEN

DIMINISHING FEARS OF THE
UNKNOWN FUTURE

APPRECIATION OF POSSIBILITIES
OF NEW WAY OF LIFE

CARE OF PERSONAL APPEARANCE

ONSET OF NEW HOPE

START OF GROUP THERAPY

PHYSICAL OVERHAUL BY DOCTOR

GUILT REDUCTION

RIGHT THINKING BEGINS

SPIRITUAL NEEDS
EXAMINED

MEETS HAPPY SOBER ALCOHOLICS

STOPS TAKING
ALCOHOL

TOLD ADDICTION CAN BE ARRESTED

LEARNS ALCOHOLISM IS AN ILLNESS
HONEST DESIRE FOR HELP

—*Modified from M.M. Glatt*

chart. Blackouts rarely give a false positive (having them means one is an alcoholic) but often a false negative (one can be an alcoholic without them). More important, the very nature of a blackout precludes one being aware of having it: One does not remember that one does not remember. Unless someone else explicitly refers to an incident that happened at eleven o'clock the evening before, one may not advert to the fact that he or she can remember nothing of the period from ten until midnight. Also, blackouts are often listed as an early sign of alcoholism, but for the above reasons they may not enter the picture until a much later stage, when a cancelled check or auto accident reveals an embarrassing hiatus in their memory. Such a blackout can be a rather disturbing or terrifying experience, although by then the illness may be so entrenched that the only reaction is to sedate the anxiety with more alcohol.

Drinking more than one intends marks the beginning of loss of control, but it does *not* mean that one gets drunk every time one drinks. One may rarely get drunk, thus avoiding the stereotype of alcoholism. This symptom is very often misunderstood, causing much confusion. At the beginning of Chapter 5 of *Alcoholics Anonymous*, the beloved "big book" of AA, alcohol is described as "cunning, baffling and powerful." Research is still trying to elucidate the precise biochemistry of cellular adaptation or whatever embodies the physiological explanation of addiction. But every alcoholic has experienced the truth of that description. The genteel housewife who pours her wine from a carafe so she can drink like a lady doesn't intend to empty it, and would be totally baffled at the suggestion that she was "one of those" (skid-road) alcoholics. The husband who starts out for the party telling his wife, "I'm only going to have two tonight, honey" really means it; they are both confused when this powerful man ends up having twelve.

Drinking alone is a misleading term. One may be quite alone in the hubbub of a crowded tavern, but deny that this is drinking alone. At that stage it is not so much that the alcoholic's friends have left him or her, although the alcoholic may think so. Rather, the alcoholic has left them. Later, they will leave in fact.

Other symptoms usually associated with the early middle stage are personality changes and "telephonitis" (lengthy conversations on the telephone, even long distance, sometimes with people the alcoholic hardly knows but usually with friends who do not enjoy the rambling barrage of words). There may be little visible interference with job performance, but some marital discord is likely. Unreasonable resentments, irritability, suspicions, and self-pity are common. Physical signs can include acid stomach with use of lots of antacids, insomnia, morning cough, sweating, elevated blood pressure and pulse. But the signs of physical addiction are usually not apparent at this stage.

Later middle stage alcoholism shows signs of increasing psychological dependence, and signs of physical dependence now begin to be observable. Hiding bottles or protecting the supply is a sure sign; one cannot bear the thought of not being able to have a drink if needed. The need will occur after a period of deprivation, usually in the morning but not necessarily. A fine hand tremor appears, developing later into "the shakes" of real withdrawal.

By now the excuses for drinking have grown into an elaborate alibi system, often centered on blaming the spouse. A "geographical cure" means changing jobs or cities, blaming the boss as focus of the alibi system. A job below one's training and education is a clue. Going on the water wagon periodically and even going to a dry-out spa or AA briefly in an attempt to prove "I can quit any time I want to" are symptomatic of the problem, but there is no real surrender at this point. Changes in drinking pattern are equally futile: switching brands, drink only beer, only with friends, or whatever. Resolutions and broken promises only increase the family frustration, and produce feelings of guilt and desperation in the alcoholic. Bringing extravagant presents home or the grandiose gesture of buying drinks for everybody in the bar betray the guilt and inner loss of self-respect. The alcoholic may not be eating properly, but signs of severe malnutrition have not yet become grossly apparent.

Late or Chronic Stage

Description here will be brief, both because the signs are all too obvious and because detailing them seems melodramatic. They include loss of family and job, trouble with bill collectors and the law, and some of the myriad physical illnesses listed in the final section of Chapter 4. Need or dependence now is palpably physical; one is caught in the vicious circle of not being able to start the day without a drink. Ethical deterioration sets in, with moral behavior at a level unthinkable a few years earlier; for example, sexual promiscuity, or the professional man neglecting clients or patients. There is irrational thinking, wide swings of emotion, persistent remorse, vague and nameless fears and anxieties. Tolerance may drop irreversibly below the initial level. Prolonged benders or constant inebriation are typical.

One way for those of us who are not alcoholics to attain some grasp of the power of this obsessive-compulsive, habitual addiction is to look at what an alcoholic will consume when desperately needing a drink. Bay Rum shaving lotion, Listerine, vanilla or lemon extract, various cough syrups and other patent medicines are all known to contain large amounts of ethyl alcohol. More toxic, with methanol or worse, are canned heat (Sterno), paint remover, liquid shoe polish, and the like. One desperate hobo drank a mixture of white (unleaded) gasoline and milk. A mechanic serving a jail sentence as a trusty working on police cars was observed to be high much of the time, in spite of being a prisoner, and this during Prohibition days at that; he was finally caught under the van with the petcock open, drinking the mixture of rusty water and antifreeze in the radiator.

Not That Bad.   We conclude this chapter with the warning that emphasis on this late, deteriorated stage can feed the alcoholic's denial and postpone acceptance of treatment. "Not that bad yet" is a phrase too often on the lips of alcoholic and spouse or employer. Alcoholics should not be encouraged by the fact that they still have a job, their health (really?), and never have been arrested or never have drunk paint thinner. The reason for our high success rates in treatment and rehabilitation is that we are getting them in treatment at an earlier stage now, before brain deterioration sets in and while there is still job, family, self-respect—all of which have no motivating force once they are lost. Perhaps it is preferable to stop referring to early, middle, and late stages and simply talk of marginal, moderate, or severe alcohol-related problems.

Sources

In spite of a proliferation of charts and lists of symptoms, the literature on progression is sparse; this may be due to great variability (from none to highly predictable) that makes generalization impossible. The works of M.M. Glatt and E.M. Jellinek have been noted.

The question of types seems equally elusive. Pages 35–41 of Jellinek's book *The Disease Concept* are brief. Two articles in the *Quarterly Journal of Studies on Alcohol* are Joan K. Jackson, "Types of Drinking Patterns of Male Alcoholics," *QJSA*, 1958, 19:269–302, and J. Rimmer et al, "Alcoholism vs. Diagnosis and Clinical Variation among Alcoholics," *QJSA*, 1972, 33:658–666. See also Jacobson (1976a) *The Alcoholisms: Detection, Assessment and Diagnosis.*

Regarding denial, perhaps the two most useful items are Kellerman's *Alcoholism: A Merry-Go-Round Named Denial*, and Wallace's chapter in Estes and Heinemann, pp. 3–14. In addition to the Lisansky (1974) article, we list a few other items:

Dealing With Denial. Hazelden pamphlet.

HEILMAN, RICHARD O., *Dynamics of Drug Dependency.* Hazelden pamphlet.

ROBE, LUCY B., "Rich Alcoholics: How Dollars Buy Denial," *Addictions*, 1977, 24 (2):43–57.

WEINBERG, JON R., *Why Do Alcoholics Deny Their Problem?* Hazelden pamphlet.

CHAPTER 7

Special Groups

IN THIS CHAPTER we survey briefly the alcohol problems of a few groups of people, who, among others, have been neglected in the research until recently, or who merit special attention.

Women

Long neglected and underestimated, alcohol problems among women are finally receiving the attention they deserve. The bibliography in Homiller's *Women and Alcohol* (1977) is testimony to how far we have progressed in a short time. Of course much more needs to be done. The picture is changing rapidly. Any definitive treatise on the subject should probably be written by a woman.

Early in Chapter 1 we listed many names in support of our belief that if fully reported the number of women alcoholics would really equal that of men, an impression confirmed by 40 percent of private physicians in one survey (Jones & Helrich, 1972). Male patterns, cirrhosis of the liver, and quantity-frequency of alcoholic beverage consumption are all misleading as indicators of female alcoholism. Although gin drinking and sherry sipping are an old story among women, there is definite evidence that the rate and amount of drinking by women has increased considerably. Women drink less beer than men, and more wine and hard liquor. Recently, greater freedom for women has included greater freedom to drink. However, to blame either the women's rights movement or the ills it opposes as the sole cause of female alcoholism is simplistic.

Myths and stereotypes about alcoholic women die slowly. The fact that their needs and problems are different from male alcoholics does not necessarily make them worse. Here we see the old double standard still operating: a man engages in "frequent extramarital relations" but a woman is "promiscuous." Another fallacy is to lump all women alcoholics into one category, when actually they vary in type and pattern as much as men. Media stereotypes that portray women alcoholics as weak, inferior, sexually loose, or drinking because they don't feel feminine only deter the woman from going into treatment because that would imply admission that some or all of this was true of her.

A false sense of chivalry and the harsh stigma attached to a woman with an alcohol problem tend to perpetuate her problems by weaving a protective circle of silence around her, rather than urging her to seek treatment. Rather than diagnosing her alcoholism problem, the physician will all too often prescribe a bottle of tranquilizers, with the result that some 80 percent of women alcoholics are said to be cross-addicted. Men are reluctant to recognize alcoholism as a primary illness in women, rather they tend to see it as a symptom of something else, and male professionals seem more easily caught up in the web of the woman's denial (Kimball, 1978, pp. 37–42).

Hypotheses that women drink because of feelings of dependency, to increase feelings of power, and to increase a sense of femininity, among others, are contradictory and lack experimental verification (Wilsnack, 1974). Some investigators assert that women, more frequently than men, start drinking heavily to cope with a specific life crisis, but this may be because the question is asked in a manner that elicits the expected response in women who are naturally looking for an excuse. Such psychologizing usually suffers from the problem of confusing cause with effect, and, in any case, it is not too helpful because alcoholics can always find a reason to drink. There are many unnecessary psychiatric referrals of alcoholic women patients.

Physical differences between male and female drinkers cannot be ignored. When women try to keep up drink for drink with men, their smaller size and higher proportion of body fat causes a higher BAC. Whereas men are more inclined to munch and snack while drinking, women are often dieting to stay thin so they drink on an empty stomach. This results in both malnutrition and quicker absorption of alcohol into the bloodstream. Menstruation can cause a higher blood alcohol level from the same amount ingested. Women tend to progress more rapidly into middle and late stage alcoholism than men do, as the physiological changes seem to occur in a shorter time span. They seem more prone to high blood pressure and cirrhosis. Hormonal changes and vitamin or mineral deficiencies connected with menopause seem to cause special problems. The Fetal Alcohol Syndrome (FAS), a source of birth defects in the children of alcoholic mothers, was described in Chapter 4.

Divorce rates for alcoholic women are much higher than for alcoholic men. Nonalcoholic wives are far more likely to remain with their alcoholic husbands, than the nonalcoholic husbands with their alcoholic wives. Men seem unable to perceive the economic problems of the recovering alcoholic woman. Far more than men, women alcoholics report a history of depression associated with their alcoholism, and this in turn leads to a greater use of psychoactive drugs.

For treatment, too few programs have aimed specifically at the needs of alcoholic women. Most women alcoholics still find themselves in treatment programs primarily designed for and run by men, where their feelings may run from fear of rape to embarrassment at walking down the corridor in a bathrobe. The treatment center is often located in a part of the city where women do not feel safe. A 1977 Wisconsin survey of women working in alcoholism rehabilitation evoked a unanimous response that women do better in all-women facilities. The coed centers that report good success rates are those where the proportion of men and women among both patients and staff are approximately equal. Women need good role models at all levels to motivate recovery.

Women need to feel comfortable with themselves and are reluctant to discuss their problems in mixed company. Hence all-women groups are important, especially in early recovery. Later, coed groups may be helpful in integrating them back into mixed society.

Lastly, child care seems to be a major need in the treatment of alcoholic women. Because the mother is with the children more hours of the day and the father is less able to shield them, it is generally conceded that children of alcoholic mothers suffer worse effects than children of alcoholic fathers. In any case, mothers cannot profit to the maximum from treatment if they are concerned about their children being with someone else. Family live-in arrangements are expensive, but this is a growing trend, and is worth the expense.

Youth

During the drug scare of the late 1960s, parents who learned that their child was involved in a drinking problem were inclined to reply, "Thank God, it's not drugs." This is understandable in a generation that grew up on the drinking song from *The Student Prince*. Now journalistic sensationalism has portrayed alcohol as the new teenage menace, and although it is a serious problem, there is always need to keep a balanced perspective. Adolescents have always drunk too much, so that is not new. Alcohol has always been the major drug of abuse among teenagers. One 1952 study showed 17 percent of high schoolers drank to forget their troubles. Even during the 1960s, one-third were drinking at least once a week and 5 percent daily. By 1974, 74 percent of high school boys and 69 percent of the girls reported having been intoxicated at least once. For most adolescents, drinking is an important part of growing up in our culture (Jessor and Jessor, 1975, 1977).

Drinking versus Alchoholism

Although Globetti (1977) and Blane and Hewitt (1977) seem to differ slightly in their impressions from reviewing the literature, there seems to be no doubt that drinking among adolescents and preadolescents has increased. Whereas some decades ago only about one-half to two-thirds as many girls drank as boys, that gap has practically disappeared. Accurate figures are hard to obtain, and researchers differ in their definitions of drinking, heavy drinking, and problem drinker. Some of the increase may reflect merely the fact that drinking is more out in the open now. Most surveys are done in schools, and it is known that the rates are even higher among school dropouts. On the other hand, data gathered on juvenile delinquents must not be generalized to all adolescents. Several local studies, notably those in San Mateo County in California and in Toronto, have been confirmed by national surveys by the Harris and Gallup polls and notably by a survey of 14,000 boys and girls, grades seven through twelve, conducted by the Research Triangle Institute (Rachal, 1975).

If the rate of increase is leveling off now, it may be because it is approaching the maximum. When 93 percent of seventeen-year-old boys and 87 percent of seventeen-year-old girls drink, there are not many left, and most of the small remainder probably will never drink. If the median age to start drinking in America is now thirteen years, that means over half our young people have been initiated into this rite of passage by the time they enter high school. We are not talking about a sip from the parent's glass given to a little child. Fifth and sixth grade teachers report that pupils in these grades, that is, as much as half the youngsters nine, ten, and eleven years old, bring bottles to school, drink during noon hour or recess, and show obvious signs of intoxication in the classroom. One-fifth of high school students get drunk at least once a month.

Is this alcoholism? No, the vast majority of kids at the Friday night kegger will never become alcoholics. Some will wreck cars and will maim others. Some will suffer other adverse effects in schooling or jobs. Among adolescents, more than anywhere else, the distinction between alcoholic and problem drinker is useful. Depending on definition, some 10 to 20 percent of adolescents report alcohol problems, including 8 percent with blackouts. One study showed that upon entry into college one-third reported some impairment due to alcohol abuse. Although true alcoholism is relatively rare in adolescents, it does occur as young as ten or eleven and cases of DTs have been reported at age nine. Some workers report a drop in tolerance at age nineteen or twenty, similar to what the Jellinek chart shows for late middle stage alcoholism. Using adult criteria to diagnose alcoholism in adolescents is misleading. Most adolescents get into a little trouble. Being stopped by the police is not the same as being arrested, and even an arrest for being a minor in possession of alcoholic beverages is not alcoholism or even problem drinking. Most important, labeling a young person as an alcoholic may be a self-fulfilling prophecy. Forcing them into treatment may only induce them to conform to adult expectations. Among juvenile delinquents alcoholism may be symptomatic of schizophrenia, of a depressive disorder, and especially of a sociopathic personality. Differential diagnosis is often difficult.

Adolescent Alcoholism Differs from Adult

Differences between alcoholism among adolescents and among adults involve most of the usual features of adolescence: rebellion against parents, poor coping skills, fewer responsibilities, hormonal changes of puberty, adolescent confusion. Adolescent alcoholism seems to be more closely tied to heredity. As with others, asking adolescent alcoholics why they drink is a waste of time. Adolescents say that adults drink to reduce anxiety or relieve personal problems, but rarely give this as a reason for their own drinking. Peer pressure and seeking adult status are no doubt very important in nonalcoholic adolescent drinking, but the adolescent alcoholic seems to drink for the effect. There seems to be less of the controlled drinking of adult alcoholics; most say they drink to get high and 52 percent of adolescent problem drinkers drink simply to get drunk. Progression seems more rapid, and organic damage especially to the central nervous system seems to be greater because the latter is still in formation. There is a lot of denial on the part of both the individual and society: "It can't happen that young"; or "They'll grow out of it." They are worse as drunk drivers because they are inexperienced both as drivers and drinkers. Because of smaller body size and tolerance, it usually takes less alcohol to inebriate them.

Most important is the polydrug complication. Almost no adolescent alcoholics use only alcohol. Combination with one or more other drugs is most common. High prevalence of polydrug abuse has lowered the age at which many individuals so afflicted must get help if they are to recover.

Treatment. Although many facilities now accept adolescents, there are less than a dozen in the country exclusively devoted to treating adolescent alcoholism. If the treatment setting is perceived as simply imposed on them by adults, it is resented and ineffective. AA lacks appeal because adolescents see it as simply another authority put-down by their elders, and the younger AA groups are still mostly young adults in their twenties and not for teenagers; so there is a real need. Adolescent alcoholics are often harder to motivate because they have not faced serious crises, saying, "I'll do something about it when it gets that bad" when they hear the stories of older AA members. They seem to have a higher relapse rate because immaturity makes successful rehabilitation difficult; most seem to have to learn the hard way. Lastly, it is harder for them to reenter their society after treatment without receiving scorn from their peers who drink.

Parents of adolescents who are in trouble with alcohol and other drugs are often not much help, as in their frustration they often take an either-or position and cannot recognize that there is a middle road between coerciveness and condoning (Ables, 1977). The parents are advised to seek help for themselves and only secondarily for the user (Huberty, 1976).

The Elderly

Even the 1974 NIAAA Second Special Report *Alcohol and Health* conveyed the impression that alcohol might be good for old people, as many physicians used to feel. Alcoholism has been underestimated among the aging partly because the picture is complicated and partly because of a reluctance to show "disrespect" by suggesting that a number of senior citizens are alcoholics. And whereas men tend to get into trouble, which exposes their alcoholism, the alcoholic woman may remain hidden for years. You won't find alcoholism if you don't look for it, and current thinking now recognizes that alcohol and polydrug problems can be a serious danger in old age. One experimental "happy hour" in a nursing home was abandoned when it was found that a few beers did not alleviate the pain and loneliness but rather awakened addiction, increased incontinence, and produced many other problems. According to some excellent and largely unpublished reviews of the literature by Marc Schuckit, much is still unknown about this topic. There are two major complications in research here: Alcohol damage is easily confused with the usual physical deterioration of aging; and there is great potential for polydrug abuse among older people.

Since "old" is a relative term, we shall arbitrarly speak of alcohol problems among those sixty-five and older. The older alcoholic is generally someone without evidence of severe antisocial or psychiatric problems. The alcohol problems began in mid or late life, and were not just a progression of early alcoholics living into old age. One reason for this, of course, is that many alcoholics do not reach old age.

But there seem to be two distinct subpopulations here. One group consists of those who began drinking as a reaction to the loneliness, depression, and lowered ego connected with retirement, widowhood, and general diminishing functions of aging. Progression in this group may be fairly rapid, although it may be that the early and middle-stage symptoms were dismissed as "just old age" and the alcoholism was not diagnosed until the person went into withdrawal. The other group are those who have been drinking for a long time, with alcohol problems progressing over the usual span. These latter usually exhibit greater organic damage. In either case, today's greater longevity means a larger population of elderly alcoholics.

Polydrug abuse among older people should always be suspected. Ten percent of the population over age sixty-five use 20 percent of the prescription drugs sold in this country, most of which potentiate with alcohol. Old people tend to hoard and swap drugs, and otherwise use them in nonprescribed ways. If they can use the sanction of "doctor's orders" for either alcohol or other drugs, it is easy to rationalize overuse. They refuse to believe that sleeping pills, diet pills, and many psychoactive drugs lose their effectiveness after five days or, at most, two weeks. They may become quite crafty at obtaining prescriptions from different doctors or having them filled at different pharmacies. Many nonprescription drugs contain large amounts of alcohol, and the combination of Nyquil or Geritol with Scope (mouthwash) can yield a 60-proof intoxicating beverage which leaves a clean breath! One alcoholism treatment center reported 85 percent of their older female patients were polydrug abusers. But a major factor remains "iatrogenic alcoholism" which Blume (1973) describes as being initiated by the physician who recommends alcohol as a tranquilizer.

Elderly alcoholics respond well to treatment, perhaps because they appreciate the added attention. But they seem to be more difficult to identify and get into treatment, requiring special outreach efforts. Society still tends to take the attitude that they should still be allowed to drink up their last days in peace and die. When younger people drink, they affect more people. When the elderly drink, they just become more isolated. Alcoholism accentuates the loneliness and suspiciousness of old age. A further tragic complication arises in a social welfare system that all too often excludes the elderly alcoholic from some old-age services because of the alcoholism, and from some alcoholism services because of the old age.

Racial Minorities

The most controversial and emotion-laden area of alcohol problems is that of racial minorities. This brief overview is drawn largely from minority sources, or from personal experiences of the author, who, more than once, found himself the only white person in a group discussing these problems. Even so, he is aware that one cannot encompass, much less please, all the subgroups that fall under this heading. The chief racial minority groups in this country are the native American Indians, the blacks, the Hispanics, and the Asiatic Americans. Each of these general headings includes numerous subgroups so diverse that one blushes to lump them together, lest he be as lacking in tact as the federal bureaucrat in the nation's capital who gave a native American from the central plains an Alaskan assignment on the assumption that "they are all Indians." Again, growing up knowing three black families well rooted in the West made the author aware that there can be greater differences between far West and deep South in both races than between black and white.

Native American Indians

By far the most literature and research concerns the aborigines of our land. A bibliography on Indian alcoholism by Patricia D. Mail and others (in press) lists over a thousand items (see Mail and McDonald, 1977). Here again diversity precludes any easy generalizations. Even the term *native American* is insisted upon by many Indian groups in the Southwest, while the Seattle group uses *Indian* by their own choice. This diversity only accentuates the basic theme of these pages: Any attempt to deal with alcohol problems in people of a particular culture must exhibit genuine sensitivity to the language, the customs, and thinking of that culture. This does not mean that only a member of that subgroup can work efficiently with their alcoholics, but it does mean that success is contingent upon being recognized as one who understands and accepts them as they are. This involves study, compassion without condescension, and, above all, the ability to listen.

American Indian leaders have long recognized that "alcohol is killing our people" and they lead the other minorities in their efforts to get training and develop programs. Figures vary with the tribe and with one's definition of alcoholism, but it is common to see reports of male alcoholism as high as 80 or 85 percent, and rates of 35 to 55 percent among females. Urban, village, and reservation natives are affected, but life-styles are so different that again the approaches must be specific.

The "drunken Indian" stereotype is both unfair and self-defeating, but the magnitude of the problem is undeniable. Alcohol is a factor in 75 percent of Indian deaths, 80 percent of their suicides, almost the only remaining prevalence of tuberculosis, and a homicide rate three times the national average (Baker, 1977, p. 195). Half of their high school students drop out because of alcoholism. Prohibition of Indian drinking was the law from 1832 to 1953, and its only effect besides high prices for the boot-leggers was to force secret and fast drinking. Customs vary and general-izations cannot be made, but some Indian languages have no separate verb for "to drink" as opposed to "get drunk." This reflects an uncritical acceptance of drunken behavior as well as widespread group pressure. Refusal to drink is an insult, or a denial of Indian identity. A drinking bout may parallel the old potlach, a ceremonial feast, in its features of prestige and reciprocity.

There is no one reason for the prevalence of alcoholism among these people. Forty-two theories have been listed under the headings of cultur-al, social, economic, biological, psychological, and combination. They include defiance to prohibition, lack of drinking norms, cultural disrup-tion, governmental paternalism, poverty, poor self-image, exploitation by the white man, and biological vulnerability or lack of immunity. Combi-nation theories center around the concepts of either a vulnerable person or conducive environment. Certainly all of these factors are important as partial causes, and we need not choose one to the exclusion of the others. We shall see in Chapter 9 that biological vulnerability must be consid-ered. Purely psychological explanations seem to ignore the fact that be-fore the white man brought his whiskey, the native American Indian was a proud, brave person who had developed high competence in coping with a difficult environment. Their current high rates of cirrhosis and other ills are clearly the result of drinking, and although there is no doubt a vicious circle at work one must look hard at the evidence that for many of their problems alcoholism is the cause rather than the effect. It is not simply a matter of tolerance, or different rates of metabolism, as there is no one "X factor" that explains alcoholism. Research on this point has tended to use simplistic logic, apparently because of reluctance to aban-don behavioristic prejudice against heredity. On the other hand, it may be that some of the evidence for rapid intoxication by Indians was a *simu-lated* drunkenness which the Indians put on for the benefit of the white observer.

Failure of earlier treatment programs should be interpreted less as a sign that the clients were hopeless or uncooperative than as a sign of our failure to involve the Indians themselves in the development of programs within their own specific cultures. A totally different concept of time, and an attitude that the white man's helping efforts were mere interference, are two characteristics of Indian thinking that were ignored. Because of a natural reluctance to go to the white man's agencies, special outreach ef-forts must be made to contact them, preferably through their own people. Understandably reticent about exposing either their inner feelings or their problems before a Caucasian group, they must be treated in centers where they can help each other within the traditions of their own culture. Every meeting on Indian alcoholism I have attended began with an invocation of the Great Spirit, and we must be careful to preserve the tradition of Alcoholics Anonymous, which gives them full freedom to speak "as they understand Him."

Blacks

The research literature of alcohol problems among blacks is less extensive than for native American Indians, with the first book appearing in 1963 by J.K. Larkins and more recently that by Frederick D. Harper, *Alcohol and Blacks: An Overview* (1976). Harper's important findings are summarized by Porter (1977) and include the following: Drinking among blacks is more social than solitary, and is more status-conscious, as evidenced by the high proportion of Scotch consumed. Problem drinking is most common among young urban black males. A much higher percentage of black women are total abstainers compared to white women, and blacks generally tend to drink either heavily or not at all. Black alcoholics admitted to hospitals and clinics show a stronger motivation for treatment, fewer complaints, and greater cooperation during the treatment process than do white alcoholics. But they are less likely to seek out treatment and need special outreach programs. Black alcoholics often feel uncomfortable at meetings of Alcoholics Anonymous dominated by whites, and the AA program is most successful for them when developed within black communities.

Writings by black authors such as Harper, Fred T. Davis, Jr., and Donald Phelps concur in linking alcoholism among blacks to problems of poverty, and there is some evidence that the upper-middle-class blacks have better attitudes and behaviors regarding alcohol than their white counterparts. But all stress that there is no simple solution and rather than just separate alcoholism programs for blacks it is important that the entire health delivery system recognize their special needs and problems and be sensitive to cultural differences. Most important is the development of prevention programs aimed specifically at these and other minority races, and the agencies funded by NIAAA are now developing posters, pamphlet material, movies, and training programs to this end. June J. Christmas, M.D., a black female psychiatrist who heads the mental health services for New York City, stresses (1978) that members of any race must not be lumped together to the neglect of important differences within the subgroups, and not merely minority but all personnel at all levels must make a real effort to understand the values, modes of communication, standards of behavior, and peculiar conditions of minority clients.

Hispanics and Asian Americans

Still less research and pertinent literature has been developed regarding Hispanic alcoholics and those whose ancestry is Chinese, Japanese, Philip-

pine, and other Pacific peoples. The language problems alone are formidable, and we can only emphasize that more consideration must be given
to both treatment and prevention. As with the blacks and Indians, excessive drinking among youth is a major and growing problem. Cultural differences and fear of discrimination make them particularly inaccessible to
prevention and outreach programs, and special efforts must be made.

The Military

The military services have long condoned, and at times encouraged, the
use of alcoholic beverages. Customs and traditions peculiar to the soldier's
environment almost dictated alcohol abuse. Even in more modern times,
military services have made regular liquor rations available to soldiers,
sailors, and airmen. During World War II, Army Air Force flight crews
were furnished with two ounces of liquor upon returning from combat
mission "to relieve the stress." Social life in the military was frequently
centered around drinking activities, from the low-priced "happy hour" to
more elegant parties where both officers and their wives were under
heavy social pressure to drink. The hard-fighting soldier was stereotyped
as a hard-drinking soldier.

Either from ignorance or from pride in the corps, alcoholism in the
armed forces was somewhat of a military secret even up to 1970, when
there had been wide publicity about abuse of other drugs among service
personnel. In that year a survey of alcoholism among civilian employees
of the army revealed that up to 8 percent had an alcohol problem. An estimate of the incidence of alcoholism in the military service was published
in 1971. The alcoholic serviceman had been generally stereotyped as the
combat-hardened veteran with many years of service; the career man
who had held responsible positions until he began to drink excessively.
Frequently he was protected and retained without treatment until retirement. This picture began to change in December 1972, when a Department of the Army survey identified alcoholics and problem drinkers to be
in their early twenties, and that the problem of alcohol abuse was on the
increase in the army. Investigations of alcoholism in all branches of the
military accelerated, culminating in the April 8, 1976 report to Congress
by the comptroller general of the United States entitled: "Alcohol Abuse Is
More Prevalent in the Military Than Drug Abuse" (MWD 76–99).

Some of the findings are that alcoholism and alcohol problems among
officers and enlisted personnel, both male and female, were far higher
than previously reported, and much above comparable civilian populations. Earlier impressions that drinking was a problem among enlisted
men far more than among commissioned officers have been corrected by
evidence that the officers are more protected and less liable to disciplinary
action. Boredom and loneliness seem to create greater drinking problems

overseas, for both service personnel and their spouses. Both in this country and abroad the social pressures and entertainment customs among wives, from the lowest enlisted man's to the highest ranking officer's, lead to serious alcohol problems. Heavy drinking and alcohol problems are not confined to the older career man; in fact, younger personnel get into alcohol-related trouble more often than those older. This latter fact may reflect, in part, a system of protection that favors the senior person. Rates of alcoholism and problem drinking were reported as high as 17 percent and even up to 35 percent in certain military populations.

All of this is now undergoing drastic change. Under the leadership of former Secretary of Defense Melvin Laird and the inspiration of men like naval Captain James Baxter, programs of education, prevention, intervention, and treatment have been initiated for the armed forces. The U.S. Navy led the way in all these areas, especially in developing excellent treatment programs. Most important for long-range prevention has been an attempt to counteract the image of the hard-drinking fighter and the easy availability of cheap alcoholic beverages. Such a reversal will take time, but great progress has been made.

Skid-Road Alcoholics

The stereotype of the alcoholic as a skid-road bum has so dominated American thinking and legislation that one is inclined to focus on its negative effects: fostering denial in other alcoholics as well as among professionals and obscuring the fact that 97 percent of alcoholics are "respectable." But these roughly 300,000 indigents are human beings, and deserve our consideration. Although for the many who have suffered permanent, irreversible brain damage, the most we can do is humane treatment and custodial care, a fair proportion are not "hopeless" and can respond to enlightened treatment methods. This means longer recovery time and more adequate follow-up rehabilitation.

Here again we must avoid generalizations. Only about 30 percent of skid-road residents are alcoholic, the remainder living there either by choice or out of financial necessity. These include many older permanent residents and some nonalcoholic transients. Among the alcoholics there are many distinct subgroups with different characteristics, designated by such names as bum, character, wino, rubby-dub (those who habitually drink nonbeverage alcohol) and lush (Jackson and Connor, 1953a; Rubington, 1973; Spradley, 1970). The lush tends to belong to a bottle gang, which has a very definite unwritten protocol and rules of conduct.

Skid-road alcoholics comprise a wide range of intelligence and mental status, from former bank presidents and professional men to mentally retarded or borderline intelligence, and including some with simple schizophrenia or sociopathic personality. They have their own language with subtle shades of meaning, for example, Spradley (1970) found them distinguishing fifteen kinds of tramp. Contrary to some romantic myths, most are not pleasantly drinking their lives away but engaged in a grim struggle for survival. Physically they are very sick men as a group. Thorough physical examinations of one hundred successive cases yielded a report that sounded like an encyclopedia of medical pathology: every organ, every known disease, many undiagnosed fractures and badly healed wounds (Ashley, 1976).

Although nobody chooses to be an alcoholic, some skid roaders apparently choose this way of life. But most are there as a result of circumstances, low intelligence, personality disorder, or alcoholism. It may be a combination of any or all of these, with alcoholism a major factor. Some want to break out of the pattern, but they have little in the way of alternatives available. The skid-road alcoholic is not necessarily an irretrievable derelict or at the final stages of a drinking career. They need hope, patience, understanding, a longer than usual treatment program, retraining to become employable, and a great deal of help in finding a place to live and a job and a new way of life. What they do not need is a social system that perpetuates and implicitly encourages their dependence, while continuing to furnish them money to drink.

Other Groups

Until very recently, physicians and members of the clergy who suffered from alcoholism were, perhaps, the subject of local gossip but they were not formally recognized as alcoholics by members of their professions, nor were formal attempts made to understand them and to help them. As the stigma has lifted from alcoholism, more and more physicians and clergy have, like women, come out of the closet. Increasingly, professional concern is expressed and appropriate actions considered. There is a group called International Doctors in AA for physicians and dentists, a treatment facility just for physicians (Caduceus Hall at Ridgeview Institute in Smyrna, Georgia), and information available through the medical component of the National Council on Alcoholism, and a special committee of the American Medical Association (Bissell and Jones, 1976; Franklin 1977; Glatt, 1977; Green, 1978; John, 1978; Medical Society of the State of New York, 1975; Seixas, 1976; Steindler, 1977).

There are at least two groups for recovered alcoholic clergy: Recovered Alcoholic Clergy Association (RACA), and the National Clergy Council on Alcoholism (NCCA). Both are quite ecumenical, but the former is predominantly Episcopal and the latter largely Roman Catholic, including religious sisters and brothers. Members of Alcoholics Anonymous who are of the clergy have been open about their occupation and are warmly welcomed by fellow members. Yet considerably less has been written about them than about physicians (Sorensen, 1976).

Both physicians and clergy share with other alcoholics, apparently to an even greater degree, their tendency to polydrug misuse. They seem especially vulnerable to the combination of alcohol with prescription drugs such as tranquilizers, sleeping pills, and reducing pills.

Sources

Women

Alcoholism and Alcohol Abuse Among Women: Research Issues, NIAAA Research Monograph No. 1 (1980), has a lengthy bibliography; Homiller (1977) has a useful list on pp. 28–35. The growing literature on this topic is reviewed and evaluated by Beckman (1975), Gomberg (1977), and Lindbeck (1972). A well-written and sympathetic journalistic work is Hornik's *The Drinking Woman* (1978); see also the writings of Bonnie-Jean Kimball, Jean Kirkpatrick, Muriel Nellis, Marian Sandmaier, Muriel Zink, and Geraldine Youcha. More technical books dealing with women addicted to alcohol and other drugs are by Eileen Corrigan, *Alcoholic Women in Treatment* (1980), Dowsling and MacLennan (eds.), *The Chemically Dependent Woman*; M. Greenblatt & M.A. Schuckit (eds.), *Alcoholism Problems in Women and Children*, and Oriana Kalant (ed.), *Alcohol and Drug Problems in Women*. The Fall 1978 issue of *Alcohol Health and Research World* is devoted to women and alcohol.

Youth

There is a vast literature on youth and alcohol abuse. An excellent review, which is both comprehensive and evaluative, is provided by Blane and Hewitt's *Alcohol and Youth: An Analysis of the Literature, 1960–1975*. Globetti's "Teenage Drinking" provides a briefer perspective on what is known to date, as does "Young People and Alcohol," in the summer 1975 *Alcohol Health and Research World*. Jessor and Jessor (1977) have done important longitudinal research. Unger (1978) and Smart (1979) discuss treatment. Barnes in "The Development of Adolescent Drinking Behavior" evaluates the data on family influences on what the young person does about drinking.

The Elderly

Although there is a substantial and growing body of publications drawing attention to the problems of substance abuse among the elderly, there are few general articles that draw together what is known about the extent of the problems and their nature. Among the few are Marc Schuckit's "Geriatric Alcoholism and Drug

Abuse"; and "Older Problem Drinkers," in *Alcohol, Health and Research World*'s spring 1975 issue.

Minority Groups

For one reason or another, Americans have been concerned for well over a century with the drinking of American Indians. As a result there is voluminous literature on the subject, much of it interdisciplinary in nature, dealing with such diverse areas as the role of drinking in Indian culture, its effects on Indian health, economics, and psychology, and in their relationships with the majority. Patricia D. Mail and her colleagues have been attempting to gather all this material into a comprehensive bibliography and have already published a preliminary annotated listing (Mail and McDonald, 1977). For an evaluation of the literature, one can turn to Heath's "A Critical Review of Ethnographic Studies of Alcohol Use," which includes what is thought about and known about alcohol and North American Indians and Eskimos, as well as other ethnic groups. There is also *Alcohol Problems among American Indians and Eskimos: Bibliography*, a listing published by the National Clearinghouse for Alcohol Information (NCALI, SAB 1-C-2). For an overview of the extent of the problem and the kinds of actions being taken to solve them, see the reports to the Indian Health Service of three task forces which were published in 1972 under the title, *Alcoholism: A High Priority Health Problem*.

In 1976, Harper and Dawkins published "Alcohol and Blacks: Survey of the Periodical Literature," pointing out that there was a dearth of research and publications dealing with the nature and extent of alcohol problems among blacks. Harper's *Alcohol Abuse and Black America* promises to deal with the findings of what research there has been and to suggest where future research efforts could be directed most effectively. Despite this lack of attention to alcoholism, there are studies dealing with drinking patterns of black youth, and these can be located by consulting Blane and Hewitt's *Alcohol and Youth. An Analysis of the Literature, 1960–1975*. See also Brunswick and Tarica (1974), Bourne (1973), and Maddox (1968). Dawkins (1980) has done sociological research.

The situation with respect to other minorities is very similar. Although occasional references occur in papers about alcoholism among Americans of Asian or Spanish origins, there has been little systematic study of alcoholism, although it is known to occur; little written about the use of treatment facilities, though they are thought to be underutilized by these groups; and some literature on general drinking practices. An example of the latter is Paine's excellent study, "Attitudes and Patterns of Alcohol Use among Mexican Americans: Implications for Service Delivery." Of interest might be Richard Stivers, *Hair of the Dog: Irish Drinking and American Stereotype*.

The Military

In "Alcohol Abuse in the Armed Services: A Review, "which appeared in two parts: I. Policies and Programs (1976), and II. Problem Areas and Recommendations (1977), Long, Hewitt and Blane have given an extremely comprehensive picture of the alcohol problems the military have faced and the solutions they are attempting. See also the entire winter 1977 issue of *Military Chaplain's Review*.

Skid-Road Alcoholics

Since the implementation of the Uniform Alcoholism Intoxication and Treatment Act, the problems faced by homeless alcoholics, and by the society that wants him or her off the streets, have been somewhat changed, but not eliminated. Being drunk in public is no longer a crime in over half the states, so that arrests have become less frequent. However, alcoholics in this category are different from other alcoholics in some important ways, have significantly different kinds of problems in treatment, and pose continuing problems for all those who exercise social control. Weisman's *Stations Of the Lost: Treatment of Skid-Road Alcoholics*, Rubington's *Alcohol Problems and Social Control*, Spradley's *You Owe Yourself a Drunk*, Bahr's *Skid Row: An Introduction to Disaffiliation*, and Schmidt's *Social Class and the Treatment of Alcoholism* throw very important light on the special characteristics and special problems of the skid-road alcoholic, despite being out of date with respect to the relationships between this kind of alcoholic and the police. A more recent work is *Liquor and Poverty: Skid Row as a Human Condition*, by Leonard U. Blumberg, Thomas Shipley, and Stephen Barsky (Rutgers Center of Alcohol Studies, monograph 13, 1978).

Other Groups

The most comprehensive single article on alcoholic physicians is Bissell and Jones, "The Alcoholic Physician: A Survey." The book, *The Care and Management of the Sick and Incompetent Physician* by Green, Carroll, and Buxton also throws light on the problems of alcoholic physicians. The article by H. John (1978) has a bibliography.

For the most part alocholic clergy are not discussed in print. Recent exceptions to this generalization are the articles by Fichter, and Sorensen's *Alcoholic Priests: A Sociological Study*. Although not for general circulation, the NCCA has published *The Blue Book* annually since 1949, and collected some of its best articles in *Alcoholism: A Source Book for the Priest*.

CHAPTER 8

The Spouse and Family of the Alcoholic

"THE FAMILY OF the alcoholic becomes as sick as or sicker than the alcoholic" has become a commonplace among workers in the alcoholism field. While, of course, this does not apply to the physical deterioration, in every other respect this will be true. The spouse and family become involved in a mighty tug of war wherein the alcoholic desperately clings to the drinking while the spouse and family try to diminish or stop it. The family as well as their alcoholic member needs help. It is futile to rehabilitate an alcoholic who returns to a family environment that is unchanged. As a result of incorporating the family into the treatment process, treatment centers are reporting a 30 to 50 percent increase in success rates. Some treatment centers have a special wing or building exclusively for the spouses of alcoholics to live in during part of the alcoholic's treatment period, and some require the spouse to be in treatment for part of that time.

Regardless of the impact on the recovery of the alcoholic, treatment of the family is important in its own right. There is a tendency to focus all attention and funding on the treatment of the alcoholic, so that the family and spouse are often the least treated and most neglected. Actually, they can often profit from treatment first. The recovery of the alcoholic can then sometimes occur as a welcome by-product, even though not the primary or direct objective. In any case, diagnosis of family problems should not be made without careful investigation of the role that alcohol might play.

Research and Theories

During the past few centuries, the alcoholic was the focus of a great deal of attention while the spouse was almost totally neglected or merely pitied. The spouse was always presumed to be the wife; the husband of the alcoholic woman was ignored entirely. When studies began to be published, they assumed that the wife was a neurotic person who married an alcoholic husband to satisfy some unconscious need to be needed, a mothering or protective impulse which could be gratified by taking care of a suffering alcoholic (Price, 1945; Whalen, 1953). Personal maladjustment was seen as the cause of being married to an alcoholic, not the result.

Dr. Joan Jackson challenged this concept in her now classic paper, "The Adjustment of the Family to the Crisis of Alcoholism" (1954), which has been confirmed by the research of others on this point, although they may disagree about her theory of adjustment stages (for example, Lemert, 1960). The principal thrust of her research was to show that although a minority of the wives of alcoholics may indeed marry because of unconscious neurotic needs, the majority were normal personalities at marriage and the neurotic behavior that they exhibit is a reaction to living with alcoholism rather than cause. This parallels a similar shift in alcoholism theory away from psychopathology as the cause of alcoholism and toward a recognition that psychopathology results from alcoholism, as we shall discuss in chapters 9 and 10.

Edwards (1973), Orford (1975), and Paolino and McGrady (1977) have systematically reviewed the controversies in the research on wives of alcoholics and have rightly insisted that the matter needs to be put in the broader perspective of psychosocial research, which includes other types of marital problems as well as alcoholism. Paolino and McGrady analyzed the research from the point of view of methodology, sampling, and theoretical context and have concluded that there is little support for the theory that wives of alcoholics need an alcoholic in order to remain psychologically stable. However, it is not necessary to make a dichotomous choice between the old *predisposing personality* theory and Jackson's *reaction to stress* theory. The wife of an alcoholic is an individual, and we must avoid stereotypes.

Predisposing Personality.   Futterman (1953) had concluded that there is much clinical evidence to suggest that the wife "unconsciously, because of her own needs, seems to encourage her husband's alcoholism." Whalen and Price went further and said that the wife of the alcoholic not only contributes to the alcoholism of the husband after marriage, but certain types of women marry alcoholics in order to satisfy deep unconscious needs. The wife, at the time of her marriage, was depicted as an insecure person who expected her husband to be strong and dependable, or as a domineering person looking for someone to mother. And so we had the stereotypes of Controlling Catherine, Wavering Winnie, Suffering Susan, and Punitive Polly.These symbolized psychological explanations of why the wife either married an alcoholic husband in the first place, or continued to live with him in spite of the misery of an alcoholic marriage, and would even include decompensation whereby she could not stand his sobriety upon recovery and would subconsciously seek to have him drink again.

No psychologist can deny the "need to be needed" nor that it is a factor in some alcoholic marriages. The wife may have a reaction formation to her own emotional deprivation in childhood, and be determined to shield others from it. The teenage daughter of an alcoholic father may receive the attention he no longer gives his wife because of their mutual animosity. As a result she may grow up thinking that she can manage an alcoholic through love, and so ends up marrying one. Likewise, we shall observe that the readjustment after recovery may involve some decompensation from fulfillment of neurotic needs, although most of it can be explained in terms of reversal of roles and readjustment.

Reaction to Stress.   The theory of a predisposing personality has largely given way to another view, one that recognized that living with an alcoholic generates instability, indecisiveness, guilt feelings, hopelessness, and a host of other reactions in an otherwise normal personality (Paolino, 1977; Reddy, 1978, p. 28). Certainly these qualities in a spouse should not be presumed at the outset to be the cause of the drinking problems, and an accurate diagnosis can only be made much later in treatment. The research of Jackson and others shows that it is more useful to conceptualize the behavior of the spouse as the reaction to a cumulative crisis in which the spouse experiences progressively more stress.

Because spouses come to the initial interview usually feeling that the alcoholic drinking is their fault, it is best not to start with a history that is only depressing and would reinforce these guilt feelings. Even when the wife's behavior is inappropriate and bizarre, we cannot assume that she is driven to act in this manner by an unconscious need to have her husband drink. There is no evidence that the husband drank because of this behavior, nor that if the wife had not so behaved he would not have resumed his drinking. We cannot demonstrate that if she were given information on how to terminate the drinking, she would not or could not make use of this information. It may be that the wife's behavior is motivated by more immediate concerns: to release situationally induced tension and to stabilize the family. If it precipitates further drinking by the husband, this is not necessarily the unconscious intent of the spouse.

Before Marriage

During courtship, the suitor tends to be on his best behavior. Problem drinking was hidden, or simply not seen because love is blind. In talking with wives of alcoholics one is astounded to hear that they suspected nothing, although any novice familiar with the early stages could have seen many warning signs of alcoholism. In other cases the alcoholism began only after marriage. These facts seem to have been overlooked in the older theories about marrying to fulfill neurotic needs, since these women did not marry known alcoholics. In cases where some awareness is reported, both wife and relatives indulge in a "love conquers all" brand of thinking, believing that "marriage would straighten him out," whereas things only get worse once the honeymoon is over.

Stages in Family Adjustment to Alcoholism

For simplicity of language, and because most of the research has been done on the wife of the alcoholic, we shall refer to her as the spouse. It is clear that the chances might be equal that the alcoholic is a woman and the spouse her husband. Similarly, our emphasis on variety of patterns and individuals should preclude any wooden interpretation of the following seven stages. They are presented as examples of how the family reacts, and not a rigid sequence of events. As such, they support Jackson's adjustment hypothesis even if the patterns vary. It is true that much of this is based on the perceptions of the wives; but these subjective phenomena are in themselves data, psychological facts that must be looked at. Most of what follows is in Jackson's own words; the author takes credit for only the shortcomings.*

1. Denial and Minimizing

Usually the first experience with drinking as a problem arises in a social situation. The husband drinks in a manner which is inappropriate to the social setting and the expectations of others present. The wife feels embarrassed on the first occasion and humiliated as it occurs more frequently. After several such incidents she and her husband talk over his behavior. The husband either formulates an explanation for the episode and assures her that such behavior will not occur again, or he refuses to discuss it at all. For a time afterward he drinks appropriately and drinking seems to be a problem no longer. The wife looks back on the incidents and feels that she has exaggerated them, feels ashamed of herself for her disloyalty and for her behavior. The husband, in evaluating the incident, feels shame also and vows such episodes will not re-

---

*Joan K. Jackson, "The Adjustment of the Family to the Crisis of Alcoholism," reprinted by permission from *Quarterly Journal Studies on Alcohol*, 1954, vol. 15, pp. 562–586. Copyright © by Journal of Studies on Alcohol, Inc., New Brunswick, N.J. 08903.

cur. As a result, both husband and wife attempt to make it up to the other and, for a time, try to play their conceptions of the ideal hsuband and wife roles minimizing or avoiding other difficulties which arise in the marriage. They thus create the illusion of a "perfect" marriage.

Eventually another inappropriate drinking episode occurs and the pattern is repeated. The wife worries but takes action only in the situations in which inappropriate drinking occurs, as each long intervening period of acceptable drinking behavior convinces her that a recurrence is unlikely. As time goes on, in attempting to cope with individual episodes, she runs the gamut of possible trial and error behaviors, learning that none is permanently effective.

If she speaks to other people about her husband's drinking, she is usually assured that there is no need for concern, that her husband can control his drinking and that her fears are exaggerated. Some friends possibly admit that his drinking is too heavy and give advice on how they handled similar situations with their husbands. These friends convince her that her problem will be solved as soon as she hits upon the right formula for dealing with her husband's drinking.

During this stage the husband-wife interaction is in no way "abnormal." In a society in which a large proportion of the men drink, most wives have at some time had occasion to be concerned, even though only briefly, with an episode of drinking which they considered inappropriate. In a society in which the status of the family depends on that of the husband, the wife feels threatened by any behavior on his part which might lower it. Inappropriate drinking is regarded by her as a threat to the family's reputation and standing in the community. The wife attempts to exert control and often finds herself blocked by the sacredness of drinking behavior to men in America. Drinking is a private matter and not any business of the wife's. On the whole, a man reacts to his wife's suggestion that he has not adequately controlled his drinking with resentment, rebelliousness and a display of emotion which makes rational discussion difficult. The type of husband-wife interaction outlined in this stage has occurred in many American families in which the husband never became an excessive drinker.

(Jackson here anticipates Orford, 1975, by two decades.)

The romantic illusions of courtship days dominate the wife's thinking in this first stage. She tells herself that he is too intelligent to be an alcoholic, forgets what he was like before problem drinking began, clings to false hopes that things will change or that it's really not that bad. She believes his excuses and accepts his promises. Reproof is met with resentment, which usually puts her on the defensive instead of him.

2. Tension and Isolation

Stage 2 begins when the family experiences social isolation because of the husband's drinking. Invitations to the homes of friends become less frequent. When the couple does visit friends, drinks are not served or are limited, thus emphasizing the reason for exclusion from other social activities of the friendship group. Discussions of drinking begin to be sidestepped awkwardly by friends, the wife and the husband.

By this time the periods of socially acceptable drinking are becoming shorter. The wife, fearing that the full extent of her husband's drinking will become known, begins to withdraw from social participation, hoping to reduce the visibility of his behavior, and thus the threat to family status.

Isolation is further intensified because the family usually acts in accordance with the cultural dictate that it should be self-sufficient and manage to resolve its own problems without recourse to outside aid. Any experiences which they have had with well-meaning outsiders, usually relatives, have tended to strengthen this conviction. The husband has defined such relatives as interfering and the situation has deteriorated rather than improved.

With increasing isolation, the family members begin to lose perspective on their interaction and on their problems. Thrown into closer contact with one another as outside contacts diminish, the behavior of each member assumes exaggerated importance. The drinking behavior becomes the focus of anxiety. Gradually all family difficulties become attributed to it. (For example, the mother who is cross with her children will feel that, if her husband had not been drinking, she would not have been so tense and would not have been angry.) The fear that the full extent of drinking may be discovered mounts steadily; the conceptualization of the consequences of such a discovery becomes increasingly vague and, as a result, more anxiety-provoking. The family feels different from others and alone with its shameful secret.

Attempts to cover up increase. The employer who calls to inquire about the husband's absence from work is given excuses. The wife is afraid to face the consequences of loss of the husband's pay check in addition to her other concerns. Questions from the children are evaded or they are told that their father is ill. The wife lives in terror of the day when the children will be told by others of the nature of the "illness." She is also afraid that the children may describe their father's symptoms to teachers or neighbors. Still feeling that the family must solve its own problems, she keeps her troubles to herself and hesitates to seek outside help. If her husband beats her, she will bear it rather than call in the police. (Indeed, often she has no idea that this is even a possibility.) Her increased isolation has left her without the advice of others as to sources of help in the community. If she knows of them, an agency contact means to her an admission of the complete failure of her family as an independent unit. For the middle-class woman particularly, recourse to social agencies and law-enforcement agencies means a terrifying admission of loss of status.

During this stage, husband and wife are drawing further apart. Each feels resentful of the behavior of the other. When this resentment is expressed, further drinking occurs. When it is not, tension mounts and the next drinking episode is that much more destructive of family relationships. The reasons for drinking are explored frantically. Both husband and wife feel that if only they could discover the reason, all members of the family could gear their behavior to making drinking unnecessary. The discussions become increasingly unproductive, as it is the husband's growing conviction that his wife does not and cannot understand him.

On her part, the wife begins to feel that she is a failure, that she has been unable to fulfill the major cultural obligations of a wife to meet her husband's needs. With her increasing isolation, her sense of worth derives almost entirely from her roles as wife and mother. Each failure to help her husband gnaws away at her sense of adequacy as a person.

Periods of sobriety or socially acceptable drinking still occur. These periods keep the wife from making a permanent or stable adjustment. During them her husband, in his guilt, treats her like a queen. His behavior renews her hope and rekindles positive feelings toward him. Her sense of worth is bolstered temporarily and she grasps desperately at her husband's reassurance that she is really a fine person and not a failure and an unlovable shrew. The periods of sobriety also keep her family from facing the inability of the husband to control his drinking. The inaccuracies of the cultural stereotype of the alcoholic—particularly that he is in a constant state of inebriation—also contribute to the family's rejection of the idea of alcoholism, as the husband seems to demonstrate from time to time that he can control his drinking.

Family efforts to control the husband become desperate. There are no culturally prescribed behavior patterns for handling such a situation and the family is forced to evolve its own techniques. Many different types of behavior are tried but none brings consistent results; there seems to be no way of predicting the consequences of any action that may be taken. All attempts to stabilize or structure the situation to permit consistent behavior fail. Threats of leaving, hiding his liquor away, emptying the bottles down the drain, curtailing his money, are tried in rapid succession, but none is effective. Less punitive methods, as discussing the situation when he is sober, babying him during hangovers, and trying to drink with him to keep him in the home, are attempted and fail. All behavior becomes oriented around the drinking, and the thought of family members becomes obsessive on this subject. As no action seems to be successful in achieving its goal, the wife persists in trial-and-error behavior with mounting frustration. Long-term goals recede into the background and become secondary to just keeping the husband from drinking today.

There is still an attempt to maintain the illusion of husband-wife-children roles. When father is sober, the children are expected to give him respect and obedience. The wife also defers to him in his role as head of the household. Each drinking event thus disrupts family functioning anew. The children begin to show emotional disturbances as a result of the inconsistencies of parental behavior. During periods when the husband is drinking the wife tries to shield them from the knowledge and effects of his behavior, at the same time drawing them closer to herself and deriving emotional support from them. In sober periods, the father tries to regain their favor. Due to experiencing directly only pleasant interactions with their father, considerable affection is often felt for him by the children. This affection becomes increasingly difficult for the isolated wife to tolerate, and an additional source of conflict. She feels that she needs and deserves the love and support of her children and, at the same time, she feels it important to maintain the children's picture of their father. She counts on the husband's affection for the children to motivate a cessation of drinking as he comes to realize the effects of his behavior on them.

In this stage, self-pity begins to be felt by the wife, if it has not entered previously. It continues in various degrees throughout the succeeding stages. In an attempt to handle her deepening sense of inadequacy, the wife often tries to convince herself that she is right and her husband wrong, and this also continues through the following stages. At this point the wife often resembles what Whalen describes as "The Sufferer."

The family has now become obsessed with the drinking problem. The question "Why does he drink?" is not only pointless but implies guilt on the part of some or all in the family. Augmentation takes place as tension mounts, so less is required to set off an emotional explosion.

3. Frustration and Disorganization

The wife begins to adopt a "What's the use?" attitude and to accept her husband's drinking as a problem likely to be permanent. Attempts to understand one another become less frequent. Sober periods still engender hope, but hope qualified by skepticism; they bring about a lessening of anxiety and this is defined as happiness.

By this time some customary patterns of husband-wife-children interaction have evolved. Techniques which have had some effectiveness in controlling the husband in the past or in relieving pent-up frustration are used by the wife. She nags, berates or retreats into silence. Husband and wife are both on the alert, the wife watching for increasing irritability and restlessness which mean a recurrence of drinking, and the husband for veiled aspersions on his behavior or character.

The children are increasingly torn in their loyalties as they become tools in the struggle between mother and father. If the children are at an age of comprehension, they have usually learned the true nature of their family situation, either from outsiders or from their mother, who has given up attempts to bolster her husband's position as father. The children are often bewildered but questioning their parents brings no satisfactory answers as the parents themselves do not understand what is happening. Some children become terrified; some have increasing behavior problems within and outside the home; others seem on the surface to accept the situation calmly.

During periods of the husband's drinking, the hostility, resentment and frustrations felt by the couple is allowed expression. Both may resort to violence—the wife in self-defense or because she can find no other outlet for her feelings. In those cases in which the wife retaliates to violence in kind, she feels a mixture of relief and intense shame at having deviated so far from what she conceives to be "the behavior of a normal woman."

When the wife looks at her present behavior, she worries about her "normality." In comparing the person she was in the early years of her marriage with the person she has become, she is frightened. She finds herself nagging and unable to control herself. She resolves to stand up to her husband when he is belligerent but instead finds herself cringing in terror and then despises herself for her lack of courage. If she retaliates with violence, she is filled with self-loathing at behaving in an "unwomanly" manner. She finds herself compulsively searching for bottles, knowing full well that finding them will change nothing, and is worried because she engages in such senseless behavior.

She worries about her inability to take constructive action of any kind. She is confused about where her loyality lies, whether with her husband or her children. She feels she is a failure as a wife, mother and person. She believes she should be strong in the face of adversity and instead feels herself weak.

The wife begins to find herself avoiding sexual contact with her husband when he has been drinking. Sex under these circumstances, she feels, is sex for its own sake rather than an indication of affection for her. Her husband's lack of consideration of her needs to be satisfied leaves her feeling frustrated. The lack of sexual responsiveness reflects her emotional withdrawal from him in other areas of family life. Her husband, on his part, feels frustrated and rejected; he accuses her of frigidity and this adds to her concern about her adequacy as a woman.

It is of interest here that marriage counselors and students of marital adjustment are of the opinion that unhappy marriage results in poor sexual adjustment more often than poor sexual adjustment leads to unhappy marriage. If this proves to be true, it would be expected that most wives of alcoholics would find sex distasteful while their husbands are drinking. The wives of the inactive alcoholics report that their sexual adjustments with their husbands are currently satisfactory; many of those whose husbands are still drinking state that they enjoyed sexual relationships before the alcoholism was established.

By this time the opening wedge has been inserted into the self-sufficiency of the family. The husband has often been in difficulty with the police and the wife has learned that police protection is available. An emergency has occured in which the seeking of outside help was the only possible action to take; subsequent calls for aid from outsiders do not require the same degree of urgency before they can be undertaken. However, guilt and a lessening of self-respect and self-confidence accompany this method of resolving emergencies. The husband intensifies these feeling by speaking of the interference of outsiders, or of his night in jail.

In Stage 3 all is chaos. Few problems are met constructively. The husband and wife both feel trapped in an intolerable, unstructured situation which offers no way out. The wife's self-assurance is almost completely gone. She is afraid to take action and afraid to let things remain as they are. Fear is one of the major characteristics of this stage: fear of violence, fear of personality damage to the children, fear for her own sanity, fear that relatives will interfere, and fear they they will not help in an emergency. Added to this, the family feels alone in the world and helpless. The problems, and the behavior of family members in attempting to cope with them, seem so shameful that help from others is unthinkable. They feel that attempts to get help would meet only with rebuff, and that communication of the situation will engender disgust.

At this point the clinical picture which the wife presents is very similar to what Whalen has described as "The Waverer."

The wife has lost her self-confidence and is unable to do any long-range planning. Her indecisiveness allows her to call the police when he beats her up, then refuse to press charges when they arrive. She may even begin to drink herself now for relief. The children feel guilty, since they have been shushed so often that they think it is their noise that causes daddy to drink.

4. Attempts to Reorganize; Shifts in Roles

Stage 4 begins when a crisis occurs which necessitates that action be taken. There may be no money or food in the house; the husband may have been violent to the children; or life on the level of Stage 3 may have become intolerable. At this point some wives leave, thus entering directly into Stage 5.

The wife who passes through Stage 4 usually begins to ease her husband out of his family roles. She assumes husband and father roles. This involves strengthening her role as mother and putting aside her role as wife. She becomes the manager of the home, the discipliner of the children, the decision-maker; she becomes somewhat like Whalen's "Controller." She either ignores her husband as much as possible or treats him as her most recalcitrant child. Techniques are worked out for getting control of his pay check, if there still is one, and money is doled out to her husband on the condition of his good behavior. When he drinks, she threatens to leave him, locks him out of the house, refuses to pay his taxi bills, leaves him in jail overnight rather than pay his bail. Where her obligations to her husband conflict with those to her children, she decides in favor of the latter. As she views her husband increasingly as a child, pity and a sense of being desperately needed by him enter. Her inconsistent behavior toward him, deriving from the lack of predictability inherent in the situation up to now, becomes reinforced by her mixed feelings toward him.

In this stage the husband often tries to set his will against hers in decisions about the children. If the children have been permitted to stay with a friend overnight, he may threaten to create a scene unless they return immediately. He may make almost desperate efforts to gain their affection and respect, his behavior ranging from getting them up in the middle of the night to fondle them, to giving them stiff lectures on children's obligations to fathers. Sometimes he will attempt to align the males of the family with him against the females. He may openly express resentment of the children and become belligerent toward them physically or verbally.

Much of the husband's behavior can be conceptualized as resulting from an increasing awareness of his isolation from the other members of the family and their steady withdrawal of respect and affection. It seems to be a desperate effort to regain what he has lost, but without any clear idea of how this can be accomplished—an effort to change a situation in which everyone is seen as against him; and, in reality, this is becoming more and more true. As the wife has taken over control of the family with some degree of success, he feels, and becomes, less and less necessary to the ongoing activity of the family. There are fewer and fewer roles left for him to play. He becomes aware that members of the family enjoy each other's company without him. When he is home he tries to enter this circle of warmth or to smash it. Either way he isolates himself further. He finds that the children discuss with the mother how to manage him and he sees the children acting on the basis of their mother's idea of him. The children refuse to pay attention to his demands: they talk back to him in the same way that they talk back to one another, adding pressure on him to assume the role of just another child. All this leaves him frustrated and, as a result, often aggressive or increasingly absent from home.

The children, on the whole, become more settled in their behavior as the wife takes over the family responsibilities. Decisions are made by her and upheld in the face of their father's attempts to interfere. Participation in activities outside the home is encouraged. Their patterns of interaction with their father are supported by the mother. Whereas in earlier stages the children often felt that there were causal connections between their actions and their father's drinking, they now accept his unpredictability. "Well," says a six-year old, "I'll just have to get used to it. I have a drunken father."

The family is more stabilized in one way but in other ways insecurities are multiplied. Pay checks are received less and less regularly. The violence or withdrawal of the father increases. When he is away the wife worries about automobile accidents or injury in fights, which become more and more probable as time passes. The husband may begin to be seriously ill from time to time; his behavior may become quite bizarre. Both of these signs of increasing illness arouse anxiety in the family.

During this stage hopes may rise high for father's "reform" when he begins to verbalize wishes to stop drinking, admits off and on his inability to stop, and sounds desperate for doing something about his drinking. Now may begin the trek to sanitariums for the middle-class alcoholic, to doctors, or to Alcoholics Anonymous. Where just the promise to stop drinking has failed to revive hope, sobriety through outside agencies has the ability to rekindle it brightly. There is the feeling that at last he is "taking really constructive action." In failure the discouragement is deeper. Here another wedge has been inserted into the self-sufficiency of the family.

By this time the wedges are many. The wife, finding she has managed to bring some semblance of order and stability to her family, while not exactly becoming a self-assured person, has regained some sense of worth which grows a little with each crisis she meets successfully. In addition, the very fact of taking action to stabilize the situation brings relief. On some occasion she may be able to approach social agencies for financial help, often during a period when the husband has temporarily deserted or is incarcerated. She may have gone to the family court; she may have consulted a lawyer about getting a restraining order when the husband was in a particularly belligerent state. She has begun to learn her way around among the many agencies which offer help.

Often she has had a talk with an Al-Anon member and has begun to look into what is known about alcoholism. If she has attended a few Al-Anon meetings, her sense of shame has been greatly alleviated as she finds so many others in the same boat. Her hopes rise as she meets alcoholics who have stopped drinking, and she feels relieved at being able to discuss her problems openly for the first time with an audience which understands fully. She begins to gain perspective on her problem and learns that she herself is involved in what happens to her husband, and that she must change. She exchanges techniques of management with other wives and receives their support in her decisions.

She learns that her husband is ill rather than merely "ornery," and this often serves to quell for the time being thoughts about leaving him which have begun to germinate as she has gained more self-confidence. She learns that help is available but also that her efforts to push him into help are unavailing. She is not only supported in her recently evolved behavior of thinking first of her family, but now this course also emerges from the realm of the unconceptualized and is set in an accepted rationale. She feels more secure in having a reason and a certainty that the group accepts her as "doing the right thing." When she reports deviations from what the group thinks is the "right way," her reasons are understood; she receives solid support but there is also pressure on her to alter her behavior again toward the acceptable. Blaming and self-pity are actively discouraged. In group discussions she still admits to such feelings but learns to recognize them as they arise and to go beyond them to more productive thinking.

How much her altered behavior changes the family situation is uncertain, but it helps her and gives her security from which to venture forth to further actions of a consistent and constructive type, constructive at least from the point of view of keeping her family on as even a keel as possible in the face of the disruptive influence of the husband. With new friends whom she can use as a sounding board for plans, and with her growing acquaintance with the alternatives and possible patterns of behavior, her thinking ceases to be circular and unproductive. Her anxiety about her own sanity is alleviated as she is reassured by others that they have experienced the same concern and that the remedy is to get her own life and her family under better control. As she accomplishes this, the difference in her feelings about herself convinces her that this is so.

Whether or not she has had a contact with Al-Anon members or other wives who have been through a similar experience and have emerged successfully, the very fact of taking hold of her situation and gradually making it more manageable adds to her self-confidence. As her husband is less and less able to care for himself or his family, she begins to feel that he needs her and that without her he would be destroyed. Such a feeling makes it difficult for her to think of leaving him. His almost complete social isolation at this point and his cries for help reinforce this conviction of being needed.

The drinking behavior is no longer hidden. Others obviously know about it, and this becomes accepted by the wife and children. Already isolated and insulated against possible rejection, the wife is often surprised to find that she has exaggerated her fears of what would happen were the situation known. However, the unpredictability of her husband's behavior makes her reluctant to form social relationships which could be violently disrupted or to involve others in the possible consequences of his behavior.

5. Separation, Escape

Stage 5 may be the terminal one for the marriage. In this stage the wife separates from her husband. Sometimes the marriage is reestablished after a period of sobriety, when it appears certain that the husband will not drink again.

If he does revert to drinking, the marriage is sometimes finally terminated but with less emotional stress than the first time. If the husband deserts, being no longer able to tolerate his lack of status in his family, Stage 6 may be entered abruptly.

The events precipitating the decision to terminate the marriage may be near-catastrophic, as when there is an attempt by the husband to kill the wife or children, or they may appear trivial to outsiders, being only the last straw to an accumulation of years.

The problems in coming to the decision to terminate the marriage cannot be underestimated. Some of these problems derive from emotional conflicts; some are related to very practical circumstances in the situation; some are precipitated by the conflicting advice of outsiders. With several children dependent on her, the wife must decide whether the present situation is more detrimental to them than future situations she can see arising if she should leave her husband. The question of where the money to live on will come from must be thought out. If she can get a job, will there be enough to provide for child care also while she is away from home? Should the children, who have already experienced such an unsettled life, be separated from her to be cared for by others? If the family still owns its own home, how can she retain control of it? If she leaves, where can she go? What can be done to tide the family over until her first earnings come in? How can she ensure her husband's continued absence from the home and thus be certain of the safety of individuals and property in her absence? These are only a small sample of the practical issues that must be dealt with in trying to think her way through to a decision to terminate the marriage.

Other pressures act on her to impede the decision-making process. "If he would only stay drunk till I carry out what I intend to do," is a frequent statement. When the husband realizes that his wife really means to leave, he frequently sobers up, watches his behavior in the home, plays on her latent and sometimes conscious feelings of her responsibility for the situation, stresses his need for her and that without her he is lost, tears away at any confidence she has that she will be able to manage by herself, and threatens her and the children with injury or with his own suicide if she carries out her intention.

The children, in the meantime, are pulling and pushing on her emotions. They think she is "spineless" to stay but unfair to father's chances for ultimate recovery if she leaves. Relatives, who were earlier alienated in her attempts to shield her family but now know of the situation, do not believe in its full ramifications. They often feel she is exaggerating and persuade her to stay with him. Especially is this true in the case of a "solitary drinker." His drinking has been so well concealed that the relatives have no way of knowing the true nature of the situation. Other relatives, afraid that they will be called on for support, exert pressure to keep the marriage intact and the husband thereby responsible for debts. Relatives who feel she should leave him overplay their hands by berating the husband in such a manner as to evoke her defense of him. This makes conscious the positive aspects of her relationship with him, causing her to waver in her decision. If she consults organized agencies, she often gets conflicting advice. The agencies concerned with the well-being of the family may counsel leaving; those concerned with rehabilitating the husband may press her to stay. In addition, help from public organizations almost always involves delay and is frequently not forthcoming at the point where she needs it most.

The wife must come to terms with her own mixed feeling about her husband, her marriage and herself before she can decide on such a step as breaking up the marriage. She must give up hope that she can be of any help to her husband. She must command enough self-confidence, after years of having it eroded, to be able to face an unknown future and leave the security of an unpalatable but familiar past and present. She must accept that she has failed in her marriage, not an easy thing to do after having devoted years to stopping up the cracks in the family structure as they appeared. Breaking up the marriage involves a complete alteration of the life goals toward which all her behavior has been oriented. It is hard for her to rid herself of the feeling that she married him and he is her responsibility. Having thought and planned for so long on a day-to-day basis, it is difficult to plan for a long-term future.

Her taking over of the family raises her self-confidence but failure to carry through on decisions undermines the new gains that she has made. Vacillation in her decisions tends to exasperate the agencies trying to help her, and she begins to feel that help from them may not be forthcoming if she finally decides to leave.

Some events, however, help her to arrive at a decision. During the absences of her husband she has seen how manageable life can be and how smoothly her family can run. She finds that life goes on without him. The wife who is working comes to feel that "my husband is a luxury I can no longer afford." After a few short-term separations in which she tries out her wings successfully, leaving comes to look more possible. Another step on the path to leaving is the acceptance of the idea that, although she cannot help her husband, she can help her family. She often reaches a state of such emotional isolation from her husband that his behavior no longer disturbs her emotionally but is only something annoying which upsets daily routines and plans.

When staying is intolerable and leaving seems impossible, the wife may try to get the counselor to make the decision for her. The answer, of course, is that she must make it herself. The counselor can assist her to work through the problem by facing squarely the consequences of separation, not to dissuade her but to help her look at them realistically. Only when she has consulted a lawyer, made decisions about the house, worked out a budget based on feasible income, and has projected schooling for the children, should the decision be finalized. The counselor can then support her in her decision. Once proposed, she must be fully prepared to go through with it. The word *divorce* should never be mentioned before this point, lest it be written off as a mere idle threat. Unfulfilled threats amount to just nagging.

6. Reorganization without the Alcoholic

The wife is without her husband and must reorganize her family on this basis. Substantially the process is similar to that in other divorced families, but with some additions. The divorce rarely cuts her relationships to her husband. Unless she and her family disappear, her husband may make attempts to come back. When drunk, he may endanger her job by calls at her place of work. He may attempt violence against members of the family, or he may contact the children and work to gain their loyalty so that pressure is put on the mother to accept him again. Looking back on her marriage, she forgets the full impact of the problem situation on her and on the children and feels more warmly toward her husband, and these feelings can still be manipulated by him. The wide circulation of information on alcoholism as an illness engenders guilt about having deserted a sick man. Gradually, however, the family becomes reorganized.

Most important is that the shift in roles described in Stage 4 now becomes complete. The wife is father and mother. She is disciplinarian, budget manager, and often the sole wage earner. The children have learned to obey only her, and ignore the father. They may be bitter against him, unless they have joined a group like Alateen and learned emotional detachment. The wife still needs her Al-Anon meetings, for not all problems are solved by separation.

7. Recovery and Reorganization with the Alcoholic

For years the spouse has prayed, begged, and hoped—always with the expectation that if the drinking would only stop, everything would be all right. Now the alcoholic has gone to treatment, joined AA, and things seem worse! There are many reasons for this paradox. Alcohol loses the role of scapegoat. The couple must face problems they haven't faced in years, discovering that not all their problems were caused by drinking. They have not really communicated for a long time, and have to learn how to talk with each other. (Hint: Don't say, "Now we are going to discuss . . ." as that will almost certainly evoke a negative response. Just start talking, preferably at a well-chosen time and place.) The mistrust that has built up for years does not dissipate overnight. He knows he is going to make it this time, but she has been burned too many times to feel his inner confidence. When he demands love from his wife, her frigidity stems not from bad will but from spontaneous feelings.

Stage 7 is entered if the husband achieves sobriety, whether or not separation has preceded. It was pointed out that in earlier stages most of the problems in the marriage were attributed to the alcoholism of the husband, and thus problems in adjustment not related directly to the drinking were unrecognized and unmet. Also, the "sober personality" of the husband was thought of as the "real" personality, with a resulting lack of recognition of other factors involved in his sober behavior, such as remorse and guilt over his actions, leading him to act to the best of his ability like "the ideal husband" when sober. Irritation or other signs of growing tension were viewed as indicators of further drinking, and hence the problems giving rise to them were walked around gingerly rather than faced and resolved. Lack of conflict and lack of drinking were defined as indicating a perfect adjustment. For the wife and husband facing a sober marriage after many years of an alcoholic marriage, the expectations of what marriage without alcoholism will be are unrealistically idealistic, and the reality of marriage almost inevitably brings disillusionments. The expectation that all would go well and that all problems be resolved with the cessation of the husband's drinking cannot be met and this threatens the marriage from time to time.

The beginning of sobriety for the husband does not bring too great hope to the family at first. They have been through this before but are willing to help him along and stand by him in the new attempt. As the length of sobriety increases, so do the hopes for its permanence and efforts to be of help. The wife at first finds it difficult to think more than in terms of today, waking each morning with fear of what the day will bring and sighing with relief at the end of each sober day.

With the continuation of sobriety, many problems begin to crop up. Mother has for years managed the family, and now father again wishes to be reinstated in his former roles. Usually the first role reestablished is that of breadwinner, and the economic problems of the family begin to be alleviated as debts are gradually paid and there is enough left over for current needs. With the resumption of this role, the husband feels that the family should also accept him at least as a partner in the management of the family. Even if the wife is willing to hand over some of the control of the children, for example, the children often are not able to accept this change easily. Their mother has been both parents for so long that it takes time to get used to the idea of consulting their father on problems and asking for his decisions. Often the father tries too hard to manage this change overnight, and the very pressure put on the children toward this end defeats him. In addition, he is unable to meet many of the demands the children make on him because he has never really become acquainted with them or learned to understand them and is lacking in much necessary background knowledge of their lives.

The wife, who finds it difficult to conceive of her husband as permanently sober, feels an unwillingness to let control slip from her hands. At the same time she realizes that reinstatement of her husband in his family roles is necessary to his sobriety. She also realizes that the closer his involvement in the family the greater the probability of his remaining sober. Yet she remembers events in the past in which his failure to handle his responsibilities was catastrophic to the family. Used to avoiding anything which might upset him, the wife often hesitates to discuss problems openly. At times, if she is successful in helping him to regain his roles as father, she feels resentful of his intrusion into territory she has come to regard as hers. If he makes errors in judgment which affect the family adversely, her former feelings of being his superior may come to the fore and affect her interaction with him. If the children begin to turn to him, she may feel a resurgence of self-pity at being left out and find herself attempting to swing the children back toward herself. Above all, however, she finds herself feeling resentful that some other agency achieved what she and the children could not.

Often the husband makes demands for obedience, for consideration and for pampering which members of the family feel unable to meet. He may become rather euphoric as his sobriety continues and feel superior for a time.

Gradually, however, the drinking problem sinks into the past and marital adjustment at some level is achieved. Even when this has occurrred, the drinking problem crops up occasionally, as when the time comes for a decision about whether the children should be permitted to drink. The mother at such times becomes anxious, sees in the child traits which remind her of her husband, worries whether these are the traits which mean future alcoholism. At parties, at first, she is watchful and concerned about whether her husband will take a drink or not. Relatives and friends may, in a party mood, make the husband the center of attention by emphasizing his nondrinking. They may unwittingly cast aspersions on his character by trying to convice him that he can now "drink like a man." Some relatives and friends have gone so far as secretly to "spike" a nonalcoholic drink and then cry "bottoms up!" without realizing the risk of reactivating patterns from the past.

If sobriety has come through Alcoholics Anonymous, the husband frequently throws himself so wholeheartedly into A.A. activities that his wife sees little of him and feels neglected. As she worries less about his drinking, she may press him to cut down on these activities. This is dangerous, since A.A. activity is correlated with success in Alcoholics Anonymous. Also, the wife discovers that, though she has a sober husband, she is by no means free of alcoholics. In his Twelfth Step work, he may keep the house filled with men he is helping. In the past her husband has avoided self-searching; and now he may become excessively introspective, and it may be difficult for her to deal with this.

If the husband becomes sober through Alcoholics Anonymous and the wife participates actively in Al-Anon, the thoughts of what is happening to her, to her husband and to her family will be verbalized and interpreted within the framework of the Al-Anon philosophy and the situation will probably be more tolerable and more easily worked out.

The illusions the spouse has had about the alcoholic, the marriage, and herself continue to create major difficulties during the readjustment process. The more idealized these were in her romantic illusions, the greater the disillusionment. For this reason the family defenses cannot be dispensed with at once, for they cannot tolerate the hurt when unmasked until time has softened it and new strengths have developed. The family is rarely at the same stage of illness as the alcoholic, who in turn may get well faster than the family.

The families of the *steady* drinker or *regular* periodic drinker usually readjust faster than the family of the irregular periodic. The families of the former learn what to expect, develop patterns of reaction, have less guilt, and are less easily manipulated by the alcoholic. The irregular periodic drinker has them in a constant turmoil, feeling very helpless and confused, and more easily manipulated because the alcoholic can somehow make them feel they must be responsible for his periodic binges. The resulting mistrust and confusion make the process of readjustment very difficult. Since he was an irregular periodic, it takes longer to be convinced that drinking will not start again.

Unwitting Sabotage.   The reversal of roles that took place during the drinking was natural and necessary. The spouse had to take charge; the children had to obey her and ignore the alcoholic. But resistance to a change back to original roles after recovery would seem illogical. Isn't this return what the spouse has been waiting for? Consciously, yes. However, there are many advantages to the spouse from the reversed roles. To revert back means to lose control of the money, to lose authority and power, to no longer be the martyr with good grounds for self-pity. She resents the fact that others have succeeded after she had tried harder than anyone else—"Why did he do it for them when I am the one who loves him?" He gets praised for his successful sobriety, while nobody praises her for her heroic management during the difficult years. After sobriety the children can no longer play one parent off against the other, and "work" the alcoholic for compensatory presents. All this adds up to powerful, if unrecognized, resentment at his sobriety and even a secret wish he would start drinking again.

The husband of the recovered alcoholic wife seems to be even more prone to this kind of subconscious illogic. With no controlled research, but with considerable confirmation from many recovered alcoholics and professionals in the field, our experience is that the role of husband as spouse is more reluctantly given up than when the wife is the spouse. He is the protector, the strong one, the martyr. All of his troubles and shortcomings can be blamed on having an alcoholic wife. In the beginning he may have found that she was most responsive sexually after a few drinks, and may fondly remember that rather than her later poor performance. Even cleaning up her vomit gives him a sense of superiority congenial to the male ego. When she recovers he can no longer baby her. In fact, when she ceases being dependent and asserts her true personality as a very capable woman, he may be totally inadequate to accepting this. For whatever reason, we have seen case after case where the husband blocks her attendance at AA meetings and subconsciously contrives a situation whereby she starts drinking again. Of course, he would deny this and protest loudly that he wants nothing more than to see her happily sober.

The psychodynamics here are very complex and subtle, which means that the counselor is wise not to attempt any conscious analysis with the spouse, be it husband or wife. Indirect means of support and constructive direction are more likely to be helpful. The spouse should be encouraged to attend Al-Anon when the alcoholic is at AA meetings, and to get involved in the out-patient aftercare or group sessions that are a vital part of the follow-up treatment in any good facility now.

Decompensation or Readjustment? If compensation for unfulfilled needs is the underlying motive for marrying or staying married to an
alcoholic, then attempts to undermine the recovery could be decompensation. This is plausible in those cases where the theory applies. However,
the evidence suggests that most of the time these subconscious efforts are
simply maladjustive reactions when a learned behavior pattern is threatened. Habit is resistant to change, and learned values can be powerful
motivation. So the spouse who once poured bottles down the sink and did
all the other wrong things may end up regretting the loss of power or self-
pity which the drinking provided. Thus Jackson's Stage 7 is not necessarily
support for the unconscious need theory.

Mutual Interaction

Although it is possible to become an alcoholic through solitary drinking
and no interaction with other human beings, this is rarely the case. Almost always there are people around who are used by the alcoholic in ma-
nipulative ways to justify the drinking or delay any surrender to treatment. Besides the alcoholic, the spouse is the principal actor in this life
drama, but there are others. We prefer the term *drama* to *games*, for this
is no fun and nobody wins. All the world's a stage, and there is a great
deal of role-playing here which must be unmasked if genuine relationships are to be restored. Otherwise the drama is always a tragedy.

J. Kellerman, in *Alcoholism: A Merry-Go-Round Named Denial*, calls
the players the Alcoholic, the Enabler, the Victim, and the Provocatrice.
Others refer to a Patsy, a Rescuer, a Persecutor, a Connection, and an Agitator, which is the language of Eric Berne's Transactional Analysis as described in Chapter 6 of his *Games People Play* (1967). Alcoholic and
spouse may reverse roles, for example each takes a turn at being the Victim or Patsy or at being the Persecutor. Any third person will usually
make a triangle out of the relationship: a child can come between the
spouses, or one spouse can set up rivalry between a child and the other
spouse. The Agitator is adept at starting fights but avoids engaging in
them. The Connection might be the friendly bartender willing to extend
credit. The Patsy or Victim may be the spouse, foreman, business partner
or whoever ends up doing the alcoholic's work when he or she is absent or
hung over. The Provocatrice or Persecutor is the spouse who ends up being blamed for all that is wrong in the marriage, in spite of heroic efforts
to make the marriage work, which only provoke resentment in the alcoholic. Nagging, hiding bottles, withholding sex, bargaining, threatening,
haggling over money, and moralizing are examples of these efforts. Alcohol through augmentation or facilitation causes a hypersensitivity and
low frustration tolerance, which in turn is displaced or projected, as when

the alcoholic kicks the cat or takes it out on the spouse, leading to to *folie à deux*, which makes their lives truly unmanageable.

The Rescuer

By far the most damaging role is that of the Rescuer, or Enabler. The spouse is the chief agent here, but other rescuers may be the clergyman, physician, social worker, lover, or parent who always comes to the rescue and never lets the alcoholic feel the full consequences of the drinking. Lying to the boss, bailing out of jail, covering up before the children and neighbors, paying debts, and reassuring the alcoholic that he or she is "not that bad" are some of the things that enable the alcoholic to continue drinking and delay the moment of truth that leads to treatment. It is not a question of causing the continued drinking, but rather of being used by the alcoholic. In the case of the secondary rescuers, that is, the professionals, it may stem from a need to play God, or a sublimation of the rescuer's own anxiety and guilt. Regardless of motivation, the Enabler never allows the alcoholic to learn from his or her mistakes.

To learn from our mistakes is the hard way, but probably the only way most of us reach maturity is by shouldering responsibility. Hence it is cruel to act as Rescuer, and really kind to exert the "tough love" that forces the alcoholic to accept responsibility and do something about the drinking. This is never easy, and always somewhat risky. Alcoholics are sick people, and the illness sometimes involves a fair degree of paranoia. The sick mind twists everything to avoid facing reality, and becomes ingenious in ways of shifting the blame. Two favorites are to accuse the spouse of infidelity, and to alienate the children. Recently we had a case where the alcoholic not only accused his wife of infidelity, but of plotting his death so that she could get his money; the means of killing him she supposedly used was to provoke fights so he would drink himself to death!

Psychotherapy for any of this is impossible while the brain is still affected by alcohol, which means not only while the alcoholic is still drinking but also in the early days of sobriety. Depth analysis is totally inappropriate during the first phase of treatment. But the counselor should be able to recognize what is happening, and to help the spouse handle some of the projected guilt and self-blame. Most important is to help the spouse abandon the role of Rescuer or Enabler, and confront the alcoholic squarely with the realities. More of this in Chapter 13.

Sources

By far the most important source is *The Alcoholic Marriage: Alternative Perspectives*, by Thomas J. Paolino and Barbara S. McCrady, which reviews all the major literature in the field and analyzes both theoretical approaches and research findings. Joan Ablon reviews the literature in her chapter in B. Kissin and H. Begleiter (eds.), *The Biology of Alcoholism*, vol. 4, pp. 205–242. The National Clearinghouse for Alcohol Information (NCALI) also has a "Bibliography on Spouses of Alcoholic Persons." Some other useful items are listed below. See the special section in the Sources for Chapter 16 for literature on the children of alcoholic parents.

AL-ANON, *Dilemma of the Alcoholic Marriage*, and other Al-Anon and Alateen literature such as listed in Sources for Chapter 16.

CURLEE-SALISBURY, JOAN, *When the Woman You Love Is an Alcoholic*.

EDWARDS, PATRICIA, and others, "Wives of Alcoholics: A Critical Review and Analysis," QJSA, 1973, 34:112–132.

JACKSON, JOAN K., "The Adjustment of the Family to the Crisis of Alcoholism," QJSA, 1954, 15:562–586. Reprinted by NCA.

KELLERMAN, JOSEPH L., *Alcoholism: A Merry-Go-Round Named Denial*. Hazelden pamphlet.

MAXWELL, RUTH, *The Booze Battle*.

McCABE, THOMAS R., *Victims No More*. Hazelden booklet.

ORFORD, JIM, "Alcoholism and Marriage: The Argument Against Specialism," JSA, 1975, 36:1537–1560.

RIMMER, J., "Psychiatric Illness in Husbands of Alcoholics," JSA, 1974, 34: 281–283.

ZINK, MURIEL, *So Your Alcoholic is Sober*; and *Ways to Live More Comfortably with Your Alcoholic*. CompCare pamphlets.

CHAPTER 9

Causality of Alcoholism

So FAR THIS BOOK has been descriptive rather than explanatory. Now we must face the hard question of etiology, or what *causes* alcoholism. Only thus can we dispel some of the myths and folklore that persist. Again we distinguish: We are not asking why people drink, or even why they get drunk. Some people deliberately get drunk for a variety of reasons, but they are not alcoholics. The alcoholics can always give a reason why they drink. Our team won, or our team lost; it's too hot, or it's too cold; women alcoholics drink because they have nothing to do at home, or because they have too much to do in a career. Analyzing the reasons why alcoholics drink is really a waste of the therapist's time. The alcoholic will play along with this for a year, drinking meanwhile or ready to start again; then decide "No, that's not it," and go off on some other alleged cause. Craving? Many an alcoholic will admit they never crave alcohol. Taste? I like the taste of T-bone steaks, but I don't eat them to the point of ruining health, job, and family. One could go on forever, or stop short with a simple answer, euphoria. That is a Greek word which simply means you drink to feel good. (In late-stage alcoholism it would be better expressed "to feel less bad.") The fact is that most alcoholics begin to drink for the same reasons as everyone else: custom, to relax, to be sociable, or whatever. The real question is not why they drink, but why do they *continue* to drink when by all reason and common sense they should not; that is, why do they drink alcoholically?

Complex Causality

To ask *the* cause of why one is an alcoholic implies that there is just one cause. Hence the current fashion of asserting with a kind of scientific hauteur that the cause of alcoholism is unknown. Although we do not fully understand and more research is needed, we do know a great deal about the etiology of alcoholism. William Madsen's book *The American Alcoholic* is mostly about causality, and it may be the best book written so far on alcoholism. The attempt to reduce all alcoholism to one explanation is a trap. For example, if there were no alcohol, there would be no alcoholism. True, but this is simplistic. If there were no money there would be no bank robberies, and if there were no marriage there would be no divorce. The fact that only one in a dozen drinkers becomes alcoholic poses the real question: Why are some drinkers alcoholic? The very fact that there are different types of alcoholics and different kinds of alcoholisms would rule out a simple answer. The question is complex, and the burden of this chapter is that alcoholism is the result of many different causes, so generalizations are impossible. Shakespeare says, "Some are born great, some achieve greatness, and some have greatness thrust upon them." The same could be said of alcoholism. In one case it might be largely physiological with an inborn predisposition; in another case alcoholism might be achieved by excessive drinking for psychological reasons; and a third case might exemplify situations whereby some have alcoholism thrust upon them.

Nearly all discussions of casuality of alcoholism pit one theory against the other, as if the reader must choose one to the exclusion of others. Worse, each writer seems determined to climb to the top of the pile by trampling on the prostrate forms of the proponents of other theories. At least they seem to take delight in pointing out that each proposal is inadequate as a total theory. Why not combine them? There is probably a grain of truth in each, or intelligent persons would not propose them. The human ego gets in the way of our brains here. It is relatively easy to go through each theory and point to evidence that shows it cannot explain all alcoholism. It is also fruitless. Yet this seems a favorite indoor sport among alcohol specialists.

We shall not only try to accept the evidence for a variety of theories, but we stress that two or more causes can work together in the same individual, and in different proportions in different individuals. It may be that no one cause is sufficient to trigger alcoholism. Let us take an apparently absurd example from an entirely different field. There is a certain chemical, which, if given to a certain hereditary strain of white mice, produces cleft palate in the next generation. You can give other mice this chemical by the gallon, or interbreed that one susceptible strain for generations, without producing a cleft palate. So it has to be the peculiar combination. This notion again need not apply to all alcoholisms, but it illustrates the thinking of this chapter. It may be that certain physiological factors, either hereditary or acquired, are combined with some psychological or sociocultural factors to produce alcoholism. And however all this comes about, the alcoholic ends up *habituated* to using alcohol in harmful ways, which result in a psychophysiological state that is unconscious, involuntary, and a self-reinforcing vicious circle.

We shall group the areas of causality under five headings. Note that these five etiological or explanatory factors in no way parallel Jellinek's five descriptive types. At least for the purposes of this chapter, any type of alcoholism could be caused by any combination of causal factors, and in any proportion.

Sociocultural Factors

There can be no alcoholism (active, not potential) if there is no drinking. In Chapter 3 we saw that different societies have different cultural attitudes toward drinking and drunkenness, which greatly affect their drinking patterns. We mentioned eight books, and there are hundreds of journal articles, that are relevant here. To ignore the importance of social pressures toward drinking in the etiology of alcoholism is to ignore facts. Craig MacAndrew's *Drunken Comportment* and studies of various native American Indian tribes show that this is true not only of drinking but also of intoxicated behavior. All this surely contributes to the development of alcoholism, and no doubt at least partially accounts for the different rates of alcoholism among different peoples.

The social psychologist Stanton Peele, in his book *Love and Addiction*, claims that addiction to a drug is largely a matter of attitudes, and points to the fact that most Vietnam soldiers who took heroin in concentrations far above street level doses were able to kick the habit easily when they returned to close contact with friends and family and productive jobs. (His claim that only a small minority of those exposed to heroin become addicts may also point to a physiological difference.) In New Zealand alcoholism is called "the Catholic disease" because so many Irish there are exposed to traditions of hospitality which demand heavy drinking. Some theories try to explain the low rate of alcoholism among Orthodox Jews as entirely due to ethnic pride and strong attitudes against drunkenness. And although the next generation will differ biologically if there is marriage with a gentile, when an Orthodox Jew leaves that culture and subsequently becomes alcoholic the change is sociocultural and not hereditary for that individual. If 57 percent of all Scotch in the United States is sold to blacks, this argues to social prestige as a strong factor. The Italians and the French, both Mediterranean and wine-drinking peoples but with different rates of alcoholism, differ notably in their attitude toward drinking outside mealtimes and especially toward drunkenness. The armed forces are (or were) a distinct subculture with heavy pressures toward drinking and a high rate of alcoholism. Joel Fort, in *Alcohol: Our Biggest Drug Problem* (1973, p.100), says that "sociological causes are preeminent" and although we might not agree entirely, we cannot rule them out. A frequent visitor to both San Francisco and Washington, D.C., two major cities with high rates of alcoholism, is always impressed with the role that alcohol plays in the social life of both; one can hardly arrange to meet someone except over a martini or a gin fizz. Intercultural diversity as to normal social drinking must be studied in order to understand differences in alcoholism.

Psychological Factors

When alcoholism first began to be seriously studied in modern times, the most common explanation was that the alcoholic drank to sedate some deep inner psychological conflict or to avoid some psychic stress, or that it was simply a behavior disorder symptomatic of the sociopathic personality. This has been proven untrue for 70 to 80 percent of alcoholics, as we shall see in the next chapter. But we must recognize that even in the research of Milam and others reported there, some alcoholism is the symptom of an underlying psychopathology. Too ardent devotion to the concept of physiological addiction can cause grave errors in diagnosis.

To begin with, psychological factors can notably alter the effects of alcohol. This parallels the research on marijuana that shows that subjective factors such as expectancy and social setting largely determine the effects. *The New Yorker* once carried a story of a New Mexico tribe in which a group mistook root beer for real beer and proceeded to get quite inebriated. A Seattle University psychology student, with parental approval, hosted a "cocktail party" for his sister's fifteen-year-old friends, during which they exhibited all the signs of intoxication although the martinis, Manhattans, and daiquiris contained no alcohol. Some iatrogenic disorders are due to the power of suggestion. We know that the amount of alcohol consumed is not nearly as important as one's reaction to the drug, and this may vary for both psychological and physiological reasons.

Partial Cause

According to all modern research, there is no such thing as an "alcoholic personality" that is *the* cause of alcoholism. But psychological factors certainly play a part in all alcoholism, and may be the major cause in some. We noted in chapter 1 that psychological dependence may be more devastating than physiological addiction. Compulsive gambling illustrates all too well the relevant psychology. The heavy smoking, coffee drinking, and compulsive talking observed in many alcoholics may indicate a personality that has at least a tangential-cause relationship to their drinking. The higher rates of alcoholism among drinkers from traditionally "dry" peoples, religious or ethnic, may well be due in great part to excessive guilt when they do drink. Parental models are a powerful influence on behavior, as evidenced by the number of mothers who treat their children exactly as their mothers treated them, in spite of loud resolves that they would do otherwise. An old adage in Alcoholics Anonymous says, "It's not your drinking that makes you stinking, it's your thinking." Although AA members generally subscribe to the disease concept of alcoholism, the AA program is very psychological and spiritual. Alcohol is mentioned only once in the twelve steps which are the core of the AA program, and much effort is aimed at eliminating the "stinking thinking." Motivation is paramount. Sobriety is recognized as being much more than mere abstinence from alcohol. Chapter 5 of the book *Alcoholics Anonymous* is a marvel of psychology, and we have used it quite successfully for other problems besides alcohol.

Most personality traits usually found in alcoholics are more the effects of prolonged drinking and reaction to drinking problems than they are the cause of alcoholism. These include immaturity, selfishness, dependence, frigidity or impotence, hypersensitivity, paranoid thinking, low self-esteem, and many others (Blane, 1968). Since we do not identify alcoholics before they develop the illness, research on personality characteristics prior to onset is difficult. Obsessive-compulsive traits, rigidity of thinking, low frustration tolerance, perfectionism and impulsiveness or short-term goal orientation are often listed, and may be either cause or effect. Ambivalent attitudes and confused thinking about the use and abuse of alcohol may be causal.

Some theories. Andrew Weil, in *The Natural Mind* (1972), theorizes that man has an innate need to get high, which he will satisfy chemically if he cannot achieve it in more natural ways. Using the psychology of Alfred Adler, David McClelland proposes a theory that explains alcoholism in terms of drive for power, frustration, and feelings of inferiority. Others propose an inner conflict between dependency and aggressive drives. All these are more accepted today than Freud's theories of slow suicide from a death instinct, fixation at the oral stage, or latent homosexuality. Of these three Freudian theories the first may have some slight foundation, the second does not explain why the oral gratification must be from alcohol and not any nipple, and the homosexual theory was pretty well refuted when some state laws were changed to allow women to drink in bars—and the alcoholics went right on drinking without paying any attention to the sex of whoever was on the next barstool.

Physiological Factors

Dr. Stanley Schacter of Columbia University, a respected clinical and experimental psychologist, reported four years of research on heavy smoking (1977) with the conclusion that we can forget all the nice psychological theories about "something to do with my hands" or Freudian oral gratification: "We smoke because we are physically addicted to the drug nicotine, period." Addiction to the drug alcohol as an explanation of why alcoholics drink alcoholically is not a new idea, having been stated in ancient times, and through the 1800s by various doctors. The psychiatrist Dr. Harry Tiebout, said to know more about alcoholism than any other psychiatrist of his time, was writing this in 1944 and 1945. Dr. Frederick Lemere, long-time staff psychiatrist at Shadel Hospital, published an article to the same effect in a 1956 psychiatric journal. Jellinek's *Disease Concept* in 1960 and his writings as early as 1945 contained much of the same idea, but the alcohol world was not ready to listen for several reasons. Behaviorism, with its stress on conditioning, dominated American social science for decades. The old psychiatric and psychological theories were there first, so were hard to dislodge. Alcohol was a controversial enough beverage without the added stigma of being an addictive drug. The notion of selective addiction had not been developed, and there was no biological evidence such as we have today that differentiates alcoholics from other drinkers.

Most previous theories, such as that of Tintera on hormones or Roger Williams on nutrition, were unable to account for all alcoholism and thus were summarily dismissed instead of being integrated into the total picture. In particular, Jellinek had postulated an unknown X factor, which sent researchers scurrying off to discover a single defect when there are actually many factors. Differences in metabolism did not materialize in sufficient degree to explain all alcoholism. Low tolerance also proved unsatisfactory, partly because early thought here missed the fact that *good* tolerance is a sign of alcoholism, and what they should have been looking for was a lack of intolerance (Goodwin, 1978a, pp. 127-129; 1978b, p. 10). The person who is allergic to alcohol, gets the characteristic Chinese flush or otherwise feels uncomfortable or even sick after one drink, is not likely to drink enough to develop alcoholism. The supposed X factor is turning out to be not a simple defect but a combination of differences in liver and brain, which are often excess (for example high tolerance) rather than defect, followed by eventual decompensation as nature can no longer adapt.

Vulnerability to Addiction

The notion of immunity versus susceptibility is a familiar one in biology. We are all exposed to the tubercular bacillus daily, but have built up sufficient immunity that we are relatively safe. On the other hand, it is said that measles, a trivial child's disease to us, killed one-fourth of the total population of Iceland when first spread from a whaling ship, because no previous exposure meant zero immunity. Diabetes runs in families, and although the parallel is not perfect, the similarity to alcoholism is striking in many ways. Dr. Roger Williams, in his book *Biochemical Individuality* and its more popular version *You Are Extraordinary*, shows that humans differ markedly from each other in both anatomy and physiology, contrary to what the textbooks might lead us to suspect: Organs are not located according to the anatomy diagrams; some people are color blind or left-handed; one person's stomach might secrete as much as one thousand times the digestive fluid of another. We know that some people get stimulated by sedatives, and a few get depressed by amphetamines. Why should we assume that all react in the same way to alcohol?

Experiments show that even within the same species, some animals adapt to alcohol at once, some slowly, and some never do. Research with humans is much more difficult since we cannot control all factors and "make" alcoholics, or measure every bit of food and drink since birth. There is always the problem of what physical differences are the result of alcoholic drinking rather than the cause of alcoholism. The research team may require years to identify and isolate just one enzyme out of the fifty or sixty involved, then longer to understand its biochemistry and transfer this knowledge from the laboratory to the living person (see Popham, 1968).

Many Factors Involved   But progress is being made. Contrary to the notion of a single X factor, we saw in Chapter 4 that every organ of the body can be affected by alcohol and also enter into the body's handling of alcohol. The body begins almost at once to adapt, so that a slight withdrawal takes place every time blood alcohol subsides. Since the obvious severe signs of withdrawal do not appear until late stages, we forget that this occurs throughout the drinking history and that much of the bodily distress is due to the adapted cell's need for alcohol to function normally. Thus almost from the beginning there are differences building up in the alcoholic in addition to, or as an increase of, any innate predisposition. What are some of these differences?

Hormonal secretion from the adrenal glands is different in the alcoholic. The liver is less able to store sugar and use it gradually, resulting in extreme swings of blood sugar level. The enzyme action in the liver differs, for example, by using catalase rather than alcohol dehydrogenase, or an abnormal form of ADH. The work of Charles Lieber and others on amino acid and liver enzyme differences may yet distinguish alcoholics from heavy drinkers, when the cause-effect time relations are fully worked out. Rats or cats who previously refused alcohol will drink it after being subjected to stress, but will prefer sugar water when given the choice. Following the discovery by Heath at Tulane that alcohol alters the pleasure center in the limbic system of the lower brain, Myers (1977) at Purdue put tetrahydropapaveroline (THP) into the brains of rats, with the result that they no longer would switch back but permanently preferred alcohol. Strains of mice that do not prefer alcohol can be converted into alcohol-craving mice by damaging their livers with carbon tetrachloride. We cannot assume perfect similarity of mice and men, but these facts are suggestive that the alcoholic liver burns alcohol in place of sugar. The hereditary aspect is reinforced by evidence that the cousins of alcohol-preferring rats develop changes in the brain rapidly upon exposure to alcohol so that they take twenty times their prior amounts of alcohol.

Most important may be the interaction of alcohol in the brain with natural psychoactive substances such as dopamine, and differences between alcoholics and nonalcoholics in the level of the relevant enzyme dopamine betahydroxylase (DBH). This seems related to the fact that alcohol is more a stimulant for alcoholics than others, and with the fact that drinking often produces anxiety rather than sedating it. Davis and others (1970) had reported on the relation of alcohol and dopamine; John A. Ewing, in 1976, showed higher levels of DBH in the blood of alcoholics, who in turn get more of a "lift" than nonalcoholics with low DBH levels, who tend to feel bad when they drink. This difference is found to vary with races. Lundquist (1975) stated that Yedy Israel's work on the permeability of nerve-cell membranes in the lower midbrain may be a key, as the alcoholic differs *initially* from the nonalcoholic in his reaction to alcohol because the nerve tissue prefers the alcohol molecule to sugar, unlike the nonalcoholic. The work of Hans Selye on *Stress* (1956) highlights innate differences in tolerance and adaptability, and is complemented by Sudduth's enterotoxemia hypothesis (1977) wherein neurotoxins from the bacteria of the gastrointestinal system are both increased by alcohol and sedated by more of the same, in a vicious circle. This conforms to the discovery of Bruel and LeCoq long ago (1939, 1947) that alcohol given intravenously does not produce the same effect as when orally ingested. Both lines of thought are congruent with the important role the liver plays in our immunity system.

We cannot recount all the details here (see Sources at end of chapter). But the exciting fact is that knowledge is rounding out a cohesive picture of addiction to alcohol, as parts of the puzzle fall into place. In the next chapter we shall see how even the psychological research confirms the notion that alcoholism is due in large part to physiological factors, innate or acquired. In relatively few cases is alcoholism merely symptomatic of personality disorder, according to that research.

Hereditary or Acquired?

The above physiological factors, which are at least a part cause of alcoholism, may be either acquired or innate. The difficulties in trying to get hard data on alcoholics before they are identified as patients leave us with the old chicken-or-egg problem of which came first. Heredity and environment are inseparable in real life, and practically impossible to disentangle in research.

Some Acquired.   Even when the biological characteristics of alcoholics are the result of drinking, this still leaves the notion of physical addiction as a cause of alcoholism: tissue adaptation with subsequent decompensation, the interaction between the chemical and the organism. Psychological and sociocultural forces are causal factors to the extent that they induced the prolonged drinking, which in turn caused the biological changes. The oxygen deprivation, magnesium loss, and general electrolyte imbalance in the brain plus the enzyme and structural changes in the liver, along with poor diet, are bound to cause deterioration in time, and nature can only compensate so much. Psychological dependence would then be more obvious in the earlier stages of the progression and physical addiction would become apparent only later in the continuum, although the physical vulnerability may have been developing very early.

Theoretically, any person who drinks hard and long enough could produce these changes and "achieve" alcoholism, even though originally not so disposed. Actually, some people seem to have such high immunity that they die of other things first, so we never know. Again, drinking may not be the only way these differences can be acquired. Gastric resection, brain injury, cross-addiction to other drugs, damage to the liver by carbon tetrachloride or the like, and other traumata all have been cited as increasing vulnerability to alcoholism. But is it always acquired?

Some Hereditary.   After Prohibition was repealed, heredity was a taboo subject in the alcohol field because it smacked of the old idea that "This child is doomed to be a hopeless drunkard like his father." Behaviorism, in its stress on environmental conditioning, had scoffed at the exaggerated hereditarianism of earlier evolutionary theory. It was not until

the invention of the electron microscope and discovery of the DNA molecule, along with other advances in the science of genetics, that there has
been a renaissance of emphasis on heredity. As this has moved into the alcoholism field, the attitude is not one of hopelessness but rather "forewarned is forearmed." If there is diabetes on both sides of my family, one
is not predestined to be a diabetic but one knows that statistically the
chances are high. Today there is a strong emphasis on children of alcoholic ancestry as high-risk candidates for alcoholism and special targets for
prevention. The time is past when we can just repeat some doctrinaire an-
tiheredity notions of twenty years ago instead of looking at the evidence.

That alcoholism runs in families is well known. The old explanations
were the alcoholic environment, imitation of parental role model, or reaction to the stressful situation. But research has controlled for these in a
variety of ways, and many lines of evidence point toward biological predisposition to alcoholism being inherited regardless of parental environment. Notice we say predisposition, for alcoholism is not inherited as a
unit Mendelian trait. At no time do we imply heredity is the sole cause of
alcoholism. Like the chemical and the mice with cleft palate, hereditary
vulnerability and alcohol ingestion must combine as part causes. Drinking
depends on many factors, as we saw. But the reason only some drinkers
become alcoholics, and many of these early on or from the start of their
drinking, is closely tied to biological lineage. A child with an alcoholic father or brother has a 25 percent chance of being an alcoholic, which is five
to eight times the incidence in the general population (Goodwin, 1978a).
The probability goes much higher if there is alcoholism in both lines of ancestry. Grandparents as well as parents must be considered, since many
hereditary dispositions tend to skip a generation.

How do we know it is heredity and not parental environment? After
all, the child speaks the same language as the parents, but nobody would
argue that this is biological. M. Schuckit (1979) summarizes evidence for
alcoholism from many studies using several different approaches. *Adop-
tion* at birth or within six weeks into a different home removes the child
from the alcoholic parent and that environment. Some of the best studies
here are Scandinavian, because records of adopted children are more
readily researched in those countries. These children develop alcoholism
at three to five times the rate of the adopting parents or adopted children
of nonalcoholic parentage. Familial predisposition is specific for alcoholism and not on a continuum of heavy drinking (Goodwin, 1978b, p. 4).
The environmental argument that alcoholics come from broken homes is
refuted by the fact that the rate of alcoholism in this case is not above that
shown by the genetic findings. Yet siblings or halfsiblings raised by the alcoholic parents were twice as likely to have broken homes as those
adopted out, and to be in poorer socioeconomic conditions. Ironically,
one study (Schuckit, 1976b) showed a higher rate of alcoholism when the
children were adopted into nonalcoholic homes than when raised by the

alcoholic parent. Studies of *identical versus fraternal twins* (who are biologically just siblings) show over twice the likelihood of alcoholism when there are identical genes. *Half-sibling* studies, where the children have one parent the same and one parent different after remarriage, again show incidence of alcoholism to be more closely related to the biological parent. *Genetic marker* studies show that alcoholism follows hereditary lines as indicated by the other characteristics known to be gene-linked, for example, blood type, salivary secretions, PTC taste response, color blindness, etc. Offspring of alcoholic ancestry get higher acetaldehyde levels after a drink than do controls (Schuckit, 1979).

The only research purporting evidence against the heredity hypothesis is one by A. Roe (1944). It has been criticized on many scores: It is based on a very small number; there was no objective definition of alcoholism; the children were adopted late rather than shortly after birth; the parents were not comparable; and it was done while the adoptees were young adults so that three of the twenty were later discovered to have developed alcoholism after the study was published and we don't know how many more could have in their lifetime. One can only say that if this is the best the antihereditarians can bring forth, they do not have much of a case. The only other opposition to heredity is from those who reject the notion of partial and complex causality, insisting that heredity be the sole cause of all alcoholism if it is to be considered at all, instead of recognizing that it is a part cause in perhaps half the cases, as Jellinek once postulated.

What is inherited? Most of the items mentioned under the subhead "Many Factors Involved" seem to be inheritable. Sudduth stresses that bacterial endotoxins vary greatly with inherited immunity systems, and this along with DBH and differences in the reaction of brain cells may be cardinal. Differences in glucose metabolism and liability to hypoglycemia (hepatic or alcoholic, not true type) seem relevant. Ongoing research will no doubt throw more light in time.

Race.   The question of racial vulnerability is a thorny one. We acknowledge the importance of cultural attitudes and drinking customs, but we cannot avoid the mounting evidence that biological factors play a part. We saw that it is simplistic to look merely at metabolism rate, and fallacious to seek for low tolerance as a danger signal when just the opposite is true. One study on rate of metabolism among native American Indians involved waiting ninety minutes after ingestion, thereby missing the most critical time for important behavioral reactions to alcohol (Bennion, 1976). There is always the question of cause versus effect. But studying racial differences is not racism, just biology. As with sickle-cell anemia among blacks, knowledge about alcoholism differences among various races can be used in preventive efforts if objectively presented.

The research is difficult, and much more needs to be learned. We know that about 75 percent of Chinese have a characteristic flush response to alcohol. We know that rates of alcoholism are very high among Eskimos and native American Indians, especially of northwestern North America, and higher among peoples of northern European stock than those of Mediterranean extraction. Alcohol-related deaths make the Indian mortality rate in the state of Washington the highest in the nation. The rate of alcohol-related deaths among the native populations of Alaska is about twice that of non-native (Kelso, 1977, vol. 4, pp. 135–143). High rate of alcoholism correlates with early onset in many peoples, in contrast to low rate and late-life incidence among others. Schaefer, Ewing, Paredes, Hanna, and many others are pursuing the problem from various angles, trying to sort out biological from cultural factors and answer questions raised by Lolli, Ladoun, and other earlier investigators. There is always the difficulty of good criteria for racial identity, more so as intermarriage and migration obscure racial lines. We said earlier that one cannot lump all members of one racial designation into a single group of Chinese, Italians, blacks, or Irish. A further complication is that hereditary diseases, including alcoholism, often skip a generation.

Rather than attempting further details, let us outline briefly one hypothesis (Milam, 1974) that might explain why racial differences could be in great part biological rather than purely sociocultural. We see a definite correlation between low rates of alcoholism and length of time in which a given people have been exposed to alcohol. Some groups have had alcohol since before recorded history, over 20,000 years. Northern Europeans have probably had alcohol for about 2,000 years, and some North Americans less than 300 or as little as 150 years. Since alcohol decreases both longevity and sexuality, the natural selection process over thousands of years could have allowed elimination of the alcoholics and the survival of the fittest, yielding low vulnerability to alcoholism among the Mediterranean peoples: Jews, Greeks, southern Italians. Since alcoholic Eskimos average fewer children than nonalcoholic Eskimos, this same kind of selective breeding could occur eventually, but it is not biologically possible in the short time that they have been exposed to alcohol. (Those American tribes who had alcohol but only used it in controlled ritual or even ceremonial drunkenness did not have free access to alcohol continuously in a way that could affect the gene pool or alter susceptibility to alcoholism, regardless of how many centuries it continued.)

One could attribute these differences to the amount of time they have had to develop social controls and drinking customs, but this theory does not square with what we know about heredity, nor with what we know about social factors and the psychological strengths and weaknesses of these races. Communist China has little alcoholism, whereas Russia has a high rate, even after the Marxists promised no alcoholism because it is a mark of a degenerate capitalist society. Sweden has a high rate of alcoholism in spite of cradle-to-grave care, whereas the very word *ghetto* tells of 2,000 years of stress and persecution that should have given the Jews a high rate of alcoholism if that is the cause. The American Indians prior to their use of alcohol were a strong people, as were the Eskimos, who survived in a hostile climate. On the other hand, Jews have the highest rate of schizophrenia and a high rate of anxiety neurosis, and Italians have the highest rate of manic-depressive psychosis, so the low rate of alcoholism in these latter peoples can hardly be credited to low psychiatric vulnerability. Lastly, the higher rate of alcoholism among the American Catholic clergy than among the Mafia is more easily explained by their respective proportions of Irish and Italian lineage than by cultural principles.

It is interesting to note that during the Prohibition fight the "drys" came largely from northern European stock, where experience said that alcohol is bad, while the "wets" were largely from southern Europe or places where drinking caused less problems. Both sides assumed that alcohol had the same effect on all, and therefore either everybody should abstain or everybody can drink. Both were wrong, since peoples differ.

Moral and Spiritual Factors

If only for the sake of completeness, we must at least raise the question as to whether some of the moral and spiritual deterioration observed in alcoholics may be part cause and not merely the effect of the alcoholic drinking. This is a delicate subject to which we shall return in Chapter 19, and certainly there is no need for a lot of false guilt arising here because most alcoholics had no idea they were heading for alcoholism during most of their drinking. We would not have dared to ask the question in the early post-Prohibition days. But the field may be mature enough now to look at the issue dispassionately.

Most of the deterioration to which we refer here is no doubt effect rather than cause. But alcoholism is an illness of the whole person. The most widely successful approach to recovery, Alcoholics Anonymous, is an intensely spiritual program and its Twelve Steps are a very practical means of refurbishing one's moral life. Religion may be a major factor in the low rate of alcoholism among Jews. The shift in moral and spiritual values that alcoholics experience in their drinking days is a psychological fact, regardless of whether there is moral responsibility for it.

Learning and Habit

Keller uses the phrase "disorder of behavior" in his definition of alcoholism. Pathological drinking behavior is certainly at the heart of alcoholism. But is it redundant to say that alcoholism is the cause of drinking alcoholically? It is not nonsense if we examine the precise nature of habit.

Habit is a key concept in personality (Royce, 1964, Chapter 3). What kind of person we are was well summed up by Aristotle and William James as a "bundle of habits," but only if one understands the term in its full richness as a psychophysiological disposition: persistent, dynamic, unconscious and often irrational. Habit is largely learned or acquired, but runs so deep that if we understand its nature we will not lightly suggest that it can be easily unlearned, if at all. Deeply rooted in the nervous and endocrine systems, human habits involve physiological changes as well as learning. Both the physiology and the psychology of addiction explain how drinking itself is a primary cause of alcoholism in those who are biologically vulnerable.

Learning

Most people do not find the taste of alcohol initially pleasant, and nobody knows ahead of time what that first drink will do for them. Even though the effects may differ for individuals because of physiological predisposition, we all *learn* to drink alcohol and are reinforced by its immediate effects. To say that this or that life trauma caused Mary's alcoholism is true only if we recognize that Mary learned that alcohol soothed life's hurts.

Animal experiments have not provided us with a good model (Lester, 1966). Mice rarely get drunk and even dogs who do so don't become alcoholics. One could argue that Masserman's (1950) cats did not develop true neurosis and the rats who learned to drink when they went to college in the experiments of Roger Williams didn't really prefer alcohol if they could get sugar water. Some recent work suggests that pigs may become alcoholics, which at least has symbolic value.

Nevertheless what we know about animal and human learning, with alcohol and in other ways, throws a great deal of light on the nature of alcoholism. Even when not primary, learning by reinforcement of the escape value of alcohol may be a part factor in the development of much alcoholism. Anxiety, tension, and guilt melt away with a few drinks, at least temporarily. Some alcoholics learn only this, and not that the troubles always come back worse.

Timing is important in learning, as any student of behavior modification knows. Drinking is reinforced quickly by a lift or glow or euphoria or tranquility or whatever. It need not always work, as the facts of intermittent reinforcement show. One does not hit the jackpot every time, but an occasional win keeps the compulsive gambler coming back. Alcoholics have selective amnesia: They remember the good times and forget the misery, looking for that illusory euphoria, when all that alcohol brings is trouble. Research by R. Smart (1968) shows alcoholics have a different sense of time than others. "A long time" is quite relative.

Timing is why a hangover does not cure alcoholism. If it did there would be very few alcoholics, because most of them eventually suffer terrible hangovers. The reason hangovers do not deter the alcoholic is the same reason you don't spank a child on Friday for eating cookies on Tuesday: If the reinforcement is to be effective it must be closely associated with the behavior. For the alcoholic, drinking feels good; next morning's hangover feels bad and is associated with not drinking; a drink makes one feel good again. The associative learning is clear. What we would need is an alcohol that made one feel bad immediately upon drinking, then good upon withdrawal. Alcoholics seem to get quicker lift or euphoria but it wears off sooner, leaving an incentive to keep drinking. The all-pervasive nature of human habit systems is illustrated in the following account, which one recovered alcoholic shared with the author.

> Why doesn't the hangover act as an aversion? A hangover acts as a powerful negative reinforcing stimulus or punishment for the act of *not* drinking. He associates the way he feels with the fact that he is not drinking. This punishing reinforcement is not absent entirely when the hangover subsides. If he is not drinking, he is uncomfortable a great deal of the time, and for many weeks, sometimes months. Many alcoholics drink to maintain a normal comfort level. Not all are seeking the euphoric level; they merely need a relief from the discomfort the absence of alcohol brings on.
>
> Let me explain the precise nature of this discomfort to the person who has never experienced it. It is akin to the emotional havoc that happens when you intensely need the love of a particular person of the opposite sex. The obsession is such that life with that person is the only thing in your mind, and life is unbearable to conceive without her. She is delight, she is solace to the soul, she is your love, she is your confidence, she is your goal, your reason for living. Life without her is empty and not worth the effort. You feel you will die without her. She is alcohol to the alcoholic, except to the alcoholic she (alcohol) is available and willing and has not rejected her lover. He must reject her. He must, or he will be destroyed himself. Magnify this emotional level a hundredfold and you can duplicate in yourself the discomfort of a nondrinking alcoholic. As with the lover, time is the only real release, but the memory is vivid all through life and release is gradual. The pain does diminish, but the emotion lies dormant.

Characteristics of Habit

Habit is *powerful*. One can resolve, pray, promise. But habit will triumph over all these unless outside leverage is brought to bear. It can lie dormant for years, as in the case of one who has not ridden a bicycle since childhood and rides off at once on his nephew's new bike without having to relearn. Compulsive gambling and heroin addiction afford comparable examples. One cigarette can rekindle a habit which the smoker paid a heavy price to extinguish. Associative learning is powerful here, as there is nothing physically necessary about the morning paper and a second cup of coffee which demands a cigarette. Heavy smokers have more knowledge and negative attitudes about smoking than nonsmokers; 90 percent in one survey wanted to quit. Yet the habit persists. I am reminded of my grandfather's story of meeting an old Irishman on the road on a Saturday evening: "Pat, where are you going?" "Sure and I'm going down to the village to get drunk, and Lord, how I *hate* it." But he went, and he got drunk.

We concluded Chapter 6 by citing examples of how the compulsion can drive one to drink everything from canned heat to antifreeze in rusty water. Denatured alcohol used in nonbeverage products contains exceedingly bitter compounds to make them undrinkable. Despite this, some people continue to drink these products. Whenever the federal government learns about beverage use of a particular product, it requires the formula to be changed, usually with a chemical named Bitrex which is about twenty times more bitter than the strychnine denaturant usually used. Yet a few will continue to drink it. Such is the power of habit.

Unconscious.   One feature of habit is that it diminishes freedom of choice, and in the extreme case can eliminate it. We are not as free to choose A rather than B if we are strongly disposed by habit to choose B. Loss or diminution of control is a sign of alcoholism; the alcoholic is not as free in the choice to avoid drink as one without the habit. Being unconscious, the habit is part of us awake or asleep, adverting to it or not. Being conscious of the alternatives is essential to choice, which is a selection between competing motives. The effectiveness of AA is partly due to keeping one conscious of the fact that one is an alcoholic. Drinking for an alcoholic is irrational, but the unconscious nature of habit means this need not be brought before the bar of reason.

One reason for the irrationality of habit is that it develops unconsciously over a period of time. Nobody deliberately and consciously chooses to become an alcoholic. The *AA Grapevine* for January 1978 tells of a psychological experiment, apocryphal or not, that illustrates the point. In the experiment, a healthy frog is placed in a pan filled with water whose temperature is raised so gradually that the rate never goes above the threshold or JND (just noticeable difference) below which an organism cannot make discriminations. The frog can never sense the increase, so although free to jump out at any time he stays until he is boiled to death. No wonder Step 2 of AA speaks of a need to be restored to sanity by some power greater than ourselves. Another example of animal behavior, closer to the self-reinforcing mechanism of the alcohol habit, is the actual work of Dr. James Olds (1960) of the University of Michigan, who connected the bar in a rat's Skinner box usually producing a food pellet to an electrode implanted at that nerve center in the lower brain which produces a sexual orgasm. Yes, the rat continued to press the bar until the successive orgasms caused him to die of exhaustion. The continued drinking of the alcoholic is not less irrational, and certainly does not involve a high level of conscious choice.

Functional Autonomy.   Habit implies a learned need; we become dependent on alcohol. Whether in response to social pressures or inner conflict is irrelevant after a while. And this fact points to the major characteristic of habit pertinent to our understanding of alcoholism. The Harvard psychologist Gordon Allport says that a habit develops "functional autonomy," which is just a fancy way of saying that habit becomes its own dynamism, a law unto itself regardless of origin. Drinking itself now leads to more drinking. Hence the habit itself, and not the original motive, becomes the main target of change. McClelland (1978) draws a parallel with the use of a device that wakes up the child when he wets the bed. This device cures 75 percent of the cases, while psychologizing about whether the child wets in order to irritate his parents or to get attention has little result. The child is unhappy because he wets; he does not wet because he is unhappy. The device does not put the child into some other substitute behavior, but rather brings improvement in all areas of life. What we need is not analysis of why one drinks but treatment that breaks the habit of alcoholic drinking, which, in turn, will bring a lot of happiness in all areas. Another example is the sailor who, at age sixty-five, comes for help on a decision whether to continue sailing. He originally went to sea at fifteen because he hated his father. Meanwhile he has sailed for fifty years, so that sailing has become his very life. His entire set of habits centers around the open sea and the adventure of far places. We say he has saltwater in his veins. All his thoughts and feelings and memories concern sailing. Is there any point in asking him whether he still hates his father? The parallel with alcoholism therapy is obvious.

It is the self-dynamism or functional autonomy of habit that explains, in great part, the answer to the question with which we began this chapter. Why does an alcoholic drink alcoholically? Gone are the reasons that our team won or our team lost; they didn't even play. An alcoholic drinks because he is an alcoholic. A combination of causes culminates in this vicious circle of wanting more of the very substance that creates the problem. Even in those cases that began as symptomatic of some psychological conflict, it is "a symptom that has become a disease," in the words of Tiebout long ago. Our next chapter examines the propriety of this designation.

Sources

The National Clearinghouse for Alcohol Information (NCALI) (see Appendix) publishes bibliographies on all aspects of causality. Not only is the literature here prodigious, but any attempt at selection means omissions that are bound to offend some. In addition to references to the General Bibliography cited in the chapter, we list a few important items.

BLANE, HOWARD T., *The Personality of the Alcoholic.*

EWING, JOHN A. and BEATRICE ROUSE (eds.), *Drinking: Alcohol in American Society.*

GOODWIN, D.W. and C.K. ERICKSON (eds.), *Alcoholism and Affective Disorders: Clinical, Genetic, and Biochemical Studies.*

JELLINEK, E.M., *The Disease Concept of Alcoholism.*

KELLER, MARK, *Some Views on the Nature of Addiction.*

LEMERE, FREDERICK, "What Causes Alcoholism?" *Journal of Clinical and Experimental Psychopathology*, 1956, 17:202–206.

MADSEN, WILLIAM, *The American Alcoholic: The Nature-Nurture Controversy in Alcoholic Research.*

MELLO N.K., "Some Issues in Research on the Biology of Alcoholism," in Filstead, William, J. Rossi, and Mark Keller (eds.), *Alcohol and Alcohol Problems: New Thinking and New Directions*, pp. 167–191.

MILAM, JAMES R., *The Emergent Comprehensive Concept of Alcoholism.*

SUDDUTH, WILLIAM V., "The Role of Bacteria and Enterotoxemia in Physical Addiction of Alcohol,' *Journal of the International Academy of Preventive Medicine*, 1977, 4(1):23–46.

Heredity

The writings of Mark A. Schuckit and Donald W. Goodwin cover the subject well. The National Clearinghouse for Alcohol Information has a "Grouped Interest Guide" and there is a bibliography on "Genetics, Heredity, and Alcoholism," in *Alcohol Health and Research World*, fall 1974, pp 31–32.

CRUZ-COKE, R. and A. VARDA, "Genetic Factors in Alcoholism," in Popham, R.E. (ed.), *Alcohol and Alcoholism*, pp. 284–289.

ERIKSSON, K., "Behavioral and Physiological Differences among Rat Strains Specially Selected for Their Alcohol Consumption," *Annals of the New York Academy of Sciences*, 1972, 197:32–41.

EWING, JOHN A. and BEATRICE A. ROUSE, "Alcohol Sensitivity and Ethnic Background," *American Journal of Psychiatry*, 1974, 131:206-210.

GOODWIN, D.W., "The Genetics of Alcoholism: A State of the Art Review," *Alcohol Health and Research World*, spring 1978, 2:2–12.

GOODWIN, D.W., *Is Alcoholism Hereditary?*

HANNA, JOEL M., "Metabolic Responses of Chinese, Japanese and Europeans to Alcohol," *Alcoholism: Clinical and Experimental Research*, 1978, 2:89 92.

KAIJ, H.L. and J. DOCK, "Grandsons of Alcoholics," *Archives of General Psychiatry*, 1975, 32:1379-1381.

LEMERE, FREDERICK and WALTER L. VOEGTLIN, "Heredity as an Etiological Factor in Chronic Alcoholism," *Northwest Medicine*, 1943, 42:110–114.

MARDONES, J., "Evidence of Genetic Factors in the Appetite for Alcohol and Alcoholism," *Annals of the New York Academy of Sciences*, 1972, 197:138–142.

PARTANEN, J., K. BRUNN and T. MARKKANEN, *Inheritance of Drinking Behavior.*

"Racial Differences in Alcohol Metabolism: Facts and Their Interpretations–A Seminar," *Alcoholism: Clinical and Experimental Research*, January 1978, 2(1):59–92.

REED, T. EDWARD, "Racial Comparisons of Alcohol Metabolism: Background, Problems, and Results," *Alcoholism: Clinical and Experimental Research*, 1978, 2:83–87.

SCHUCKIT, MARK A., D. W. GOODWIN and G. WINOKUR, "A Study of Alcoholism in Half-Siblings," *American Journal of Psychiatry*, 1972, 128:1132–1136.

SEIXAS, FRANK A., "Nature and Nurture in Alcoholism," *Annals of the New York Academy of Sciences*, 1972, 197:1–229.

WILLIAMS, ROGER, *Biochemical Individuality: The Basis for the Genetotrophic Concept.*

CHAPTER 10

The Disease Concept of Alcoholism

THIS MAY WELL BE the most important chapter in this book. A great engineer once said, "There is nothing so practical as a good theory." Understanding what kind of an illness alcoholism is has very important practical applications. Not that a counselor goes into a long academic disquisition about five part-factors of etiology. But philosophy and goals of prevention and treatment, length of recovery period, and attitudes regarding return to life in a drinking society all depend on one's conception of the nature of alcoholism. Actually, the foundation for this concept was laid in the previous chapter, which will be presumed here. Alcoholism was portrayed there as a complex, psychophysiological dependence upon alcohol which ends up being its own obsessive-compulsive dynamism. Should this be called a disease? If so, what kind of a disease is it?

Pros and Cons of Disease Concept

June 17, 1968 was a black day for most of those interested in helping alcoholics. In early 1966 two U.S. district courts of appeal had raised the hopes of most workers in the field that the U.S. Supreme Court would soon declare it unconstitutional to jail an alcoholic for drunkenness, on the grounds that it is cruel and unusual punishment to jail a man for ex-

159

hibiting the symptoms of a disease. But in the 1968 case of *Powell* v. *Texas* our highest court ruled that it is *not* unconstitutional to jail an alcoholic. It was close, a five-to-four decision, with Justice White concurring but writing a separate opinion which indicated that except for some legal technicalities he would have dissented and thus thrown the decision the other way.

The decision was based largely on our failure to establish the disease concept of alcoholism. The court said,

> The inescapable fact is that there is no agreement among members of the medical profession about what it means to say that "alcoholism" is a "disease." . . . There is no agreement among doctors and social workers on the cause of alcoholism, there is no consensus as to why certain treatments work in certain cases, and facilities for treating impoverished alcoholics are woefully lacking throughout the country.

(Instead of using the lack of existing treatment facilities as a reason for putting alcoholics in jail, the court might have put the burden on the public for developing adequate facilities, much as the great civil rights decisions forced the issue of racial justice. Eventually this began to happen because of the passage of the Uniform Act, to be discussed in Chapter 20.)

The main reason given by the court is a challenge: either validate the disease concept or abandon it. The majority opinion in *Powell* v. *Texas* suggested that the current disease concept was too narrow, and stimulated rethinking of the whole problem in terms of *disorder*, or self-destructiveness (suicide is against the law), or socially inappropriate *behavior*. This rethinking does not imply rejection of the illness concept. But let us review the pros and cons of calling alcoholism a disease and see where this leads us.

Pro

It was a great step forward to replace the view of alcoholism as a crime, a species of moral depravity or weak will, with the view that it is an illness to be understood and treated rather than punished. Put in the setting of post-Prohibition uneasiness redolent of the bitter wet versus dry controversies and religious partisanships, it helped to clear the air and give the problem dignity. It made it the respectable object of scientific research, which had apparently been afraid to step out of its ivory tower and dirty its white coat with a problem that had so many religious, moral, and emotional implications. We saw toward the end of Chapter 3 how the concept was accepted by the various professional organizations and fostered by Jellinek's book. Calling alcoholism a disease encouraged a professional attitude among doctors, nurses, social workers, the police and courts, and hospitals. We don't punish a disease. Marvin Block, M.D., headed an

American Medical Association team to educate physicians and hospital administrators to this effect. It has been important in getting medical insurance coverage for alcoholism treatment, and acceptance of occupational alcoholism programs for employees.

The disease concept has great psychological advantages for the victim who is sincere about helping himself. It disarms denial, enabling one to admit needing help; nobody takes out his own appendix. It facilitates the realization that one is different, that one cannot drink like others. It removes the sting of the moral degeneracy or weak will theories; it replaces guilt with the self-respect that is so essential for coming back. It reassures alcoholics that they are not crazy. It makes alcoholism seem less ghostly and mysterious; it makes it something we can fight. It is face-saving for the family, too. "Mom is sick" sounds acceptable.

Alcoholism has been compared to diabetes. Like all comparisons, this one limps; but there are similarities. Neither alcoholism nor diabetes is cured, but both can be controlled. Both have aspects of compulsion, and both involve behavior that is socially acceptable for others but harmful to these victims. There is evidence for physical factors as part cause, and that these may be inherited as a physiological predisposition in some cases.

Bodily damage is certainly part of the picture. These are *sick* people, regardless of whether this is cause or effect. The Supreme Court argued that a disease ought to be more identifiable; but they focused too much on the early stages, where other diseases also escape detection. Alcoholism does follow a somewhat identifiable course of progressive and even degenerative history, at least within a variety of types, which makes it a syndrome with fair predictability if untreated. There are many varieties of cancer, many of them undetected in early stages; this does not keep cancer from being a disease.

Lastly, in the area of prevention and public education it reduces the social prestige of the early symptoms, and dispels a lot of folklore about drinking and the macho image.

Con

It is necessary to examine the arguments contrary to the disease concept even if one favors it, for several reasons. We must be able to answer the objections of insurance companies who do not want to include medical benefits, and industrial interests who do not want to pay premiums for this coverage. We have to be able to defend in court, perhaps under cross-examination, the fact that our client is sick, not criminal. We have to answer the fallacious arguments against the disease concept as well as recognize its true weaknesses.

Invalid Arguments.   We have already noted that some of the arguments are fallacious; for example, that alcoholism must be a single disease entity like smallpox rather than a multiple illness like cancer. Some argue that to call alcoholism a disease implies that it is hopeless; but many diseases are eminently treatable, including alcoholism. Alcoholism is not an allergy, in the technical sense of antigen-antibody response. But many diseases are not allergies. (To say alcoholism is "like" an allergy may be a useful, if inaccurate, analogy, which helps some people and harms no one.) It is sometimes said that the disease concept is incompatible with certain treatment approaches, from aversion conditioning to the spiritual program of AA. This is not true. AA tradition prohibits espousing any causes, but members usually accept the disease concept and even insist on it. The same is true of those who prescribe Antabuse or aversion techniques, which can quite logically be used to fight a disease. The disease concept does not absolve one from all responsibility for getting help, as we shall see.

It is naive to argue that alcoholism cannot be a disease because it is self-inflicted; any experienced physician has seen many self-inflicted illnesses. You don't buy disease in a bottle; you buy a drink. Similar is the argument that you can't give up a disease but you can give up drinking. These arguments confuse alcoholism with drinking, as warned against early in our first chapter. One never gives up alcoholism any more than one gives up diabetes. One does not choose whether or not to be an alcoholic. Even to give up drinking is a problem for which the alcoholic requires help, as the very nature of the illness limits one's ability to control drinking. Would you tell a hay fever victim to use will power and not sneeze?

Like Diabetes.   The comparison with diabetes does limp, as all analogies do. There is no insulin and no natural need for alcohol as there is for carbohydrates. More important are the psychological differences: The diabetic does not get the same degree of lift or sedation from sweets that the alcoholic gets from alcohol, nor does he experience the same compulsion, go to the same extremes, bring the same tragic harm to his family, or undergo the drastic personality changes we see in alcoholics. One bite of a rich dessert may make it psychologically harder for the diabetic to refuse a second bite, but there is not the quick effect on the brain that makes the alcoholic unable to refuse a second drink. Nonetheless the analogy does have some value.

What's in a Name?   Of similar mixed validity is the objection that alcoholism is not just physical, hence undeserving of the name disease. A trip through the dictionary reveals that disease, illness, sickness, and disorder are really synonyms, differing only in connotation. Thus "disease" connotes bacteria, and hence is inappropriate for alcoholism. We might wish that Jellinek had chosen one of the others, but none is quite satisfactory. A holistic view of human nature avoids mind-body dualism, and puts the disorder in the whole person. One could ask, is compulsive gambling a disease? It is certainly sick behavior. Whether you call the addiction a disease or not, you can substitute gambling for alcohol or heroin and get exactly the same tale of repeated promises, threats of divorce, relapses, remorse, resolutions, renewed efforts, wrecked lives and families. "Sick" for many connotes mental illness, and for this reason would be misleading because alcoholism is usually the primary pathology rather than symptomatic of mental disorder. "Behavior disorder" connotes a purely learned reaction, which can be unlearned, missing the peculiar psychology and physiology of addiction, which is an apparently irreversible habit state even when the act or behavior is controlled as in abstinence. "Illness" again connotes only the physical to some people, missing the psychological and spiritual dimensions of alcoholism. There seems no *word* which will please everyone, but this does not invalidate the *concept*.

Reasons Contra.   Some arguments against calling alcoholism a disease cannot be dismissed as fallacious. The alcoholic still caught up in the web of denial and rationalization can use as an excuse: "I'm sick, feel sorry for me, I can't do anything about it"; and to avoid all responsibility for recovery: "I'm sick; *you* cure me." (These phrases do not usually come from the alcoholics we see in treatment. Like the diabetic or cancer patient, they know they must cooperate in the recovery process.) The alcoholic might excuse himself from all responsibility for debts incurred and injuries inflicted, on the grounds that he was sick. Prevention efforts can be harmed because people use the disease concept to excuse heavy drinking instead of exerting social pressures against it.

The disease label can feed the denial of the early-stage or upper-class alcoholic who identifies disease with the skid roader, since he sees no serious physical symptoms in himself (yet). Even if applicable to primary alcoholics, it may be that *secondary* alcoholics fare worse under a disease model. In family therapy it creates a false dichotomy of "You're sick, I'm well" thinking. It creates guilt feelings in the spouse who divorces the one he or she vowed to keep "in sickness and in health." It can generate a fatalistic hopelessness in those who do not understand it is a treatable illness. It can slight the importance of sociocultural factors, miss the psychology of addiction (Peele, 1977), and omit the whole spiritual dimension.

Lastly, the word *disease* suggests full acceptance of a medical model. While this may have the advantage of motivating physicians to treat the alcoholic in a nonjudgmental way, cognizant that relapse is common in any chronic disease, it has some distinct disadvantages. In spite of the recent rapid growth of the American Medical Society on Alcoholism (AMSA) and a general awakening of interest in the medical profession, several surveys have revealed that the average American physican is still both reluctant to treat alcoholics and often ignorant about alcoholism. This is not said in disrespect, and is based on reports from the medical profession itself; as one medical school dean put it, his students, until recently, had fewer clock hours of instruction on alcoholism than on some obscure tropical diseases they will never see. Medical models tend to put the physician in full charge, focus almost exclusively on physical damage, and perpetuate a medical "revolving door," which is more humane than the drunk tank but equally ineffective for long-range treatment. It implies that nonmedical persons are unable to treat the illness; yet AA, with one million members, has been the single most successful treatment, and other group therapies, recovery houses, and out-patient centers staffed by trained but nondegreed professionals are achieving recovery rates far better than the old medical approach. Worst of all, "medical" suggests "medication": substituting another addictive drug like Valium or Librium for alcohol. The result, as a member of AMSA told his medical colleagues, is that "your patients don't get better, they just *smell* better." As another physician puts it, treating alcoholism with Valium is like treating lung cancer with cigarettes.

Holistic Disease

Rather than a naive acceptance that "everybody says" it is a disease, alcoholism must be understood in the full light of its many-faceted nature and complex etiology. We need not choose between heredity and environment, or between medical model and psychological approach. A holistic view takes into account all aspects. But this must be grounded in the fact that alcohol is a drug introduced into a living organism—with all the physiological and psychological factors this involves. Addiction is more than physical, and learned habit goes deeper than psychology. Most human behavior is a complex resultant of physical, psychological, social, and learning factors. Alcoholic drinking is no exception.

Thus we do not say simply that 70 to 80 percent of all alcoholism is physical, or that 20 percent of alcoholics are psychiatric cases. In the former group physiological addiction may be primary, but psychological and sociocultural factors are also at work. In the latter group stress or conflict may be the major cause, but physiological vulnerability and the dynamism of acquired habit also contribute. Granted multiple causality in each case, with the various factors contributing in different proportions for individuals even within the same category, present evidence seems to favor roughly the above proportions.

Dis-ease

The question is the appropriateness of calling this complex phenomenon a disease. As we saw, troublesome connotations make any word a poor choice. But going to the root meaning of the word, what is disease? Note that health is not a mere absence of disease, but vice versa. Health is functioning according to the design of nature. Disease, illness, sickness, disorder all mean a lack of this integral and purposive functioning. Disease is lack-of-ease in functioning. Alcoholism is a state of not being able to function "with ease" in regard to alcohol: any loss of control, notable interference with life, however you define it. The decision not to drink does not eliminate the disease, any more than the decision not to eat strawberries eliminates the allergy; the inability to handle alcohol endures.

Is Drug Addiction a Disease?   Some seem to feel that as high as 90 percent of true alcoholics are not physically addicted, at least in the early or early-middle states. These theorists are using manifest criteria such as withdrawal symptoms, but we have seen that from the onset of drinking there may be subtle adaptive changes occurring in both liver and brain. Older people who develop alcoholism as reaction to crises of retirement may have been physiologically vulnerable all along, but their bodies had never been exposed to heavy doses of alcohol. The youth who smokes to prove he or she is mature ends up thirty years later addicted to the drug nicotine, though the original motive has long since gone. Nobody can say when psychology ended and physiology took over. It makes no difference whether the alcoholic hides bottles because the dependence on alcohol is psychological or physical. If one needs alcohol to feel "normal," that *is* addiction.

Gary Miller (1970) objects to the inconsistency of calling heroin misusers addicts and not calling alcoholics addicts. Perhaps the same kind of reluctance keeps us from accepting the word *disease*. Obsessive-compulsive mental patients are sick, psychosomatic illnesses are very real, alcoholism is dys-functional. It may seem to be stretching the word a bit to call this disease, but the concept seems clear enough. Alcoholism is a physical, emotional-psychological, and, as we shall see, a spiritual disease.

Emerging Consensus

The alcohol field is seen by some as divided. At the risk of sounding arrogant, it might be more accurate to say that the split is not within the ranks of alcohol specialists so much as between those who understand alcoholism and those who don't. This sounds perilously like an argument of "either you agree with me or you're wrong," but a closer look reveals a fair consensus emerging among those working in the field. Theoreticians are showing a renewed interest in the work of Tiebout, rereading Jellinek, capitalizing on the broad perspective of social scientists like Madsen, who put a balanced but strong emphasis on physiology and heredity, and accepting the views of psychiatrists and psychologists who have rejected the older psychiatric theories in the light of both psychological and biological research. The work of Lieber, Israel, Ewing, Myers, and many others on liver and brain differences in alcoholics points more and more toward a confirmation of this view. The evidence for a hereditary factor reinforces it from another angle. This convergence in theory corresponds to two trends in the realm of practice that foster consensus. One is the disappearance of the old dichotomy between degreed professionals and recovered alcoholics, as more recovered alcoholics with doctor's and master's degrees get active professionally. The other is that degreed people are coming out of their traditional clinics and working in recovery programs that use newer and more successful approaches based on the experience of recovered alcoholics.

Pathological Drinking is Primary

This view is holistic, psychobiological if you will. With variations, there is substantial agreement that alcohol is an addictive drug, so that the concepts of tissue tolerance, cellular adaptation, withdrawal, and the rest all apply. Moreover, the whole psychology of addiction also applies: the notions of compulsion, augmentation, habituation, denial, learning, and sociocultural pressures.

But chiefly it considers alcoholism as a pathology in its own right, not merely a symptom of something else. The American Medical Association's interpretation of alcoholism as a disease says that ". . . the treatment primarily involves merely not taking a drink," and we must presume that physicians are treating illness and not just symptoms. But they add that "most alcoholics cannot break the cycle alone." Treatment facilities and AA report high rates of success, whereas, according to Tiebout, psychiatry helped only 3 percent of alcoholics. The reason is that the mechanics of psychotherapy may be inherently self-defeating. If the anxiety and tension are the result of drinking and what ultimately bring alcoholics to treatment, then reduction of these may function more to sustain drinking than promote recovery. Worse, a probing psychotherapy can be very threatening and can literally drive one to drink. The patient often continues to drink while the psychotherapist is trying to uproot the causes. "Meanwhile the patient gets sicker and sicker," said Dr. Luther Cloud, then president of the National Council on Alcoholism, with agreement from Dr. Marvin Block, chairman of the AMA Committee on Alcoholism.

Toxicity, Not Personality.   The literature is full of reports on psychological tests of alcoholics, which exhibit a formidable array of psychopathology. We would indeed be inclined to infer from this that one is an alcoholic because of personality problems, especially because alcohol is a tranquilizer. Unfortunately, most of these tests were administered during the first ten days of sobriety. Milam (1970, revised 1974) and Farmer (1973) were among the first to challenge the apparently obvious inference by repeating the tests after three months of sobriety. Milam used standard personality tests like the Minnesota Multiphasic Personality Inventory (MMPI) on three different populations, from skid roaders to upper class; Farmer replicated his study using Bender-Gestalt, a test sensitive to brain damage. The results were consistent: Between 70 and 80 percent of the "alcoholic personalities" in all these studies turned out to be quite normal when residual toxicity had been given a chance to subside. Only about 20 percent were personalities that may have caused the alcoholism. This is congruent with the reports of EEG brain wave changes and brain scan tests requiring up to six months or a year to return to normal after drinking ceased. It also coincides with the fact that 90 percent of alcoholics can be color-blind ten days after drinking, but most will recover normal vision in time (Smith and Brinton, 1971).

This concept is not new. The psychiatrist Tiebout was writing about alcoholism as a primary disease as early as 1944 (see Sources). E.M. Jellinek (1952) said,

> The aggressions, feeling of guilt, remorse, resentments, withdrawal, etc., which develop in the phases of alcohol addiction are largely consequences of the excessive drinking. . . . By and large, these reactions to excessive drinking which have quite a neurotic appearance—give the impression of an "alcoholic personality," although they are secondary behaviors superimposed over a large variety of personality types which have few traits in common. . . . (p. 683)

Frederick Lemere (1964), long-time staff psychiatrist at a hospital for alcoholics, held that psychiatric consultation should be available, but "I do not believe, however, that psychiatry should dominate the treatment of alcoholism" (p. 559). Marty Mann, commenting favorably on the research of Milam, relates how for five years she thought she was crazy, and when psychiatrists did not confirm this she decided that "my insanity is of such a severe nature they don't dare tell me"—only to discover that she was perfectly normal after getting sober. Unfortunately, the psychiatric label often clings to the patient even after a return to normalcy. Many an alcoholic has spent a fortune on psychiatric analysis, only to discover that their symptoms disappeared when they got direct treatment for their alcoholism. One alcoholic spent $3,000 for psychoanalysis undergone during blackout.

There is no research evidence that proves that the psychopathology observed in alcoholics precedes and causes alcoholism (Malzberg, 1960). Contrariwise, psychometric research (Milam, Farmer, White, White and Porter, Rohan) as well as the experience of psychiatrists working with alcoholics (Tiebout, Fleming, Lemere, Heilman) show that recovery from alcoholism results in disappearance or marked diminution of these symptoms, which are therefore logically effect and not cause. Even the minority who will need psychotherapy can neither be identified nor treated until the residual toxic effects have disappeared. Success is highest in therapies that attack the drinking-habit pattern itself, whether by Antabuse, aversion conditioning, AA, or whatever. The analysis of personality defects in Chapter 5 of *Alcoholics Anonymous* is aimed at prevention of relapse, not at the original causality. The focus is on helping the alcoholic to avoid drinking, which is seen as the basic problem. (Always fascinated by psychiatry, it took Bill W. until 1968 to admit that Dr. Silkworth was right on this point, according to histories of AA.) Westermeyer (1976, p. 27) and Mello (1972) attest to the common opinion that there is no such thing as the alcoholic personality.

Needless Psychologizing.   Paresis or syphilis of the brain is called "the great simulator" because it can imitate the symptoms of any psychosis. Brain tumors can do the same, and so can alcohol. Hence the need for retesting three months after sobriety. We don't treat paresis by inquiring why one went to a brothel where the syphilis was contracted. Very few personality traits have been identified as existing prior to alcoholism rather than subsequent to it. One of these is a slightly higher average IQ which would only confirm the idea that alcoholism is not caused by inferior personality. If we blame shyness and being left out for causing alcoholism, what about the one who develops alcoholism because of being very popular and always invited to parties? Adolescent alcoholics are immature and confused; but so are most adolescents. The reason why only some become alcoholic would seem to lie elsewhere, since nearly all adolescents drink. Ironically, when we carefully explored a relapse with one alcoholic, not unique in this, she could say only that things were going too well, she couldn't stand everything going right.

Analyzing causes can be a game both psychotherapists and alcoholics love to play, with little fruit. Various motives can be augmented or facilitated by the alcoholic state, just as a minor remark gets blown up into a horrendous attack when one is sick or tired. The psychological causality is in no proportion to the effect, which must be attributed in great part to the physical condition. Here again the question is not Why does one drink? for which the incident could be reason enough; but Why get drunk? The reason for that is not in the incident, but in the augmentation that facilitates the alcoholic's motivation to drink, much as you get a bigger knee jerk if you tense your arms.

The adage *in vino veritas*—when one is in his (wine) cups the truth comes out— is sometimes taken as evidence that alcoholism is the result of inner repressed urges or conflicts. To begin with, there seems to be a contradiction here. Does alcohol sedate the repressed material, or the inhibitions that prevented it from coming out? Actually, both may be true. Alcohol is a tranquilizer, and it can also act as a "truth serum" by sedating inhibitions so that defenses are down. But what comes out is not necessarily the "true" personality but a toxic version: drug-affected emotions and irrational thinking or behavior. The result can be most unrepresentative of the person's true inner feelings. In any case, there is no proof that what comes out was somehow the cause of alcoholism rather than the effects of alcohol. Moreover, if alcohol is a stimulant initially, especially for alcoholics, they would therefore seem less likely to use it to sedate inner conflict. MacAndrew (1969) showed that in many cultures alcohol does not sedate inhibitions.

Alcoholism is Cause, Not Symptom.   All this parallels what we saw in Chapter 4, that the alcoholic does not drink because he is impotent, but is impotent because he drinks. "Stinking thinking" can lead to a relapse, but it is no more the cause of alcoholism than "diabetic thinking" is the cause of diabetes. One of the few longitudinal studies is by the Harvard psychiatrist George Valliant (1977), who studied 202 men for 35 years, starting as college sophomores in 1940. He came to a similar conclusion, that "alcohol is the antithesis of a tranquilizer and the average alcoholic does not drink because his childhood was unhappy; he is unhappy because he drinks." To put it another way, alcoholism is indeed usually a symptom— of a deep, underlying *drinking* problem!

Practical Applications

Implications for Therapy

As a licensed psychologist and a clergyman, this author would be the last to neglect emotional and spiritual aspects; but these approaches are inappropriate until the brain clears. You don't *counsel* a caterpillar on how to fly; you wait for the needed physiological changes to occur. For this reason it is ridiculous to attempt depth psychotherapy in early stages of recovery, nor are newly sober alcoholics ready for "hot seat" encounters or insight therapy. They need to learn that they are sick, not weak or crazy or morally bad people. Dredging up the past may produce guilt and remorse, which can do more to occasion a relapse than to promote sobriety. They need to learn that their irrational behavior, including drinking behavior, is the result of the illness of alcoholism. To feel so badly about a friend who drank himself to death that you go get drunk is not very sane.

Nor is drinking out of remorse for drinking too much. But it is equally ir-rational to attack the behavior instead of the alcoholism. We know cases where patients, upon admission to the hospital on the verge of alcoholic seizures, were referred to the psychiatric ward because of their alcoholic hallucinations. In other cases four or five major complications of alcohol-ism were treated, such as liver disease and bleeding ulcers, without any attempt to treat the alcoholism that caused all this. In still others the so-cial worker attributed to "bad luck" a string of accidents, lost jobs, bad marriages and the like without once seeing whether these might be the re-sult of alcoholism rather than the cause of the drinking.

Prevention

This conception of alcoholism as a disease is seen by some as inimical to prevention efforts. On the contrary, since it points to physiological differ-ences as a reason why only one in twelve drinkers become alcoholic, that should answer the frequent question, "Why don't you drink like others do?" It is not that alcoholics don't want to, but that they can't. They may have the same reasons for drinking as everybody else, but their reactions to alcohol are not the same. Urging them to drink responsibly is futile. Many responsible drinkers develop alcoholism, and many irresponsible drinkers do not, even though drinking heavily all their lives.

If early, even hereditary, predisposition is a factor in about half the cases, it is fallacious to talk about a prealcoholic stage for them. Research on the many physiological factors mentioned in the previous chapter could give the examining physician palpable objective evidence of early alcoholism whereby he could penetrate the alcoholic's denial, without haggling over subjective factors or a rationalized drinking history. The differences are often imperceptible except in retrospect, but this should not deceive us into thinking that everyone reacts similarly to alcohol until late-stage alcoholism is manifest. Much of the early adaptation is nonpa-thological; for example, thickening of the lining of the bowel. Tolerance is not a defect but a plus. Thus it is important for people at the onset of drinking to be aware that they may be more vulnerable than others, espe-cially if their ancestry suggests this.

Heredity is now being studied as a causal factor in schizophrenia and manic-depressive (affective) psychosis, but in these the precipitating envi-ronmental causes are nebulous and diffuse. In alcoholism we know exact-ly what the agent is: alcohol. Prevention can thus be much more specific. What is inherited is not a compulsion to drink, so learning and sociocul-tural factors still play a part. An orthodox Jew who leaves his orthodoxy does not change biologically but may develop alcoholism, whereas a Na-tive American Indian is not necessarily an alcoholic in spite of his biological heritage. But just as a disposition to diabetes or an allergy to strawberries can run in a family, so those of alcoholic ancestry should be told that statistically the chances are much higher that alcohol is dangerous for them. This avoids both moralistic and racist overtones. If my body breaks out in ugly red hives every time I eat strawberries, the safest answer is not to eat strawberries. This does not make me bad or weak, just physiologically different. It really makes no difference whether it is because I am like my grandfather in this, or had a brain or liver injury, or broke down my strawberry-immunity system by eating too many. And if my compulsion for strawberries is so strong that I cannot avoid them without help, then I should take Anti-Strawberry-abuse and join Strawberries Anonymous.

Rehabilitation

Focus on alcoholism as not only a primary but a *chronic* disease has important implications for long-term recovery. Where before they drank because of alcoholism, alcoholics must now stay sober in spite of alcoholism (Madsen). It may take years for the body to return to normal, if ever. Adaptation can be so profound that even after two years of sobriety alcoholics need a little alcohol to approach normal on some functions. The drop in tolerance common in late-stage alcoholics seems to be irreversible. And after even years of sobriety, a relapse does not put them at the start of social drinking, but at the stage they were when they quit. (The further theory that they are not only at that stage, but at the same stage of progression where they would have been had they not stopped meanwhile, is not proved and may be just a function of the deterioration attached to aging.)

Other drugs will likewise act on this chronic condition. We mentioned the recovered alcoholics who relapse when given a painkiller by the dentist, and have seen long-recovered alcoholics whose doctor prescribed tranquilizers after a mild heart attack relapse into alcoholic drinking within three weeks. It is not true that one drink will always trigger a relapse, but sooner or later, if continued, the drinking gets out of control. (It is often asked how the recovered alcoholic priest can drink wine at Mass without relapse. Most recovered priests agree that a thimbleful of dry wine at Mass is neither physiologically nor psychologically an adequate stimulus for a binge: The few molecules of ethanol when diluted in many pints of blood are unable to make any impact on the brain, and for a priest who believes that the wine is the blood of Christ it is simply *not* "a drink." The problem is the bottle of wine in the sacristy, but that is the same problem every recovered alcoholic has of living in a society where alcohol is always available.)

Enduring Disposition.   Habit is a state or disposition, a quality of the person, semipermanent in nature. Actions come and go, but the habit is disposing us to a certain way of acting at all times. Thus a man is good or wise even though sound asleep and performing no acts of goodness or wisdom, because when he awakes he does not start from zero to acquire these dispositions but has had them all along. Hence a person says, "I *am* an alcoholic" rather that "I *was*" even though sober for twenty years. They know they are the kind of person who will not drink in moderation over the long haul, but are disposed to drink alcoholically. After twenty years of no hives, I still say, "No thanks, I am (*not* was) allergic to strawberries."

Recovering?   For the above reasons, members of AA often prefer to call themselves "recovering" rather than "recovered," lest the latter term cause them to let down their guard as if the process were over and the disposition were no longer there. (Thirty years ago "cured" was forbidden and "recovered" was insisted upon, for exactly the same reason!) This is perfectly intelligible within the fellowship. However, the *AA Guidelines* (rev. 1977, p. 5, n.) warn that others may interpret "recovering" to mean that one is still drinking, and recommend "recovered" as more intelligible to outsiders. Marty Mann strongly concurred. The designation *alcoholic* maintains the concept of permanent quality or disposition. The word *recovering* could cost one a job if the person hiring did not understand this language, antidiscrimination laws notwithstanding.

Can Recovered Alcoholics Be Conditioned to Drink Socially?

The furor aroused by the Rand report (Armor, 1976) has subsided, thanks, in part, to a second report (Polich, 1980), which largely erodes the original findings. Akin to the fear that computers would take over the world, the notion of behavior modification as some Orwellian ogre is ridiculed by the psychologist, who "is much more impressed by how difficult it is to produce any behavioral changes at all, let alone manipulate people without their consent" (McClelland, 1978, p. 201). Even with their consent, to attempt to condition alcoholics to drink socially may be asking behavior modification more than it can do.

Actually, most uses of conditioning in this field have been to create an aversion against drinking, and to condition alcoholics to live comfortably in a drinking society, to learn how to resist pressure to drink, and to develop self-management skills aimed at more than just staying sober (for example, Miller and Mastria, 1977). Steps 4 through 10 of AA use what in behavioral terminology would be described as reinforcement, operant conditioning, modeling, incompatible response method, etc. In this we have been reasonably successful, as this is in accord with the physiology and psychology of addiction as just described. But can we turn recovered ·alcoholics into social drinkers?

Davies (1962) and Cain (1964) started the discussion, but except for some work by Mendelson and Mello no scientific research had been attempted until Drs. Marc and Linda Sobell, in 1969, at Patton State Hospital in California, began to explore how alcoholics drink at the onset of a bout, which is often lost in a blackout. In early 1970 the Sobells attempted to modify the drinking of chronic alcoholics, not as a treatment goal but just to see whether it could be done at all. They used only chronic alcoholics who had failed many times in all other programs and who explicitly rejected abstinence as a goal. Other experimenters used only indirect means of testing desire, with no actual drinking. One researcher used controlled drinking to entice the reluctant into treatment, in the hope that they could be sold on total abstinence later. Two researchers thought one value of controlled drinking experiments could be that the patient learns for himself what he has not been able to accept from others, namely that he cannot drink in moderation: Giving all this extra scientific help might destroy the rationalizations of the alcoholic who still thinks he can drink socially "if I *really* tried." Lastly, some have tried to avoid polarization by suggesting a compromise whereby total abstinence be the agreed goal for treating alcoholics, but experiments on controlled drinking continue for nonalcoholic problem drinkers, drunk drivers, etc. Scientific caution and concern for the experimental subjects could thus combine with pushing back the frontiers of knowledge and freedom of research.

Controversial.   With these exceptions, the literature is largely a record of failure. Although never quoted by advocates of controlled drinking, Davies (1963), Cain, and Selzer (1963) whose research Cain had cited, have all repudiated it except as a speculative concept, and have stated that the only realistic goal in treatment is total abstinence (Paul, 1973, pp. 101–103). Drs. Ruth Fox, Harry Tiebout, Marvin Block and M.M. Glatt were among the thirteen authorities who responded to the Davies article in a special reprint from the 1963 *Quarterly Journal of Studies on Alcohol* to the effect that never in the thousands of cases they had treated was there ever a clear instance of a true alcoholic who returned to drinking in moderation. Madsen, in Chapter 5 of *The American Alcoholic* (1974), concludes one of the better reviews of the Sobell experiments by saying, "In no place does the experiment demonstrate that a single alcoholic has learned to control his drinking totally" (p. 75). But the most thoroughgoing experiment was that of Ewing (1975, 1976), who was determined to prove it could be done by using every technique known to behavior modification, but also did the most careful and lengthy follow-up. Where others had reported success after periods as short as three months and several after a year or so, at the end of forty-five months every one of Ewing's subjects had gotten drunk and he called off the experiment with the declaration that it would be unethical to attempt any more.

In contrast, the Rand report (*Alcoholism Report*, July 9, 1976; Emerick, 1977) and other studies have been criticized for being too short a time period, for using inadequate care in followup, for subjective reporting, small number, sampling fallacies, lack of control group, and employing absurdly artificial settings. The Sobells (1974, 1978) give a well-reasoned defense of their work, but questions remain about selective sampling and adequate criteria. Pattison and the Sobells (1977) seem to make a "straw man" of the disease concept by incorrectly assuming that alcoholism is always progressive, that alcoholics are all of one type, and that craving, compulsion and loss of control are uniform all-or-none phenomena (Maisto, 1977). There is a vast difference between a nonalcoholic getting drunk and an alcoholic doing so; for the former it may be a minor incident, but for the latter it is pathological behavior. Many researchers lumped all alcoholics together, ignoring the fact that there are many different types. Thus craving is entirely different in a progressive Gamma, a maintenance Delta, and a periodic Epsilon. Craving also varies with the individual; it may not automatically be set off with one drink, but can build up. The research of Peter Nathan indicates that whereas others may be able to use internal cues (subjective feelings of intoxication) to estimate BAC while drinking, alcoholics cannot and so this method of control is not available to them.

Loss of Control.   A major fallacy concerns loss of control (Keller, 1972). *All* alcoholic drinking is "controlled" drinking, until the last deteriorative stage. There is some partial control at various stages and at some periods, so experimenters took too literally the idea that one drink always means getting drunk. Madsen suggests (pp.68–69), and quotes Marty Mann to corroborate, that this misinterpretation resulted from listening to the preventive philosophy of Alcoholics Anonymous rather than to the actual experiences of members. His own research shows 97 percent of AAs reported ability to quit drinking after one drink at some stage and under sufficient motivation, yet every one of them knew that if they continued they would eventually lose control. Many research projects set out to disprove the "one drink" hypothesis in laboratory or hospital settings so artificial and with criteria so wooden that nobody with real experience in alcoholism could take the results seriously. As Madsen says, any heavy smoker can avoid smoking during High Mass.

Conclusion.   It is unfair to imply that all researchers advocate social drinking for alcoholics. And nobody with lengthy experience in treating alcoholics would find it hard to agree with Dr. Ernest Noble, former director of the National Institute on Alcohol Abuse and Alcoholism (NIAAA), that "it would be extremely unwise for a recovered alcoholic to even try to experiment with controlled drinking." To ask a recovered addict to engage in "responsible heroin shooting" or a compulsive gambler to just play for small amounts is to ignore the whole psychology and physiology of addiction. Even if a tiny fraction of alcoholics could, in fact, return to normal drinking, many alcoholics, through denial and rationalization, would immediately place themselves in that fraction. The Rand report does have some cautions, and if scientific pursuit of truth could be confined to the ivory tower, it might be easier to understand Pattison (1968) when he "deeply regrets" the relapses, but says "they are the result of misinterpretation." It seems most unpsychological to furnish the rationalization and then call the result a misinterpretation. Pattison's arguments against the disease concept only confirm the importance of a psychological and motivational approach stressing abstinence. This, of course, is exactly what the AA program does, so it cannot be dismissed as holding a simplistic disease concept that is purely physical. Physiology aside, the compulsive gambler had better be motivated to accept the idea that he should avoid gambling entirely.

Add to this the statement of Dr. Nicholas Pace, former president of the National Council on Alcoholism (NCA), that "you can't teach a sick liver to drink again" and recall what happened when Myers put THP into the rat's brain. Alcoholism is not a simple learned behavior that can be unlearned, but a habitual disposition that has profoundly modified the whole person. This explains the admitted failure of psychoanalysis to achieve any notable success in treating alcoholics, and renders vapid the notion of Claude Steiner in *Games Alcoholics Play* that the alcoholic is a naughty child rather than a sick adult. Even Sobell's successful cases are now reported to have given up controlled drinking; for them abstinence is easier (Caddy, 1979). Once you have turned a cucumber into a pickle, you cannot change it back.

One need not question the sincerity of the experimenters, but one can question their good judgment and their unconscious motives. Must they cling to an out-moded behaviorism that impels them to prove the efficacy of conditioning at the expense of the alcoholic? When he assumed directorship of NIAAA, Dr. Noble repudiated the former slogan of "responsible drinking" because it is neither possible for all nor desirable. For this reason Dr. Marvin Block (1976) of the American Medical Association Committee gives perhaps the best answer to our question by saying, "Don't place alcohol on a pedestal." Not everybody *has* to drink.

Sources

Probably the best overall comment is the article by M.M. Glatt, "Alcoholism Disease Concept and Loss of Control Revisited," *British Journal of Addiction*, 1976,

71:135-144. Selden Bacon reviews the pros and cons well in his chapter "Concepts" in Filstead (1976), pp. 88–96, 112–116. One can purchase from NCA a package of nine important contributions by H.M. Tiebout as "The Tiebout Papers" (for titles see General Bibliography). Jellinek's classic *Disease Concept* (1960), Madsen's *The American Alcoholic*, and Milam's monograph (1974) have been referred to. We list a few other pertinent items.

BELL, ROBERT G., *Escape from Addiction*.

EMRICK, CHAD D., *"The Rand Report," JSA*, 1977, 38:152–163. See also his earlier articles in QJSA, 1974, 35:523–549 and JSA, 1975, 36:88-108.

EWING, JOHN A., *Psychiatric News*, Sept. 17, 1975, 10, n. 18.

EWING, JOHN A. and B. ROUSE, "Failure of Experimental Treatment Program to Inculcate Controlled Drinking in Alcoholics," *British Journal of Addiction*, 1976.

GERMAN, WILLIAM P.Z., JR. "An Analytical Survey of the Rand Report on Alcoholism and Treatment," Fundamental Research Organization, 2365 N. Oakland St., Arlington, VA 22207. This monograph concludes that the Rand report findings about normal drinking by alcoholics have no scientific validity.

HEILMAN, RICHARD O., *Dynamics of Drug Dependency*. Hazelden pamphlet.

ISRAEL, Y. and J. MARDONES (eds.), *Biological Basis of Alcoholism*.

KELLER, MARK, "Disease Concept of Alcoholism Revisited," *JSA*, 1976, 37:1694–1717.

ORFORD, JIM, "The Future of Alcoholism: A Commentary on the Rand Report," *Psychological Medicine*, 1978, 8:5–8.

VALLIANT, GEORGE, "Alcoholism Not a Symptom of Neurotic or Psychotic Disorders," *Alcoholism and Alcohol Education*, May 1977, 11–12.

PART III

Prevention and Intervention

CHAPTER 11

Prevention

WE HAVE COMPLETED our survey of the problems arising from excessive use of alcohol. As it was only a survey, it left many questions unanswered. But the big question remains, What are we to do? This second half of the book is a brief look at some solutions.

Quite understandably, the humane thing to do seems to be to help the sick alcoholic. This is important, and a large portion of the remaining chapters will be devoted to treatment and rehabilitation. But at the risk of being accused of insensitivity to the suffering alcoholic and his or her family, we put an even higher value on prevention.

You do not win a war by treating its victims. It is a fact of medical history that no major public health problem was ever solved by treatment. Smallpox has been practically wiped off the globe, not by daubing the pockmarks with medicine but because Jenner discovered vaccination. Malaria has been greatly reduced, not by soothing the fevered brow of the malaria victim but by discovering the role of the mosquito and taking appropriate action. Jonas Salk and his polio vaccine did more than all the devoted therapists massaging the muscles of polio victims. Even tuberculosis, although medical and surgical treatment techniques have greatly improved, has been minimized largely through the education-prevention campaign of the Anti-Tuberculosis League. The analogy is trite but still appropriate: Putting the bulk of our alcoholism funds into treatment rather than into prevention is like running an ambulance at the bottom of the cliff instead of erecting a barricade at the top.

Mention of funds usually raises the question of what this will cost. But the real question is how much it will save. The National Institute on Alcohol Abuse and Alcoholism (NIAAA) estimated in 1977 that alcoholism costs this country $42.75 billion a year. Preventing even a small part of that loss would save far more than the total we have spent so far on prevention. Regardless of cost, heroic efforts and huge expenditures on treatment are like bailing a damaged ocean liner with a teacup if society continues to turn out alcoholics faster than we can rehabilitate them. The answer seems to lie in the community rather than in institutions, in long-range prevention rather than in stopgap measures.

But is prevention possible? Probably not with 100 percent success. But that is no reason not to try; only that we need to be realistic in setting goals. Where possible we should set specific goals, whose achievement can be evaluated by objective measures.

Some object to prevention because they think it means a return of Prohibition. It must be made clear that what is to be prevented is alcoholism and alcohol problems, not drinking. And in our present polydrug culture we need to enlarge our target to include the misuse of other drugs, especially the combined dependency on alcohol and prescription drugs.

Current terminology distinguishes primary, secondary, and tertiary prevention. We shall define each briefly before going into detail.

Primary prevention means to forestall or reduce the incidence of new cases in a population at risk *before* the development of alcoholism, even in its early stages. This means stopping it before it gets started.

Secondary prevention, or early intervention, refers to measures taken to arrest or interrupt the progression of symptoms in the alcoholic before they reach the middle or late stages.

Tertiary prevention is actually treatment and rehabilitation, which prevents further progression of the illness and spread of its effects to others.

Primary Prevention

Specific, or *direct*, primary prevention aims at removing or blocking the causes of alcoholism to the extent that they are known, or become known as research progresses.

Nonspecific, or *indirect*, primary prevention refers to means that have the prevention of alcoholism as a desired by-product, even though they are not aimed directly at factors known to be principal causes of alcoholism. For example, developing adequate social skills and better ways of coping with stress are legitimate goals in themselves, but they may also be cultivated in the hope that thereby some alcoholism may be prevented.

A major obstacle to open discussion about primary prevention has been the tendency to make it synonymous with education or information. In exploring the means of primary prevention it shall become clear that much more is involved. Granted we cannot eradicate alcoholism at one stroke; we must use any and all means to reduce the incidence. Toward this goal the National Council on Alcoholism (NCA) Education-Prevention Committee lists strategies that attempt to:

1. Alter public attitudes, sociocultural factors, and environmental conditions conducive to alcohol misuse and alcoholism.
2. Educate the community and especially high-risk populations concerning the addictive properties of the drug alcohol and the varying susceptibilities of individuals to its use.
3. Influence positively the individual's decision-making skills regarding the use, misuse, or nonuse of alcohol.
4. Provide adequate role models and other means of developing social skills and ways of coping with stress so as to include alternatives to alcohol.

This is obviously a big order. It may be true that once alcohol has been introduced into a preliterate society, it has never been eliminated. But Moslems, Jews, Buddhists, the Pioneer Society in Ireland, and Maoist China all exemplify the fact that patterns of excessive use can be changed (Keller, 1976a, p. 14). There have been massive changes in our own country in the last three centuries regarding patterns of use, preferred beverage, place and amount of consumption, age and sex of consumer, tolerance of drunkenness, and many other aspects of drinking. For the most part these changes have not come about through legislation, but through social groups and personal motives, including religion. Government *control* has been largely a failure, but much might be accomplished if we could agree on methods and objectives and then use government *help*.

Since there is no one cause of alcoholism, there will be no one way of prevention. Complex etiology demands multiple preventive approaches. Using a public health model, we can list strategies according to their relation to the *agent* (alcohol), the *host* (that one in ten or twelve drinkers who seems most susceptible) and the *environment* (conditions conducive to interaction of the host with the agent).

The Agent: Alcohol

Perhaps the biggest reason why prohibition did not work was the infringement on personal freedom, the fact that it was imposed by law. Even if in theory nobody is absolutely immune, in practice we know that many people drink all their lives without developing alcoholism. This makes it difficult, if not impossible, to eliminate alcohol entirely. Yet it is still true that there would be no alcoholism without alcohol, and many are taking a second look at the relation between per capita consumption of alcohol and rates of alcoholism. It is true that the alcoholics will always get liquor, regardless of cost or availability; but we are talking here about primary prevention, before one becomes alcoholic.

To some this smacks of prohibitionism, but rather than a curt dismissal it deserves careful appraisal to assess the effect of limited times and place of purchase, legal age of purchaser, and price in relation to available income. Although per capita consumption is not always in direct proportion to alcoholism rates, much evidence indicates that the relation is hardly zero. In fact, some claim there is more evidence for this hypothesis as a basis for prevention than for any other preventive measure. Formerly dismissed as an approach the public would not stand for, its feasibility seems confirmed by the increase of those who favor some restrictions. The very mention of this approach naturally sparks powerful lobbying from the alcoholic beverage industry. In any case, it must be accomplished largely through public acceptance rather than simply by law. No aspect of prevention can be effective in isolation from the total picture.

Those who favor moderate legal restraint on availability, chiefly writers associated with the Addiction Research Foundation of Toronto (Archibald, 1975; Popham, 1976; Schmidt and Popham, 1978; de Lint, 1974, 1975), view their position as being tied to a uniform distribution model in opposition to a bimodal model showing a high-risk population. Perhaps the two theories are not that irreconcilable in practice. Decrease in overall availability could reduce consumption among the high-risk group before they develop alcoholism, especially if combined with a "forewarned is forearmed" approach, which the bimodal model favors. We need to try combining efforts rather than putting them in opposition. When the "wets" say everybody should drink and the "drys" say nobody should, there seems need to make some differentiations among people.

At least the controversy over reduction of per capita consumption has caused us to examine certain events, such as the 1918 taxation increase in Denmark, the Ontario beer strikes of 1958 and 1968, the Finnish experience with "medium beer" in 1969, and the lowering of the drinking age in many parts of North American in the early 1970s. One result is to question the hypothesis that alcohol problems can be reduced by substitution of new drinking patterns; they seem just to add on to the old. Moveover, attitudes and life-style are changing so rapidly, especially among young drinkers, that prevention efforts cannot be focused exclusively on the host without regard to availability of the agent (alcohol) and to the environment. See the section on "Regulation of Sale" in Chapter 20.

The Host

Even though we do not understand fully the biochemical mechanisms of immunity and susceptibility, we have a fair amount of data that identify certain populations as at high risk of alcoholism if they drink. We said in chapters 9 and 10 that no child is doomed by heredity to be an alcoholic. But we know that statistically the children of alcoholic ancestry are much more vulnerable. The NIAAA 1977 prevention plan (*Alcoholism Report*, January 14, 1977, p. 6) also mentioned truants and school dropouts, and native American youth, among others. Liver enzyme tests or other indicators may eventually enable us to identify those more likely to develop alcoholism, who would then be educated as to the nature of the illness without using scare tactics. The current interest in nutrition and good health habits can be used here.

Another approach is law. The legal drinking age was lowered in many states as part of a move to accord adult status to young men involved in the unpopular Vietnam war. It now seems that several assumptions were false: a) that most teenagers were already drinking, so changing the law would not alter their drinking patterns; b) that removing the motive of rebellion might actually reduce their alcohol consumption; c) that alcohol-related auto accidents by teenagers would not increase; and d) that lowering the legal age to eighteen would not affect the high school population because those over eighteen would have left school. Various researchers have shown all four assumptions to have been wrong, and the trend to lower the legal age is being reversed in many states.

The Environment

To say that we live in a drinking society describes only a part of the reality. Social pressures to drink, and sometimes to drink heavily, converge on us from all sides. The alcoholic beverage industry in the United States spends over $800 million a year, $2.2 million a day, in advertising. Presumably these businessmen get what they pay for, $800 million worth of pressure on us to drink. They claim it is not aimed at consumption but only at choice of brands; yet the net effect cannot help but promote drinking rather than abstinence. The atmosphere this creates is bolstered by the attractive cocktail waitress who appeals to your machismo with the subtle implication that you are not much of a man if you don't order up; by the modeling of parents who make hospitality synonymous with offering a drink; by the portrayal of alcohol drinking on television shows out of all proportion compared to the actual rate of nonalcoholic beverage use; by our tolerance and even admiration of excessive drinking; by slogans and customs that make the nondrinker feel unsophisticated and antisocial.

Customs.   Suppose you invite me to dinner and serve carrots as a vegetable, which I politely refuse. You do not spend the rest of the evening telling me that I *must* have a carrot, that I can't fly on just one carrot, to have one for the road, be a man and have a carrot. . . . Ridiculous, or course; yet this is the way we all too often treat a guest who wishes to drink moderately or not at all. We seem afraid of being thought stingy or unhospitable or morally overrighteous, of favoring prohibition or of being against fun and enjoyment. Given that alcohol is a drug, we are a nation of pushers. The host urges "one more won't hurt you" when he has no certainty as to whether this guest might be developing a problem, or cries "bottoms up" when he has not assessed whether some in the group should not continue drinking. Rarely does "a drink" mean anything except alcohol.

A major feature of this environment is its inconsistency. Even our jokes reveal a certain uneasiness and mixed attitudes about drink and drunkenness. Drinking straight gin is considered vulgar, but the very, very dry martini is sophisticated—and practically straight gin. Adult luncheon groups that welcome a speaker who expatiates on "youth and drugs" will reject the suggestion of a speaker to talk about "middle age and martinis." We are not sure whether Joe is the life of the party or an embarrassment. We deplore the problems that alcohol causes, yet fear to lose the revenue that alcohol taxes bring in. We still have a double standard regarding women and alcohol misuse. And those who work in the alcoholism field know that heavy drinkers are not the jolly people we hear described in the popular drinking songs; we see much more of loneliness, tension, fear, anxiety, frustration, resentment.

This inconsistency, combined with divergence in use patterns, makes impractical the suggestion of those who feel that alcoholism can be prevented by simply letting children grow up learning how to drink moderately. This might make sense in a population that has consistent attitudes, does not condone excess, and attaches no great social significance to drinking. Even there it does not seem to work too well for the one group with whom we are concerned, the alcoholics. Social and recreational use may be the reason why others drink, but even in adolescence those who are headed for trouble with alcohol seem to be those who drink for the effect. Apparent contradictions in the research regarding parental models might be explained by noting that research that describes youthful drinking as an imitation of adult drinking has often been done where adult social drinking is the norm, whereas studies that ascribe youthful drinking to rebellion have usually been conducted where adult abstinence is the norm. Moreover, adults have been more permissive recently about adolescent drinking because of their concern over adolescent misuse of other drugs.

The Media.   Athletes often serve as models for youth, and for years American youth have been exposed, often during broadcasts of athletic events, to famous athletes advertising a favorite beer. Full pages of color in the slick magazines advertise hard liquor as associated with adventure, sexual attractiveness, or sophisticated entertainment. A few years ago the industry introduced drinks of 30 proof, almost four times the alcoholic content of beer, with flavors for adolescent tastes: chocolate, mocha, strawberry, banana. In addition, the so-called pop wines appeal largely to the youth market, and we know that beer has always been popular with young people. So in spite of disclaimers by the alcoholic beverage industry, there seems little doubt that this barrage of advertising is, in great part, aimed at young people, regardless of the legal age for drinking.

Quite apart from advertising, several studies of prime-time television shows *(Report on Alcohol,* Fall 1975, 22–28; Breed, 1978) reveal that the drinking of alcoholic beverages is portrayed on the screen with a frequency that is totally unrepresentative of American drinking practices. Coffee and soft drinks are both consumed far more frequently than alcohol in real life, yet the impression conveyed by television is that the exact reverse is true. Moreover, drinking alcohol is pictured as not only a constant feature of American life but as refined, as manly, or as useful in relief of stress, with no suggestion that for some it could be dangerously addictive.

An encouraging contrast is the Code of Advertising Standards adopted by the Wine Institute (1978), which could well serve as a model of responsible advertising for the entire alcoholic beverage industry. Subscribers to the code agree not to use athletes or other youth heros to advertise their products, not to imply health or problem-solving benefits, not to exploit sex, not to appeal especially to youth, and other laudable cautions.

Indirect, or Nonspecific, Prevention

The above discussion of agent, host, and environment has been largely in the area of direct, or specific, prevention. Indirect, or nonspecific, primary prevention refers to means of improving the quality of life, which could have the prevention of alcoholism as a desired by-product, even though not directly aimed at factors believed to be principal causes of alcoholism. For example, if environmental stress may be a part cause of some alcoholism, then achieving a stressless society might prevent some alcohol problems. Impossible? It might be worth exploring, rather than our concentrating exclusively on picking up the pieces afterward.

But only if stress were the only cause of alcoholism, and only if we could raise an entire generation completely free of any need to anesthetize themselves against stress, would this be a final solution. The result would be a nicer world, but the fact is that life does bring stress. As one writer puts it, "ecstasy without agony is baloney." What we really need is to help young people develop better ways of coping with stress so they will not turn to alcohol.

Adolescence is an awkward age, and adolescents are socially clumsy. It is easier to dull one's sensitivity with alcohol than to develop social graces. The result is much like the boy with ambitions to be a baseball pitcher who decides to save his pitching arm by putting it into a sling: the muscles atrophy. Drinking in the formative years atrophies the development of coping mechanisms and social skills. Psychologists know from imprinting experiments that some needs must be met at a certain developmental stage or it is too late. The same may be true of these social needs if not developed during adolescence because of reliance upon alcohol as a substitute or escape. Add the evidence that the nervous system is still in its formative stages during the teen years, and the importance of delaying the use of alcohol until maturity becomes even more clear. The big problem is to convey this to young people without putting a premium on drinking by making it adult behavior, a sign of maturity, which they will immediately try to prove by drinking. We shall return to this topic in the latter part of the chapter, which deals with means of prevention.

Secondary Prevention

Alcoholism can be prevented from developing into serious problems through intervention, whereby it is interrupted in the early stages. Although not as ideal as primary prevention, it may be more realistic in our present state of knowledge. The American Cancer Society has not conquered cancer yet, but it has saved a lot of lives by early detection and treatment. The elements in successful secondary prevention include public education, which will both alert to the dangers and make treatment more acceptable; the education of key persons such as physicians, nurses, clergy, social workers and others as to the early signs of alcoholism; and development of skills in intervention or confrontation.

Public Education

The communications media can do more than the classroom to educate the public, but all avenues must be used. The distinguished citizens who have publicly identified themselves as recovered alcoholics have done much to break down the stigma and make treatment for alcoholism no more a disgrace than treatment for appendicitis. Alcoholism is now being recognized as our nation's biggest public health problem, and myths that clouded the early signs are being dispelled. But much more needs to be done. An objective, scientific approach, rather than scare tactics in the classroom or a preachy, moralizing tone in the pulpit, needs to be combined with a nationwide effort to change the image of drinking in both entertainment and advertising. Ignorance is still widespread. We hear too often, "I was married to an alcoholic for twenty-five years and never knew it." One client was drinking a fifth of vodka a day for over a year before her husband had any idea she had a drinking problem. Many spouses relate in retrospect that they saw none of the obvious signs of developing alcoholism during the dating period.

Early Detection

Industry and business (occupational alcoholism programs) can provide a major source of secondary prevention. Workers are still motivated, the alcoholism can be caught before there is deterioration of brain or other organs, and a good policy can set up strategies for getting them into treatment.

Courts, especially *family* and *traffic courts,* are good places for early detection and intervention if judges, attorneys, and court workers are skilled in detection and alert enough not to be fooled into thinking that other problems are the cause of the drinking instead of its result. We cannot assume that all persons arrested for drunk driving are alcoholics, but the question of drinking problems should be explored. Deferred prosecution or diversion plans may put the suspect into an Alcohol Information School (AIS) or treatment clinic, rather than jail, which solves nothing and may only perpetuate the problems. One judge has the DWI offender write out a detailed essay on the twelve hours preceding his arrest, indicating not only the amount of alcohol consumed but all the circumstances that may have contributed to the consumption.

Physicians and nurses, especially public health nurses and other outreach workers, can uncover many cases of hidden alcoholism and get the patient into treatment before it has reached middle stage. Now that some knowledge of alcoholism is required in the licensing examination for physicians, we need to look at making it a requirement for psychologists, lawyers, and other professions.

Teachers and counselors in schools need to become aware of early signs. Gulping and sneaking drinks are typical symptoms of early alcoholism, and for youngsters they have a thousand special meanings. A drop in school grades, sleepiness in the classroom, irritability, and many other signs may tip off an alert teacher or counselor to look for incipient alcohol problems.

Driver education classes are a prime opportunity for alcohol education. Teenagers are highly motivated at the time of obtaining their first driver's license, and much more likely to be impressed by scientific facts about the effects of alcohol on behavior than by scare lectures on how their liver will look forty years from now. The factual approach can show that alcohol causes more problems than alcoholism, and that alcoholism is not confined to the late organic stages but includes psychological or social dependence and other aspects of interest to the adolescent.

Tertiary Prevention

Since tertiary prevention is actually treatment and rehabilitation, one might ask how this can be considered prevention, since the alcoholism has already occurred. First, it prevents further damage to the alcoholic and those affected, and prevents relapses. Next, it prevents further ill effects on the children, and the spread of harm to others not yet affected. Third, it gives a model of alcoholism as a treatable illness, thus motivating others to seek help. Lastly, it prevents the alcoholic from recruiting others to his rationalizations, and rather adds weight to the trend toward abstinence or nonabuse.

All of the above aspects of prevention need to be considered as applying not merely to the alcoholic, but also to the spouse and family. Many systems within the community promote or facilitate either continued drinking or treatment. Prevention includes, for example, educating a personnel manager to the idea that a recovered alcoholic is a good employment risk, as opposed to a hidden drinker.

Means of Prevention

To reduce or eliminate the incidence of alcoholism in a drinking society is a huge task, and nobody has a magic wand. Authoritarian answers imposed by experts, whereby the populace is to be manipulated for its own good, have little hope of success. A self-correcting system in which the people themselves work toward desirable changes should be more fruitful, but this requires knowledge and resources from both public and private agencies. No one means will be effective; it requires well-orchestrated cooperation on many sides.

Information

Factual information is basic to all prevention efforts. Myths must be dispelled, and there are probably more myths and false folklore about alcohol than about any other drugs. The information must be correct, current, objective; otherwise credibility is lost. It should not be just about alcoholism, but about alcohol and alcoholic beverages and the problems caused by alcohol to alcoholics and others.

This information needs to be disseminated both through the popular media and in the classroom. We must remove the mystery about why people drink and stress that the principal reason why most people (including alcoholics) drink is for euphoria, which makes alcohol a psychotropic drug. Since alcoholic beverages are readily available and known to the smallest child, there is not the same danger in giving information about alcohol as there is about other drugs. Hence the information can be given very early. High school is too late to start, as most have their attitudes formed before that and half our youngsters are drinking by age thirteen. The preschooler can recite or sing all the beer ads from TV and tell you what brand of whiskey his daddy drinks. The five-year-old knows that what her mommy is drinking while she irons is not Seven-Up but gin.

But mere facts can be quite ineffective. We learned this in the big drug scare of the late 1960s, when schools rushed into a program of factual information that not only failed to prevent but often added fuel to the flames. Youngsters learned how to shoot heroin into the vein, others learned about glue sniffing or other things they would never have dreamed of without this "drug education" (Bard, 1974; Brecher, 1972). We have abandoned a stress on mere facts, showing students the different colored pills and the like. After all, most heavy smokers know more about smoking than the nonsmoker. And most have tried to quit: 90 percent in one survey had tried more than once. Doctors and nurses know more about drugs than most other people, yet their rate of addiction problems are not less than for others. The horrors of delirium tremens in the vague distant future makes no impact on the teenager. Important as facts are, mere knowledge has never guaranteed behavior, any more than knowing how to do it makes me shoot par golf.

Education

Imparting facts is an integral part of alcohol education, but it lacks the educational process. Alcohol *education* is the development of appropriate habitual knowledge, principles, attitudes, and motivated behavior regarding alcohol and alcoholism. It may be formal or informal, in the classroom, through mass communications media, or in homes. It adds to factual information the elements of experience, appropriate role models, values and decision-making skills, attitudes, and the whole process by which these are internalized so as to motivate behavior. The question is whether alcohol education is using the best that we know about the education process. It is certainly more than writing one more curriculum guide which nobody uses. All fifty states have some law requiring alcohol education, often honored in a perfunctory way by having a speaker come in once a year, with little effect. Private schools have often been more progressive in this matter than the public schools, especially at the college level.

Unenforceable laws against underage drinking are not the answer, but neither are scare tactics, biased opinions, or what students perceive as just one more authoritarian figure telling them what to do. Studies that show that many adolescents lower their rate of drinking after reaching legal age suggests that at least some adolescent drinking is just rebellion. *Self-activity* of the learner is an established principle of educational psychology. Rather than telling them, let them find out and tell us. There is plenty of factual material available today. Talking *with* students is much more effective than talking *at* them. Another neglected principle is *individual differences:* Adolescents are not all the same, and adolescent alcoholism is not the same as adult alcoholism.

This latter is one reason why Alcoholics Anonymous warns its members that if they are invited to a school they should not give the same type of talk they might give in meetings. The students cannot identify with the recital of either drunken escapades or misery. Sometimes the result is, "I'm going to drink and have all those adventures, and if I get into trouble I'll join AA and then everybody will admire me."

Four possible approaches can be listed.

1. Total abstinence. This is unrealistic in a drinking society, and denies personal freedom.

2. Avoid the question, because it is controversial. This would force the schools to abandon nearly all teaching, since most subjects arouse some difference of opinion. What is conveyed is not the personal value judgment of the teacher, but a basis for choice. To exemplify how divergent and controversial views can be, note that while white parents are being permissive about alcohol and very concerned about abuse of other drugs, some Indians are telling their children to use peyote and avoid alcohol.

3. Teach pupils to drink responsibly, since alcohol use is widely accepted. This was the approach favored by the first director of NIAAA, Dr. M. Chafetz, and repudiated by his successor, Dr. E. Noble, and by the NCA. The slogan "responsible drinking" sounds good, and this approach certainly would make a lot of fifth graders happy. But there are many reasons for rejecting it. It puts a premium on drinking as proof of responsibility, and subtly implies that nondrinking is a mark of irresponsible people. It assumes that everybody drinks, which is not true because a sizable minority of Americans do not drink at all and over 70 percent do not drink more than once or twice a month. It assumes that everybody *should*

drink, confusing average with normal and giving no freedom to minorities. Worse, it assumes that everybody *can* drink, ignoring the one in ten or twelve who cannot drink without problems. It ignores the role of drinking in the etiology of alcoholism, and the fact that every alcoholic does a lot of "controlled" drinking before reaching the final stages. There is no special skill or ability to drink without danger than can be developed by practice. Even if "responsible drinking" were not a possible trap for the rest of us, it is totally inept for the group we are most concerned about: the potential alcoholics.

4. Alcohol education integrated into all subjects in a factual way that leaves pupils free but gives the basis for an informed choice. This is the ideal, but in reality requires that teachers are all not only well informed but have their own attitudes well in hand. They must be able to admit the diverse opinions of a pluralistic society, with no emotionalism and with no pretense that differences do not exist. It must not focus just on alcoholism, but on beverage alcohol and a recognition that this causes more problems than alcoholism. It can be done not only in health education classes but in literature, history, chemistry and biology, sociology, economics, psychology, anywhere. Until that ideal day when all teachers are so prepared, at least it can be done by a growing corps of teachers who have been trained to use an integrated curriculum guide that provides for alcohol education from kindergarten through senior high school, such as that developed for NIAAA by Roberts and Mooney (1976).

Alcohol-specific education is needed, not mixed in with education about other drugs. Otherwise we foster the erroneous assumption that alcohol is used in the same context as other drugs, instead of being socially acceptable. We lose sight of the fact that the kinds of decisions made about drinking are often quite different from decisions about other drugs. When lumped with other drugs, alcohol tends to be minimized and taken for granted instead of being seen as our major drug problem, and focus on populations at high risk for alcohol problems is lost.

Rather than how to drink, what is needed is to teach how to live in a drinking society, how to make responsible decisions or personal choices about use and nonuse of alcohol. Young people need to develop skill in exercising options, to know that instead of saying, "I can't," they can say, "I prefer not to" or "I'll have a coke, please." They need to see that they are being used if they pay the beer company to advertise its product on their T-shirt, instead of the beer company paying them. In other words, independent decision-making means more than being swept into the assumption behind the liquor industry's slogans such as "Know your limits"—that everyone should drink up to their limit. It means being your own person. The aim is not to make people feel guilty if they drink, but to help them not feel guilty if they don't drink.

Values Clarification

Popularized in the writings of Louis E. Raths and Sidney B. Simon in the 1960s, values clarification is as old as the role of motives in the process of choice and was thoroughly studied by the German Jesuit psychologist Johann Lindworsky around the turn of the century. This technique enjoyed a vogue in which it was mistakenly touted as some kind of magic, then debunked as a passing fad. Both reactions are mistaken. Some see it as moral relativism, teaching that any behavior is permissible as long as you clarify your purely subjective values to justify it. On the contrary, it can be used to promote objective values rather than mere feelings as the basis for choice. It is not the whole of primary prevention, but an important step. It moves beyond factual information to the process of applying such knowledge in everyday choices, to sort out the information and set priorities. Every choice involves a preference, and we need to learn to decide what is more important than what. Starting with "how alcohol touches your life" one can go on to learn how to ask, "Is it worth it?" The danger of alcoholism forty years from now is small motivation; we need to assess our values and motives for our actions right now.

Peer counselors can play a role in this as in other approaches. Young people will often be more effective with those their own age than older people are, because they are more trusted and because they know the age level.

Alternatives

A most valuable part of prevention is helping people to realize that there are alternatives to drinking, that you don't have to drink to have fun. A natural high can be a bigger thrill, and leave you with happy memories instead of a hangover. As one learns interpersonal skills, there is less need for alcohol as a social lubricant. Some cynic has suggested that we anesthetize ourselves with martinis at social gatherings because we can't stand each other. Certainly we don't need alcohol if we truly enjoy someone's companionship, and are doing something that both find pleasurable in itself.

Enjoyable activities need not be expensive. During the Depression people made their own fun, and seemed to enjoy themselves more than is indicated by the faces of those sitting around smoke-filled bars and taverns today. Conversation, like letter writing, is in danger of becoming a lost art. Dancing, sports, camping and hiking, hobbies, volunteer work in institutions, and a thousand other things can be enjoyed for their own sake and actually go better without alcohol. At least drinking should never be the sole or even primary function of a social activity, but at most an incidental accompaniment, which is optional and could be dispensed with if the occasion arises. Young people especially need to learn how to turn on to life, to cope without the crutch of alcohol, to develop a zest for living.

Enhancing Self-esteem

One of the big reasons why people find it hard to make their own choices about drinking instead of letting the crowd sway their behavior is that they lack a sense of self-worth. If they have confidence that they are somebody who deserves respect, who can live their own lives and not worry about what others think, they can say, "No thank you" with poise and self-assurance. We have to like ourselves. We have to know that we are each a unique individual, that there is nobody in the whole world quite like ourself. Children need to be taught that. Then what others do or think becomes less important. Whatever is too much for you becomes the norm, regardless of others.

Secondly, enhancing one's sense of self-esteem removes a reason for excessive drinking. Some people develop alcoholism by using alcohol to compensate for poor feelings about themselves.

Changing Public Attitudes

Lastly, a key factor in prevention is to reverse current public attitudes about drinking and drunkenness. Instead of condoning drunken behavior as comic, it should not be tolerated. Instead of looking upon drinking as a social necessity and a sign of sophistication or manliness, and pushing drinks as a sign of hospitality, we need to see these attitudes as both silly and dangerous.

But is it possible to change public attitudes? It is not easy, and Prohibition made it a lot harder. But it can be done. It has been done with regard to other things. We take air travel for granted, for instance, and forget it was not too many decades ago that people were saying that human beings were not made to fly. People once argued against the automobile because it would ruin the livery stable business. Today, nonsmoking is becoming almost a prestige symbol instead of making one a social outcast.

A school education program can scarcely be effective if the parents and the community at large are still set in the opposite opinion and customs. Parent-Teacher Associations have joined with the Jaycees in a national educational effort, and local cooperation can often be enlisted simply by inviting the parents to find out what their children are being taught about the number-one drug among youth. Those parents who say they don't want their child talking about the drinking that goes on should be informed that children do talk regardless. Parents and business can cooperate in objecting to advertising and entertainment programs that push drinking or tolerate drunken behavior as funny. Attractive role models must be provided; for example, by bringing out that many top athletes and popular girls might not drink at all. We need ads portraying the beautiful people enjoying themselves and saying, "What do we need beer for anyway?" and the group agreeing.

"You don't drink! Why not?" puts the nondrinker on the defensive. This burden should be reversed: "You drink, why? I don't need it." Business needs to show that alcohol is not necessary for success in certain jobs such as selling. We need to point up the inconsistency of looking down on an Indian custom of drinking to get drunk while we condone the bachelor party, which often has exactly the same intent. Instead of too much emphasis on drunk driving and alcoholism, we need to stress positive things, such as alternative forms of entertainment, how to handle somebody who wants to drive while impaired, how to promote good family relations. To be a good host or hostess one must learn some basic rules: a) Always offer soft drinks and/or coffee as choices; never force your guest to have to ask. b) Serve some food so that one need not drink on an empty stomach. c) Don't push drinks, or serve doubles, or rush refills. d) Serve dinner on time; don't prolong the cocktail hour. e) Don't allow an intoxicated guest to drive home; call a taxi, or take him or her home yourself. Ideally, we can look forward to the day when one can order a plain ginger ale without embarrassment or need of explanation, without having to resort to ridiculous names like a "Shirley Temple" or a "Horse's Neck," without fear that some ignoramus will spike it with vodka, and without having to pay an exorbitant price just because it is served in a bar.

One means of changing public attitudes and spreading information is through community outreach programs such as the Cottage Meeting Program developed in Salt Lake City (Boswell, 1976) and the Harmony Program developed in California. This approach has the strong endorsement of the National Council on Alcoholism. It consists of small, informal gatherings held in the homes of interested residents of a neighborhood, and conducted by a trained volunteer. The host invites the group members, who learn how to discuss alcohol problems in a knowledgeable and comfortable manner with friends and peers. The intent is to eliminate moralizing, stigma, and myths, while promoting healthy attitudes.

Primary prevention involving such massive changes in attitude will take a long time, so we must not expect instant results. The pessimists are all too quick to point to a lack of results so far. (And if "responsible drinking" was the theme, one need not be surprised.) We must keep the long range goal in sight, which should not be hard if we recall Chapter 2 on the magnitude of the problem.

Sources

Alcohol Education Materials: An Annotated Bibliography by Gail Milgram (Rutgers, 1975), and Samuel Miles' *Learning about Alcohol: A Source Book for Teachers (* (NEA, 1974) are two most useful sources. New materials are coming out rapidly, some needing careful evaluation according to the concepts in this chapter. The chapter by Joseph R. Gusfield "The Prevention of Drinking Problems" in Filstead (1976), pp. 267–291, and that by Howard T. Blane "Education and Prevention of Alcoholism" in Kissin and Begleiter (1975), vol. 4, pp. 510–578 present balanced discussions.

BEAUCHAMP, DAN E., *Beyond Alcoholism: Alcohol and Public Policy.*

BOSWELL, B. and S. WRIGHT, *The Cottage Meeting Program.*

BURCENER, V.E., *Alcohol and Highway Safety Curriculum Workshops for K-12,* U.S. Department of Transportation, Washington, D.C., 1974. (Report No. DOT HS-149.)

CALAHAN, D., "Drinking Practices and Problems: Research Perspectives in Remedial Measures," *Public Affairs Report,* 1973, 14(2): 1–6.

FINN, PETER, *Alcohol: You Can Help Your Kids Cope. A Guide for the Elementry School Teacher.* NCA pamphlet.

GLOBETTI, GERALD, "An Appraisal of Drug Education Programs" in R.J. Gibbins (ed.), *Research Advances in Alcohol and Drug Problems,* vol. 2, pp. 93–122.

MALFETTI, JAMES L., *Instructor's Manual for DWI Mini-Course for High School Driver Education Program.* American Automobile Association, Chicago, 1976.

O'GORMAN, PATRICIA A. and PETER FINN, *Teaching About Alcohol: Concepts, Methods, and Classroom Activities.*

PLAUT, THOMAS F.A., *Alcohol Problems: A Report to the Nation by the Cooperative Commission on the Study of Alcoholism,* p. 119 ff.

ROBERTS, CLAY and CAROL MOONEY *Here's Looking at You: Teacher's Manual for K-12 Alcohol Education.* Educational Service District 121, Seattle, WA 98148

WILKINSON, R. *The Prevention of Drinking Problems.*

College Students

The Whole College Catalog about Drinking: A Guide to Alcohol Abuse Prevention. HEW Publ. No. ADM-76-361., U.S. Government Printing Office, 1976.

ANDERSON, D.S. and A.F. GADALETO, *That Happy Feeling: An Innovative Model for Campus Alcohol Educational Programming.* Southern Area Alcohol Education and Training Program, Inc. 4875 Powers Ferry Rd. N.W., Atlanta, GA 30327

GONZALES, G.M. *Procedures and Resource Materials for Developing a Campus Alcohol Abuse Prevention Program: A Tested Model.* Univ. of Florida, Gainesville, FL 32611

KRAFT, D.P. "College Students and Alcohol: the 50 plus 12 project," *Alcohol Health and Research World*, Summer, 1976, pp. 10–14.

NORTH, G. *Alcohol Education for College Student Personnel.* 338 Student Services Bldg., Michigan State University, East Lansing, MI 48824

CHAPTER 12

Occupational Programs

SECONDARY PREVENTION was defined in the previous chapter as early detection and intervention, preventing progression of the illness to middle or late stages. Perhaps the best opportunity for this is through employee programs in business and industry. They are better called *occupational* alcoholism programs, because they include the armed services and government employees at all levels, from local to federal, as well as other employment situations that are neither business nor industry. The reason why secondary prevention is so successful in occupational programs is twofold: the alcoholism is nipped in the bud before severe deterioration develops, and the person is highly motivated by the desire of keeping a job. Hence there is much more to work with in the person than after brain damage or a loss of major incentives has occurred.

"We don't have alcoholics in our company; we fire them" is a fairly typical response when this topic is first broached to corporate executives. There is a double fallacy here. First, any company of any size is almost certainly employing a number of alcoholics, whose presence is kept hidden through fear of the very policy just stated which discourages them from seeking treatment. Secondly, these hidden drinkers, driven underground by the above policy, continue as troublesome, half-efficient, accident-prone employees until they are terminated, often after some tragedy.

More enlightened employers recognize that in America 6 to 8 percent of the work force at all levels is having problems with alcohol; one study gave 5.7 percent as the most conservative estimate. It may vary geographically, but recall that alcoholism rates are higher among the so-called drys who do drink, even in the "dry" areas. It is statistically most improbable that any organization of sixteen persons will not have at least one alcoholic, or that a group of one hundred will not have about six alcoholics, or a company of one thousand about sixty alcoholics. They may range from bank presidents and chief surgeons to secretaries and maintenance personnel. Probably there are as many women as men, in proportion to numbers employed. The more denial at top level management that there is a problem, the more likely it is that the problem is being kept hidden by both employee and immediate supervisor.

Costly Alternatives

Some executives see themselves as having only three choices regarding an employee with a drinking problem: termination, early retirement, or continue employing a half person. All three are costly. Termination is costly because valuable employees are lost by this policy. Their knowledge and experience are real assets to the company, and represent a big investment in training. For example, the average client in the Great Northern Railroad's alcoholism program had been twenty-two years with that railroad. Early retirement is costly for this reason, plus the fact that pension benefits must be begun earlier than budgeted. But more costly than turnover is keeping the alcoholic on the job. Aside from humanitarian considerations of either the person or the family, let us examine the cost in hard dollars.

Excessive drinking was estimated in the 1950s to cost American business and industry annually some seven billion dollars. The National Institute on Alcohol Abuse and Alcoholism (NIAAA) in 1977 put the figure at $19.64 billion. These are not wild guesses. Earlier cost-accounting studies by Dun and Bradstreet and by the Yale Center for Alcohol Studies were followed by a three-year study at Johns Hopkins University. More recently Luce and Schweitzer (1978), health economists at the University of California at Los Angeles, put the figure at $20.6 billion. The General Accounting Office (GAO) of the federal government (U.S. Comptroller General, 1970) reported on a similar study done on federal civilian employees. These figures are conservative. Many costs are not recorded, such as number of work errors. Some costs cannot be measured, such as employee morale or customer good will, and loss to the corporate image when a drunken executive lands on the front page of the local newspaper or makes unfulfilled promises during a blackout. But some we can count:

1. Lost hours of work. This can be through absenteeism, tardiness, interruptions. Alcoholic employees average more than twice the sick leave

of other employees. Time lost in arguments with fellows or supervisor is often not recorded and added to absence and tardiness.

2. Half work on the job, through diminished efficiency or time-wasting habits. Closer supervision, correction of errors, and especially slowing down the whole production line are all costly.

3. Wasted time of supervisor and discipline board.

4. Excessive sick benefits and higher insurance premiums, usually paid by the employer. Recall from Chapter 4 the long list of ailments that can be due to alcohol.

5. Costly errors from either hangover or drinking on the job. Two actual examples will illustrate. A layout man ruined $30,000 worth of materials before a large press could be shut off. The vice-president in charge of investments for a large insurance company returned from a three-martini lunch and made a foggy-minded decision that cost the company two million dollars.

6. Accidents. In addition to the worker who literally drops a wrench in the machinery, causing costly repairs and lost production time, there is a massive cost in personal injuries and damage suits. Allis Chalmers reports 56 percent of waste loss was eliminated after they put in a good company alcoholism program. The Oldsmobile plant of General Motors cut accidents by 82 percent. Most sensitive here is the transportation industry, where there was reluctance to initiate a program for fear the public might take this as an admission there were alcoholics running the train or plane, with subsequent loss of patronage. Actually, just the opposite occurred. The president of the Great Northern Railroad three decades ago had the vision and courage to put in a program, with the result that his company had the best safety record in the country for five of the next six years. In contrast, another railroad, which did not put in a program, had two freight train wrecks within one year in which the engineers had been drinking. Added to the deaths of several railroad men was damage to track and trains, plus the contents of a dozen loaded freight cars. One shudders at the hundreds of lives lost if these had been passenger trains. The commercial airlines, the Air Line Pilots Association (ALPA), and the Federal Aviation Administration have all now recognized that a happily recovered alcoholic is a much safer pilot than a hidden alcoholic who is still drinking but afraid to ask for treatment for fear of reprisals.

A simple yardstick to measure what all this probably costs an organization is to take 6 percent of their total employees, including administrators, and multiply that figure by 25 percent of the average annual salary. Thus 6 percent of 1,000 persons equals 60 probable alcoholics; 25 percent of an average salary of $12,000 equals $3,000 per person; 60 times $3,000 equals $180,000 probable loss due to excessive drinking in that organization of 1,000. In a small company of 100, the cost would be $18,000 per year. This formula applied to 93 million employed persons in the country yields just under $17 billion loss annually.

A Fourth Choice

From this it is clear that the question is not how much an occupational program would cost, but how much it would save. The 1970 GAO report (p. 10) estimates that if alcohol affects 6 percent of federal civilian employees, it costs us $410 million annually. Assuming only a 54 percent success rate, this means a saving of $221 million from an alcoholism program that might cost $15 million. On this basis a company that invested $15,000 in a program would save $221,000, for a net gain of $206,000, which is a very profitable investment. It is expensive *not* to rehabilitate alcoholic employees.

Because of early intervention, success rates in business and industry are usually higher than the 54 percent which the conservative GAO report used. Recovery in 60 to 80 percent of cases is common, some companies reporting 85 or 90 percent, and the pioneer program in one of the companies listed below reports 93 percent success using stringent criteria. A U.S. Navy cost-benefit study (Borthwick, 1977) reported 83 percent success using a two year followup, saving $23.8 million. One company spent $65,000 on a program that saved them $750,000 in sick pay alone. That this is good business policy is evidenced by naming some of the corporations that have adopted enlightened policies regarding alcoholic employees: Eastman Kodak, DuPont Chemical, Allis Chalmers, Burlington Northern R.R., McDonnell-Douglas, Standard Oil of California, Caterpillar Tractor, Kemper Insurance, Oldsmobile, American Airlines, Hughes Aircraft, Con Edison, and many members of the Bell Telephone system, starting with Illinois Bell. About three hundred programs are now in operation, so these are only a sample. The U.S. Navy has an excellent program; the other armed services and some branches of federal civilian employment are developing alcohol programs, with the postal system taking the lead here.

Two elements are essential for success: a policy and a program. A policy without a program to implement it is just a sheet of paper. A program without a firm policy to back it up will never be effective.

Policy

A 1971 statement from the prestigious investment firm of Merrill, Lynch, Pierce, Fenner and Smith describes the unwritten policy all too often still extant in many companies, and well known to the employees: The company will award sick leave, paid vacations, and promotion to any employee who can successfully conceal his alcoholism from the attention of management; when the employee can no longer conceal it, his employment will be terminated. Since this situation is assumed unless otherwise corrected, a firm policy must be promulgated widely and clearly to educate the whole company: all members at all levels. A policy of "quit drinking or we fire you" implies that the employee *can* quit, missing the compulsive nature of the illness as well as the social respectability of alcohol.

Instead of this negative approach, a positive policy states that alcoholism is a treatable illness entitling one to the same sick leave and benefits as any other illness, with no penalty or stigma attached to seeking treatment. This policy statement provides a basic frame of reference for the development of procedures and a guide for uniform administration by all concerned. It encourages the individual's voluntary use of the program, and serves as a valuable training tool for all employees and managers.

The policy must state early that there is no intrusion on the private life or personal habits of the employee. The focus is on job performance, and relates to alcohol only to the extent that drinking on or off the job affects this performance. It does not create a witch-hunter looking for drunks, but offers assistance to those whose job is imperiled in whatever way. It must make clear that the fact of seeking help will not become a part of one's personnel record, and will pose no threat to job security or promotion. In fact, the whole purpose is to save the job, and more importantly to save the person who, when sober, will be a far better candidate for promotion than when drinking. The U.S. Navy proved this by showing that 46 percent of those who accepted treatment were promoted, as opposed to only 44 percent of the comparable navy population.

Participation is voluntary, in the sense that the alcoholics make the choice. In that sense they fire themselves by refusing to take the necessary means to remedy deficient job performance. The policy must be clear that firm and consistent action will be taken on this basis. Saving the job and the person is always paramount, so the individual acts for his own good.

Cooperative Effort

Experience has shown that it is important that the policy statement be drawn up by a joint committee representing both labor and management. This is very feasible, because it is in the best interest of both parties. Even when at odds over the bargaining table on other issues, labor and management can and do cooperate well here. The union knows it is protecting the jobs and health of its members just as clearly as the organization knows it is protecting its image and fiscal viability.

Although this is a matter of good management and not for negotiation at the bargaining table, it is important that labor be involved from the outset. Otherwise the policy could be misinterpreted as something imposed upon labor from above instead of a matter of mutual interest and concern. Two examples at the national level of this cooperation are the

National Council on Alcoholism (NCA) Labor-Management Committee and the Association of Labor-Management Administrators and Consultants on Alcoholism (ALMACA). The former represents the volunteer sector but includes many professionals. The latter is a professional society of those who work full time in the occupational alcoholism field, with associate membership for those who work part time and for other interested individuals.

Against this prestigious background it is clear that a new joint committee in any company need not start from scratch in writing a policy, but can draw on the accumulated experience and readily available materials of these and other organizations. They will still be free to adapt the policy statement to the particular needs of their organization and their community. Perhaps the most useful starting point can be the "Joint Union-Management Statement of Policy" on page five of the NCA (1976) booklet *A Joint Union-Management Approach to Alcohol Recovery Programs*. (This publication also contains a practical guide for developing the program.) In line with the policy positions already enunciated here, the statement includes the following among its thirteen principles:

(2) Alcoholism is defined as a disease in which a person's consumption of any alcoholic beverage definitely and repeatedly interferes with that individual's health and/or job performance.

(3) Persons who suspect that they may have an alcoholism problem, even in its early stages, are encouraged to seek diagnosis and to follow through with the treatment that may be prescribed by qualified professionals, in order to arrest the disease as early as possible.

(8) Neither supervisors nor union representatives have the medical qualifications to diagnose alcoholism as a disease. Therefore, referral for diagnosis and treatment will be based on job performance, within the terms, conditions and application of the union-management agreement.

Top-Level Endorsement. It is most important that this policy statement, although the work of a joint labor-management committee, be promulgated as having the endorsement of management at the highest level. Otherwise there will always be doubt about whether middle management will back up a supervisor who relies on it. It must apply to all levels, so that a vice-president is given the same alternatives as anyone else. It is true that an industrial nurse or personnel manager who is trained in alcoholism can do a lot of good in a company that does not have a policy, but this is not a good substitute for a full program.

Women. A proper policy does not single out women alcoholics, but neither does it make any special concessions to them. Both errors have been made in the past, and constitute unjust discrimination. The old double standard is too often still operative, even when the policy is clearly based on job performance. A woman may make a mistake on her job and is rated "not qualified" where a man making the same mistake simply "needs more training." Women may be more prone to polydrug misuse, but this in turn is usually the result of a patronizing attitude by the physician who looks on her complaints as psychosomatic, or by a psychologizing approach that more often analyzes "female" reasons for drinking instead of facing the nature of addiction in itself. Thus a forty-four-year-old office worker dressing for work one day realized she didn't remember where she worked; instead of recognizing blackout or alcoholic stupor, a therapist told her that she hated her job so much she had blocked it out of her mind. Male protectiveness here can only harm the woman by avoiding the issue of alcoholism. On the other hand, sex discrimination has put added pressure on the woman who tries to climb the corporate ladder. She may compete at the bar as she has to elsewhere, drink for drink with the men, but her smaller size and hormonal differences put her at a distinct disadvantage in this dangerous competition.

Program

> The counselor in business and industry is asking management to let him identify a disease that has not really been defined, to treat a victim who really does not want to be treated, and to educate a population that really does not want to believe that the disease exists. (Dorris and Lindley, 1968, p. 56)

The situation may have improved somewhat in the decade or so since the above was written, but it points out that implementation of even the best-written policy drafted by the best joint committee is fraught with difficulties. Developing a program takes time and expertise. After the policy is written and means of promulgation agreed upon, supervisors must be trained, treatment facilities selected, procedures arranged whereby the employee is referred to treatment through the medical department or personnel office, means of payment for treatment worked out, and record-keeping routines established as a basis for follow-up and evaluation. Many states now require that all group health insurance policies include coverage for alcoholism. Often it can be shown that it is cheaper to treat the alcoholism than the medical complications or injuries resulting from accidents. In all this the joint committee can call on occupational alcoholism consultants, for example those now available through local NCA affiliates in most parts of the country.

Job Performance is the Criterion

As stated in the policy, decline in job performance is the basis for any action taken, and restoration of job performance to proper level is the measure of success. This is crucial, because it takes supervisors out of the role of diagnosing or counseling, and keeps them in their proper role. Besides expecting a function for which they are neither trained nor paid, any other approach invites untold problems. It can lead to arguments: "You were drunker at the staff party than I was." It introduces subjective and emotional factors into arbitration which do not fit with contractual agreements and union-management understandings. Unsatisfactory work performance is the concern of management; protection of the employee's job and health is the concern of labor. Both have the same result here: co-ercive action if alcohol interferes with job performance of the employee or others. This latter is relevant because the alcoholic is more likely to get into fights or disturb others at their work. This criterion also applies to drinking behavior off the job that either cuts efficiency or reflects on the company. The alcoholic often carries his problem to the job in the form of hangovers, headaches, nervousness, money worries, and wage garnish-ments—all of which waste time and cut down productivity. Union's role and right is to be present during a supervisor-employee interview, to pro-tect the employee from unjust action, and to assure that coercive action is clearly based on the work record of the employee.

Supervisors can thus be trained in a two-hour session to carry out the policy, since they do not need to be experts in alcoholism. Their task has four functions: to observe, to document, to confront, and to refer. Their observations can be sharpened by alertness to on-the-job signs of alcohol-ism, especially early signs not usually recognized by those who think in terms of a falling-down drunk, or even bleary eyes and shaky hands. They must learn to document behavior precisely, so that confrontation is not a fiasco of assertions and denials. The exact dates of absences and tardiness, the excuses given for sick leave (twenty-three tooth extractions or three grandmother's funerals are suspect), the exact time and place of fights and the name of the other party should all be recorded. Notes on the confront-ing interview should document the fact that the shop steward or other union representative was present.

The supervisor can look for and document many things not usually thought of as symptomatic of alcoholism. Absenteeism, especially on Monday mornings, is a late sign; the alcoholic knows enough to punch in bright and early and to avoid having a record of Monday morning delin-quency on file, at least until the illness has progressed to the point where this gets very difficult. Personality change may be more important than physical signs at first: irritability, especially in one previous pleasant, moodiness, procrastination, sloppy dress, undependability, blaming oth-ers when things have been put off or done poorly, avoiding others. To be noted is improvement in personality after lunch or a break where one might sneak a drink from thermos jug or in the washroom; this shows de-pendence on alcohol to function normally. There may be the usual signs of hangover: red or bleary eyes, hand tremors, flushed face, mistakes or errors of judgment, intolerance of fellow workers. Instead of a steady work pace, the alcoholic may work furiously for a while but spasmodically slow down in both quantity and quality of work. Excessive use of breath purifiers can be obvious, but so is always needing a loan until payday, and even having one's wages garnished. Being indignant at any mention of one's drinking is significant, as are drinking at lunch, or arriving at work with liquor on the breath. Accident proneness can be due to either drinking or hangover.

Confrontation is aimed at referral, not counseling or even diagnosis. After a warning session, likewise documented, the second interview puts it squarely to the employee: either improve job performance or be terminated. It is strongly urged that the employee use the help provided by the company program, whether it be an employee assistance counselor, the medical department, or whatever. They are to do the diagnosis, not the supervisor. However, without violating confidentiality he can confer with the counselor and discuss the reasons for the referral. Since alcoholics are usually great con artists and the supervisor is naive in this area, any other approach can eventuate in the alcoholic convincing the supervisor that it is the supervisor who has the problem. Or the supervisor feels sorry for the employee and agrees to help out or cover up in ways that only prolong the alcoholism or defer real help. Promises, idle threats, resolutions and bargaining are most ineffectual here. The supervisor should never ask why; stick to facts, not reasons. Moralizing and debating with the employee are to be avoided.

Forced Treatment Works.   But doesn't the alcoholic have to hit bottom and want help before it is effective? This myth has been thoroughly exploded by occupational programs. Actually, it has long been known that most alcoholics come into treatment under some duress: threat of job loss, divorce, ruined health, or the like. Nobody seeks help if there is no problem. A director of one large and successful treatment facility in the Midwest stated that every patient came in angry at being forced into treatment, but left grateful that somebody cared enough to act for his own good. Research is not unanimous on the point, but most evidence suggests *higher* rates of recovery in forced treatment. This, of course, may be at least partially due to the earlier arrest of the illness. The real danger is that not only the spouse but also fellow workers and the immediate supervisor will deny the problem or cover up for the alcoholic, shielding from higher management in a misguided form of help, which may actually be lethal. Whether it is called tough love or constructive coercion, the experience of many programs confirms the fact that forcing an alcoholic into treatment as an alternative to job termination is saving jobs and lives.

Part of the policy, clearly promulgated and then rigidly adhered to, should be a statement on relapse. The Great Northern (now Burlington Northern) policy explicitly provides for rehiring once only, with no exceptions. Experience has shown that deviations from such a policy backfire and create worse problems. With this policy, they report 88 percent success in their overall program with over 2,000 cases.

Confidentiality

A most important feature for the credibility of any program is that the employee must know that seeking help will not hurt a future career. In some programs the office and records are in the home of the alcoholism counselor, and in any case should never be part of the personnel file. This is not the same as the anonymity tradition of AA, but there are some common features. The fact that the supervisor referred the employee to a counselor is a matter of company record, as is any subsequent job improvement or deterioration. But the diagnosis or nature of the treatment is strictly between the counselor and the employee, and even higher management has no right to that information. Exception could be for proven imminent and serious danger to a third party, or to the employee himself or herself.

The above, of course, will vary with conditions, and is sometimes governed by law. It is a particularly difficult problem in the armed services, but every effort should be made to protect the individual seeking treatment. The model Uniform Act provides for secrecy of records.

The Family

We have stressed that it is almost pointless to treat alcoholism and ignore the family environment in which the recovered alcoholic must live. Since the trend is toward family involvement in all treatment, occupational programs should be no exception. The counselor, of course, must have the employee's permission to contact the spouse. This is usually granted once a good relationship has been established and the client is assured that cooperation is to his or her benefit. In some programs the alcoholism counselor and spouse form an AA and Al-Alon team, which has proven very effective. Family group sessions can add much to a program. Special provision for child care may be necessary.

Alcoholic Spouse.   The program ideally should provide for the alcoholic spouse of a nonalcoholic employee. This is related to work performance. If the alcoholic calls frequently during business hours, or is just on the employee's mind as a source of worry, this cuts down efficiency. The employee is afraid or unable to take a trip for either vacation or company business, for fear the alcoholic will burn down the house or have an accident. One is ashamed to bring the alcoholic spouse to the company picnic or office party. If there are children, the anxiety is increased. Al-Anon and Alateen (Chapter 16) can be a major asset to any alcoholism rehabilitation program, without adding to the budget.

Follow-up

It is not sufficient to refer the alcoholic employee to the proper source of help. The counselor must keep in contact for at least two years, being careful not to give the impression of spying or mistrusting. The contact should be friendly, encouraging, with the offer of help on any of the myriad problems that can linger after recovery. Legal, medical, family and financial problems may plague the recovered alcoholic for some time. Loan sharks, child support or visiting privilege wrangles, social pressures to drink, and the restoration of reversed marital roles described in the last section of Chapter 8 can all demand continued support and counsel. Without being overprotective, the supervisor must do everything to insure that fellow employees welcome the recovered alcoholic back with warmth and encouragement, and counteract any suggestion from the group that recovery means that the alcoholic can drink again.

Renewal.   An ongoing training program is needed to bring new supervisors in line with the policy and sharpen the referral skills of all. Promulgation to new employees, and an occasional reminder for the entire organization, will keep both supervisors and union representatives aware, so that the program does not die through neglect. Education should always be a function of the program.

A much-neglected need is counseling for the supervisors themselves. Like the spouse, the supervisor, at any level, may become emotionally involved in the problem, get caught up in the alcoholic's denial system, develop denial that the supervisor himself or herself may indeed be part of the problem, experience guilt or anxiety, and be inept at handling the situation when the alcoholic returns to work from treatment. Even when well trained in confrontation and referral, the supervisor may need individual counseling and help with these and other problems. Presumably the trained alcoholism counselor to whom the employee is referred can also help the supervisor.

Evaluation.   Although names must be kept strictly confidential, records must be kept so that number of cases and rates of success can be communicated to higher management and indeed to the whole organization. This means establishing definitions and criteria in keeping with the policy statement, and avoiding bias in reporting results.

Referral Procedure

If, upon confrontation, employees agree to seek help, to whom does the supervisor refer them? It should be someone within the company who is trained to make a diagnosis. It must not be assumed that the average physician, nurse, social worker, or counselor has specific knowledge and skills regarding alcohol and other drug addiction. It must be someone who knows not only early signs and patterns of progression, but also the tricks of denial and manipulation by which an alcoholic can usually outmaneuver the unwary professional. Regardless of profession or title, the person must be prepared to recognize that perhaps 90 percent of the problems referred are caused by alcohol. And above all, one must not fall for the rationalization that the problems caused the drinking, when really the drinking caused the problems.

The location and title of this person will depend on the size of the organization and other circumstances. It would be impractical for a small company to establish its own alcoholism program. A clear alcoholism policy will provide a channel to resources available in the community, once the problem has been identified. A large organization could profitably have its own full alcoholism program staffed by one or more alcohol specialists, with AA and Al-Anon meetings on location. But even in this case, counselors must accept their limitations and possess a thorough knowledge of other treatment facilities for appropriate referral. In neither case does the supervisor refer to a person or office entitled "alcoholism," because this presumes a diagnosis not yet made. Even those who reject a "broad brush" approach agree on this.

Broad brush is a term used to describe programs that do not carry the word *alcoholism* in their title, but go by such names as employee assistance, occupational health services, or guidance and counseling. ("Troubled employee" and other negative terms are unacceptable. "Chemical dependency" and "substance abuse" are criticized by some because they obscure the primacy of alcohol as a problem.) Strong authorities and research evidence support both sides of the broad brush controversy; for example, whether a program should be called employee assistance or alcoholism. Recall the pros and cons of dropping the term *alcoholic* listed toward the end of Chapter 1. The opponents argue that the broad brush approach only feeds denial, perpetuates the stigma, and weakens the whole preventive and educational effort (Roman, 1979). The proponents claim that many people will accept the more neutral title who would refuse to walk through a door with *alcoholism* on it. They argue that as long as the counselor is skillful in diagnosing alcoholism once the client is inside, it will catch more alcoholics than a program whose title deters them. A strong consideration is polydrug abuse, since there are really very few "pure" alcoholics anyhow. As indicated above, the two positions may not be as far apart as either side would make it appear; a forthright policy on alcoholism still calls for procedures that permit the supervisor to refer to a counselor without the supervisor making the diagnosis.

Sources

Much of the material quoted in this chapter is derived from a long acquaintance with the programs of private industry for helping their alcoholic employees. Some, if not most, of the companies mentioned in the text are willing to share with genuinely interested persons the excellent materials they have developed. Much useful material is also in pamphlet form, published by organizations such as the National Council on Alcoholism, the National Institute on Alcohol Abuse and Alcoholism, the Christopher Smithers Foundation, Association of Labor-Management Administrators and Consultants on Alcoholism (ALMACA), and insurance companies such as Kemper and Metropolitan Life. In addition, The National Council on Alcoholism publishes *Labor-Management Alcoholism Journal* and ALMACA publishes *The ALMACAN*. This is an aspect of alcoholism on which there are also excellent 16 mm. films such as: *Alcoholism: The Bottom Line*; *The Dryden File*; *Weber's Choice*; *One Company's Answer*; *We Don't Want to Lose You*; *Alcoholism: Industry's Costly Hangover*; *A Firm Hand*; *Business with a Twist*; and *Need for Decision*.

There is less bibliography in book form and in technical journals. The following books are recent and deal with occupational programs rather than the program of a specific company. They also contain good bibliographies.

BRISOLARA, ASHTON, *The Alcoholic Employee*.

SCHRAMM, CARL J., *Alcoholism and Its Treatment in Industry*.

SORENSON, DARRELL, *Employee Assistance Program, The Art of Preserving Human Resources*.

TRICE, HARRISON and PAUL ROMAN, *Spirits and Demons at Work: Alcohol and Other Drugs on the Job*.

WILLIAMS, RICHARD L. and GENE H. MOFFAT (eds.), *Occupational Alcoholism Programs*.

Additional Sources

BERRY, RALPH E. and JAMES P. BOLAND, *The Economic Cost of Alcohol Abuse*.

CODORKOFF, B., H. KRYSTAL, J. NUNN and R. WITTENBERG, "Employment Characteristics of Hospitalized Alcoholics," *Quarterly Journal of Studies on Alcohol*, 1961, 22:106–110.

HEYMAN, MARGARET, "Employer-sponsored Programs for Problem Drinkers," *Social Casework*, 1971, 52:547–552.

LONG, J.R., I. E. HEWITT and H. T. BLANE, "Alcohol Abuse in the Armed Services: A Review. I. Policies and Programs," *Military Medicine*, 1976, 141:844–850;

and "Alcohol Abuse in the Armed Services: A Review. II. Problem Areas and Recommendations," *Military Medicine*, 1977, 142:116–128.

MOREE, GERALD B. and ROBERT J. JERNIGAN, *Treat Alcoholic Workers and Stop the Dollar Drain*. CompCare pamphlet.

NATIONAL COUNCIL ON ALCOHOLISM, *A Joint Labor-Management Approach to Alcoholism Recovery Programs*. NCA pamphlet.

CHRISTOPHER D. SMITHERS FOUNDATION, three booklets: *The Key Role of Labor in Employee Alcoholism Programs*; *A Company Program on Alcoholism*; *Alcoholism in Industry*.

STANDARD OIL COMPANY OF CALIFORNIA, *Special Health Services and Troubled Employee: A Supervisor's Guide*. Booklet.

UNITED STATES GENERAL ACCOUNTING OFFICE, *Comptroller General's Report to Special Subcommittee on Alcoholism and Narcotics, Committee on Labor and Public Welfare, United States Senate: Substanial Cost Savings from Establishment of Alcoholism Programs for Federal Civilian Employees*, U.S. Government Printing Office, Washington, D.C., 1970.

WRICH, JAMES T., *The Employee Assistance Program*. Hazelden booklet.

CHAPTER 13

The Art of Referral

How do we get alcoholics into treatment? Perhaps the best answer is, "Any way we can." Individuals and situations differ. Referral is more than merely giving someone a name and phone number. All the skill and tact one can muster might be necessary to get the client to accept help, and a thorough knowledge of available facilities is essential to making an appropriate referral.

In social welfare agencies, alcoholics are said to be the most referred and the least helped of all clients. This is true if they are shunted from one agency to another, instead of entering a system that tailors an integrated continuum of care for each individual. Too often they are lost in transition from one stage of treatment to the next. A good referral includes follow-up from detoxification through intensive treatment to rehabilitation and return to full life in the community. This ideal is sometimes thwarted by bureaucratic structures that restrict functions and make difficult or impossible the continuity which is so necessary; if so, we must all work to change the system. Continuum of care also means that it is rarely a matter of choosing one means to the exclusion of all others, but rather a sequence or combination of several.

Timing is vital in the referral process. Obviously, it is useless to discuss anything with a person who is intoxicated. Later, when alcoholics are sick, sad, and sorry is often the best time to refer; don't wait until they are neither sad nor sorry, as they will feel little need for treatment. And, we must see them when they need help, not at our convenience. "Next Tuesday at two o'clock" often means "never" to a person in crisis.

Initial Evaluation

Regardless of how the person makes the contact, the skilled alcoholism worker is alert not to presume that the client is an alcoholic. The spouse or clergyman may say so, but this does not make it true. Overenthusiasm may cause some to see every DWI offender or drunken adolescent as alcoholic; this only destroys the credibility of alcoholism workers in the eyes of judges and others. Snap diagnoses, sometimes over the telephone without having ever seen the client, often based on hearsay evidence or solely on amount of alcohol consumed, discredit the whole alcoholism profession.

We have already pointed out that hanging the label *alcoholic* on a client may only get defenses up if he or she is in a denial phase. Rather, we just explore together whether excessive drinking is causing any problems in major life areas, or whether there is any basis to the complaints of spouse or employer. Better that label comes later, from the clients themselves. A major reason for avoiding the word *alcoholic* at this stage is the stereotype of the skid-road bum, or at least the vision of late-stage alcoholism; we *want* to contact alcoholics while they are still "not that bad."

Sometimes inquirers will try to hide their own problem by beginning with "I have this friend . . ." while feeling out the counselor to test acceptance. Or she may say, "My husband says I drink too much" when actually it is she who is worried about her drinking. And to lie about one's drinking is a classic symptom of alcoholism; the counselor can usually double or quadruple the amount. But it must not be assumed that the person is lying; one may be unaware of how much was consumed in a blackout.

A drinking alcoholic is not always rational. He or she may sound very logical and convincing. Often the spouse or family have become enmeshed in the alcoholic's rationalizations. If the counselor falls into the same trap of accepting the twisted explanations and distorted views of a toxic mind, little help will result. The counselor who agrees that the client wouldn't drink excessively if only he or she could find the right job, or if only a spouse would be more responsive sexually, has been conned.

We must relate the drinking to the life history. For example, how likely is it that a string of bad marriages, lost jobs, accidents, and poor health is anything but the result of the drinking? Those who have never been fired because of drinking should be asked how often they quit first to prevent being fired. Alcoholics may be much more willing to talk about their sex life, and must be made to stick to the drinking history. Asked if they have ever quit drinking, they must be shown that this is a classic symptom, not proof of control. The same must be said for good tolerance, or ability to function better after a drink or two. Changing jobs, working below one's level of competence or education, loss of friends and family disruption must all be related in the client's eyes to the drinking, contrary to the fine rationalizations the client may present.

Drinking problems in one's ancestry, heavy smoking and coffee consumption, breath purifiers, excessive makeup on the woman, bruises, puffiness, slight tremors or nervousness, clamminess or perspiring are all telltale signs. Review the patterns in Chapter 6. Significant is the giving of reasons why one drinks, which the social drinker does not have to do. Relief from worry, depression, low self-esteem or tension, and any "use" of alcohol as opposed to merely enjoying it are symptomatic of alcoholism. Blaming the wife's nagging or the unreasonable boss usually betrays a drinking problem rather than explaining it away. Every clue must be brought to bear in order to unmask the denial and rationalization. Is it really true that the neighbors don't know? the children? They probably know far more than the alcoholic dreams. There should be no argument; just description based on what we know of the symptoms and patterns.

Selection of Treatment Approach

Once a diagnosis of alcoholism is made, a decision must be reached on where to go for help. A smorgasbord of choices only confuses the client; decide on the treatment modality and offer a choice of facilities within that category. A rule of thumb is: The sicker the client, the fewer the choices. If the exploratory evaluation has been well done, the authority of the counselor should emerge. This expertise has the following facets.

Knowledge of Facilities.   Here specific and current information is essential, not guesswork. To keep a list up to date requires constant effort. One must know admitting procedures of hospitals, extent of group insurance coverage, policies of welfare agencies and major employers, local meeting times and places of AA and Al-Anon. One must know physicians and clergymen whose attitudes and knowledge about alcoholism can be relied upon, including psychiatrists and clinical psychologists who will help instead of complicate matters if called. Acceptability to the client may depend not only on cost but on tone or climate of a treatment center, or the personality of the therapist. Not everyone is suited to every personality. Whether a bed is available must be checked, as well as the ability of the client to meet the financial arrangements at admission. Knowledge should include not only alcoholism facilities but other community resources: public assistance caseworkers, child care, food stamps, Homemakers, medical coupons, social security benefits, skid-road centers, Medicaid and Medicare, senior citizens groups, and all kinds of helping agencies.

Skill in Selection.   Equipped with this information, the counselor must still exercise judgment in picking a particular facility for this individual. Contrary to some mythology, a trip to the county detoxification ward will *not* scare the upper-class patient into doing something about his or her problem, but will probably scare them out of any other kind of treatment if they conclude that this is typical of all treatment facilities. Besides, it reinforces their rationalization that they are not "that bad" when they see the late-stage derelicts being treated. Conversely, hospitals may be threatening and "middle class" to some indigents. A coed facility may terrify a timid female patient. Choosing the right group and finding a suitable sponsor is paramount for a favorable introduction to AA.

Stage of progression is a major factor. A hospital may be the only choice if the patient is extremely ill. Late-middle stage alcoholics need a physical examination and structured residential treatment with good follow-up. Early and early-middle stage clients are often best treated in outpatient centers, with a strong educational component to help them understand the nature of their illness, and intensive AA participation. Within these categories, the client may be offered a choice, but ordinarily should not be asked to choose between hospital and outpatient treatment, for instance. Few alcoholics need medical detoxification, but a physical examination is always wise to rule out medical complications. Psychotherapy is usually best postponed until there has been enough sobriety to see if it is necessary, and to allow the brain to reach a point where it can be effective. If there is a spouse or family, Al-Anon and Alateen are very important.

Psychiatric assessment may be helpful in selection of treatment modality. The aggressive and stubborn patient usually has a good prognosis, as does the slightly neurotic. More severe mental disorder and sociopathy indicate a poorer prognosis. Adolescents are typically unstable, confused, egocentric; of greater diagnostic importance is what they were like before the onset of drinking. But in any case we cannot assume all alcoholics will respond equally well to the same approach. In addition to form of treatment and the psychological characteristics of the patient, the social components of the treatment setting may also be important. Extroverts do better in AA than introverts, while psychotics and borderline psychotics don't do well there. The socially competent do better than those less adept. Other factors in suggesting a type of treatment are level of intelligence, family and job stability, active religious participation, and degree of emotional control.

It is a mistake for any one treatment center to attempt to handle all types of patients, either through a single approach or by trying to give a little of everything, for the simple reason that both client population and residential tone must be matched with the individual client. Unfortunately we have not yet developed the matching process with scientific precision, but experience and good judgment along with a knowledge of the characteristics and client populations of each local facility can result in a fair degree of accurate matching. Jacobson (1976a) and others mentioned in the Sources can be helpful.

A common mistake is to recommend outpatient treatment in a futile effort to save the client's job when intensive residential treatment is needed. This sets up the client for failure, and the job is lost anyhow. Since most alcoholics are short on self-confidence, they need maximum help and assurance of a successful outcome. It is better to overtreat than to undertreat.

Objectivity.   The worst mistake is to assume that all alcoholics are alike, and that all will respond equally well to the same rehabilitative effort. Membership of the helping person in a particular profession may be a hindrance here, creating a tunnel vision unless specialized training in alcoholism has broadened one's horizons to the panoply of approaches other than one's own. Similarly, recovered alcoholics have a very understandable loyalty to the particular means that saved their life, but this may blind them to the fact that what worked for them may be totally inappropriate for somebody else. This is true regardless of how they got sober; one hears equally enthusiastic loyalty to Antabuse, to AA, to aversion conditioning, or to any one of many fine treatment centers throughout the country. It is the mark of the real professional to rise above personal bias and choose what is best for the client. Inability to do so disqualifies one from working in the field, according to all national norms and codes.

This is not only a matter of professional integrity; it may be crucial in saving a life. More than one alcoholic has turned suicidal after being told that AA, for instance, is the only way to sobriety; when AA fails to appeal they decide they are hopeless and take their own life. Some may need to buy time through Antabuse or aversion conditioning in order to achieve enough sobriety to profit from a program such as AA. Here the choice is not to the exclusion of one means or the other, but may involve several. Others may need to find out for themselves that they cannot do it alone, and need some physical leverage such as Antabuse, or some group support like AA. The counselor should always leave open the possibility of alternative treatments, although the interviewer should focus on the most appropriate at this time.

Motivation For Treatment

It is now recognized that to say the client is not motivated is an escape on the part of the counselor. It is our job to motivate them. In AA there is much talk now of "early bottom" or "high bottom" or even "forced bottom." Since we know that forced treatment works, once we are sure of the diagnosis we do not passively sit by and let them hit bottom. Referral at this point becomes motivational counseling. Great as the contribution Carl Rogers has made to counseling neurotics with his client-centered and nondirective approaches, with an alcoholic we usually have to be quite directive. A crisis never cures anyone, but usually a crisis is the only thing that will bring someone to seek treatment. A crisis can be forced. The effective motive will differ for each one, as a divorce (not an idle threat), loss of job, jail, or loss of health may move one client while another may say he wants to die anyway. But something can do it, if we can only find the key. Timid, halfway measures are ineffective.

Some counselors are too quick to reassure, to relieve anxiety. At this point a little fear can be useful. To say "Don't worry" may feed denial and make the client feel good, but it doesn't save a person's life. Likewise, one must avoid being caught in the client's web of excuses. If they have been told that drinking is not their problem, that they are oral-dependent, fixated-Oedipal, latent homosexual, they may just use that as an excuse for excessive drinking. And if it is the spouse who is the client, their anxiety and guilt should be utilized to get them some help whether the alcoholic seeks help or not.

Someone else may have to make the decision. Just as some patients are not able to decide if surgery is needed, an alcoholic is usually far too sick to make a major decision regarding a terminal illness or choose between a lot of alternatives. Of course, we have to motivate the person to cooperate, and eliminate the attitude of "What are *you* going to do about my drinking problem?" The cancer patient has to agree to submit to surgery, and the alcoholic should not be relieved of all responsibility but be expected to cooperate in his treatment. They must be motivated on the basis of their own welfare, not do it just for someone else's sake. This can backfire: "I'll get drunk and show you."

Intervention

Very often the most effective way to motivate a person to go into treatment is by a group confrontation. Of course, diagnosis must be certain, or tragic harm can be done to family relations. This must be carefully planned, under the guidance of a trained alcoholism worker. For example, every member of the family over age five should come to the counselor's office, where the process is explained. As in an employer-employee interview, documentation is important so that there are specific facts and not vague general allegations. It is useful to have each family member write out and read a list of times and events, which makes the encounter less emotional and more factual. Since they know about it anyhow, small children can have a powerful part to play, as when daddy's girl says, "Why do you drink that stuff when it makes you talk so funny or hurt mommy?" For whatever chivalrous reasons, a son may find it harder to join the confrontation of his alcoholic mother, and husbands are usually more reluctant to confront alcoholic wives. Significant others besides family members may be able to make a useful contribution. The employer or a competent professional (physician, clergyman, friend) may add authority to the group.

The alcoholic will try to play the confronters off against one another. Each must agree to maintain a united front; no one party can feel sorry for the alcoholic and spoil the unanimity. The counselor should warn them in the briefing session what to expect: The alcoholic will cry, accuse them of picking on him or her, of being unfair, of exaggerating, etc. But they must promise not to settle for anything less than agreement to enter treatment. Sometimes there is refusal to enter treatment but a strong promise to join AA. Confronters can agree only under the firm condition that if the alcoholic has a single drink he or she will enter treatment immediately. It must be explained that their fear of losing the alcoholic's love is unfounded; they will earn undying gratitude. There may be fear of failure, or that the confronters will weaken and lose their nerve. Even if the person threatens to leave home, he should be told that it is better to do so sober and be able to earn a living, so he had better go to treatment first. Mostly, the family must be warned not to be taken in by promises without agreement to a specific course of action, or to allow the discussion to be diverted to other problems. They must not bluff, bargain, or debate. The tone must not be anger or punishment, but of positive concern and hope. In the planning session the group should face the fact that this will be an emotional drain; the counselor would be wise to schedule a debriefing session for after the confrontation. There they must agree to forget the past, and hope for the future regardless of previous disappointments.

Although we have used this method successfully for decades, it has been most usefully described in recent writings and films of the Johnson Institute of Minneapolis. Their research is reinforced by the even stronger conclusion of Rosenberg (1976) and others that results with coerced patients can be superior to results with voluntary patients.

Confrontation can come from unexpected sources. There is a move across the country, as exampled in San Mateo, Racine, Anchorage and other cities, to train bartenders in the art of counseling alcoholic customers into treatment, with some success reported. A powerful ploy is to videotape alcoholics, with their permission, upon admission into the detoxification center and then play it back to them twenty-four to thirty-six hours later; denial is largely eliminated in the ensuing confrontation (Thomas, 1978). A similar use of the videotape or movie camera is made in arrests for drunk driving, when the suspect appears later with her hair nicely done, or the man clean-shaven, and is confronted by the contrasting behavior and appearance at the time of arrest, always with a view to forcing treatment for the alcoholism rather than mere conviction and fine for the traffic violation.

The Drinking Test for Alcoholism

Most alcoholics can be reached through an explanation of the symptom progression charts, but a few whose denial prevents them from seeing that they have the symptoms of a disease can sometimes be reached by a test proposed by Marty Mann and others, whereby they find out for themselves. This test is only for these denying alcoholics, and after all other attempts have failed. After explaining that there is the same alcohol in a bottle of beer, a glass of wine, and an ounce of hard liquor (not a "drink" or cocktail containing more), give the client a strict quota of two of these drinks per day, every day, for six months.

If they can do this and never exceed two, they are probably not alcoholic. But they must be absolutely honest, making no exceptions and never transferring one's day's ration over to the next day. It is not valid as a test if someone else doles it out, or makes sure they stop, or if they have to take means such as leaving a party in order to keep within the quota. They must agree to come back if they exceed two even one time, for whatever reason or in whatever way. It may appear to be sending an alcoholic out to do more drinking, but for these cases it may be better than letting the client leave without any commitment.

Process of Referral

Instead of just giving someone a name and phone number, referral requires considerable attention to detail. Explicit instructions on how to get there may still not be enough, especially if shaky motivation fosters escape. In the light of good client-counselor rapport, actual transportation to the treatment facility can be considered an integral function of the counseling process rather than above and beyond one's duty. It is a more efficient use of the agency's time than losing the client after spending an hour or more motivating for treatment. At least the treatment center should be alerted to expect the client and agree to confirm arrival.

The client must be helped to know what to expect, as the fear of the unknown terrifies. Prior information on some detail about the personality or appearance of the therapist (for example, obesity or a beard) can engender a sense of confidence and prevent a negative impression. While generating a positive attitude, the counselor can moderate excessive expectations by noting limitations of a treatment facility and warning that progress will not be instantaneous. Clients must be encouraged to realize that there is not so much a fear of *facing* reality without alcohol as it is inability to *imagine* reality without it, finding it hard to believe that they can function without a drink.

The counselor should avoid giving the impression that referral is a means of getting rid of the patient, much less a matter of last resort. Referral should be made while the relationship is good, not when it is going sour. The door should always be open for a return visit, and interest shown in the client's long-range recovery. If there is to be a next appointment, make the day, date, and time clear and explicit. In either case a good rule is always have the client walk out of the office with a card or pamphlet that has the counselor's name and phone number; it may be the bridge to sobriety when the client finds it in his pocket after a lost weekend, or at least some insurance against taking a drink whem tempted. And to protect against the accusation of violating confidentiality, the counselor must get a signed release if records are to be forwarded to the new facility.

Lastly, referral is a two-way street. Too often alcoholism workers complain about lack of referral from other professionals, but forget that they try to play God themselves and fail to refer clients to nonalcoholism agencies for problems that are beyond their scope.

Evaluation of Treatments

The referring counselor is not in a position to do evaluation research on the comparative effectiveness of various treatment facilities, nor is this the place for an elaborate treatise on research methodology. But a few cautions may assist the counselor or inquirer in judging reports of claimed success.

There are four factors not quantifiable: First, each individual being unique, and alcoholism being so complex and variable with individuals, one can never be dogmatic about the effectiveness of any treatment for any individual. Secondly, what industrial psychologists call the Hawthorne effect means that a certain number of people are going to get well no matter what is done for them, just from the fact that somebody is at least paying attention to them. Thirdly, spontaneous remission does occur in alcoholism, although rarely. My barber was a "hopeless" skid-road alcoholic who woke up from a binge one day and decided this was nonsense; he has not had a drink in over fifteen years, though he did not join AA or go to any treatment center. Fourthly, subjective bias and loyalty to one treatment modality may introduce subconscious distortions into one's perception of success rates. While the staff of facility A is gloating that they have succeeded in the treatment of x number of patients whom their rival modality B had failed to help, they forget that over at B, the staff may be recounting a similar number of A's failures with whom they have had success using the B approach.

When quantitative data are presented, a certain healthy scientific skepticism is justified in scrutinizing the claims that N number or percentage of cases have been successfully treated. Is N large enough to be valid? If N is small, the results could be sheer chance. If N is a round number, one wonders how precisely the data were gathered; 200 does not sound as scientific as 217. Is the sample a representative cross section of the alcoholic population, or were selective factors at work which yielded a particularly apt group? These factors can be the reputation of the facility, high cost, early case-finding, nature of referral source, etc. Does N include those who refused treatment or dropped out before completion? One claim of 80 percent success turned out to refer to the 10 percent who stayed for treatment, yielding really 8 percent success rather than 80 percent. Another reports success with 75 percent of the "well-motivated" patients, which leaves one wondering how many did not fit this category. Comparable control groups are difficult to find, since we are reluctant to refuse treatment to some just for the sake of experimental design.

Most important is the time elapsed since completion of treatment. Many alcoholics, except those of the Delta or maintenance type, stay sober for varying periods regardless of treatment. One year after discharge is the minimum time to have any significance; two years would be preferable, but problems of follow-up make this less practical. For evaluation research purposes (not AA birthdays), sobriety should be counted from the date of leaving a residential treatment center, not entry date. This is because most people can stay sober within the sheltered environment and strong pressures of a treatment center; the real test is how well they do living in the real world of taverns and cocktail bars. If a median time of sobriety is presented, one must look at how much the curve is skewed toward the short end of the sobriety period. If a range of three months to one year of sobriety is given, a large number of cases may be bunched near three months and relatively few sober for nearly a year.

The criterion of success to be used is a matter of dispute. The final section of Chapter 10 made it clear that total abstinence is the only sensible goal to be proposed to patients, given the nature of the illness. Researchers may wish to consider additional criteria that are less stringent, such as reduction in drinking or improvement of function in major life areas. And, of course, comfortable sobriety means more than just abstinence. These other criteria are much harder to measure quantitively, and are much more liable to subjective perception and self-fulfilling prophecy. At least any research attempting them should use a double-blind experimental design so that the rater does not know which cases are alcoholics and which are controls. Compared to total abstinence as a criterion, "improved" sounds too much like being just a little pregnant. Substitute addiction to tranquilizers is a complicating factor.

Nature of the follow-up is crucial. Mail or secondhand reports that a subject is "doing all right" are too easily falsified, by either the subject or spouse who is ashamed to report failure. Purely negative criteria, such as not returning for treatment or not being arrested again, should not be taken as positive evidence of success: they may be in jail or in treatment somewhere else. Those who have died or are lost are sometimes allowed to appear as successes by the way the percentage of failures is reported. A second or third report is often more accurate but seldom forthcoming. In one's first enthusiasm there is a danger of reporting doubtful cases as successful, and to use a shorter time as a criterion of success. Later reports can give a less rosy picture, if they ever appear.

Sources

The material in this chapter draws heavily on personal clinical experience. For the reader who is interested in delving further into the subject of referrals, a sampling of the extensive literature is given below. Such a reader might also find it helpful to explore the social work journals, which often focus on techniques of referral that would be useful with alcoholics, as well as on the whole problem of making good referrals of alcoholics and members of their families. In addition, the literature on alcoholism, both in journals and texts, contains much on this subject that will help the referrer.

BISSONETTE, RAYMOND, "Bartender as a Mental Health Service Gatekeeper: A Role Analysis," *Community Mental Health Journal*, 1977, 13:92 99.

CORRIGAN, E.M., "Linking the Problem Drinker with Treatment," *Social Casework*, 1972, 17:54–56.

FINDLAY, G.D., "Effect of Role Network Pressure on an Alcoholic's Approach to Treatment," *Social Casework*, 1966, 11:71–77.

GIBBS, LEONARD and JOHN FLANAGAN, "Prognostic Indicators of Alcoholism Treatment Outcome," *International Journal of the Addictions*, 1977, 12:1097–1141.

JACOBSON, GEORGE R., *The Alcoholisms: Detection, Assessment and Diagnosis.*

JOHNSON, VERNON, *I'll Quit Tomorrow.*

KRIMMEL, H., *Alcoholism: Challenge for Social Work Education.*

LEMERE, FREDERICK et al., "Motivation in the Treatment of Alcoholism" *Quarterly Journal of Studies on Alcohol*, 1958, 19:428–431.

MCLACHLAN, JOHN F.C., "Therapy Strategies, Personality Orientation and Recovery from Alcoholism," *Canadian Psychiatric Association Journal*, 1974, 19: 25–30.

PATTISON, E. MANSELL, "Population Variation among Alcoholism Treatment Facilities," *International Journal of the Addictions*, 1973, 8:199–229.

RAPPOPORT, LYDIA, "Crisis Intervention as a Mode of Treatment," in Roberts, Robert W. and Robert H. Nee (eds.), *Theories of Social Casework*, pp. 265–311.

Rosenberg, Chaim M. and Joseph Liftik, "Use of Coercion in the Outpatient Treatment of Alcoholism," *Journal of Studies on Alcohol*, 1976, 37:58–65.

Selzer, M., "The Michigan Alcohol Screening Test: The Quest for a New Diagnostic Instrument," *American Journal of Psychiatry*, 1971, 127:1653–1658.

Spicer, Jerry, "Assessing Client Outcome: The Role of Client Self-Selection and Motivation," *Addictions*, 1977, 5:16–17.

Thomas, Sam D. and Warren C. Lowe, "Acute Treatment as Motivation for Rehabilitation," *Alcohol Health and Research World*, 1978 (Spring), 2:38–40.

Tiebout, Harry M., "Intervention in Psychotherapy," *American Journal of Psychoanalysis*, 1962, 22:74–80.

Weinberg, Jon R. *Helping the Client with Alcohol-Related Problems* (an excellent guide for attorneys). CompCare pamphlet.

Evaluation

Although there are innumerable articles that evaluate specific forms of treatment for alcoholism, or the results of specific treatment settings, relatively few deal broadly with the issues of evaluation. One of the most extensive and thoughtful articles about evaluation is "Methods for the Treatment of Chronic Alcoholism: A Critical Appraisal," by Frederick Baekeland, Lawrence Lundwall and Benjamin Kissin, which appeared in volume 2 of R.J. Gibbins (ed.), *Research Advances in Alcohol and Drug Problems*, pp. 247–327. The bibliography for this article contains most of the relevant literature up to 1974. Throughout B. Kissin and N. H. Begleiter (eds.), *Treatment and Rehabilitation of the Chronic Alcoholic,*which is volume 5 of their *Biology of Alcoholism*, the methodological problems of evaluation are attended to. In addition, the following may prove to be useful references to the reader interested in pursuing this area further:

Anderson, Daniel J. et al., *Applied Research: Impact on Decision Making*. Hazelden booklet.

Booz-Allen and Hamilton, Inc., *Model Benefit Costs in Alcohol Treatment Programs*, 2 vols.

Caddy, Glenn, R., *Problems in the Field of Alcoholism Treatment Outcome Evaluation: A Review with Special Reference to Blind and Independent Research Programs*. Conference on Alcohol and Treatment Outcome Evaluation, Nashville, 1977.

Costello, R.M., "Alcoholism Treatment and Evaluation: In Search of Methods," *International Journal of Addiction*, 1975, 10:251–276.

Ruggels, W.L., Ann Mothershead and Ronald Pyszka, *Follow-Up Study of Clients at Selected Alcoholism Treatment Centers*. NIAAA, 1977.

Sedlacek, David, "Evaluation of Residential Alcoholism Treatment Programs," *Alcohol Health and Research World*. 1975 (Summer), 24–26.

Smart, Reginald G., "Spontaneous Recovery in Alcoholics: A Review and Analysis of the Available Research," *Drug and Alcohol Dependence,*1975/1976, 1:277–285.

PART IV

Treatment and Rehabilitation

CHAPTER 14

Overview of Treatments

BEING ONCE ASKED, "Just what *do* you say to an alcoholic?" reminded me of the great surgeon, who had spent thirty years developing his techniques, being asked at a cocktail party, "Doctor, just how do you take out a gall bladder?" Alcoholism is complex, and each alcoholic is a unique individual. Add the individuality of the therapist, and it is clear that nobody can lay down a simple set of rules. One can only develop as broad and deep a knowledge as possible, and apply it as best seems fit.

Besides the alcoholism, each patient brings a unique set of other problems which must be attended to if successful rehabilitation is to occur. The "whole person" is a concept to which we often pay only lip service. And we have already pointed out the need to assist the family with the problems they have developed as a result of living with an alcoholic. Treatment thus becomes far more than the simple application of one approach to patient after patient.

Continuum of care means that for each patient an individualized treatment plan is formulated, providing for the gradual transition from detoxification through intensive treatment to long-range rehabilitation and restoration to normal living in the community. It may utilize a problem-oriented medical record rather than a conventional file, which in any case would be geared to continuity between the different treatment phases. Since any adequate discussion of treatments would constitute a separate book, we can only list them briefly and make a few comments.

Detoxification

The percentage of alcoholics coming into treatment who need detoxification, withdrawal from the drug alcohol in a hospital setting, has been reported at 4 percent, 5 percent or 7 percent—at most a very small minority. But these do need it very acutely, as it may be literally a matter of life and death. Getting blood alcohol level down to zero for other alcoholics is largely a matter of time and commonsense care. Much of this is being done now in subacute (not "nonmedical") dryout centers, which are not part of a hospital but have medical supervision and backup arrangements in case of need for quick transfer to a hospital

The decision whether to hospitalize depends on many factors. Alcohol poisoning constitutes a medical emergency, especially since tolerance to a lethal dose does not increase proportionately to behavioral tolerance. Here a stomach pump, airway tube, life-support measures, and vigilance lest they choke on their own vomit are called for. Violent nausea may cause ruptured esophageal varices or Mallory-Weiss syndrome, and there is always danger of respiratory failure. In *chronic* alcoholism, anyone drinking over one fifth of liquor a day will certainly need medical supervision. Numerous complications, including undiagnosed fractures and internal hemorrhage, may require hospital care but go unnoticed because the alcohol masks the pain. Alcoholic seizures and DT's can be prevented by skilled medical management, which means specialized knowledge and experience the ordinary physician may not have. We have noted that polydrug cases may exhibit a second withdrawal several days after the first is over, and other drug use must be routinely checked upon admission.

Withdrawal by complete abstinence ("cold turkey") rather than by gradually tapering off is preferred if done at home, because neither the patient nor the family can control dosage well. But in either a hospital or a subacute detoxification center, the more addicted alcoholic is less liable to severe reactions if withdrawal is gradual. In these settings "tapering" may be appropriate. Some experienced physicians even use decreasing doses of oral alcohol in a controlled environment to achieve DT-free withdrawal. Others prefer to give ethanol intravenously, arguing that this route offers freedom from gastrointestinal irritation while giving less positive reinforcement for drinking. Still others borrow a principle from the established techniques of withdrawal from narcotics or barbiturates; that is, the substitution of a calculated dose of a less addicting tranquilizer or sedative in controlled and decreasing doses to achieve withdrawal.

No matter which drug is chosen it is mandatory that all staff personnel be aware of the dangers of substitute addiction, and protocol must include a finite date on which the patient is to be completely off such medication. Clearly a substitute addiction is neither helpful to the patient nor ethical for the physician. Hippocrates observed that "therapy" ought not make a patient worse.

Medical Management. Dehydration is not to be assumed (Knott, 1967). The diuretic effect of rising BAC may be counteracted later by an antidiuretic hormone from the pituitary gland, which results in hyperfluidity (puffiness, edema) even if thirst is a complaint. Excessive urination, perspiration, diarrhea, and vomiting all have contributed to loss of body salts. These will be aggravated by the presence of kidney dysfunction or diabetes mellitus. Screening should be done for abnormal sugar, potassium or nitrogen in the blood. Although the literature speaks of magnesium deficiencies in alcoholism, it is prudent to avoid magnesium administration unless a deficit can be proven. Many American alcoholics self-medicate with magnesium-containing antacids (for example, Milk of Magnesia) and deficiencies are rare; overdoses of magnesium can be lethal. Another caution is not to give iron unless iron deficiency is present. The alcoholic population has blood loss from the stomach or trauma plus folic acid deficiency as common causes of anemias. They also have a high incidence of liver damage. Inappropriate administration of iron can precipitate the irreversible condition of hemosiderosis.

In general, medical management of withdrawal is concerned with controlling or preventing 1) nausea and vomiting, 2) "shakes," 3) seizures of a grand mal type, 4) hallucinosis, and 5) sleeplessness. *Nausea and vomiting* can be controlled with a nonsedative antinauseant such as Tigan. Some prefer frequent small doses of the phenothiazines because of their sedation. *"Shakes"* and *seizures* can be managed with the benzodiazepine derivatives, of which Valium and Librium enjoy the widest acceptance. Taractan, a phenothiazinelike drug, is also widely used, but it does not have anticonvulsant effects and, in fact, may lower the convulsive threshold. Some have chosen to stay with the standard Dilantin for anticonvulsive management. If this drug is chosen one must use another rapidly absorbed, short-acting, anticonvulsant in conjunction, because it requires three to five days of Dilantin to achieve therapeutic blood levels for seizure control. *Hallucinosis* is best controlled by vitamin B_1 (thiamine), and prevention or control of hypoxia to the brain. In practice this means management of pneumonias, obstructive lung diseases, anemias, and shock conditions concomitantly found with the condition of alcohol withdrawal. *Sedation* is perhaps most prudently managed by choosing a drug for either control of vomiting and/or seizures that has an adequate sleep side reaction. Some general rules apply: If nausea and vomiting are present or if the level of consciousness is compromised, the intermuscular or intravenous route is preferable to anything given by mouth. Doses must be individualized and are known to vary with sex, age, smoking, body weight, and the health of the liver. Most drugs depend upon the liver for excretion. Duration of action of any such drug will be modified in the presence of compromised liver function.

There is evidence that addiction to alcohol is really a dependence on the breakdown product of ethyl alcohol: acetaldehyde. For this reason these drugs that also break down to acetaldehyde, such as the barbiturates and paraldehyde, are suspect in managing withdrawal. Since paraldehyde is chemically almost identical with acetaldehyde, it should never be given to an alcoholic. Tranquilizers with no anticonvulsant capability and with high risk of addiction have little place in the management of alcoholism; for example, meprobamate (Miltown, Equanil). The patient needs to be educated to expect disturbance of sleep pattern for six months or more. Any sedative needs to be used sparingly, in a strictly controlled fashion and must not lead to a new addiction.

Malnutrition and vitamin deficiency, especially of the vitamin B complex, have already been noted as common in alcoholics because of inadequate diet, excessive kidney excretion, and poor absorption from the gastrointestinal tract. For this last reason the needed vitamin supplement should be given either by injection or intravenously in the early phase of recovery. Later a good balanced diet with minimum added daily oral vitamins should suffice.

Lastly, there is some evidence that plenty of TLC (tender loving care) can reduce the need for medical aids during withdrawal. Thus having a light in the room can prevent hallucinations, warm reassurance can reduce tremors, and understanding encouragement can dispel fear or despair, with resulting positive attitudes that speed up the body's recovery processes. Some claim that these factors can decrease the incidence of DT's. At least good nursing, and the shared experience of recovered alcoholics with some training, seem to make a major contribution in this first phase of recovery. (See O'Briant, 1973.)

Alcoholism Treatment Methods

None of the above is really treatment for alcoholism, only for its immediate effects. The most important function of the detoxification center is not to bring the alcoholic through one more crisis, but to serve as a bridge to definitive treatment, which should begin as soon as the patient's mental condition allows. Treatment may involve several different modalities, simultaneous or successive. These may be inpatient or outpatient, short-term intensive treatment or long-term care, medical or psychological or spiritual, and in any combination. Never should we think we are restricted to a choice of just one modality. The treatment plan should allow for flexibility if a change is required.

Inpatient or residential settings, whether in a hospital or an alcoholism treatment center, have the advantages of better control of the patient and maximum opportunity to build up physical health, which are so important for the mental attitude of the patient. Since the body of the alcoholic has adapted to the point of needing alcohol to function, the period just after withdrawal may require more difficult bodily adjustments than withdrawal itself; the recovering alcoholic may thus need inpatient care even more from the third to the tenth day than during the first two or three days. A structured program puts order into the alcoholic's life after perhaps years of irregular living habits. Diet, exercise, recreation, sleep, and medication can all be managed. An interdisciplinary team from the various professions can still have a unified philosophy of treatment, which is important to avoid further confusing the patient, who is already confused enough by alcoholism. These centers usually require a minimum stay of ten to ninety days, averaging twenty-one to twenty-eight days, but often open to extension.

Outpatient treatment, however, even right from the start, has certain advantages (Ruprecht, 1961; V. Fox, 1974). It is less expensive, does not create overdependency in patients but rather enlists their cooperation, may provide an occasion to involve the family earlier (for example, if they engage in transportation of the patient), does not give the impression that release from the hospital means the end of treatment, can be integrated with mission or shelter type management (for example, the Salvation Army), allows participation in a suitable local AA group, thus insuring continuity, and is more acceptable to those who find a hospital threatening.

Alcoholics Anonymous

AA will be dealt with in a later chapter. Numerically by far the most successful in dealing with alcoholics, AA does not always immediately appeal to every patient, and some preparation is often necessary for its attraction to work. If patients cannot stay sober for at least five days on their own, they will need some other help in breaking the habit-pattern so as to clear their head enough to engage in the AA program. AA can be an integral part of a treatment plan that includes prior or concomitant approaches.

Antabuse (Disulfiram)

In 1947 it was accidentally discovered that workers in the rubber industry had absorbed the sulfur compound disulfiram (tetraethylthiuram disulfide), which made them hypersensitive to alcohol. Jacobsen, a Danish physician, did controlled experiments after experiencing unpleasant effects himself from drinking alcohol while disulfiram was in his body, and published the results as evidence that it might be useful in the treatment of alcoholism. By 1950 it was being marketed in America under the trade name Antabuse. Unfortunately, the dosages used then were too high and caused serious side effects, diminishing its popularity for a while. A similar drug, Temposil (citrated calcium carbimide), is used in Canada and elsewhere but not in the United States. It is said to build up to an effective level sooner than Antabuse but not to last as long, to have no odor, nor to cause low blood pressure, but to cause a high white blood cell count in a fair number of users. Another drug, Flagyl (metronidazole), was thought for a while to be useful but has been abandoned for this purpose. Certain mushrooms and other drugs are being explored. Antabuse remains the primary drug of this class and is now widely used with excellent results, in lower doses and with practically no side effects (Martin H. Keller, 1976; R. Fox 1967a, 1973).

Dr. Ruth Fox, certainly an ardent admirer of AA, made a strong case (1958) that far from any antagonism there is perfect compatibility between AA and Antabuse. This chemical may be the most useful means of breaking the habit and buying sober time in order to participate in AA. To those who call it a crutch, the obvious answer is that prescribing a crutch is good medicine while a broken leg heals, and alcoholism is a far more serious ailment than a fracture. One physician credits Antabuse with saving over a quarter of a million lives, for which all alcoholics should be grateful. Purported dangers and side effects are largely related to its earliest use when dosage was much higher than what is common now. Others objected to the practice, now largely abandoned, of giving the patient a little experience of the Antabuse reaction as a deterrent. In short, one suspects that opposition to its use today could be symptomatic of resistance to the idea of sobriety, or denial. This is so true that the suggestion of Antabuse serves as a good test of one's motivation for recovery.

Antabuse blocks the enzyme action necessary for the breakdown of acetaldehyde, a product of alcohol metabolism. Harmless as long as no alcohol is imbibed, it causes acetaldehyde to build up in the body if one drinks alcohol. The resulting reaction is characterized by flushed face, rapid pulse, pounding headache, difficult breathing, nausea and vomiting, sweating, blurred vision, etc. Since it takes at least five days for the Antabuse to be eliminated from the body, the alcoholic knows he will have this reaction if he drinks before that time. It thus acts as a guard against drinking, with the advantage that the decision is made only once a day, usually in the morning and away from temptation to drink. This frees the mind of any consideration of drink for the next four or five days or even up to two weeks.

Antabuse should never be taken without a doctor's prescription, based on a medical examination and the patient's consent after a clear explanation to the patient of how Antabuse works. The patient must be willing to use it as an aid toward desired sobriety. Otherwise he will resent it and soon find an excuse to stop. If given without his full knowledge, he might drink and precipitate a reaction. He must understand that he cannot take foods or medicines containing any alcohol (except foods cooked so that the alcohol has been evaporated out). Paraldehyde must be avoided. A few people do not absorb Antabuse into the bloodstream, which can be checked by a test of breath, urine, or blood. The European technique of implanting a pellet of disulfiram in the skin of the abdomen has not been approved for American practice, for technical reasons.

Disulfiram is not a total therapy in itself, but can be extremely useful in early stages of recovery. It cannot stop a person who wants to drink, for all the patient has to do is stop taking the Antabuse for five days or longer. But it can help those who want to avoid alcohol and cannot do it alone. Some take it as insurance before holidays or stress times. The unwilling can pretend to swallow the pill and spit it out later, or even swallow it and vomit later. For this reason mandated Antabuse is crushed and given in orange juice. The impotence attributed to Antabuse is probably psychic, possibly also due in part to the sex partner's reaction to the bad breath it initially creates in some patients. There are very few, if any, for whom it is dangerous (R. Fox, 1973), and in any case it is far less dangerous and damaging than alcohol or even aspirin.

Aversion Conditioning

In 1935 Charles Shadel, a recovered alcoholic, began treating alcoholics by establishing a conditioned response whereby the alcoholic experiences nausea at the sight, taste, or smell of alcoholic beverages. He compared it to Pavlov's conditioning a dog to salivate at the sound of a bell. An injection of the drug emetine, which naturally produces nausea and vomiting, is used as the unconditioned stimulus. The conditioned stimulus is exposure to the whole range of alcoholic beverages, especially to one's favorite. This eventually produces a reaction of nausea even without the emetine, resulting in a deterrent against drinking. It differs from Antabuse in being psychological instead of physiological, since it is the sight or smell of liquor that triggers the reaction and not the actual presence of alcohol in the body.

The idea goes back to ancient times, when the Romans tried to deter alcohol abuse by putting a tiny scorpion in the bottom of a wine glass. The reason this did not work is basic to understanding the Shadel process: any amount of alcohol in the bloodstream spoils the conditioning. Since one had to drink the wine in order to get to the scorpion, alcohol had already been absorbed. At Shadel Hospital any alcohol swallowed is immediately vomited before absorption, and if some is accidentally absorbed the conditioning session is canceled. Timing is crucial here, as we saw when explaining why a hangover does not act as a deterrent. For the same reason many attempts to use this approach in other treatment centers have shown poor results, since so much depends on precise technique.

Like Antabuse, aversion conditioning is not a total therapy. But especially when coupled with other means and good follow-up, it has resulted in recovery rates as high as 64 percent and 75 percent using stringent criteria of two and even four years of total abstinence (Dunn, 1971, p. 104; Smith, 1979). It is not infallible, and patients are told that they can break down the conditioned response. It does not make it impossible for one to drink, but possible for one not to drink. Like taking golf lessons to correct a bad slice, it is a learning process one freely chooses in order to achieve a desired end. The aversion counteracts the craving or appeal of alcoholic beverages and the many stimuli that have conditioned the alcoholic to drink; for example, at certain times or places. It serves to break the pattern, and provide a nondrinking life-style as a condition for pursuing permanent recovery. In common with Antabuse and AA, it attacks alcoholism as the primary problem, assuming that even if it were originally due to some psychic trauma at age two, it is a little late to do anything about that but one can do something about the pathological drinking.

Other forms of aversion conditioning are sometimes used. Carbon dioxide inhalation and momentary paralysis from anectine have been abandoned as conditioning stimuli. A mild faradic sting (not electric shock as usually understood) has been successfully substituted for emetine in the Shadel conditioning process when vomiting is contraindicated (Jackson and Smith, 1978). Covert sensitization, wherein the patient pairs a mental image of nausea and vomiting with an imagined drink, it reported to have some success but takes a great deal of time and is less effective unless the patient has a very vivid imagination. In no case is the aversion conditioning considered a punishment, but simply an associative learning process to counteract an undesirable habit.

Chemotherapy

Disulfiram is a deterrent drug, more akin to aversion conditioning in its treatment role than to the psychotropic (mind altering) drugs sometimes used in an attempt to treat alcoholism. We have stressed the danger of substitute addiction to sedatives and tranquilizers, while noting their legitimate use during withdrawal; they have no place in long-term therapy of alcoholics. Even nonaddictive tranquilizers are more harm than help, since they can tranquilize to the point that the patient does not care very much about anything, including recovery. At one time LSD (lysergic acid) was used in the hope that the psychedelic experience would give a self-actualizing insight that would obviate any future need to drink. Several reviews (for example, Ditman, 1967; Costello, 1969; Smart and others, 1966, 1967) of the literature concur that the percentage of success is no better than without LSD; those few who get well are the stable personalities who recover from alcoholism regardless. The same is true of other hallucinogens; and marijuana, if anything, seems to lead to relapse in recovered alcoholics. In short, there is no psychotropic chemotherapy known at this time to be specific for alcoholism (see Viamontes, 1972).

Psychiatrists use a wide array of drugs for various neurotic and psychotic conditions: major and minor tranquilizers, antidepressants, stimulants, antipsychotics, hypnotics, antianxiety. And other drugs are being developed continually. Many of these are addicting, most potentiate with alcohol, and none are specific therapy for alcoholism. A few used for treating conditions other than alcoholism, for example, lithium carbonate for affective (manic-depressive) psychosis and the tricyclic anti-depres sants (Elavil, Triavil, Tofranil, etc., but not the MAO inhibitors), may be legitimately prescribed for recovered alcoholics who have these problems. The prescribing physician should be aware that the patient is a recovered alcoholic, and dosage must be carefully monitored. In general, alcoholics need to be educated that amphetamines do not succeed in controlling weight and only make depression worse on the rebound; sleeping pills and antianxiety pills only work for a short time; and that there is no magic pill for alcoholism.

Physical Rehabilitation

Psychosomatic medicine has taught us that feeling good physically can do wonders for mental attitudes, just as psychological factors can greatly modify physical health. Recalling from Chapter 4 the damage that prolonged drinking can do to every organ of the body, it is clear that a major part of treatment is restoration of the alcoholic to good physical health. Directors of treatment centers are often so occupied with specific therapies that they lose sight of the importance of the following.

Diet.   Malnutrition, and especially vitamin deficiency, have been mentioned frequently. While avoiding fads, such as massive dosage of vitamins, a well-balanced diet is important. To avoid big fluctuations in blood sugar, avoid all refined sugar and carefully balance carbohydrates with proteins. (A badly damaged liver cannot handle the amino acids from too much protein.) Since meat, fish, eggs, and cheese are more expensive than macaroni and other staples of institutional food, this will increase treatment costs. But the importance of eating well cannot be overemphasized. The same is true of fresh fruits and vegetables. Food should also be attractively served, as the recovering alcoholic often lacks an appetite. Excessive coffee, unless decaffeinated, should be avoided.

Because the vitamin B complex is so important for neural functioning, its administration was observed to work dramatic improvement in routinely undernourished alcoholic patients. This, along with the facts of general nutrition, led to the advocacy of massive doses of vitamins. Now a good vitamin supplement is certainly called for in these patients, but one cannot abuse nature with impunity. Megavitamin therapy using massive or gross doses became a fad, with predictable reactions. Except for people with inborn defects of vitamin metabolism, these massive doses have been shown to be not only unnecessary and useless, but also harmful and possibly fatal. Thus large doses of vitamin B_1 may destroy vitamin B_{12}. Excessive vitamin C can destroy 50 percent or more of the vitamin B_{12} in a meal, cause kidney damage, and cause "rebound scurvy" in newborns of mothers taking massive doses, since nature apparently stops supplying it in the child. Several vitamins, including niacin, when taken in excess are known to cause liver damage, and gross dosage of vitamins A, D, and E have all been indicted as harmful. Careful reading of one popular book on megavitamins (Adams and Murray, 1973) leaves the distinct impression that the "cures" are not due to megavitamins but to the well-balanced, low-carbohydrate, high-protein diet the book advocates.

Nevertheless, many nutritional diseases in alcoholics are treatable by vitamin therapy, when prescribed by a physician after a specific diagnosis. Thus pellagra, with its symptoms of diarrhea, gross skin disorders, and mental confusion often responds quickly to the vitamin B complex. The Wernicke-Korsakoff syndrome and beriberi are other examples. Polyneuropathy with impaired walking can be alleviated by vitamin B_1 treatment.

Recreation and Exercise.   Alcoholics may have been getting little more exercise than sitting on a bar stool, and no other recreation than drinking. They need help in developing ways to entertain themselves, and opportunities for play. We can recommend outdoor exercise, a variety of sports, and an appreciation that walking is not only good physical exercise but also a way of getting back in contact with their world. Good conversation activates one's potential more than passively watching television. Hobbies, arts and crafts, music, and a library of books and magazines can all contribute to recovery. All this may have the added benefit of promoting a good night's sleep without any pills. A regimen of regular hours and good living habits is important for sleep and general health. Learning a trade or refurbishing old skills can serve the double purpose of occupying one's mind and preparing for future employment.

Education

We referred in the Preface to a national study that placed "learning about alcoholism" as the most important part of therapy. One can question the ability of minds to absorb very much while the brain is still toxic; certainly much repetition will be needed before it sinks in. And mere passive attendance at dull lectures is not education. Nevertheless, it is of utmost importance that the patients be made to understand what alcoholism is and how their bodies react to alcohol. The folly of trying to drink like other people will be apparent only when these facts are understood. The disease concept of alcoholism will alleviate much guilt and shame. A sense of self-esteem can be promoted through realization that alcoholics are neither weak-willed nor crazy, but just physiologically different from nonalcoholics. Education for all these reasons is an important part of therapy.

Psychotherapy

Individual and group counseling have always been major components of alcoholism treatment. Each takes many forms. As *individual*, it may range from the motivational counseling at referral or intake as described in the previous chapter, through intensive sessions with a trained alcoholism counselor during treatment proper, to depth psychotherapy for underlying problems later by a psychiatrist (M.D.) or clinical psychologist (Ph.D.) or psychiatric social worker (M.S.W.). As *group*, it most commonly occurs under a trained alcoholism worker in either inpatient or outpatient alcoholism treatment settings, but AA meetings may be considered a form of nonprofessional group therapy. Always there should be individual contact with a counselor throughout treatment; lack of this is a severe deficiency in some treatment centers.

Individual. From its own literature, psychiatry, and especially psychoanalysis, admits a very poor rate of success as a therapy for alcoholism. This is due largely to the old tendency to conceive of alcoholism as a symptom of inner conflict or escape from psychic stress, rather than as a primary pathology (see chapters 9 and 10). Analysis of hidden motives or past causes is not only ineffective but can even worsen the drinking. At best, this approach only produces a better adjusted alcoholic, not a recovered one.

However, at least 20 percent of alcoholism is secondary or reactive, and the primary psychopathology must be treated. In addition, many recovered alcoholics will need psychotherapy for residual problems after sobriety has been achieved, and most will need some kind of counseling in vocational, marital, or other adjustments. Obviously, this is best done by a therapist who understands the nature of addiction and the danger spots for a recovered alcoholic. For all this the time sequence is clear. There is ample research evidence (for example, see Chapter 4, on brain) to confirm the commonsense observation that a toxic brain can neither absorb nor remember the insights achieved in psychotherapy, nor project them for future behavior. This is true not only while the patient is still drinking, but also for weeks after the last drink.

Group.   There are some distinct advantages to therapy in small groups, whether AA or otherwise, which are largely composed of alcoholics who are either recovered or recovering (here the distinction is meaningful). There is a sense of belonging and acceptance that puts the newcomer at ease, a depth of understanding rarely achieved by one who has not experienced alcoholism personally, and a penetration of defensiveness and denial because an alcoholic is more likely to accept insights or criticism from a fellow alcoholic. Some even feel that there should be no individual psychotherapy for the first few months, just because recovery occurs best through a program. Groups are the best way to involve the family in treatment.

We must warn, however, that useful as a strong confrontation can be in getting a person into treatment, there is little place for it in recovery. The newly recovering alcoholic is too sick and lacking in self-esteem to be stripped of defenses when there is insufficient time to rebuild ego strength. Suicide can be the result. When president of the American Association of State Psychology Boards, this author was privy to knowledge about serious abuses of encounter, marathon, sensivity training or T group methods (see Hartley, 1976). The Synanon "hot seat" approach may or may not be effective on hardened street-drug addicts, but it is inappropriate for most alcoholics (O'Leary, 1977).

Positive Therapy.   Whether group or individual, it seems that the most appropriate psychotherapeutic modes for alcoholics are those that focus on the present and future rather than on the past. Examples are the reality therapy of William Glasser, the existential or logotherapy of Viktor Frankl, the rational-emotive therapy (RET) of Albert Ellis, and other such nonanalytic therapies. Self-management, positive motivation, and attitude change—especially in building up one's sense of self-esteem—are the cardinal features in most of these approaches, along with learning some good problem-solving techniques. Psychodrama (Weiner, 1967) and role playing can be very useful under a skilled therapist, because of their appeal to both imagination and emotion. Transactional analysis (TA) is a simplified form of psychoanalysis wherein Id, Ego and Superego are translated as the Child, Adult and Parent within each of us; it can be useful provided one does not get too involved in analyzing the games people play, or think of alcoholic addiction as merely learned behavior that can be easily unlearned.

Because of the toxic action of alcohol on the brain, alcoholics may be less able to function than they appear. The result is that we may have unrealistic expectations of their performance, which can only mean frustration, sense of failure, and lowered self-esteem for the patient and therapist. Cognitive and "insight"-oriented therapies may require more verbal mediation or abstract thinking than the patient can master; patients may resort to just repeating key words without inner growth. Behavioral and social-skill approaches may be more efficacious. Readiness for a particular treatment approach may depend on many factors, such as degree of awareness of drinking problem, dissatisfaction with present style of life and achievement, and willingness to takes serious steps toward change.

Just as no dosages were given when outlining medical management, no details of counseling will be attempted here for the same reason—that this is a general survey and not a treatment manual. In any event, one does not become a trained counselor-therapist by reading a book anymore than one becomes a surgeon by reading a medical treatise. Alcoholism counseling differs from other therapy, and demands knowledge and training from alcohol specialists. Alcoholics are usually skilled manipulators or con artists and have their own forms of rationalization. The counselor does well to listen rather than talk; in that sense the session should be client-centered even though it cannot be nondirective. The patient should never be allowed to dump all responsibility on the counselor, which many are prone to do. Transference and countertransference should be thoroughly understood; sexual attraction between therapist and client does occur, and a genuine interest must never be misinterpreted as a romantic interest. Termination techniques and the need to release rather than hold on to clients, or allow them to hold on to you, can be another area requiring special training.

Hypnosis.   In the past some have strongly advocated the use of hypnosis for the treatment of alcoholism. When used by a responsible professional, the technique has some value as an adjunct to therapy. During the hypnotic trance, posthypnotic suggestions are given to associate the offer of a drink with vomiting or the choice of another beverage. This is sometimes used as a reinforcement for aversion conditioning. But its limitations are now recognized, chiefly because the effects do not last. As in other therapeutic uses, hypnotism by itself is too artificial and superficially imposed, in contrast to real growth from within. However, it is useful for diagnostic investigation of deep-seated problems while defenses are down, and for promoting relaxation. Intravenous sodium pentothal is useful for the same two purposes, and is not addictive when used in this way (Smith, Lemere and Dunn, 1971).

Relaxation is important in the recovery of alcoholics, most of whom have been anxious and tense, which inclines them to turn to alcohol to relax. Self-hypnosis can be taught for this purpose, individually or in groups.

Records or tapes, deep-muscle relaxing exercises, biofeedback for tension control, transcendental meditation (TM) and any drug-free means of promoting relaxation are to be encouraged.

There are many methods of learning impulse control and developing one's inner psychic life without chemicals. Values clarification and active religious participation can make a distinct contribution to recovery. A marathon encounter may assist an alcoholic in advanced stage of recovery who is stuck on a plateau. Behavior modification techniques of all kinds can be used to condition a person for living without alcohol; this should not be confused with conditioning alcoholics to drink socially.

Other Proposed Treatments

Nearly every possible approach known to human ingenuity has been proposed as a treatment for alcoholism at one time or another. Most have not stood the test of time. We have already noted the demise of LSD, anectine, Flagyl and Carbon dioxide, and can list others that have joined them in obscurity: lobotomy, electroconvulsive shock, spinal puncture, animal charcoal, salt, benzedrine, hormones such as ACTH and thyroid extract, and propranolol (Inderal).

A few have promise, or at least cannot be discarded without further testing. When *biofeedback* is used to control certain semiautomatic body functions, it gives some people a new sense of mastery over themselves rather than being at the mercy of forces beyond their control; they thus gain more control over the choice not to drink. It requires persistent effort and a skilled instructor, but is worth pursuing. *Acupuncture* has been used in China; nobody seems able to explain how or why it works in terms of Western physiology, but direct observations by Dr. William Lukash, the White House physician, and others attest to its success.

A disputed question is whether alcoholics and street-drug addicts should be treated in the same facility (Ashley, 1978). We say street drugs, because if we ask about prescription drugs the question is moot; most alcoholics also misuse prescription drugs. The staff of Eagleville Center in Pennsylvania claim their experience favors treating alcoholics and addicts together, and that they mutually benefit. Certainly the psychology and physiology of addiction to alcohol and to other drugs are very similar in many respects. The problem is more socio-cultural, as the two populations differ notably in attitudes and values. There is a tendency for each to look down on the other as inferior, or weird. Life-styles are so different that there are serious problems of living together. A review of the literature indicates that the majority experience, including that of the Veterans Administration hospitals (S. Baker, 1977), favors separate treatment. At least coordinated planning is called for, but alcoholism workers fear that even this may obscure the numerical preponderance of alcoholics and dilute their education and prevention campaigns.

Conclusion

Again we insist that no one treatment approach should be thought of to the exclusion of combining with others. Whether from a desire for omnipotence or a lack of appreciation of how they can work together, many therapists seem afraid to complement their professional efforts with referral to Alcoholics Anonymous (Curlee, 1971), while many members of AA seem unaware of their own long tradition of cooperation so earnestly advocated in the writings of their cofounder, Bill W.

Those who report that no treatment is as good as "standard" treatment are no doubt referring to outmoded approaches with 10 to 15 percent recovery rates, perhaps unaware of newer methods which yield 70 to 90 percent success. Within this broad framework there is room for a variety of treatments, and there is some research evidence that choice between them is less important in predicting outcome than variation in patient characteristics (Smart, 1978). One might add that individual personalities of treatment staff might again be more important than differences in treatment modality.

Like patients with any chronic illness, alcoholics can be frustrating at times, and can relapse in discouraging ways. Psychotics who have been tranquilizing themselves with alcohol will erupt into bizarre symptoms. But the work can also be very gratifying. Years ago physicians commonly avoided treating alcoholics because they smelled up the office waiting room, didn't pay their bills, and got drunk again. Now a growing number of physicians say they enjoy treating alcoholics because they like to see patients get well. Whereas other patients often die, it is most rewarding to see alcoholics recover the glow of health and a zest for living.

Sources

The National Clearinghouse for Alcohol Information (NCALI) publishes a Grouped Interest Guide (bibliography), entitled *Alcoholism Treatment Modalities*. Frederick Baekeland, L. Lundwall and B. Kissin present "Methods for the Treatment of Chronic Alcoholism: A Critical Appraisal," in R.J. Gibbins (ed.), *Research Advances in Alcohol and Drug Problems*, vol. 2, pp. 247–327. Jean Rossi and William Filstead discuss " 'Treating' the Treatment Issues: Some General Observations about the Treatment of Alcoholism," in William Filstead et al. (eds.), *Alcohol and Alcohol Problems: New Thinking and New Directions*, pp. 193–227. Part IV of Estes and Heinemann, *Alcoholism: Development, Consequences, and*

Interventions contains eleven chapters with ample references. Some general books on the treatment of alcoholism are:

BELL, ROBERT G., *Escape from Addiction.*

BOURNE, PETER and RUTH FOX (eds.), *Alcoholism: Progress in Research and Treatment.*

CATANZARO, RONALD J., (ed.), *Alcoholism: The Total Treatment Approach*, rev. ed., 1972.

EDWARDS, G. and M. GRANT (eds.), *Alcoholism: New Knowledge and New Responses.*

FILSTEAD, WILLIAM, JEAN ROSSI and MARK KELLER (eds.), *Alcohol and Alcohol Problems: New Thinking and New Directions.*

FORREST, GARY G. *The Diagnosis and Treatment of Alcoholism.*

GIBBINS, ROBERT J., Y. ISRAEL, and O. KALANT (eds.), *Research Advances in Alcohol and Drug Problems*, 5 vols.

GLATT, MAX M., *The Alcoholic and the Help He Needs;* and *A Guide to Addiction and Its Treatment.*

GROUPE, VINCENT (ed.), *Alcoholism Rehabilitation: Methods and Experiences of Private Rehabilitation Centers.*

JOHNSON, VERNON, *I'll Quit Timorrow.*

KISSIN, B. and H. BEGLEITER (eds.) *Biology of Alcoholism*, 5 vols.

LARKIN, E.J., *The Treatment of Alcoholism: Theory, Practice, Evaluation.*

POLEY, WAYNE et al., *Alcoholism: A Treatment Manual.*

RITSON, BRUCE, and C. HASSAL, *Management of Alcoholism.*

SEIXAS, FRANK A. (ed.), *Currents in Alcoholism*, 4 vols.

STRACHAN, J. GEORGE, *Practical Alcoholism Programming;* and *Alcoholism: Treatable Illness.*

TARTER, R., and A. SUGERMAN (eds.), *Alcoholism: Interdisciplinary Approaches to an Enduring Problem.*

ZIMBERG, SHELDON, JOHN WALLACE and SHEILA BLUME, *Practical Approaches to Alcoholism Psychotherapy.*

Some Special Topics

AMERICAN PSYCHIATRIC ASSOCIATION, "Megavitamin and Orthomolecular Therapy in Psychiatry," *Nutrition Review*, 1974, 32 (Suppl.): 44–47.

CURLEE, JOAN, "Combined Use of Alcoholics Anonymous and Outpatient Psychotherapy," *Bulletin of the Menninger Clinic*, 1971, 35:368–371.

FOX, RUTH, "A Multidisciplinary Approach to the Treatment of Alcoholism," *American Journal of Psychiatry*, 1967, 123:769–778.

GALLANT, D.M. et al., "The Revolving-Door Alcoholic: An Impasse in the Treatment of the Chronic Alcoholic," *Archives of General Psychiatry*, 1973, 38: 633–635.

GITLOW, S.E., "A Pharmacological Approach to Alcoholism," *AA Grapevine*, October 1968, or AA reprint.

GITLOW, S.E., (ed.), *Alcoholism: A Practical Treatment Guide.*

GLASER, FREDERICK B. et al., *A Systems Approach to Alcohol Treatment.*

GROSS, MILTON M. (ed.), *Alcohol Intoxication and Withdrawal.*

HARTMAN, B.J., "Approaches to the Treatment of Alcoholism," *Journal of the National Medical Association*, 1976, 68 (2):101–103.

HINDMAN, MARGARET, "Rational Emotive Therapy in Alcoholism Treatment," *Alcohol Health and Research World*, 1976 (Spring), 13–17.

JACKSON, THOMAS R. and JAMES W. SMITH, "A Comparison of Two Aversion Treatment Methods for Alcoholism," *Journal of Studies on Alcohol*, 1978, 39:187–191.

KENDIS, JOSEPH B., "The Effect of Attitudes in the Therapy of the Alcoholic," *British Journal of Addiction*, 1967, 62:307–315.

O'BRIANT, ROBERT G. and H.L. LENNARD, *Recovery from Alcoholism: A Social Treatment Model.*

ONTARIO MEDICAL ASSOCIATION, *Diagnosis and Treatment of Alcoholism for Primary Care Physicians*, Addiction Research Foundation booklet.

SMITH, JAMES W., "Abstinence Oriented Alcoholism Treatment Approaches," In Ferguson, J. (ed.), *Advances in Behavioral Medicine*, 1979.

Disulfiram (Antabuse)

BUSSE, S. et al. *Disulfiram in the Treatment of Alcoholism*, a 363-page bibliography, 1979.

DOHERTY, JAMES, "Disulfiram (Antabuse): Chemical Commitment to Abstinence," *Alcohol Health and Research World,*, 1976 (Spring), 2–9.

FOX, RUTH, "Disulfiram," in Peter Bourne and Ruth Fox (eds.), *Alcoholism: Progress in Research and Treatment*, pp. 236–239.

FOX, RUTH, "Disulfiram (Antabuse) as an Adjunct in the Treatment of Alcoholism," in Ruth Fox (ed.), *Alcoholism: Behavioral Research, Therapeutic Approaches*, pp. 242–255.

KELLER, MARTIN H., "Reports of Antabuse Depression Debunked," *The Journal*, July, 1976.

SAUTER, A.M. et al., "Reevaluation of the Disulfiram-Alcohol Reaction in Man," *Journal of Studies on Alcohol*, 1977, 38:1680–1695.

CHAPTER 15

Alcoholics Anonymous

SINCE ALCOHOLICS ANONYMOUS is numerically by far the most successful program of recovery from alcoholism, no one can claim a knowledge of the field without knowing what AA is and how it works. No physician would write a prescription and hand it to the patient remarking, "I don't know what this is or how it works; but take it, it will be good for you." No professional should recommend AA who has never attended AA meetings nor read "the big book," *Alcoholics Anonymous*, much less the mass of literature produced both by the fellowship and by scholars who have studied it. Since each member and each group is different, one should both read AA literature and attend open meetings of several groups in diverse settings, to savor the variety while perceiving the basic uniformity of the program.

Even long-time members sometimes betray a lack of familiarity with their own "official" literature, the AA Conference-approved books and pamphlets published by AA World Services, Inc. in New York. Not being a member, this author feels it even more imperative to base his description on that literature, in spite of close association with AA since 1942. For all, a thorough study of AA can be most rewarding. The nonalcoholic founder of one famous treatment center is said to have taken off an entire year just to study AA.

What Is AA?

Nobody can speak for AA. Members usually begin a talk by stating that this is just their view. Nobody needs to speak for AA—it speaks for itself. One million success stories (estimated worldwide membership from the latest survey) and the Twelve Steps that constitute the heart of the program speak more eloquently than any description.

Alcoholics Anonymous is a self-help group that combines many facets of good group therapy. But it is not therapy in any professional sense. It is universally available, meeting in about one hundred countries and listed in the telephone book of practically every city of any size in the world. There is no requirement for membership except a desire to stop drinking (originally they said "honest desire" but dropped the adjective to avoid judging who might be honest). One does not have to declare oneself an alcoholic, and there is no membership card. One is a member if one says so. It is free, supported only by voluntary contributions of the members. Being anonymous, there are no member lists and hence accurate statistical data are difficult to compile. But surveys in 1968, 1971, 1974, and 1977 by the organization have yielded considerable information about the group while protecting the anonymity of individual members.

AA is both a fellowship and a program. The program of Twelve Steps can be used successfully by those isolated from the group either by geography or personal temperment. Yet the mutual support and fellowship are most important aspects, as depicted by Madsen in his excellent Chapter IX on AA in *The American Alcoholic* (1974). Founded shortly after the repeal of Prohibition, it was careful to avoid any semblance of partisan involvement. Members often say, "If you want to drink, that's your business; if you want to stop, we can help." Alcohol is mentioned only once in the Twelve Steps; AA is a whole way of life. Although an intensely spiritual program, it is careful to avoid affiliation with any sect or religion. As they describe themselves,

> Alcoholics Anonymous is a fellowship of men and women who share their experience, strength, and hope with each other that they may solve their common problem and help others to recover from alcoholism.
>
> The only requirement for membership is a desire to stop drinking. There are no dues or fees for AA membership; we are self-supporting through our own contributions. AA is not allied with any sect, denomination, politics, organization, or institution; does not wish to engage in any controversy; neither endorses nor opposes any causes. Our primary purpose is to stay sober and help other alcoholics to achieve sobriety. (Copyright © and reprinted by permission of the A.A. Grapevine, Inc.)

Perhaps the greatest contribution of AA is hope. Most alcoholics feel pretty hopeless, and the old moralistic and prohibitionistic approaches only accentuated that feeling. The disease concept is not new, as we saw, but it had never been widely promulgated until AA began to spread. To see thousands of alcoholics recover and lead happy lives, and without great monetary cost, gave reason for hope to every alcoholic. Physicians and clergymen were at first chagrined and then delighted to see success where they had failed, and endorsed the program enthusiastically. Where each recovery seemed to some a miracle, the story of growth without either promotion or money was to others a greater miracle.

A Bit of History

It all started when a New York stockbroker named Bill W., who had lost everything but discovered he could stay sober by trying to help other alcoholics, found himself alone and desperate in Akron, Ohio, on the eve of Mother's Day, 1935. He called a clergyman and asked to be put in touch with another alcoholic with whom he could talk. He was referred to Henrietta Seiberling of the rubber manufacturing family, who arranged a meeting the next day with Dr. Bob S., a "hopeless" alcoholic surgeon. The two talked for hours, and agreed that they needed each other for the sake of their own sobriety. Dr. Bob had one relapse a few weeks later, and on June 10, 1935 began complete sobriety, which lasted until he died. Thus AA was born, though the anniversary is usually celebrated on the Fourth of July.

The Washingtonian movement in Baltimore in the early 1800s had helped some alcoholics with a religious approach, but soon destroyed itself by getting too involved with politics and prohibitionism. The Oxford groups (not the Oxford movement in England), started by the Protestant clergyman Frank Buchman early in this century, had tried a program of surrender, conversion, and confession, but insistence on rigid "moral absolutes" made the groups repulsive to many, and they advocated prominence rather than anonymity. Bill W. was aware of these movements through his alcoholic friend Ebby and the Episcopal clergyman Reverend Sam Shoemaker, and Dr. Bob had attended Oxford group meetings; it was not until 1939 that AA entirely disengaged itself from the Oxford groups, which metamorphosed into Moral ReArmament (MRA). Bill W. was also influenced by his physician, William D. Silkworth, by the psychologist William James through his book *The Varieties of Religious Experience*, and by the great Swiss psychiatrist Carl Jung's observation that no profound change in the latter half of life takes place without a religious conversion. Dr. Bob and Bill W. were greatly aided by Sister Ignatia of St. Thomas Hospital in Akron, and in 1939 the cofounders became very close friends with Father Edward Dowling, S.J., a St. Louis Jesuit priest who pointed out the remarkable similarity between the Twelve Steps of

AA and the Spiritual Exercises of St. Ignatius Loyola, founder of the Jesuit order. This history is recounted in *Alcoholics Anonymous Comes of Age* (1957), and by Kurtz (1979).

But it should be made clear that the program of Alcoholics Anonymous was not borrowed from any of these. It grew out of the actual experiences of the founders and early members. The similarity with other movements is largely due to the basic psychological and spiritual soundness of what they have in common. That is why the Twelve Steps are not a statement of what anyone should do, but simply a record of what these people did: "We admitted . . . came to believe . . . made a decision . . . " These experiences were formulated into the twelve suggested steps in December 1938, and published in the book *Alcoholics Anonymous* in 1939, which has been added to several times since but never essentially changed. The source of AA's appeal was not its origins or its philosophy, but that it worked.

Growth at first was slow. Only forty members were staying sober in the first two years, and a bare one hundred by the fourth anniversary. Brief articles in *Liberty* (Markey, 1939) and in *Collier's* (Anonymous, 1939) gave them some notice, but their rapid growth really began when Jack Alexander wrote an article in *The Saturday Evening Post* for March 1, 1941 (reprint available from AA). In 1944 a monthly, *The AA Grapevine*, commenced publication, and in 1953 a book, *Twelve Steps and Twelve Traditions*, set forth the workings and spirit of the group. The Twentieth Anniversary Convention at St. Louis in 1955 saw membership at about 200,000. Here the three legacies of recovery, unity, and service were turned over by its founders to an elected General Service Conference. By 1967 *The AA Way of Life* was published, and a large number of pamphlets were appearing. By then the movement, at first largely in the United States and Canada, had 20 percent of its membership in overseas groups. The 1973 booklet *Came to Believe* expressed the wide range of individual members' spiritual views, smoothing the way for many doubters. In 1980 the Forty-fifth Anniversary Convention was attended in New Orleans by 25,000 people, and total membership reached the one million mark in 1977.

The AA Program

One way to grasp quickly how AA works is to list the things it does not do, contrary to some assumptions. It does not solicit members, promote any religion or abstinence movement, provide social service such as housing or jobs, run hospitals or any treatment services, follow up or try to control its members, claim to be a cure-all or help with any other problem except excessive drinking, accept any money for services or contributions from outside sources, make medical or psychological diagnoses, prescribe or pay for treatment, claim to be the only successful approach or that one must be an alcoholic to deal with the problem, engage in or sponsor research, affiliate with any other organization, nor hire professional field workers.

How it Works

Dr. Bob and Bill W. did not succeed with anybody else for théir first six months, but they noticed that as a result of their efforts they were staying sober themselves. AA members share their experience with anyone else seeking help with a drinking problem, and offer the alcoholic an opportunity to develop a satisfying way of life free from alcohol. They sponsor new members and discuss their program at AA meetings, which may be either *open* to anyone or *closed* except to members. Meetings are either *speaker* meetings, in which members tell their stories, *discussion* meetings, which may center either around their experiences in recovery or around some topic such as humility, faith, resentments, etc., or *step* meetings, which explore in depth one of the Twelve Steps. The recital of personal history ("drunkalog") is to encourage newcomers to realize that no matter how bad they may seem, others have recovered who were worse off. It also serves as an emotional catharsis, and enables them to build self-respect by having their story accepted by the group. But the essence of the AA program is not these recitals; it is in the serious study and personal application of the Twelve Steps. This is how Chapter 5 of the book *Alcoholics Anonymous* presents them:

> Our stories disclose in a general way what we used to be like, what happened, and what we are like now. If you have decided you want what we have and are willing to go to any length to get it—then you are ready to take certain steps.
>
> At some of these we balked. We thought we could find an easier, softer way. But we could not. With all the earnestness at our command, we beg of you to be fearless and thorough from the very start. Some of us have tried to hold on to our old ideas and the result was nil until we let go absolutely.
>
> Remember that we deal with alcohol—cunning, baffling, powerful! Without help it is too much for us. But there is One who has all power—that One is God. May you find Him now!
>
> Half measures availed us nothing. We stood at the turning point. We asked His protection and care with complete abandon.
>
> Here are the steps we took, which are suggested as a program of recovery:
>
> 1. We admitted we were powerless over alcohol—that our lives had become unmanageable.
> 2. Came to believe that a Power greater than ourselves could restore us to sanity.

3. Made a decision to turn our will and our lives over to the care of God *as we understood Him.*
4. Made a searching and fearless moral inventory of ourselves.
5. Admitted to God, to ourselves, and to another human being the exact nature of our wrongs.
6. Were entirely ready to have God remove all these defects of character.
7. Humbly asked Him to remove our shortcomings.
8. Made a list of all persons we had harmed, and became willing to make amends to them all.
9. Made direct amends to such people wherever possible, except when to do so would injure them or others.
10. Continued to take personal inventory and when we were wrong promptly admitted it.
11. Sought through prayer and meditation to improve our conscious contact with God *as we understood Him,* praying only for knowledge of His will for us and the power to carry that out.
12. Having had a spiritual awakening as the result of these steps, we tried to carry this message to alcoholics and to practice these principles in all our affairs.

Many of us exclaimed, "What an order! I can't go through with it." Do not be discouraged. No one among us has been able to maintain anything like perfect adherence to these principles. We are not saints. The point is that we are willing to grow along spiritual lines. The principles we have set down are guides to progress. We claim spiritual progress rather than spiritual perfection.

Our description of the alcoholic, the chapter to the agnostic, and our personal adventures before and after make clear three pertinent ideas:

(a) That we were alcoholic and could not manage our own lives.

(b) That probably no human power could have relieved our alcoholism.

(c) That God could and would if He were sought.

(From Alcoholics Anonymous copyright © 1939, by Alcoholic Anonymous World Services, Inc. Reprinted by permission of Alcoholics Anonymous World Services, Inc.)

Why It Works

It is indeed quite an order. The fifth chapter continues with an analysis of selfishness and egocentricity that is a marvel of commonsense psychology. Reading the AA literature one is struck by the constant emphasis on humility, a favorite theme of cofounder Bill W. This is not to further beat down already-discouraged alcoholics, but to inject some perspective into their self-esteem by an honest acceptance of limitations and acknowledgment of God rather than self as the ultimate source of assets. The founders' psychiatrist friend Harry M. Tiebout wrote much about the role of egotism and the need for surrender. Pride, it seems, is the chief obstacle to sobriety as it is to progress in the spiritual life. Here psychology and spirituality meet in a common recognition of the need for dependence on a Higher Power, apart from any religious dogma. Ego, far more than libido, was seen as the great enemy of adjustment and serenity.

But simplicity of purpose rather than psychological analysis is the great strength of Alcoholics Anonymous. The fellowship concentrates on achieving and maintaining sobriety to the exclusion of other enterprises. Some criticize the use of clichés and simpleminded slogans, but the desperate alcoholic recovering from a foggy haze needs some simple hooks to grab on to, not complexity and subtlety. Moreover, simplicity tends to be a hallmark of greatness in art, philosophy, and science as well as in successful social movements. It is certainly no obstacle to being profound.

In keeping with this simplicity, we suggest that one reason why AA is so effective is because it applies the basic psychology of motivation. Lindworsky (1928) had shown that there is no such thing as raw will power, that the key is not strength of resolution but keeping the motive in consciousness. Attendance at meetings and other contacts have the net effect of keeping the alcoholic always conscious of the danger of taking that first drink, and the need to nip in the bud any resentments or egotism that could lead to drinking. Add to this the whole psychology of surrender and the spiritual experience of turning one's life over to God as each understands Him, and you have a combination that is highly effective. The Sources at the end of this chapter indicate many more profound analyses, but this seems to put it in a nutshell.

Surrender, of course, demands humility, and this is never easy for human pride. The encouragement and experience of others is helpful here, and the counsel of one's AA sponsor can keep things on an even keel. The inventory of Step 4 is not all negative, but reveals positive assets as well. Focus is on staying sober, not analysis of why one drank. The self-examination is aimed at preventing relapse, not harping on the past. "One day at a time" is a motto that has practical psychological value. A major boon is also the discovery that one is not alone, that others have had the same problems and discouragements. Sharing helps others, but the first benefit of twelfth step work is that it keeps oneself sober. For this reason members call it a selfish program, in that primacy is always given to maintaining one's own sobriety, even as a prior condition to helping others. This kind of enlightened selfishness naturally benefits everyone in the long run. Honesty, open-mindedness, and willingness are key words.

If there is a sense of grim earnestness in the members at times, it is because they know they are battling a "hard" drug: hard on the body, hard to overcome, hard on their lives, families, friends. They know they need total surrender, total commitment, no half measures. But along with this is a lighthearted good humor, a sense of friendliness and fellowship, dances and breakfasts and picnics, where even complete strangers can relax and enjoy each other without fear that excessive drinking will spoil the fun.

The Three Legacies

Bill W. made three talks at the Twentieth Anniversary Convention in 1955 describing three legacies bequeathed to the membership. The talks constitute Chapter 2 of *Alcoholics Anonymous Comes of Age*. The first legacy is Recovery, focusing on personal survival. It is embodied largely in the Twelve Steps and in the book *Alcoholics Anonymous*. It may not have invented, but at least it recognized, assembled, and applied some great psychological and spiritual principles.

Twelve Traditions. The second legacy is Unity, looking to the survival of AA as a whole. It is embodied principally in the following twelve traditions.

The Twelve Traditions of AA
1. Our common welfare should come first; personal recovery depends upon AA unity.
2. For our group purpose there is but one ultimate authority—a loving God as He may express Himself in our group conscience. Our leaders are but trusted servants—they do not govern.
3. The only requirement for AA membership is a desire to stop drinking.
4. Each group should be autonomous, except in matters affecting other groups or AA as a whole.
5. Each group has but one primary purpose—to carry its message to the alcoholic who still suffers.
6. An AA group ought never to endorse, finance or lend the AA name to any related facility or outside enterprise lest problems of money, property, and prestige divert us from our primary purpose.
7. Every AA group ought to be fully self-supporting, declining outside contributions.
8. Alcoholics Anonymous should remain forever nonprofessional, but our service centers may employ special workers.
9. AA, as such, ought never to be organized; but we may create service boards or committees directly responsible to those they serve.
10. Alcoholics Anonymous has no opinion on outside issues; hence the AA name ought never to be drawn into public controversy.
11. Our public relations policy is based on attraction rather than promotion; we need always maintain personal anonymity at the level of press, radio and films.
12. Anonymity is the spiritual foundation of all our traditions, ever reminding us to place principles above personalities.
(Copyright © and reprinted by permission of Alcoholics Anonymous World Services, Inc.)

We shall comment briefly on only two features: poverty and anonymity. Voluntary poverty (Tradition 7) is a characteristic of AA that is striking in a materialistic age. During its early struggle for existence AA had asked John D. Rockefeller for $50,000, which he refused lest it ruin their singleness of purpose, giving them only a $5,000 emergency grant. They acknowledged the wisdom of his decision and agreed to avoid accumulating any wealth which might be a source of contention or create a conflict of interest. Pride and ambition have little to feed on in AA. Authority is nonexistent. Leaders are but trusted servants—they do not govern; each group is autonomous except in matters affecting other groups or the whole (Traditions 2 and 4). The result (Tradition 9) is referred to by the members with loving humor as "the most unorganized organization in the world" but at least it presents no obstacles for the newcomer and no chance to build a power structure.

The anonymity implied by its name is another strong feature of the fellowship. Not intended to perpetuate the stigma of alcoholism but to protect the humility of its members, it has the great advantage of making membership no threat to the newcomer who might fear for his reputation. A General Conference leaflet, *Understanding Anonymity*, based largely on writings of Bill W., lays out a balanced middle course between grandiosity, which might lead to relapse, and secrecy, which could prevent suffering alcoholics from receiving the message. In brief, Traditions 11 and 12 forbid self-identification with AA at the level of public communications media such as film, press, radio or television, while allowing one to identify oneself as a recovered alcoholic. They forbid disclosure of the identity of another member outside the meeting, but allow one to identify oneself as a member below the level of public media. Within the fellowship customs differ, some groups using only first names at meetings but the majority apparently using full names within the group.

The third legacy is that of Service. Originally this meant service to AA itself, from making the coffee to acting as an elected representative to the General Service Conference. More recently it has included the whole matter of serving other alcoholics who need help, not only in twelfth step work, which must remain forever nonprofessional according to Tradition 8, but also by the activity of AA members working professionally in the field. Evolution of this latter situation has been gradual and sometimes painful, but a clear tradition has emerged and is expressed in AA literature, especially *AA Guidelines for Members Employed in the Alcoholism Field* (rev. 1977), which again reveals the eminent common sense of the group conscience. This will be discussed further in Chapter 21.

AA Today

Over the years many changes have taken place, although the basic soundness and spiritual wisdom of the Twelve Steps have not changed. AA has come of age, professionalism has entered the field, those once in the honeymoon stage are now the entrenched old guard. This is inevitable because AA is a living organism, not a corpse, and change is characteristic of living things. "There are no rules in AA, and God help anybody who breaks them." In other words, there are always the liberals and conservatives in any group, with resultant need for tolerance, a balance between the old and the new.

Change is also inevitable because each member is allowed to apply the steps as he or she sees fit: one million interpretations of a single program. Too often AA is stereotyped, by both professionals and its own members, on the basis of single or limited contacts. The wide variation between individuals and between groups must be stressed. Each member is unique, and one research study showed individuals in the same locality to vary on an important characteristic between zero and 86 percent. Another example is the fact that although some have had an ecstatic spiritual experience such as Bill W. had, most members have a gradual, less dramatic spiritual awakening and many find the spiritual aspects difficult to accept at first.

Membership in AA today is younger, getting away from the old stereotype that one has to drink for a long time in order to be an alcoholic, or that one must lose everything in order to "hit bottom." Talk now is of an "early" or "high" bottom, indicating that surrender can come at any age and there are many young alcoholics. The proportion of women in AA is steadily increasing, as the double standard lessens. There is more emphasis on the steps and less on the drunkalogs. There is more openness to working with professionals, and cooperation (but not affiliation) with other approaches to recovery. There is more awareness of the role of the family, and joint meetings with Al-Anon, the subject of our next chapter. At least one large AA regional conference recently had the major Al-Anon presentation on the main program, not in a concurrent session.

Rate of Success

In addition to the tradition of anonymity, which means no member lists, another reason why it is hard to assess the success rate of AA with any accuracy is that today there is a tendency for alcoholics to utilize several approaches. The 1974 survey showed a surprisingly high percentage of members had been referred to AA by professionals, and a large number had combined AA with other helps. Depending on criteria, success rates in AA have been put at 75 to 89 percent, after one relapse for about half of these. That is, the first year is the hardest and about half relapse once; eventually a high percentage stay sober for five years or more. But keeping score is less important than people getting well. AA never claimed 100 percent success; the sheer numbers attest to the impact of the movement.

Not Perfect

AA has, of course, been criticized. Some of this may be due to professional jealousy, some to impatience with the non-scientific and unstructured nature of its operation, some to uneasiness with the spiritual, some to misunderstanding or ignorance. The Twelve Steps are not something to be read, but to be lived. Outside observers can hardly be expected to grasp them readily. Being human, the members themselves make it quite clear that their adherence to the program is not perfect. When cofounder Bill W. saw that some of the criticisms had foundation in fact, he urged that they be taken with humility for what might be of profit, in "Our Critics Can Be Our Benefactors" (AA Grapevine, April 1963) and elsewhere.

Some of these criticisms include rigidity and literal-mindedness both in the interpretation of the steps and in the conducting of meetings. It is true that each member may interpret the steps at will, and the group conscience can decide how to conduct the meeting, so that theoretically this objection should not hold water. But in practice it is sometimes true. Although AA never claimed to be the only means of recovery and explicitly rejected this position, some individual members talk this way. Likewise in the matter of cooperation with the medical profession. There have always been close ties and much cooperation, from the days of Dr. Bob and Sister Ignatia, but individual members sometimes speak as if the opposite were true. It might be noted that one-half of the founders of AA belonged to the medical profession (Dr. Bob), and the first two counselors were non-alcoholic women (Henrietta Seiberling and Sister Ignatia). Dogmatism and smugness are, of course, the direct opposite of the humility and tolerance advocated by the AA slogan "Live and let live." More important, they tend to drive those who are unattracted to AA into despair, presuming that if AA is the only way, then for them there is no hope. Recall the section on "Objectivity" in Chapter 13. If one gets to the right meeting at the right time, AA will work—but that is a lot of ifs.

Psychotherapists sometimes object that there is too much repression of emotion and not sufficient room for catharsis. This may be true for some individuals, but that is probably best handled by professional psychotherapy later and would be dangerous for amateurs. In general, alcoholics have led an undisciplined life and need some controls rather than uninhibited expression. Some criticism stems from the fact that professionals get a distorted sampling because they rarely see those who find a happy sobriety in AA. Perhaps a more valid criticism is that AA prolongs dependence on the group for some and prevents their growth back into full involvement with society. This again is not intrinsic to the AA program, which is one of true growth. It may apply to some individuals, but we must recall that any chronic disease needs lifetime care and some persons will always need more care than others. The same is true of the concentration on mere avoidance of drinking; alcohol is mentioned only in the first step, and the remaining steps have to do with total personality development. But some groups or individuals forget that sobriety is more than mere abstinence. *Twelve Steps and Twelve Traditions* (1953, pp 116–120) speaks of "two-steppers," members who seem to know only Steps 1 and 12 and ignore the demanding regime of Steps 2 through 11.

Some poor impressions of AA stem from unskillful referrals. One should prepare the prospect by careful explanation of AA (or Al-Anon), with special stress on anonymity and one's complete freedom in how they understand the Higher Power. The sponsor plays an important role, and should be carefully selected. A sponsor should be matched to the client so there is at least some compatibility of age, occupation, or other common interest, and always be of the same sex (by an unwritten tradition). An appropriate sample of meetings should be given, with explanation of the choice between open and closed, stag, women, or mixed, and special-interest groups. Many alcoholics need to break the habit-pattern and achieve some sobriety through other means first, and then find AA most helpful for long-term follow-up and a new way of life.

A Personal Impression

It is impossible to put on paper the electrifying excitement of those 20,000 AA members at Denver in 1975; the warm acceptance upon addressing 1,300 AA and Al-Anon members at Honolulu in 1976; or the sense of universal understanding when one walks into an open meeting of total strangers a thousand miles away without any identification or even being a member and finds himself at home. For all these experiences and many more the author is profoundly grateful, and feels that not only his knowledge of alcoholism but also his spiritual life is the better because of them.

Sources

AA can be looked at from several perspectives. The first is from within AA, then how others see it. The AA Conference-approved literature is obtainable locally at AA intergroup offices listed in most telephone directories, or from AA World Services (see Appendix) which will furnish a complete list. Books include:

The AA Way of Life (A Reader by Bill)
Alcoholics Anonymous
Alcoholics Anonymous Comes of Age
Came to Believe
Living Sober
Twelve Steps and Twelve Traditions

Their pamphlets cover every phase of AA activity, and are too numerous to list here. We mention a few introductory items; see also the items about cooperation with professionals listed in Sources for Chapter 21.

The AA Group: How a Group Functions, How to Get One Started
44 Questions and Answers about the AA Program of Recovery from Alcoholism
A Member's Eye-View of Alcoholics Anonymous
Questions and Answers on Sponsorship
Understanding Anonymity

Non-AA Sources

In addition to a wealth of pamphlet material (Hazelden, CompCare, NCA and others listed in the Appendix), we list a few items depicting how others see Alcoholics Anonymous:

BAEKELAND, FREDERICK et al., "Methods for the Treatment of Chronic Alcoholism: A Critical Appraisal," in R.J. Gibbins (ed.), *Research Advances in Alcohol and Drug Problems*, vol. 2, pp. 247–327.

BEAN, MARGARET, "Alcoholics Anonymous: Principles and Methods," *Psychiatric Annals*, February-March, 1975, vol. 5, nn. 2 and 3.

BLUMBERG, LEONARD, "The Ideology of a Therapeutic Social Movement: Alcoholics Anonymous," *Journal of Studies on Alcohol*, 1977, 38:2122–2143.

C., BILL, "The Growth and Effectiveness of Alcoholics Anonymous in a Southwestern City," *Quarterly Journal of Studies on Alcohol*, 1965, 26:279-284.

CLINEBELL, HOWARD J., "AA Our Greatest Resource," Chapter 5 in *Understanding and Counseling the Alcoholic*, rev. ed., 1968.

CURLEE, JOAN, "Combined Use of Alcoholics Anonymous and Outpatient Psychotherapy," (NCA reprint from *Bulletin of the Menninger Clinic*, 1971, pp. 368–371).

CURLEE-SALISBURY, JOAN, "Perspectives on Alcoholics Anonymous," Chapter 25 in Estes and Heinemann. Has 20 references.

DELEHANTY, EDWARD J., "The Therapeutic Value of the Twelve Steps of AA," Utah Alcoholism Foundation, n.d. Hazelden reprint.

GELLMAN, I.P., *The Sober Alcoholic: An Organizational Analysis of Alcoholics Anonymous*.

JOHNSON, VERNON, *I'll Quit Tomorrow*.

JONES, K.J., "Sectarian Characteristics of Alcoholics Anonymous," *Sociology*, 1970, 4:181–195.

KURTZ, ERNEST, *Not-God: A History of Alcoholics Anonymous*.

LEACH, BARRY, "Does AA Really Work?" Chapter 11 in P. Bourne and R. Fox (eds.), *Alcoholism: Progress in Research and Treatment*. Ample references.

LEACH, BARRY and J.L. NORRIS, "Factors in the Development of Alcoholics Anonymous (AA)," in Kissin, B. and H. Begleiter (eds.), *The Biology of Alcoholism* (1977), vol. 5, pp. 441–453.

LEE, JOHN PARK, "Alcoholics Anonymous as a Community Resource," *Social Work*, October 1960, 5:20–26. NCA reprint.

MADSEN, WILLIAM, "AA: Birds of a Feather," Chapter IX in *The American Alcoholic*.

MANN, MARTY, *New Primer on Alcoholism*, Chapter 11; *Marty Mann Answers Your Questions About Alcoholism*, Chapter 13.

MAXWELL, MILTON A., "Alcoholics Anonymous: An Interpretation," in D.J. Pittman and C.R. Snyder (eds.), *Society, Culture and Drinking Patterns*.

NORRIS, J.L., "Alcoholics Anonymous," in E.D. Whitney (ed.), *World Dialogue on Alcohol and Drug Dependence*.

NORRIS, J.L., "Alcoholics Anonymous and Other Self-Help Groups," in R. Tarter and A. Sugerman (eds.), *Alcoholism: Interdisciplinary Approaches to an Enduring Problem*.

RIPLEY, H.S. and JOAN K. JACKSON, "Therapeutic Factors in Alcoholics Anonymous," *American Journal of Psychiatry*, 1959, 116: 44–50.

STEWART, DAVID, *Thirst for Freedom*, Chapter 7.

STRACHAN, J. GEORGE, *Alcoholism: Treatable Illness*, Chapter 22; also treats relation of AA to public programs in his *Practical Alcoholism Programming*.

THOMSEN, ROB., *Bill W.* (biography).

TIEBOUT, HARRY M., "Therapeutic Mechanism of Alcoholics Anonymous," *American Journal of Psychiatry*, 1944, 100:468–473; also "Alcoholics Anonymous: An Experiment of Nature," *Quarterly Journal of Studies on Alcohol*, 1961, 22:52–68.

TRICE, HARRISON M., "A Study of the Process of Affiliation with Alcoholics Anonymous" *Quarterly Journal of Studies on Alcohol*, 1957, 18:39–54; also his "Delabeling, Relabeling and Alcoholics Anonymous,"*Social Problems*, 1970, 17:4; and "The Affiliation Motive and Readiness to Join Alcoholics Anonymous," *Quarterly Journal of Studies on Alcohol*, 1959, 20:313–320.

ZINBERG, N.E., "Alcoholics Anonymous and the Treatment and Prevention of Alcoholism," *Alcoholism: Clinical and Experimental Research*, 1977, 1:91–102.

CHAPTER 16

Al-Anon and Alateen

IN VIEW OF shortages in funds and personnel, the dismaying statistics on the number of alcoholics have one bright aspect: the more people who join Alcoholics Anonymous, the more people there are to help other alcoholics. Granted that funding for treatment of the alcoholic is still inadequate, the family gets even less help. Here again, volunteers with the AA philosophy fill the gap—this time in the form of two offshoots of the Alcoholics Anonymous program. Al-Anon is for husbands, wives, other relatives, or friends of the alcoholic, and Alateen is for children of alcoholic parents. In some cities there are special groups of Alatots, for children younger than teenage, though they often meet together with the Alateens and prefer to be called Preteens.

Just as we have emphasized that an alcoholic is not necessarily a skid-road male, so we must stress that in some Al-Anon groups today the majority are husbands of female alcoholics. The alcoholic may or may not have achieved sobriety and may or may not be in AA. In any case, the family and those close to the alcoholic need help with their own problems and must learn to cope whether the alcoholic gets well or not.

Origin. In the late 1930s, when Alcoholics Anonymous was beginning, close relatives realized that they too needed help and sought solutions by following the principles of AA in what they called Family

Groups. In 1951 several wives of AA members formed a committee, which was incorporated in 1954 as a non-profit organization now known as Al-Anon Family Groups. Thus Al-Anon started as an outgrowth of AA, though it is a completely separate organization.

By 1978 Al-Anon had extended to over seventy countries. Some 14,000 groups worldwide include 2,200 Alateen groups. Lone members serve as referrals where groups have not yet formed. As in AA, some meetings are held in institutions, such as hospitals and prisons. Al-Anon has produced six books, over forty pamphlets, a monthly publication and a bimonthly newsletter, as well as cooperating with the public media in the production of TV films. magazine articles, and other materials.

Alateen started in 1957 when Bob, the seventeen-year-old son of an alcoholic, hoped to find the serenity his mother found in Al-Anon and his father found in AA. He decided to apply the Al-Anon program to his own life, and contacted five other teenagers with alcoholic parents. They chose the name Alateen and became a component of Al-Anon. Although both groups began with families, the fellowship now extends to anyone who suffers because of someone close.

What is Al-Anon

Al-Anon Family Groups are a fellowship of relatives and friends of alcoholics who have banded together to solve their common problems. Al-Anon is a recovery program for people who suffer because someone close to them drinks too much. At Al-Anon meetings members learn, through mutual aid and loving interchange, that their own recovery is possible whether or not the drinker seeks help or even recognizes that a drinking problem exists. Al-Anon groups are nonprofessional, nondenominational, self-supporting and have no opinions on outside issues. Anyone who feels his/her personal life is or has been deeply affected by a problem drinker is eligible for Al-Anon membership.

The Al-Anon purpose is threefold: to offer comfort, hope and friendship to the families of compulsive drinkers; to learn to grow spiritually by living the Twelve Steps adopted from Alcoholics Anonymous; to give understanding and encouragement to the alcoholic.

What It Is Not.   It is clear that the group does *not* have as its purpose to "reform" the alcoholic. Their primary purpose is to improve themselves and work on their own defects. If the recovery of the alcoholic is hastened indirectly by changes observed in the member, this is a welcome by-product. But the image of Al-Anon as a group who sit around and complain about how much their spouse drinks or how badly they are treated is a stereotype that must be exploded at once. The new member is allowed to vent feelings on this subject just once, and the second time it comes up the group kindly but firmly directs the conversation to what the new member should be doing about *self*-improvement.

How Al-Anon Works

Detachment—the First Step.   Al-Anon and Alateen use the same Twelve Steps as Alcoholics Anonymous. In the first step they admit that they are powerless over alcohol, that they cannot control the excessive drinking of their spouse, parent or friend. After years of manipulating, nagging, worrying, and feeling guilty, this is as big a step as the admission is for the alcoholic. But the sense of relief when they move on to the second and third steps is equally great: They turn the matter over to a Higher Power as they understand Him, and then go about the business of correcting their own defects (Steps 4 through 10).

We saw in Chapter 8 that for the most part the old psychological theories of alcoholic marriages put far too much stress on the predisposing personality of the spouse. Most of the spouse's apparent neuroticism is not the cause but the result of living with the problem, being obsessed with it, feeling guilty because surely the problem would not exist if only they could do the right thing or avoid doing the wrong thing. Recognizing in Step 1 that they cannot control the drinking means less guilt feeling in the Al-Anon member, but correspondingly a recognition of the inability to do much about the drinker. They learn that their alcoholic is sick, not ungrateful or malicious. This is a relief, but it also shifts the focus from the alcoholic to learning how to manage their own lives properly. No longer can they blame the alcoholic's drinking for their own shortcomings.

As Al-Anon and Alateen members learn more about the illness of alcoholism, they stop fighting a lot of ghosts and come to grips with real issues. They learn that scolding or arguing does not help, and only hurts both parties. Most important, they learn that shielding the alcoholic, lying to the boss, paying bail or fine, and all forms of smother love only encourage the alcoholic behavior. Letting alcoholics feel the full responsibility for their actions had seemed cruel, but it is now seen as kindness because it hastens that moment of truth that is the beginning of recovery. Detachment is not cold and selfish, but a form of the "tough love" that has proven so beneficial in confronting alcoholics through occupational programs and elsewhere. Members detach from the problem, not the person.

Denial of alcoholism plays a big role in the family, as it does in the thinking of the alcoholic. The group helps to penetrate this denial because they can share insights. For the spouse the denial is more likely to be interwoven with self-pity. Again the group can often work more effectively on the "poor me" syndrome than an individual therapist can. Resentments and blaming the alcoholic need to be aired, and the group is able to put these feelings in an objective light because they have all been through them. The fact that they are not alcoholic has been used subconsciously to mean that all the family troubles stem from the drinking. Although this may be true to a great extent, the picture has become distorted.

Spiritual.   Like AA, Al-Anon is compatible with all religions and offends none. It is a spiritual program that allows all to conceive of God in their own way, careful not to affiliate with any sect or denomination. Skeptics and agnostics are accepted, and allowed to work out their own program as they see fit. Tolerance and good humor are evident at every meeting, and in the social events they often sponsor jointly with AA.

Sharing is Beneficial.   The fellowship of Al-Anon does two things. It lets people know they are not alone, that others have the same fears and frustrations and have made the same mistakes. And it gives the opportunity to get involved in helping others, a source of personal satisfaction as well as a distraction from one's own troubles. The warmth and genuine friendship one observes among Al-Anon members is somewhat unique, in some ways more striking than that among members of Alcoholics Anonymous. Probably it stems from the sense of mutual understanding, after years of thinking that nobody could possibly know what they were going through. Alcoholics can anesthetize themselves to much of the misery simply by drinking, and might find at least superficial companionship in their drinking buddies. The spouse or child of the alcoholic lacks both of these cushions. Joining Al-Anon or Alateen does not provide the anesthesia, but it does give a much deeper companionship.

The new member says, "My case is different from any of yours because my husband says if he weren't married to me, he wouldn't need to drink." The person in the chair replies, "That's the cop-out every one of us has heard." The new member raises her head and sees members nodding in agreement all around the table, some with soft smiles of reassurance. She is not alone. She learns to accept with serenity the things she cannot change, while praying for the courage to change the things she can, and the wisdom to know the difference. Soon she will enjoy the thrill of helping others achieve the same realization. But each needs to tell their story, no matter how often others may have heard it.

Differences from AA

Although they use the same Twelve Steps and basic philosophy, Al-Anon differs from Alcoholics Anonymous in some minor respects. We have already noted that there seems to be more intimate warmth. There are more daytime meetings, and more attention to such arrangements as baby-sitting. Anonymity is a more sensitive issue, and there are fewer open meetings. This is understandable. "The whole town knew I was a drunk," says many an alcoholic; "I don't care who knows I'm happy to be a member of AA." But the spouse says, "If I am identified as Al-Anon, that could hurt my marriage partner's business or career." Visitors at open meetings are well advised not to bring notebooks or cameras, and to be very discreet about even the semblance of violating anonymity. As the stigma of alcoholism decreases and the benefits of Al-Anon become more widely known, this difference may diminish.

A special problem for Al-Anon is the detachment called for in Step 1 (Reddy, 1978). After years of feeling responsible for the alcoholic's drinking, it may be as difficult to break this habit as it is for the alcoholic to stop drinking. By first admitting in Step 1 their own powerlessness to control the alcoholic, they are able to turn the matter over to God (Step 3) and learn to live their own lives. A delicate question is whether Al-Anon sometimes prolongs the detachment of the first step to the point of missing the chance for a confrontation with the alcoholic, which might get him or her into treatment. One must balance a respect for the traditional emphasis in Al-Anon on that first step against what we now know about the success rates of forced treatment. We repeat, this is a delicate issue, to be raised only when the surrender is complete, detachment has been achieved, and the false guilt problems have been well worked through. For example, Jane learned that to detach is not to ignore, and that Step 1 does not mean she must let her husband drink himself to death. When she finally spoke to him directly, he went immediately into treatment

Varied Membership

The Al-Anon philosophy can apply in a wide variety of situations. Attendance at meetings may be helpful while the alcoholic is still drinking, during the early days of recovery, as the period of sobriety lengthens even into years, if the alcoholic is no longer in the home, if the alcoholic is the parent of an adult Al-Anon member, and if the alcoholic is a woman. People in any of these or similar circumstances may attend. The point is to recognize that they need help as much as does the alcoholic. An increasing number of parents of alcoholics are finding help in Al-Anon, especially with problems of stigma and false guilt about the alcoholism of their offspring.

Problems after Recovery.   The last section of Chapter 8 detailed the family problems that arise in Jackson's Stage 7, after recovery and reunion. Although one may be a member of Al-Anon whether the alcoholic is in AA or not, the following advice applies especially if the alcoholic is an AA member:

The Al-Anon member should be willing to cooperate with the alcoholic's efforts to get and maintain sobriety in AA, but should not interfere or advise. Alcoholics have a better chance of success when the family leaves them free to work out their own problems. Overcoming the obsession to drink requires an equally strong drive toward involvement with something positive like Alcoholics Anonymous, so one must accept graciously the need for spending much time at meetings and in doing Twelfth Step work helping others. When the alcoholic is busy with AA, one can cure the lonely, left-out feeling by becoming active in Al-Anon. Sometimes the AA member, elated with the achievement of sobriety, may assume a superior attitude. This is a natural reaction to former inferiority feelings; AA is a spiritual program, and as one grows in humility one's attitude will moderate. We must have patience, and then more patience. Sometimes it is harder to bear with daily petty irritations than it was to deal with the big problem of alcoholism. So don't be discouraged if progress is slow. Some alcoholics are sicker than others and take longer to get well. As an Al-Anon-leaflet suggests,

> *Don't expect immediate personal readjustment.* The distorted relationships which resulted from drinking will still leave many personal problems to be ironed out. Patience and understanding will do it! *Have faith in the alcoholic.* Don't let yourself doubt, even if he slips back one or more times. The AA fellowship has a long history of successes with cases that seemed hopeless. *

Husbands of alcoholic wives seem to have special problems, which are only now beginning to be studied. It has long been known that they are far more prone to divorce their wives, whereas the wife of an alcoholic husband will tend to hang on to the marriage. How much of this is feminine loyalty and how much is sheer economic dependence is not known. Denial seems stronger in the husband. Perhaps the male ego still holds him to the role of protector and head of the household. His wife's alcoholism is an affront to his management ability and pride of leadership. Perhaps chivalry prevents him from admitting that the lady he vowed to love and cherish is an alcoholic. While the wife of the alcoholic husband finds sympathy from family, friends and the clergy, the husband of the alcoholic wife too often out of pride refuses to discuss his secret with anyone. Without the help of Al-Anon the resentments build up until he simply packs up and leaves. If the alcoholic wife is also a career woman, the competition and overlapping of roles may make the situation extremely complex.

"*Double Winners*" is the title of a 1977 Al-Anon leaflet addressed to those who have reason to belong both to Alcoholics Anonymous and to Al-

*From "Purpose and Suggestions," p. 13, copyright © 1969 by, and reprinted by permission of, Al-Anon Family Group Headquarters, Inc.

Anon: recovering alcoholics who are also married or close to an alcoholic. Experience suggests that when both parties to a marriage are alcoholics, even recovered ones, the chances of marital difficulties increase notably. But likelihood of success can be enhanced by the dual membership in AA and Al-Anon. Even the person who is working the AA program well can learn how to take a different inventory (Step 4) as an Al-Anon spouse or family member rather than as an alcoholic. Release or "detachment with love" can eliminate a lot of marital friction. "Double winners" often say that in AA they learned how to accept themselves, and in Al-Anon they learned how to accept their spouse.

Alateen

The Alateen program uses the same Twelve Steps and much of the literature of Al-Anon, but has also developed its own traditions and materials. Usually the sponsor of an Alateen group is a member of Al-Anon who helps the Alateen leader arrange the time and place of the meeting and sometimes helps conduct it. This group sponsorship is necessary to insure continuity (teenagers soon outgrow this period), and to lend adult status to meeting arrangements and permissions to be out at night. But the Alateen group runs its own meetings and develops its own leadership. Meetings at school can have the advantages of not having to be out at night, not requiring transportation to another site, and not antagonizing the alcoholic parent.

Children of Alcoholics

Having an alcoholic parent can have devastating effects on a child. They may become confused, withdrawn from other children and afraid to bring companions home. They may be divided in their loyalty between their two parents, and mistrusting of all adults. They are often inattentive in school, physically abused and perhaps sexually molested by the alcoholic parent, hostile and rebellious, lonely, insecure, defensive. They may feel neurotic guilt about their parent's drinking, and develop a wide spectrum of psychosomatic disorders, such as skin rashes and stomach upsets. They may be happy at school early in the week, and grow more tense as the weekend approaches. They may constantly fear being abandoned. They may try to compensate with bizarre attempts to win or buy acceptance from the other children. They may avoid alcohol entirely until their thirties or start drinking very early, but in either case then tend to become alcoholics in a higher proportion than average. They will deny and conceal their parent's alcoholism, with boys more likely to be chivalrous about their mother's drinking. They may act out their resentment and frustration by vandalism, truancy, shoplifting, early marriage, drinking or other drug abuse. Alateen helps them to acknowledge that these behaviors are mere escapes, and to take responsibility for their own lives regardless of whether the alcoholic parent stops drinking or not.

Too often the above serious symptoms signal the first time anyone realizes that the children need help. The alcoholic mother may compensate by sending the children off to school well dressed and scrubbed, so that signs of neglect do not appear until the problems are well advanced. This delay until late stage is fostered by the fact that their experiences as children of alcoholics result in earlier maturity. Having to take responsibility as substitute parent, adjusting to frequent moves, learning to subsist in spite of poverty or desertion, and trying to prevent their parents' fights may force them to learn how to cope with the world very early. They may be more aware of the cold facts of real life than their counselors.

It is generally agreed that when the mother is the alcoholic the effects on the children are worse, since she is usually more often with them and more directly involved in their care. She may alternate between being cross and overloving, belligerent while drinking and irritable during the hangover, with periods of overcompensation in between. She may fail to hear an infant cry or leave it wet and hungry, drop lighted cigarettes or hurt herself in falls, and otherwise keep the children in a constant state of anxiety, confusion, repressed rage, and rejection. She creates guilt feelings in the children by seeming to blame them for everything. She often throws a burden on the oldest girl as substitute mother, who shoulders it well at the time but resents it bitterly later.

Sharing all this in Alateen helps children to understand and handle these disturbing emotions. It must be emphasized that Alateens do not criticize the alcoholic's behavior, but learn to live less affected by it. They learn that they are not responsible for their family situation, and that they are not crazy, in spite of having been told that by their alcoholic parent.

Referral to Al-Anon and Alateen

As with referrals to AA, merely giving someone a phone number of Al-Anon is not enough. Referral should be based on a good understanding of the Al-Anon program, awareness of different groups and their characteristics, the mechanism of sponsorship, and with some preparation of the client through prior explanation and reading of the Al-Anon literature. If the spouse is already in therapy, the professional can use Al-Anon as supportive or adjunctive therapy and long-term follow-up. Clergy, skilled alcoholism counselors, and, surprisingly, even members of AA working professionally in the field sometimes neglect to use Al-Anon as a resource.

Occupational alcoholism programs in business and industry now see the value of engaging the spouse in Al-Anon, both for the spouse's own sake and for the added understanding support it gives the alcoholic. Al-Anon is prepared to furnish speakers and otherwise cooperate with health agencies, recovery centers, and institutions, making it a valuable adjunct without adding to budget.

Alateen referrals take special care. Teenagers need to be told that it is free, that it is strictly anonymous, that attendence is not a sign of disloyalty to their parents. Reassurance that it is okay to have an alcoholic parent is coupled with the idea that it is not okay to do nothing about it. All adolescents have troubles and doubts, so others can understand and help. The child is better off knowing that alcoholism is the problem, rather than remaining baffled by the unknown and risking greater danger of alcoholism themselves later. Referral must have the explicit permission of the child before contact is made with a sponsor, either Al-Anon or Alateen. Rather than driving the newcomer to a meeting, it is better to take them on the bus if that is the way they will be going to meetings. Although not necessary for participation in Alateen, if the nonalcoholic parent can be referred to Al-Anon, so much the better.

Ala-Family?

Alcoholics Anonymous, Al-Anon, and Alateen have all proven their worth in assisting with alcohol problems. The original name, Family Groups, in the early days of AA seems to support a recent proposal by Father Joseph Martin of *Chalk Talk* film fame. Given the tremendous advantage of group sharing and the importance of the family as a unit, we should promote joint meetings of all three and call them Ala-Family.

Sources

The primary source here is the Al-Anon and Alateen Conference-approved literature available locally from the groups or from Al-Anon Family Groups, Inc., 1 Park Avenue, New York 10017, and to which we are greatly indebted in the writing of this chapter. Books include:

Al-Anon Faces Alcoholism
Al-Anon's Favorite Forum Editorials
Alateen—Hope for the Children of Alcoholics
Dilemma of the Alcoholic Marriage
Living with an Alcoholic
One Day at a Time in Al-Anon

Pamphlets and leaflets explain every phase of Al-Anon and Alateen activity, some addressed to the new inquirer and some to those who wish to know more about how to form or sponsor groups. A few of the many Al-Anon titles include:

Alcoholism: The Family Disease
Al-Anon Family Groups at Work
Al-Anon, You and the Alcoholic
Blueprint for Progress (Al-Anon Step 4 Inventory)
"Double Winners" (dual membership in AA and Al-Anon)
Homeward Bound (for relatives of returning alcoholics)
Living with Sobriety: Another Beginning
A Teacher Finds Guidance in Al-Anon
Twelve Steps and Twelve Traditions for Al-Anon
Why is Al-Anon Anonymous?
(For men) *Al-Anon Is for Men*; *"My Wife Drinks Too Much"*; and *"What's Next?" Asks the Husband of an Alcoholic*
(For parents) *To the Mother and Father of an Alcoholic*; and *How Can I Help My Children?*

Alateen Conference Approved Pamphlets

A Guide for Sponsors of Alateen Groups
If Your Parents Drink Too Much (color cartoon booklet)
It's a Teenaged Affair . . .
Operation Alateen
Twelve Steps and Twelve Traditions for Alateen
Youth and the Alcoholic Parent

Non-Conference Sources

ABLON, JOAN, "Perspectives on Al-Anon Family Groups," in Estes and Heinemann, pp. 274–282.
BAILEY, M.B., "Al-Anon Family Groups as an Aid to Wives of Alcoholics," *Social Work*, 1965, 10:68–74.
HAZELDEN FOUNDATION, *Guide to the Fourth Step Inventory for the Spouse.*
KELLERMAN, JOSEPH L., "AA—A Family Affair," *Addictions*, Spring 1974, 21(1):19–33. See also his *Al-Anon: A Message of Hope*, and *Guide for the Family of the Alcoholic*, both Al-Anon pamphlets.
REDDY, BETTY and O.H. McELFRESH, "Detachment and Recovery from Alcoholism," *Alcohol Health and Research World*, Spring 1978, pp. 28–33.

Children of Alcoholic Parents

We list only a few items, some with only tangential relation to Alateen. Many of these contain further references, and a bibliography is available from the National Clearinghouse for Alcohol Information (NACLI).

An Assessment of the Needs and Resources for Children of Alcoholic Parents. NTIS, PB 241-119A/S.

ACKERMAN, ROBERT J., *Children of Alcoholics: A Guidebook for Educators, Therapists, and Parents.*

BLACK, CLAUDIA, "Innocent Bystanders at Risk: The Children of Alcoholics," *Alcoholism: The National Magazine*, January/February, 1981, 1(3):22–26.

CORK, MARGARET, *The Forgotten Children.*

CRAMER, PATRICE A., *An Educational Strategy to Impact the Children of Alcoholic Parents: A Feasibility Study.*

FOX, RUTH, "Treating the Alcoholic's Family," in R. Catanzaro, pp. 105–115. See also her NCA pamphlet, *The Effects of Alcoholism on Children*, and her chapter in William C. Bier (ed.), *Problems in Addiction*, pp. 71–96.

HINDMAN, MARGARET, "Child Abuse and Neglect: The Alcohol Connection," *Alcohol Health and Research World*, Spring 1977, pp. 2–7.

HOMILLER, JONICA, *Women and Alcohol*, bibliography pp. 28–35.

HORNIK, EDITH LYNN, *You and Your Alcoholic Parent.*

HUGHES, J.M., "Adolescent Children of Alcoholic Parents and the Relationship of Alateen to These Children," *Journal of Consulting and Clinical Psychology*, 1977, 45:946–947.

NCA, *The Lollipop Program: Alcohol Education for Young Children of Alcoholics.*

SAUER, JOAN, *The Neglected Majority.*

SEIXAS, JUDITH, "Children from Alcoholic Families," in Estes and Heinemann, pp. 153–161.

SEIXAS, JUDITH, *Living with a Parent who Drinks Too Much.*

CHAPTER 17

Rehabilitation

JUST AS DETOXIFICATION without definitive treatment for the alcoholism is just a more humane revolving door than the jail drunk tank, so treatment without long-range rehabilitation is largely a waste of time and money. Intensive treatment is not necessarily effective treatment. For lasting results, treatment requires at least one year. The first twenty-one or twenty-eight days may be in a treatment center and the remaining eleven months on an outpatient basis, but we should never allow talk of the twenty-eight-day treatment as if it were all over upon discharge. Given the chronic nature of the illness, it is wiser to think of the recovery process as lasting not one but two to three or even five years. Probably one reason why some research suggests that "all treatments work equally well" is because what one does to stop drinking is less important than what one does to remain stopped.

"White knuckle sobriety" refers to people who are barely hanging on to abstinence but are not comfortable in their sobriety. In contrast, truly recovered alcoholics move easily in a drinking society, serenely accepting the fact that others drink while they choose not to. Happy in their sobriety, these people do not consider themselves as unfortunately deprived of the pleasures of drinking, but rather as free of its compulsion and misery. Those who in the spirit of the Rand report picture all recovered alcoholics as pining for some way to drink again successfully have not known the many who are delighted that they have no need to. Not martyrs, all that they have given up is hangovers and headaches. And the gains far out-weigh any loss. "I'm glad I'm an alcoholic" is a shocking statement the first dozen times it is heard at AA meetings, until one comes to appreciate the joy of living and spiritual growth these people might otherwise never have known. Enjoying beauty or friendship to the full, or having what the psychologist Maslow calls peak experiences, involve a "natural high" not achieved through a chemical.

Recovery Takes Time.   All this does not occur automatically when one stops drinking. Alcoholism is diffuse, encroaching upon every aspect of one's life. Even if intervention arrests the progression in its early or middle stages, many changes in life habits have occurred over a fair length of time. It may require a comparable length of time to reverse these changes. The modified Glatt chart in Chapter 6 lists in its second, or ascending, half the many steps involved in full recovery. Admission of the problem and cessation of drinking, by whatever means, are only the be-ginning.

One must learn that alcoholism is an illness, see recovered alcoholics functioning, discover that one is not alone or hopeless. Fears begin to di-minish, physical appearance improves, sleep and meals start to become regular. A new hope dawns, and belief that a different life is possible gen-erates the optimism known as the honeymoon stage. Thinking begins to clear and become realistic, as various adjustments are faced and self-dis-cipline grows. A returning sense of self-esteem is bolstered by acceptance from others, including, perhaps, initial reconciliation with the family. Emotional stability is enhanced, as one learns to trust and is trusted. The desire to escape passes, as the old rationalizations are unmasked and one accepts both oneself and new way of life. Appreciation of real values and a rebirth of ideals may lead to a new interest in spiritual values, which lifts one beyond the level of predrinking years.

Physical, Mental, Social

The accompanying chart by Dr. Margaret Mantell, adapted from Dr. Robert Gordon Bell, depicts three phases of recovery that occur over two to three years. The chart shows the first year is predominantly physical re-covery, which continues through three years. About halfway through the first year emotional-psychological recovery gains in importance, and dominates the second year. Toward the end of the first year maturation and integration into full social living begins, and reaches full bloom in the third year. There is, of course, much overlap and individual variation. Mantell generalizes that only 10 percent of total recovery takes place in

FIGURE 7. The two- to three-year recovery process

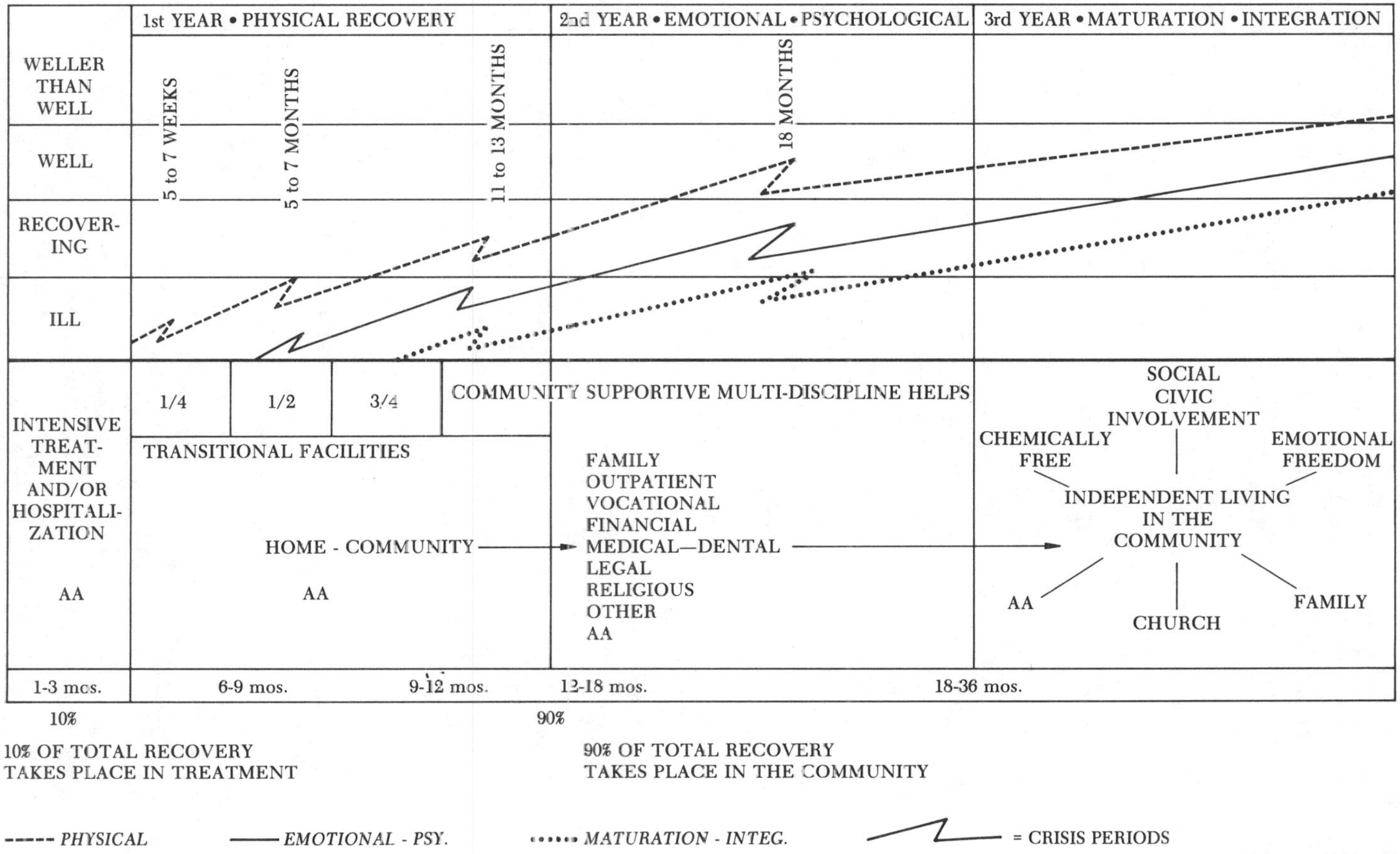

Margaret Mantell
(adapted from R.G. Bell)

269

the treatment center, 90 percent after returning to the community. After inpatient treatment, the process may continue in recovery homes (halfway houses or more graduated after-care transitional facilities called quarter or three-quarter houses) where regimen is gradually relaxed and more autonomy given. This supportive environment is more necessary when the alcoholic has been a homeless drifter or otherwise leading an unstructured life. For others the family home may provide the support and stability needed. Scheduled return visits with a counselor or therapy group after discharge should be included in the package cost of treatment. Outpatient clinics and Alcoholics Anonymous meetings can provide invaluable guidance and serve as fixed navigational points as the new voyage through life gathers momentum. Return to fully independent living in the community is a gradual process, with many facets, requiring a continuum of care. Some few may require permanent custodial living arrangements.

Not All Smooth Sailing.   Note that the Mantell chart does not graph progress as a smooth upward line, but realistically indicates occasional slumps and crisis periods. These do not occur at exactly six months or one year of sobriety, for example, but as she indicates they tend to occur at around five to seven months, or eleven to thirteen months, etc. The recovering alcoholic becomes as restless as a caged lion, moody, depressed, or grandiose. Sobriety may still be shaky and there may even be a brief relapse, but this may just serve to confirm what is being heard in the group sessions about the need for total surrender and avoidance of compromise. Those crisis periods are typical of all human development; the normal growth curve is never a smooth line, and occasional backsliding and plateaus are common. Too much attention to them could result in a self-fulfilling prophecy, but, in general, some knowledge of this by both counselor and recovering alcoholic eliminates the surprise factor and reassures that progress is normal.

"Weller than Well"   on the chart conveys the notion that recovered alcoholics must not only get well, but must become better adjusted than nonalcoholics, because they must learn how to cope with life's stresses without the moderate use of alcohol, a tranquilizer available to others. This is somewhat controversial, but is not unique to Mantell. Milam (1974) and other authorities speak this way. Without encouraging a "healthier than thou" attitude, we tend to agree.

Sensibly pursued, this is a much sounder ideal than the opposite: Those who hide from reality behind their illness and use it as an excuse for not coping. This is the point of a brief but forcible article in the July 1971 *AA Grapevine*, reprinted in the November 1976 "classic" issue of that monthly, entitled "Reality Can be Uncomfortable" (M. McF., 1976). The author recounts cases where members refused to take Steps 4 and 5 because it makes them uncomfortable, or avoid twelfth step calls and even employment because they are "not comfortable around non-AA's," or otherwise keep themselves wrapped in the cocoon that is their idea of AA. Contrariwise, the article contends, learning to cope with life, people, and situations is vital to growth, which means accepting the challenges of life even though perhaps uncomfortable.

Physical

We have seen that there is considerable evidence now that the residual toxic effects of alcohol, especially on the brain as shown by both brain wave studies and psychological tests, persist long after detoxification has reduced blood alcohol level to zero. With great variation among individuals, this period may generally be thought of as three to six months or up to two years. Add the damage, even reversible, which we saw in Chapter 4 can occur to every other organ in the body due to both alcohol and malnutrition. The conclusion is that rebuilding physical health as outlined in the section on "Physical Rehabilitation" in Chapter 14 must be attended to for a minimum of one year and probably two or three.

This should be with as little medication as possible, and a maximum stress on good health habits. Exercise, recreation, relaxation exercises, and a balanced diet are far more useful than any chemical help, to which alcoholics seem vulnerable. This includes not only strict avoidance of sleeping pills but also moderating excessive use of coffee and cigarettes. It is true that avoidance of alcohol may seem to be enough of a problem at one time, but moderation in other areas often makes sobriety easier because of a general sense of well-being. Even physicians sympathetic to Alcoholics Anonymous point to the irony of their imbibing huge quantities of one drug while discussing avoidance of another, and laud the growing use of decaffeinated coffee at AA meetings. One caution cannot be put too strongly: Whatever one may feel about marijuana for others, it is very dangerous for recovered alcoholics. This author has no desire to become involved in the controversy over marijuana because alcohol is a more serious problem. But experience confirms reports in the literature (see *Patient Care Magazine*, January 1975 for a summary) that even mild marijuana use can lull one's defenses and eventually lead to a relapse. The artificial euphoria may be considered a boon to others, but even mild unrealism is something the recovered alcoholic cannot afford.

The above cautions do not rule out the continued use of medicines that a knowledgeable physician may prescribe for a recovered alcoholic's persistent or recurring medical problems. As in any chronic illness, continued contact with the physician is called for. The treatment center should make an informative referral back to the client's own physician upon discharge. The doctor should understand the emotional aspects of living as a recovered alcoholic, the family and other interpersonal relations, the employment or vocational implications. Medications to prevent heart attacks, strokes, or chronic seizures, some nonaddictive antidepressants, or medicine for diabetes and other metabolic or nutritional disorders may be necessary for the remainder of one's life and are not to be construed as inimical to sobriety.

Mental

If alcoholism is not in the bottle but in the person, rehabilitation of mental and emotional states is vital. Positive attitudes, renewed self-esteem, and emotional stability must be built up if sobriety is to be permanent. Alcoholics must be satisfied that life without alcohol is preferable; they must want to be sober more than they want to drink. This entails a "play for keeps" attitude coupled with a conviction that they can stay sober, in spite of previous discouragement. Any notion of weak will must be shown false in view of their strength in getting a drink when they wanted one. But no pledges or promises or other added hurdles need be introduced.

It is not enough to spend the rest of one's life running away from alcohol. Some positive goals and a new life plan need to be explored. This can be threatening in early stages of recovery, but one means is to have recovering alcoholics write out two lists: one of what alcohol had been doing to their lives, and one of what they would like for the future. The former might list damage to health, the cost of liquor, family disruption, loss of memory, morning depression, and the like. The second could list not only financial goals, but such things as hobbies, enjoyment of beauty, friends, fun—many cannot remember having fun without liquor. In many ways they have to learn to live all over again. This may seem a gigantic task, and needs to be mollified by "one day at a time" realism.

Conflicts must be resolved and resentments removed, or relapse is inevitable. Escapism and self-deception diminish as one learns to stop playing games with oneself. This growth is often achieved best in groups. The discovery that one is not alone, that others have the same fears, is not only reassuring but can banish self-pity. Most good treatment centers have follow-up or after-care groups meeting regularly, and group sessions are a regular event in halfway houses. Many of these groups include the spouse or whole family, which has great value for lasting adjustment. The Twelve Steps of Alcoholics Anonymous are highly useful in this process, even if one does not attend meetings. The AA member will say, "Yes, you might do it on your own, but if you do it with us it will be fun."

Dr. Robert Gordon Bell of the Donwood Institute near Toronto hit upon an ingenious and successful means of follow-up. Al-Anon members,

usually housewives with time at home, volunteer to make a friendly telephone call to discharged patients at regular intervals. This assures them
that someone is interested, gives an opportunity to air minor problems,
and nips major problems in the bud. It has the obvious advantage of costing nothing. Both AA and Al-Anon members might be encouraged to expand this novel form of twelfth step work.

Grief.   Much is being written today about the necessity of "doing
one's grief work" after the loss of a loved one. That is, to accept and work
through a normal series of emotions rather than repressing these feelings
with a show of bravery. This latter path can lead to psychosomatic conditions such as ulcers or high blood pressure as well as to lingering emotional
repercussions and resentments, which are much worse than a frank expression of sadness or anger at the time. Kellerman (1977), Bellwood
(1975), and others have drawn an interesting parallel in a need for the recovering alcoholic to go through a similar process of grief work in accepting the losses attendant upon the transition from alcoholic to sober living.
These include not only giving up some real or imagined conviviality, but
perhaps loss of health, job, family, memory, or moral respectability and
sense of self-mastery. The normal reactions here are shocked disbelief,
anger, depression, guilt, hostility, and inability to return to one's old self.
Failure to accept and express these feelings stems from false pride, which
says, "I should not feel that way" when in fact you do, or "I must act like
my old self" when in fact you are not. If these feelings are vented with a
skilled counselor or experienced AA or Al-Anon sponsor, they can be then
understood and accepted. The ultimate result of this painful process is the
ability to face a new life. The past is truly forgiven if not entirely forgotten, and one begins a better life with hope. Kellerman notes a similar
need for the family, especially the spouse.

Clinical Depression.   Prolonged and continuous depression without any palpable cause, especially if accompanied by thoughts of suicide,
is reason for seeking psychiatric help. This is not just the emotional flatness that most recovering alcoholics experience when they discover that
the honeymoon stage is over and they are back to day-to-day living. Here
it helps just to understand that this emotional flatness is a common occurrence. One should get active in doing things, especially for others.

Sex after Sobriety.   Recovery often means the emergence of problems connected with one's sex life, which need to be faced frankly. One is
the feelings of guilt over any promiscuity during the drinking years; the
principles pertinent to this problem are given in Chapter 19, chiefly that
one must not judge oneself in the light of present sober realizations but in
the light of one's illness at the time.

Other problems stem from developments after sobriety. We noted in Chapter 4 that alcohol depresses sexuality, especially male, in several ways. This may have become unimportant as alcoholism progresses to the point where the bottle took priority over all else. Recovery may bring a dramatic reversal. Feeling good again and looking better than they have for years, patients may experience a renewed interest in and from the opposite sex. The breakup of their previous marriage may not have led to any immediate sexual frustration while they were drinking, but now there can be strong resurgence of the sex drive.

This leads to three problems. One is readjustment of sexual relations with the spouse, if the marriage is still intact or if reconciliation has occurred. If the husband is the alcoholic, the wife may be understandably slow to welcome his advances after years of hurt and revulsion. She may not even want him to touch her. It may take a long time to rekindle a close, delicate, loving sexual relationship. The needed patience is difficult for him, because he feels confident in his sobriety now and cannot appreciate her mistrust from having been burned so often. It is not bad will on her part; she simply does not feel responsive. If the wife is the alcoholic, the husband may have to overcome disillusionment in his once-idealized loved one. Or conversely, he may jeopardize her sobriety by remarking, "You were more fun in bed when you were drinking." In any case we recommend frank discussion with a good counselor, by the couple and individually. There is also a wealth of literature on sexual adjustment available.

The single or divorced person in recovery faces two problems. One is promiscuity. The renewed interest in sex, linked with undisciplined behavior and lack of respect for others during the drinking years, may result in a wild fling of sexual adventures. Regardless of one's moral code on this point, the emotional fluctuations and unstable interpersonal relations that this entails can be a serious obstacle to the maturity and psychological growth essential for a solid sobriety. If guilt over the moral aspect is added, relapse becomes even more likely. "First things first" suggests that staying sober be given top priority, and sexual activity be postponed. For those who question the biological wisdom of this, the answer is that physicians who have treated celibates have testified unanimously for decades that there is no evidence of any physical detriment as a result of controlling the sex drive. Not all people experience a strong urge, and to them Dr. Jon Weinberg, in *Sex And Recovery* (1977a, p. 24) sagely remarks, "If you are enjoying life without sex, don't feel something must be wrong with you. Not everybody likes apple pie either."

The other problem of the unmarried person in recovery is the prospect of marriage. This, of course, may be a very laudable goal for the future, but if it comes too early it can be a disaster. Those involved are usually deaf to advice here, but counselors should make every effort to forestall an early marriage by warning against any romantic involvements for at least a year after recovery. Rebound marriages have a poor rate of success, and rebound from alcoholism is similar. Weinberg (1977a, p. 32) echoes the experience of many AA members and all professionals: that the risk is greatly increased if both parties are recovering alcoholics (see L.S., "That Thirteenth Step," *AA Grapevine*, February 1978). Any one alcoholic has enough problems to sort out and cope with; marriage between two of them just multiplies the chances of trouble. There are exceptions, but the problem is that everyone likes to believe they will be that rare exception. Here love can be not only blind but stupid.

Social

Under this heading we will include all of the aspects of rehabilitation involved in returning the recovered alcoholic to full life in the community: employment; housing; health, including teeth and eyeglasses or hearing aid; legal, including probation and parole as well as wage garnishments and divorce settlements; church affiliation; family, including reconciliation with children who have left the home; finances; recreation; education or retraining; and a host of others. Many of these are dealt with elsewhere, and none can be fully treated in this survey. A few general guidelines may be indicated.

First, easy does it. The above list can be overwhelming to the newly recovered alcoholic. New skills must be learned, or old ones refurbished. Some may have to learn for the first time how to handle money, manage a checking account, shop and keep house, apply for a job. The transition to independent living must be paced to the degree of readiness and stage of recovery. Better to start with a job as janitor-custodian, even if one has been a bank president.

In the early stage they will need a lot of help. One cannot apply for a job if one has no decent clothes to appear in or no means of transportation to get to the job interview. The recovering alcoholic may not know how to get public assistance or veterans' benefits, how to contact the Division of Vocational Rehabilitation, or what sheltered workshops and retraining opportunities are available. Continuum of care means that the system somehow provide these helps, in contrast to the case of a patient who left the treatment center alone, on a bus that by incredible coincidence discharged him directly in front of his favorite old tavern.

Some education on the nature of alcoholism as a treatable illness and the nature of recovery may have to be conveyed to any or all of the people contacted in the foregoing. Judges, parole officers, employers or job interviewers, family, friends, former drinking pals, clergy, physicians, and others may not understand the need to avoid all alcohol and other psychoactive drugs, the impossibility of a return to social drinking, the time required for gradual recovery, the fact that declared sobriety means a better employment risk than hidden drinking. All must learn not to harp on the past but hope for the future. The married couple should agree never to bring up the past except in the presence of the counselor. Emphasis should be on personality assets rather than failings.

A part of the past that must be faced is the effects on the children from living in an alcoholic home. To begin a new life after recovery as if the past never existed may sound fine for the alcoholic, but the damage done to the personality development of the children must be rectified to the extent that is possible. Too often all the focus is on the recovery of the alcoholics, and on the acceptance and support the children are supposed to give them in their new sobriety. This is merely continuing the role reversal that had been so damaging to the children all along. Parents are to accept and support children, not vice versa. The responsibility of parents who have abused and neglected their children needs to be included in the educational phase of rehabilitation. One way is by incorporating Parent Effectiveness Training (PET) or by membership in Parents Anonymous for child abusers. Alcoholic parents are in need of specific training in how to parent.

Life in a Drinking Society.   A major adjustment is learning how to conduct oneself at social gatherings, where drinking is a common feature. Our society does not make this easy, and there are always ignorant boors who will push drinks at the recovered alcoholic. One can begin by recalling that about 30 percent of American adults are nondrinkers, and that nobody has to drink. Recovered alcoholics are more welcome at a party now that they don't get obnoxious. One should tell friends bluntly that alcohol is out; those who cannot understand or accept this are not worth keeping as friends anyhow. The host who says, "One won't hurt you" or "This is just sherry" is fortunately becoming more rare as the public becomes better educated about alcohol.

In public, there should be no lame excuses about ulcers nor any suggestion of weakness or inferiority. Not "I can't" but "No, thank you"— which can indicate strength and independence. The brevity and a calm poise with which it is said keep it from sounding like a prohibition lecture. This comes with practice; during early sobriety it is difficult, and cocktail parties might better be avoided. For some, it is fun to stay sober and watch others make fools of themselves. As for being conspicuous, this author often gives up alcohol as a Lenten practice and is repeatedly impressed how easy it is to rattle a few ice cubes in a highball glass full of ginger ale with nobody in the room aware of the difference. One should fix the drink oneself or observe its preparation, to prevent it being spiked.

The only danger here is that unknowing spouse or friends might worry that one is having a relapse. Eventually one may feel comfortable enough to serve alcoholic drinks at home if appropriate; the spouse must let the alcoholic decide when. All this is well presented in an article "My Trials as a Nondrinking Alcoholic" by a recovered alcoholic physician (Tabor, 1959).

Mention was made above that feeling conspicuous need not be a problem. Short of the actual need that only an alcoholic can experience, the author, during Lent, finds that the major hurdle is the pressure to drink arising in certain social situations. Preparation to handle this should be a part of the final treatment stage. Antabuse or aversion conditioning may put up a helpful physical barrier, but this can break down eventually unless one is practiced in the ways of *how* to refuse a drink gracefully. Restored self-esteem and assertiveness training should be implemented by actual role-playing sessions at the treatment center, where one rehearses for concrete situations. Let another patient act the role of waiter, boss, escort, or friend offering a drink; what do you say? Similarly, one should develop specific action plans for those times of the day or week that will be the most likely occasion for a drink: five o'clock closing time, end of a three to eleven shift, Saturday night. What will you do, where will you go and how? Positive use of leisure time must be planned.

Relapse

In a chronic illness there is always the possibility of decompensation and relapse. This does not mean total failure of treatment, and may even be the beginning of lifetime sobriety. It is a warning to stress the quality of sobriety rather than measuring in months or years. Sometimes it is more effective not to push treatment too soon after a relapse, and, in any case, the type of alcoholism and treatment modality need to be reexamined.

Although we have stressed that analyzing why one drinks is largely a misleading therapy, causes for an actual or potential relapse can be profitably looked at. Specifically, one needs to learn certain dangerous fallacies of thinking. Thirst can be mistaken for a cue to drink, when body fluid is all that is needed. Hunger is a danger; here good nutrition and even the guidance of a dietitian may be helpful, and at least excessive sugar should be avoided. False notions about weak will, hopelessness, or social unacceptability need to be corrected. Lack of attention from family does not mean less appreciation now that sobriety is taken for granted. We all like a pat on the back now and then, but it is childish to expect constant praise for just living. Sometimes the only prelude to a relapse seems to be that everything is going well. Is this reason for drinking? Anger and loneliness must be understood as normal human experiences, not cues for a drink. These are not alcoholic problems, but human problems. The acronym HALT sums up four danger signals: be on guard if one is Hungry, Angry, Lonely, or Tired.

The Dry Drunk

Under the heading of "Relapse" is a phenomenon that is inimical to sobriety even if abstinence is retained. "Dry drunk" is the term applied to an episode in which one may exhibit any or all the feelings and behavior associated with intoxication, but no alcohol is consumed. Formerly it implied grandiosity; currently it more often connotes moderate to severe depression. It commonly occurs about six months after detoxification or around the end of the first year of sobriety, but can happen up to six years later or at any time. Shakes, insomnia, stiffness, headaches, and other flulike symptoms may accompany the irritability, fatigue, depression, hunger, egocentrism, overreaction, unexplained sadness, aimless puttering or wandering, and a host of negative emotions. Sometimes the resemblance to actual intoxication is remarkable. A "dry hangover" may follow.

Analysis of what leads up to a dry drunk reveals great similarity to the antecedents of relapse, but a caution against generalization and psychologizing is in order. "Stinking thinking" can indeed be a prelude, but the concepts of buildup and binge do not apply to all alcoholics, or in the same way. At least the rationalizations are quite foreign to a comfortable sobriety, and betray a lack of surrender or honesty of which the person may be unaware. Lurking indecision about commitment to a life of sobriety may be the basic cause, but a thousand factors can trigger the dry drunk. Resentments and self-centeredness are common causes.

A pamphlet *How to Beat the Blues* (Prasch, 1977) describes the symptoms and causes of the dry drunk phenomenon, and gives some practical suggestions. To understand what is happening removes the mystery and leads to acceptance. Talking it over with an alcoholism counselor or AA sponsor will usually help. Self-pity is countered by resisting the urge to remain alone. Getting busy, and especially helping others, has therapeutic value. But recreation and relaxation are also important. Going through the Twelve Steps of Alcoholics Anonymous as if for the first time can evoke new light and incentives. Lastly, mood can improve through prayer and meditation on spiritual perspectives.

Sources

Most books dealing with alcoholism, and particularly those concerned with treatment, have recently come to include sections on rehabilitation. For example, see

Heinemann and DiJulio's article, "Assessment and Care of the Chronically Ill Alcoholic Person," in Estes and Heinemann, pp. 239–248. Especially useful is Strachan, *Practical Alcoholism Programming.*

In the area of rehabilitation, much of the most valuable information is available in pamphlets, rather than in the technical literature. For those sufficiently interested to write for materials, the following references will be of interest. The National Clearinghouse for Alcohol Information (NCALI) has several bibliographies which contain relevant materials, two in particular which are recommended: Part IV, pp. 133–165 of NIAAA, *Alcoholism Treatment and Rehabilitation: Selected Abstracts* (1972); and *Selected Publications on Rehabilitation Strategies for Alcohol Abusers* (1977). NCALI has also published an excellent pamphlet by Ernest P. Noble, entitled *Role of Halfway Houses in the Rehabilitation of Alcoholics* (1977).

The Association of Halfway House Alcoholism Programs publishes: Diane Fontaine, *Analysis of the Recovery Process*; T. Richards, *So You Want to Start a Halfway House for Alcoholics?*; M. Rudolph, *Therapeutic Intervention: Counseling in Post-Treatment Programs*; and *Standards for Halfway House Alcoholism Programs.*

Hazelden is the publisher of the following sensitively understanding pamphlets: D. Anderson, *The Joys and Sorrows of Sobriety*; J. Kellerman, *Grief: A Basic Reaction to Alcoholism*; B. Kimball, *Aftercare: Blueprint for a Richer Life*; and B. Kimball, *Counseling for Growth in a Halfway House for Women.*

Two other very useful and understanding statements are available in pamphlet form: Jon Weinberg, *Sex and Recovery* (1977), available from Recovery Press, P.O. Box 21215, Minneapolis, Minnesota 55421; and Muriel Zink, *Recovery: Turning Negatives into Positives*, CompCare pamphlet.

The following are a sampling of what is available in alcoholism and rehabilitation journals and in the popular press: Ogborne, "Evaluating Halfway Houses," in *Addictions*; Jacquelyn Small and Sidney Wolf, "Beyond Abstinence," in *Alcohol Health and Research World*; Jonathan Tabor, "My Trials as a Nondrinking Alcoholic," from the *Saturday Evening Post* originally and republished in *Reader's Digest*; and Marc A. Schuckit, "The Identification and Management of Alcoholic and Depressive Problems," in *Drug Abuse and Alcoholism Review.*

Relapse and Dry Drunk

As this chapter has indicated, recovery is often by fits and starts, and rarely a straight line process. Relapses as a stage in recovery, the "dry drunk," and other keenly felt subjective problems during recovery have not been given formal attention in the technical literature. Notable exceptions are: Flaherty, "The Psychodynamics of the 'Dry Drunk'," which appeared in *The American Journal of Psychiatry*; Ludwig and Stark, "Alcohol Craving—Subjective and Situational Aspects," in the *Quarterly Journal of Studies on Alcohol*; and Scott and others, "Flare-Up: Stress Time in Recovery from Alcoholism," in *The Osteopathic Physician* (reprint).

Vivid subjective accounts of these experiences have been provided, however, by recovered and recovering alcoholics. Almost any issue of *The Grapevine*, a monthly publication of Alcoholics Anonymous, will have at least one article dealing with such problems. The March and April 1976 issues contained a series of articles dealing with "slips" (returns to drinking after a period of abstinence), and depression. Two others were mentioned in the text: L.S., "That Thirteenth Step" (February 1978); and M. McF., "Reality Can be Uncomfortable" (July 1971, reprinted November 1976).

In pamphlets, there are: Crewe, *A Look at Relapse*; Grimmett, *Barriers Against Recovery*; and Solberg, *The Dry-Drunk Syndrome*; all published by Hazelden. From the Daughters of St. Paul, 50 St. Paul's Avenue, Boston, MA 02130 there are: Prasch, *How to Beat the Blues* (1977) and Prasch, *Ten Steps to Serenity* (1975). The following books contain materials on the "dry drunk" also: Blane, *The Personality of the Alcoholic*; Meyer, *Off the Sauce*; and two by Valles, *From Social Drinking to Alcoholism* and *How to Live with an Alcoholic*.

CHAPTER 18

Spiritual Aspects

ALCOHOLISM HAS BEEN described as an illness: physical, mental-emotional, and spiritual. But few have analyzed the precise nature of this spiritual illness. One is tempted to look at the fellowship of Alcoholics Anonymous, for instance, and say, "Here are a lot of wonderful people who have recognized their problem and have done something about it, helping each other and making progress. But why all this God stuff? Why drag religion into it?"

One can get fellowship in a tavern, but not sobriety. This chapter will analyze the spiritual needs of alcoholics as they describe themselves. This is not theory, but the experience of a million people. The founders of Alcoholics Anonymous found no lasting serenity until they came to believe that no human power is adequate to the alcoholic's problems. But it is important to recognize that AA is not the only or necessary way to approach the spiritual aspects of this problem. Many people work their own spiritual program toward rehabilitation without joining AA.

The counselor may or may not consider spiritual values important; the question is how the client feels. The great psychiatrist Alfred Adler called himself an atheist, yet he was careful to respect the faith of his patients and use it to best advantage. The counselor must look at the client's needs, and at least understand them well enough to make a good referral.

AA Is Not Religion.   Before beginning our description of the alcoholic's spiritual needs in general, a word about the spiritual in Alcoholics
Anonymous itself. Psychologists and clergy have good reason to be wary
of religious movements that smack of mere emotionalism, so it is gratifying to state as a professional psychologist and a clergyman that in this author's opinion the AA program is both psychologically and spiritually
sound. It does not feature ecstatic emotional experiences, but is rather a
sensible facing of the spiritual realities that are in all lives, even of the
avowed atheist. It avoids the old revival-meeting emotionalism, which
was short-lived and superficial even when sincere.

AA is not a religion in the sense of any organized institution, or a particular creed, cult or code. God is always referred to as one's Higher Power, as the individual wishes to understand Him. The AA program does not
favor a white man's God, for instance, but can apply equally well to the
God of those moving Southern spirituals that have been an important part
of our American musical heritage, or to the Great Spirit of our native
American Indians. Where custom has it to close the meeting by reciting
the Our Father, nobody is obliged to join in. (When one Jewish member
objected to the custom, another retorted, "That prayer was composed by
a Jew to teach other Jews how to pray.")

AA is very tactful in handling the skepticism of the agnostic or atheist,
and is careful not to impose any sectarian religion on anyone. But AA is an
intensely spiritual program, God being mentioned explicitly in six of the
Twelve Steps, and implicitly in two others. Acceptance for some is not
easy. There is no pressure, and each comes to understand in his own way,
at his own pace.

Role of the Church

In the realm of organized religion, on the other hand, we note some remarkable changes in church policy and activity during the past few decades. The image of the church was formerly associated with the judgmen-
tal crusading of the Prohibition era, but a more enlightened attitude is
rapidly erasing that. There is better cooperation with the health and social service professions, with Alcoholics Anonymous and Al-Anon, and
with national or local organizations, both governmental and volunteer.
We list briefly some of the contributions the churches are making.

The church can be a strong influence in changing public attitudes. Instead of the hypocrisy in former moralistic condemnations of all drinking,
many churches are now expressing genuine concern over excessive drinking and are promoting reasonable guidelines for alcohol use (for example,
those developed by the Episcopal Church in Maryland and California).
Alcoholism is recognized as an illness, and cooperation with the profes-

sional agencies is encouraged. Strong support is given to AA, and the clergy are learning to use Al-Anon as a spiritual resource in their family counseling. Positive spiritual values are being substituted for feelings of guilt and discouragement, which did little more for the alcoholic than to provide an excuse to drink again. Members of the Pioneer group, not alcoholics themselves, pledge total abstinence as a witness of concern and to help those who have the problem. Some churches are including educative tidbits of information about alcohol and alcoholism in their parish bulletins or other publications. Most important, instead of leaving the problem to treatment centers, individual church members are beginning to understand and help the alcoholic within the parish community.

Self-Description Reveals Needs

Rather than any program, we shall examine spiritual needs as embodied in the characteristics reported by alcoholics. Much of this is also true of their spouses and children. This is how they describe themselves.

Faith.   First, they are *confused*. They don't know what to think. Spouse, doctor, boss, and friends give advice that is often contradictory. They need a new set of values and principles, something to believe in. William James talks about the sick soul that needs to be reborn. Viktor Frankl talks about one being in an existential vacuum. Into this emptiness comes faith. Belief in God can put a new meaning into life, clarify some of the confusion, and establish a set of values. They need something more solid than the "easy glum, easy glow" of alcoholism.

Hope.   Secondly, they are *discouraged*. Whether or not they admit being powerless over alcohol, they are often in despair. At this point the need is hope. It can be a turning point in one's life to discover, with St. Paul, that however powerless, "I can do all things in Him who strengthens me." With this admission comes hope. For the first time one may experience the freedom to determine whether or not one will get drunk.

Faith and hope are the two basic points in the relation of person to Creator. This is basic spirituality, not organized religion. Some psychologists have raised the question whether this relation to God admits a kind of neurotic dependence or escapism. But if God is the supreme reality, it is not an escape from reality to acknowledge this fact. Rather, it is unrealistic if one fails to face God as part of the whole of reality. We are all dependent on oxygen. This is not neurotic; it is simply realism. We all depend on many things and many people. AA is careful to avoid any description of God other than as a power higher than oneself. It is hard to imagine anyone so egotistical as not to recognize there is a power greater than himself. One can even tell him that alcohol is greater than he is, since it has been running his life, and that he needs somebody or something bigger than either himself or alcohol to straighten him out. Faith and hope in God can give a sense of freedom not experienced in years, a way out of that sense of powerlessness over either the alcoholic's compulsion to drink or the spouse's obsession with the problem. They get a great sense of freedom by turning their lives over to God as they understand Him.

Perhaps one should say God as we *don't* understand Him, since the biggest obstacle to a spiritual program is not God but our own distorted image of Him, our failure to understand even the basic concepts of what God really is like. To acknowledge that one's life is unmanageable is to admit the need for a new manager. The famous Chapter 5 of the book *Alcoholics Anonymous* describes what happens when one tries to run the whole show himself. The antidote is to turn one's life over to God—let Him run the show, since He can do a much better job than the mess we have been making of it. But to turn our lives over to God with trust and hope and faith means having a God in whom one can trust. We have trouble here because of our horribly childish and inadequate concepts of God and what He is like.

Useful here is a book by the Anglican clergyman J.B. Phillips, entitled *Your God Is Too Small* (1954). It is not about alcoholism. It is a marvelous analysis of all the stupid and childish ideas we have about God. No wonder people have trouble! Our God is so often a little egotistical pipsqueak who needs to be adored on Sundays to gratify His own ego; one can hardly respect such a God, much less adore. Or our God is an old man with a long white beard, some father image from childhood. Or He may be an unreasonable God, a tyrant who will not let us have any fun. This is the way we see God when He permits things to happen in our lives which are not immediately gratifying. Some people know only an avenging God. One neurotic patient could not conceive of God as having any other function than to put people in hell. Philosophy may give us the concept of an infinite and reasonable God, but often He is a cold, abstract principle of causality far away from our personal lives. Faith tells us that God is a God of love, a Good Spirit that is wise and providing.

A priest with sixteen years in AA is reported by Fichter (1977a, p. 458) as making a salient observation about the current vogue that pictures the God of our childhood religion as stern and harsh. He grants some of this is valid, and makes the distinction between spirituality and institutional religion. But, he questions, was God really portrayed that way? How much of this is a party line, which newcomers hear at meetings and repeat? We alcoholics, he says, are prone to blame others for all our troubles—so why not blame the clergy, nuns, church, and even God? A similar note is sounded by Grateful Members (1977, p. 5).

Successful recovery from alcoholism usually requires a spiritual program, but it must not be moralistic, holier-than-thou attitudes. It should be enhanced by clergy with an understanding of the illness, who do not approach it with threats of hellfire and damnation, nor with prayerful pat phrases, pity, do-goodism, or moralizing exhortation and sentimentality. We don't need the psychiatrist who answered the question of why he did not confront his patient with her alcoholism, by saying, "My job is to treat, not condemn," as if diagnosis was a condemnation. As we shall see in Chapter 19, the disease concept of alcoholism does not eliminate moral responsibility, but it clearly distinguishes between responsibility for being an alcoholic and responsibility for doing something about it. From the remainder of this chapter, and from AA Steps 4 through 10, it is clear that there is no question of just dumping all on God. Common sense and sound theology concur that "God helps those who help themselves."

Guilty.   This leads us to the fact that the alcoholic is guilt-ridden: alienated from God, himself, and his fellow man. He needs *forgiveness.* Otherwise guilt about drinking just leads to more drinking. He needs the infinite mercy of God. He needs to know that no matter what he has done, if he acknowledges this and asks for forgiveness an infinitely loving and merciful God cannot possibly refuse him. No finite human being can flatter himself by thinking that he has committed sins so great that they exceed the forgiving power of a deity who is infinite. In the next chapter we shall elaborate on the distinction between guilt based on objective responsibility and subjective or neurotic guilt feelings. These latter are a psychological problem, not a spiritual one. But if there is true guilt, then the answer is forgiveness, not psychotherapy.

Reverend Samuel Shoemaker, an early friend of AA, made the statement that there is probably more confession going on in bars than in churches. In any case, alcoholics, like any human beings, need to unload their guilt and find forgiveness. There is a definite psychological value in making this confession, not merely to God in the secrecy of one's own heart, but also to another human being. To make a fearless and searching moral inventory and to confess the result of this to another person is being authentic, a reality therapy encounter. Although it is a mistake to do this too soon in recovery, except as a preliminary test of honesty and growth in stability, it eventually is necessary if one is going to achieve lasting and comfortable sobriety.

Lonely.   Both alcoholics and their spouses have a sense of being nobody, of not fitting in. Although the talk about identity crisis may be a bit overdone, people do need to feel they are somebody. For those who feel that no one loves them, perhaps the first glimmer of hope in their lives comes when they realize that they are children of God, and that at least God loves them no matter what else. For some people who have lost everything and everybody, it is all they can hang on to. The rebirth, the transcendence when people make this startling discovery is amazing. They have someone to love, and they love God because they have discovered that God loves them. Loneliness has been defined as being alone with yourself, but solitude as being alone with God. In addition, there may be group prayer, common spiritual growth, profitable confrontations, and a going out to others as a result of this discovery.

Anxious.   In addition to being confused, discouraged, guilty, and lonely, those affected by this problem are also very tense and anxious. They need *serenity*, peace of soul. They can achieve this by turning their lives over to God. "Let go and let God" is a favorite axiom. Their serenity comes not from perfection, since they are not saints, but is rather based on their tranquil acceptance of their human weakness in the light of a loving God who now takes care of them. This spiritual serenity explains how recovered alcoholics can laugh and joke about even the very tragic past in their lives. They know there is no sense crying over spilled milk and that it would be sick to do so. Instead, they laugh about it because with God's help they have put it all in the past. Most recovered alcoholics are not blue-nosed, lugubrious, prune-faced killjoys. They are very happy people. They have peace of soul.

Resentful.   Next, alcoholics and their spouses have described themselves as having a lot of resentments. They need *resignation* to God's will and to the realities of human nature. They tell how they turned their lives and their will over to God, and were entirely ready to have God remove their defects. "Thy will be done." As a result, resentments disappear and serenity reigns. They humbly asked God to remove their shortcomings, made a list of all the people they had harmed, became willing to make amends to them all. Note the word *willing*. It is a great clean feeling when you at least make the attempt. They made direct amends to such people wherever possible, except when to do so would injure them or others. This shows good sensible balance. Easy does it, don't push. If the person doesn't want to accept your money or apology, at least you made the effort. Now you can have perfect peace of soul.

Impatient.   Rehabilitation of one's whole life-style requires a lot of *patience*. It demands that one continue to take personal inventory and when wrong, promptly admit it. One picks up his cross and accepts the wisdom of "Sufficient for the day is the evil thereof." We learn to live one day at a time. Anybody can stay sober for just twenty-four hours, and there are no one-year pledges. It goes without saying that the virtue of temperance is fostered by sobriety, and the alcoholic has been intemperate in many ways beyond that of intoxication.

Pride. To promptly admit that we are wrong is a mark of *humility.* One of the most characteristic features of the alcoholic is hurt pride. It is known that alcoholics tend to run above average in intelligence, to be talented and worthwhile persons. But they also have a lot of sensitivity and pride. And this is perhaps the toughest thing to handle in all of human nature. Sigmund Freud thought he had the basic human motivation identified in the sex drive or libido. Certainly the sex drive is a very strong and important one, and the source of a lot of human difficulties. Most psychologists today, however, agree with Alfred Adler, that pride or ego is a deeper basic motivation, a stronger drive and a source of much more difficulty than sex or libido. Even a lot of apparently sexual difficulties are not sexual. This is the most delicate intimate relationship two people can have, and if there is a personality conflict it will manifest itself there. But remove the hurt pride, the domination, the submission, the resentment and jealousy, and the sex activity pretty well takes care of itself.

Humility is the most fundamental virtue in the spiritual life, but it is also the most misunderstood. Humility is truth. It does not consist of saying, "I'm no good." That is a lie. Rather it is simply acknowledging that one is not perfect, that one is not all powerful, that one is dependent on God, that whatever good one has is thanks more to one's parents and to God than any credit to oneself. The truly humble person is not self-conscious about it, making no pretense of being obsequious. Happy and joyful persons have usually achieved genuine humility. It is the only remedy for hurt pride, because pride never goes away and needs constantly to be worked on even in a comfortable sobriety. Otherwise one ends up like the rather accomplished old-timer who, having finished giving his talk and was returning to his seat, heard the remark in the back row, "There, by the grace of God, goes God." Humility is also the remedy for the self-pity the spouse often feels when the alcoholic gets all the attention, both while drinking and after recovery. It puts one in proper perspective in relation to God, self, the alcoholic, and all who benefit from the recovery.

Dishonest. Largely because of pride, alcoholics tend to be dishonest. They have lied, cheated, and covered up. They need the virtue of *justice*, a program of honesty. Having been immature and irresponsible, they need to make amends. But they should *not* reveal to a present spouse any past sexual indiscretions, out of a false sense of honesty.

Fearful. A large part of the life of the alcoholic is fear. This is one reason for drinking; it tranquilizes the fears. One needs the virtue of *fortitude*, getting strength from a relationship with God so as to face life's troubles. We all have troubles. Instead of trying to run away from them by "better living through chemistry," we learn how to cope. Maturity demands facing life and employing our social skills without the crutch of alcohol. It means courage, fortitude, strength of character, a way of meeting people and of meeting life. Fortitude can come from confidence in God and in having turned one's life over to God.

Selfish.   Lastly, we are all selfish; but perhaps more than others, alcoholics have allowed their lives to center around self, to the neglect of consideration for others. Love, the antidote for this unselfishness, is not always easy for those who doubt whether they might be loved in return and who fear the sting of rejection. This need is met when they realize that they can love others because God has first loved them and they have come to love God.

But in order to love God one must get to know Him. Hence the one million recovered alcoholics in AA discovered the need of prayer. They found that prayer is not a matter of reciting long formulas, folding one's hands, or saying a lot of *thees* and *thous.* The very mention of prayer terrifies some people, but it is simply a matter of talking with God as one speaks with a friend. Interestingly, one of the great masters of the spiritual life, himself a great mystic who had visions and ecstasies, describes prayer in just this way. For many this means talking over with God whatever is of interest or concern. The musical *Fiddler on the Roof* illustrates this well in the conversations between Tevye, the leading character, and God. Conversation being two-way, one should not just talk but also listen for God to talk. This is rarely in the form of a special revelation such as Bill W. experienced and some few others have had. More often it comes as a quiet realization of some truth, or a growth in our own strength.

The eleventh of the suggested steps of the AA program says that recovered alcoholics "sought through prayer and meditation to improve their conscious contact with God as they understood Him, praying only for knowledge of His will and the power to carry it out." Meditation is a thoughtful reflection in God's presence, seeking to know His will through communion with Him. Nobody lifts himself up by his own bootstraps. We all need to transcend ourself, our own loneliness, our own selfishness. AA members have learned that it is not demeaning to submit to the Author of the universe upon whom all things depend, from magnificent galaxies to brilliant intellects. The alcoholic who feels discouraged and admits his dependence finds in this very dependence the emotional support he needs. After years of tension, anxiety, and guilt, the kind of psychological growth and deep personality change necessary for successful rehabilitation is often and perhaps only achieved by letting God seep slowly and quietly into the thirsty soul of the alcoholic.

Sources

Few books or journals treat the spiritual aspects of alcoholism, but there is an occasional chapter. Paperbacks and pamphlets contain some valuable material. We divide our sources into those dealing primarily with the spiritual, independent of organized religion (including a subsection on the atheist), and those dealing with church and clergy. We have found no good recent overview of the former, but the article by Harrison John (1977) summarizes the latter topic.

Alcoholism as a Spiritual Illness

CLINEBELL, HOWARD J., "Philosophical-Religious Factors in the Etiology and Treatment of Alcoholism," *Quarterly Journal of Studies on Alcohol*, 1963, 24:473–488.

CLINEBELL, HOWARD J., *Understanding and Counseling the Alcoholic through Religion and Psychology*, rev. ed.

FICHTER, JOSEPH H., "Spirituality, Religiosity, and Alcoholism," *America*, 1977a, 136:458–461.

GRATEFUL MEMBERS, *The Twelve Steps for Everyone . . . Who Really Wants Them*. CompCare paperback.

JOHNSON, VERNON, "The Dynamics of Forgiveness," in *I'll Quit Tomorrow*, pp. 99–110.

KENNEDY, RAYMOND J.H., *Steps to Sobriety*. Paperback.

"Search for Spiritual Experience," *AA Grapevine*, April 1978, 2–16. Six brief articles on alcoholism and the need for spiritual experience.

TAYLOR, G. AIKEN, *A Sober Faith: Religion and Alcoholics Anonymous*.

Some useful pamphlets are *A Clergyman Asks about Alcoholics Anonymous*, from AA World Services, Inc.; *Guide to the Fourth Step Inventory*, and *A New Fourth Step Guide*, also Reverend Suzanne Smith, *Working the Steps*, all from Hazelden. For the spouse or family there are *Blueprint for Progress: Al-Anon's Fourth Step Inventory*, from Al-Anon, and *Guide to the Fourth Step Inventory for the Spouse*, from Hazelden.

Regarding the atheist, a Hazelden pamphlet by Jon Weinberg, *AA: An Interpretation for the Nonbeliever* and Chapter 4 "We Agnostics" in the book *Alcoholics Anonymous* speak directly to the issue, as do parts of the AA pamphlets *Do You Think You're Different?* and *A Clergyman Asks about Alcoholics Anonymous*. The AA booklet *Came to Believe* shows how broadly the Higher Power can be taken, as does an article by an atheist, "Sober for Thirty Years," *AA Grapevine*, November 1976, p. 2. *Your God is Too Small* by Phillips is a Macmillan paperback that is relevant, as are parts of the six articles in *AA Grapevine*, April 1978, pp 2–16, and parts of *The Twelve Steps for Everyone . . .* , a CompCare paperback.

Religion and Alcoholism

CLINEBELL, HOWARD J., *Understanding and Counseling the Alcoholic through Religion and Psychology.*

CONLEY, PAUL AND ANDREW SORENSON, *The Staggering Steeple: The Story of Alcoholism and the Churches.*

JOHN, HARRISON W., "The Church and Alcoholism: A Growing Involvement," *Alcohol Health and Research World*, Summer 1977, 2–10.

KELLER, JOHN E., *Ministering to Alcoholics.*

KELLERMAN, JOSEPH L., "Pastoral Care in Alcoholism," *Annals of the New York Academy of Sciences*, 1974, 233:144–147.

LINCOLN COUNCIL ON ALCOHOLISM AND DRUGS, *Parishioner's Assistance Program*. Lincoln, Nebraska, 1976, a program package.

LUM, DOMAN, "The Church and the Prevention of Alcoholism" *Journal of Religion and Health*, 1970, 9:138–161.

MCKINSEY, JOHN P., *Handling the Alcoholic Man: A Guide for Pastors.*

NAVY ALCOHOLISM PREVENTION PROGRAM, *The Chaplain's Role*. Bureau of Naval Personnel booklet.

Proceedings of the Symposium on the Role of the Christian Churches in the Recovery of the Alcoholic. DePaul Rehabilitation Hospital, Milwaukee.

SCHNEIDER, KARL A., *Alcoholism and Addiction: A Study Program for Adults and Youth* (for parish use).

SHIPP, THOMAS J., *Helping the Alcoholic and His Family.*

Some NCA pamphlets:

KELLERMAN, JOSEPH, *Alcoholism: A Guide for the Clergy.*

LEE, JOHN PARKS, *The Church's Ministry to the Alcoholic.*

VERDERY, E.A., *Pastoral Counseling and the Alcoholic.*

CHAPTER 19

Alcohol and Responsibility

PROBABLY THE MOST sensitive aspect of the problems arising from the overuse of alcoholic beverages is the area of moral responsibility. How guilty should one feel—if at all—for the drinking, for the subsequent behavior, even for being an alcoholic? There is an understandable reluctance even to mention these issues, both because of bitter emotional controversies that surrounded Prohibition, and because the recovering alcoholic is already burdened with unnecessary guilt feelings to which we do not wish to add. But a mature look at alcoholism demands that we consider the moral side, if only for the sake of completeness.

In former days alcoholism was a sin, and fell in the province of the clergy. Today most have gone beyond the preachy, moralizing approach of the mission flop houses, when men made a "nose dive" sham conversion just to get a free meal. Pledges, promises, and pious resolves not backed by sound remedial approaches have been found to be equally ineffective.

Dr. John C. Ford, the Jesuit moral theologian who was one of the few ever to write professionally about the moral aspects of alcoholism, once wrote an article, "Clerical Attitudes on Alcohol" (1953), with the delightful subtitle "—Most of Them Wrong." He talks about clergy attitudes, which are Unformed (immature, confused), Uninformed (ignorant), Misinformed (erroneous, myths), Deformed (extremes on either side of the drinking question—either it's *the* moral issue, or it's no moral issue at all), and Reformed (holier than thou, hard to live with).

When alcoholism became a civil crime, it was handled by the police, courts, and jail—the "drunk tank." But the model Uniform Alcoholism and Intoxication Treatment Act provides that the alcoholic be taken to treatment rather than be punished. The person is not bad, but sick.

Nature of Alcoholism

As necessary groundwork for addressing the moral issues, we first have to review from Chapter 10 the kind of a disease alcoholism is. The usual answer is, "Physical, psychological-emotional-mental, and spiritual." Alcoholism is neither weak-willed moral depravity nor usually the symptom of a psychiatric conflict, but rather a pathology in its own right: a compulsive addiction to alcohol, with its concomitant drinking behavior, which is indeed sick. This addiction is an habitual disposition or state-of-the-person. The compulsion to drink is now rooted in the whole complex of mental and biological changes already referred to. This means that in asking questions of moral responsibility we must clearly distinguish between *drinking, drunkenness,* and *alcoholism.* Obvious as these distinctions are, they are constantly ignored in moral discussions, with resulting disastrous confusion.

Drink versus Abstinence

This, of course, is the area where American churches have disagreed widely and even bitterly. Even when they agreed about drunkenness (abuse or overuse or misuse), they differed on drinking (use). The clergy has taken all positions on the issue of drinking, from the one extreme of saying that even one drink is morally wrong to the other extreme of saying that it is permissible to get deliberately drunk on occasion, and not just for medical purposes (alcohol was once used as an anesthetic, though it is a poor one for practical reasons as well as because it is addictive). The battle went on for over a century. The pendulum never stops in the middle; extreme positions breed extreme reactions.

The intent here is not to dictate anyone's morals, but to promote thinking objectively and in terms of moral principles instead of emotion or blind loyalty to a tradition. We might even swing the pendulum back toward the middle, which could possibly prevent some alcoholism in the light of Ullman's research (1953), which showed one common factor in a lot of cases was confused or ambivalent attitudes about drinking and drunkenness at the time one took the first drink in his life. The T in WCTU did not mean temperance but abstinence, causing one authority to remark that the "identification of total abstinence with the Christian Ethic was the basic fallacy of the temperance movement."

There seems to be neither historical nor theological basis for the total abstinence movement, since historically we saw in Chapter 3 that the Jews, Christ, and the founders of the major Protestant denominations all drank. Although drunkenness is condemned in both the Old and New Testaments, there is no condemnation of drinking in either . The wedding at Cana and the Last Supper are not isolated incidents in Christ's life, but reflect the ordinary life-style of His day, as seen in the customs of Orthodox Jews down to this time.

H.L. Mencken once defined Puritanism as "the haunting fear that somewhere, someone might be having fun." Extreme Puritanism would make anything pleasurable a sin. Now since God made sunsets and mountains beautiful, and food taste good, that makes Him out to be a fool. Most of us would be undernourished if food didn't taste good, and it would be a dreary world without flowers or sunsets. Because they confuse use and abuse, people wonder if there is something wrong with alcohol, or with God, or even with themselves (see Gallagher, *Pleasure Is God's Invention*, n.d.).

Scriptural scholars affirm there is no biblical justification for using grape juice rather than wine in the sacrament, and it was wine that Christ used when He instituted it. The same Hebrew and Greek word is used for the wine that made Noah drunk as that which Isaiah considers a special sign of God's favor for His chosen people—"pure, choice wines"—and which the Psalmist praises as "wine that gladdens the heart of man."

We conclude that drinking itself (for the nonalcoholic) is not wrong. The Judeo Christian tradition, which sees drink as "lawful but not expedient," makes total abstinence a matter of ascetic counsel rather than precept. Our point here is simply that drinking is not alcoholism; it is not even drunkenness. Use of alcohol is one thing, excessive use is something else.

Drunkenness versus Temperance

Whatever disagreements there are about use, most agree about misuse. Although the Jewish, Roman Catholic, Orthodox, Episcopal, and Lutheran traditions generally allow moderate drinking for those who can do so, it is simply incorrect to accuse them of condoning drunkenness. Temperance is an accepted Judeo-Christian virtue.

In this section we are talking about drunkenness in nonalcoholics; the case of the alcoholic is special and will come later. Seneca calls drunkenness "a temporary insanity, deliberately assumed." Ethically, it seems clear that to *deliberately* deprive oneself of one's rationality and self-control by a chemical is an abuse. And if it is the design of nature that human beings have the ability to exercise rational control, then drunkenness is obviously contrary to the intent of the Author of nature and therefore morally wrong.

Short of severe loss of the exercise of rational control, to be slightly drunk has some moral implications, too. For one thing, lesser degrees do not excuse one from all guilt. Secondly, there is the danger of going further once one starts to drink, because control and inhibitions are dulled. Thirdly, short of being drunk, one can be just relaxed enough by alcohol that poor reaction time or perceptual judgment might kill someone in an auto accident.

Alcoholism

If we say that it is not wrong to have a drink (for nonalcoholics), and agree that to choose to get drunk deliberately is wrong, we still have not examined how much free choice and, therefore, how much responsibility there might be for these actions on the part of alcoholics.

We have already made the distinction between choosing to drink and choosing to be an alcoholic. Nobody chooses to be an alcoholic, anymore than one chooses to be a diabetic. In this sense alcoholism is not a moral problem and there is no question of responsibility or guilt here. We shall return to this distinction in the next section when dealing with controlled drinking by alcoholics.

Freedom over Drinking

But are alcoholics, when sober, free in the choice to drink, and in control over getting drunk? Here we have a paradox. There is least responsibility in the precise area where there was once the most moralizing: excessive drinking by the alcoholic. Hence the importance of applying the concept of alcoholism delineated above as an obsessive-compulsive habit, an addiction with powerful psychological and physiological dynamics that greatly diminish one's ability to control behavior.

If it were merely a matter of sin, we would say, "Use your will power." The alcoholic has tried that, only to find that he is powerless over alcohol and that his life has become unmanageable. An old adage says, "A drunk could quit if he would, an alcoholic would quit if he could." Willpower is not the issue here. Clergymen have drunk themselves to death while clinging to the old idea that they could lick the problem if they just prayed more and tried harder.

Rather, we must apply what we know of the nature of the illness. Of its very nature, habit diminishes freedom. If we are powerfully disposed through habit to act in a certain way, then we are not as free to choose the opposite as we would be without the habit. We do not start at zero or from a neutral position, but as already disposed by habit so that we may be almost there before we begin. Choice means selection between alternatives, and to the extent that we are unable to consider alternatives fully, or see them clearly, our free choice is limited. Now habit is unconscious; what is conscious is habitual behavior or action. Therefore the full force of habit does not appear in consciousness and hence cannot enter into any clear deliberation between alternatives. Habit does its work in subtle, unconscious ways, which render choice exceedingly difficult. Moreover, addiction has physiological components, and nobody is aware of their cellular or hormonal state, so again much of the impact of the addiction is in a dark, murky area of which we are largely unaware. This further restricts the conscious deliberation that is essential for full freedom of choice.

All this means is that an alcoholic is less free, and hence less responsible for drinking and getting drunk, than one who is not an alcoholic. We must further distinguish between drinking by an alcoholic before recovery and after recovery.

Before Recovery.   If alcoholism is an illness, then it seems we should apply the same reasoning we use in other illnesses, namely the concept of *diminished* responsibility. We say with perfect understanding, "Joe's sick today; don't pay any attention if he's a bit grouchy." We do not tell a tubercular patient not to cough, a starving man to just use willpower. Alcoholics have a similar lack in freedom of choice.

Reverend John P. Cunningham, long-time director of the National Clergy Conference on Alcoholism, rightly asks whether those persons are capable of making a responsible moral decision who have been living for years with an overwhelming need for a chemical and in constant fear of the pain its deprivation would entail, hopelessly frustrated by their inability to control it, unaware of the deterioration it has caused until too late to turn back, convinced that they are worthless, suspicious of others, alienated from everybody including God. For such a person the ordinary concepts of guilt and responsibility may not apply at all, or only to a limited extent. It is humanly impossible to measure guilt here with any precision. But certainly they should not be told just not to drink, as if it were that simple.

A further question is whether a disease concept of alcoholism absolves one of *all* moral responsibility. A diabetic must still take insulin and follow a diet, and a cancer patient may still have to choose to undergo surgery. To the extent one is able, an alcoholic may have some obligation to get help for overcoming the illness. In light of the foregoing discussion on diminished freedom, an alcoholic before recovery should not be faced with a choice to stop drinking, only to accept help.

But alcoholics live in an alcoholic fog much of the time, and even in their sober periods their thinking is distorted by denial and rationalization. Cancer patients may find it as difficult to undergo surgery as alcoholics to go into treatment. But there is nothing about cancer that makes it attractive for cancer victims to continue it, whereas the vicious circle of alcoholism causes alcoholics to feel a strong if not uncontrollable urge to imbibe the very cause of their ills. Hence their responsibility is greatly diminished, and it may devolve more on others who are in a position to confront alcoholics effectively.

After Recovery.   The aim of treatment is to restore freedom of choice. Some say that an alcoholic is not free to take or not take the first drink. The sobriety of one million AA members and many other recovered alcoholics shows that at least with God's grace and the help of the fellowship or some other means, they can successfully choose not to drink. It is true that for recovered alcoholics the choice is much harder, the temptation much stronger, so they are less free. But we all struggle with temptations of various strengths: sex, stealing, whatever. The alcoholics' compulsion (perhaps not craving) may seem almost insuperable at times, and certainly their guilt is far less than if they did not have the enduring habitual disposition. But they do have some freedom and therefore some moral responsibility for taking the means or getting the help to avoid that first drink.

A true alcoholic probably has no free choice over whether he takes a third drink. By the time he has two in him he is not free to choose. This is because the direct absorption of alcohol into the blood stream can quickly affect the brain centers that mediate control and judgment as to whether he ought to have another one. In that sense he should be treated as a sick person and not as a criminal.

Controlled Drinking by Alcoholics

In saying that alcoholics have some choice over taking the first drink, and none over taking the third, the second drink was omitted. This is a gray area where literally "God only knows." There is some responsibility, in some cases, maybe. But far less than for the nonalcoholic. The very nature of the illness is some loss of control, some degree of psychological and/or physiological dependence whereby the alcoholic drinks not because he wants to but because he needs to. One Catholic alcoholic was given in confession the penance to say certain prayers "for the grace to drink like a lady." Such advice ignores the basic psychology and physiology of addiction. Whatever other choices she might have, that is precisely the one thing she *cannot* do.

The concept of alcoholism as a compulsive addiction raises questions of professional ethics about attempts at controlled or moderate drinking by alcoholics. Alcoholism treatment centers all over the country reported relapses attributable to publication of the Rand report (Armor, 1978). Academic freedom for scientific investigation and freedom of the press in reporting must be balanced against the Hippocratic oath to "do no harm" to patients. Injudicious publicizing of such experiments can literally kill alcoholics by feeding their denial that they have a terminal disease. For both psychological and physiological reasons, the only safe choice is to avoid drinking. Behavior modification can help them choose not to drink, but it is vapid to "choose" to change the nature of alcoholism. One might as well choose to change the laws of gravity, and then wrangle about why one hits the pavement every time one jumps out of a tenth-story window. Failure to make this basic distinction is behind much of the confusion about free choice and alcoholics (see Chapter 10).

A Paradox.   In the recent controversies over conditioning alcoholics to drink, several paradoxes have emerged. The most fascinating paradox is the reversal of roles regarding free choice. The behaviorist is usually pictured as favoring a mechanistic determinism by external stimuli in the old S-R (stimulus-response) paradigm, while those who favor a spiritual view of man think of him as possessing intellect and will by which he has the power of free choice. Yet it is the behaviorists who talk frequently of self-control, choice, strategies of self-management, "control by the subject," and so forth, whereas AA members talk about being powerless. An attempt to resolve this particular paradox follows, largely by using the distinction between surrender and compliance that appears in the writings of Dr. Harry Tiebout.

Drs. Marc and Linda Sobell (1974, p. 21), who are well known for their advocacy of conditioning alcoholics to drink socially, exhibit an interesting embodiment of this paradox when they defend free choice, or at least repudiate the old "weak will" theory, and to that extent are in agreement with AA. The answer may lie in the difference between surrender and compliance. The choice not to drink (so neglected in talk about responsible drinking) is *conscious*. But this may be merely superficial compliance if the alcoholic has *unconsciously* refused to accept a life of total abstinence; that is, if there is no surrender. He makes promises in all sincerity, but fails again and again. Why?

He is not powerless over the choice about drinking, but about being an alcoholic. One can choose to eat candy or not to eat candy, but one has no choice about being a diabetic. This is not an object of choice but of feeling. To save his ship in a storm the captain may choose to throw his cargo overboard, but he doesn't *feel* like it, and reason does not change his feeling. Surrender here is not defeat, but acceptance of reality. An alcoholic does not give up the power of choosing to drink or not to drink, but accepts the fact that he has no choice over whether he is an alcoholic or not.

Compliance at the conscious level without surrender at the feeling and unconscious levels not only has the alcoholic divided against himself, but the superficial compliance actually blocks the surrender. Psychologically, it would be better that he made no promises, as they only prolong his denial. This is a compromise reaction. (Tiebout is speaking of the *psychology* of compliance without surrender; he would not deny that actual sobriety might buy time to get the toxic effects of alcohol out of one's brain so that one's thinking could be straightened out.) Consciously, the alcoholic may want to drink socially, but unconsciously the desire is for inebriation.

In contrast, surrender or acceptance leads not to a sense of crushing defeat but to a sense of freedom, of completeness, serenity, and a sense of honesty, because now the alcoholic's conscious and unconscious are in harmony. He no longer lies to himself, which is what denial or rationalization is. He accepts his limitations with humility, the antithesis of pride which would lead to drinking again. Now he can identify with the speaker at the AA meeting—he feels at home. The emotional aspects of the fellowship have a most important psychological function, since surrender is at the feeling level rather than at the level of reason. Analysis of the *reasons* why one drank cost thousands of dollars in psychiatrist's fees and did not buy sobriety. Being a member helps one *feel* good about choosing not to drink.

Consequences

So much for drinking and drunkenness. But a very large area of moral responsibility has to do with the consequences of our choice. Here ethics gives a basic principle: One is responsible only to the extent that one knows *at the time* of the choice what the consequences are, and deliberately chooses a course of events *then* under his or her control.

The time factor is important, because many recovered alcoholics suffer needless guilt feelings over consequences they now see through sober eyes. They must not judge themselves in the light of their present knowledge, but according to what they knew at the time. Most did not foresee the consequences clearly, or were unable to control them. For example, this is true of the recovering alcoholic woman who reads about the fetal alcohol syndrome and feels guilty about having risked deformity for her baby. She is to judge in light of what she knew at the time she was pregnant, not her present knowledge. (What she now knows should govern her choice of whether to drink, especially during the first trimester, in future pregnancies.)

But suppose a man, cold sober and fully conscious, knows for certain that if he goes into this bar or tavern with these companions on Friday and has even one beer, he will end up drinking and gambling away his week's paycheck, come home drunk and beat up his wife, and his children will have no food next week. Suppose that in light of this knowledge he deliberately chooses to have the beer regardless of the consequences. Would just the fact that he is an alcoholic automatically acquit him of all responsibility?

We have painted the extreme case to make the point; in real life it may be more gray and fuzzy. Thus, in this case, the degree of responsibility will vary with whether one is an alcoholic or not, and if so with whether one is in early or late stage of progression, the length and quality of sobriety since last drinking, the influence of companions, one's physical condition, including fatigue, and other factors. For a woman alcoholic the menstrual period can vary her reaction to alcohol and her actual blood alcohol level, to say nothing of her emotional sensitivity.

Note that the question is not whether the man in our foregoing example is free to choose at the time he comes home and beats up his wife. The villain in the Gay Nineties melodrama who ties the heroine to the railroad track and cuts the boxcar loose has no control when it is halfway down the incline; yet he is guilty of her death because he deliberately set in motion this chain of events (he, of course, doesn't know the hero is going to rescue her at the last second). It is his conscious control at the time he makes the choice that determines his degree of guilt. Recall that although alcohol's net effect, after perhaps some initial stimulation, is to depress or lower performance, it mostly depresses our ability to judge how well we are doing. Hence, after a few drinks the person is less able to rationally control behavior, including drinking behavior.

All this must be kept in mind when attempting to assess guilt for the consequences of one's drinking. One is not a bad person, but may have done some bad things. We must distinguish between true responsibility and irrational feelings. If one has done something wrong and knew at the time it was wrong, to feel responsible is not neurotic but realistic. On the other hand, it is irrational to feel guilty if the act was not really wrong, or if one did not know at the time that it was wrong, or if it could not have been avoided, or if one has every reason to believe that it has long since been forgiven. These are baseless guilt feelings, a frequent symptom of neurosis. The spouse or children may have special problems of false guilt. They often feel it must be their fault that the alcoholic drinks. Al-Anon and Alateen can help them detach from these feelings, to accept their inability to control the drinker, and to know they are not responsible.

Psychologists and psychiatrists sometimes reject the whole notion of guilt, because they deal with so many patients obsessed with neurotic guilt feelings over past deeds for which they were not really responsible and should therefore not feel guilt. The answer is not to attack the notion of guilt but rather the neuroticism. A parallel is in the case of a woman patient obsessed with anxiety about the gas being turned off. When the family started out on an outing she would make her husband go back not once but three times to check. The solution here is not to attack modern gas appliances. It is equally unreasonable to attack the concept of guilt because of neurotic guilt feelings. Albert Ellis, in his system of Rational-Emotive Therapy, applies the term *guilt* only to the latter. But he does talk of *responsibility*, which we can call objectively based guilt as opposed to purely subjective guilt feelings. The difference here may be purely semantic. Some recent authors more to the point are Menninger (1973), Campbell (1975, presidential address to the American Psychological Association), and Becker (1977).

Again, we must distinguish regret from guilt. If I acidentally kill a little girl who ran in front of my car with no neglect on my part, I naturally regret the fact. But I am not guilty of her death. Likewise, the desire to make amends must not be confused with guilt. Even though one was not culpable, he may still want to try to make up for the effects of his drinking.

The question of whether intoxication is an excuse comprises a complex portion of criminal law. Here the best legal minds run into that murky area we pointed out when showing how habit in all its unconscious psychophysiological aspects can reduce freedom of choice, without necessarily eliminating it. Culpability is always tied to the degree of awareness one has at the time the choice is made, and to the degree of control over behavior and its consequences even when known. Obviously a thousand factors can be at work here, most of them unmeasurable and some unknown. Human prudential judgment, rather than scientific precision, must rule in such a situation.

It is important to note that the new Uniform Act explicitly disclaims any change in criminal law. It affects only the simple act of being drunk in public, as exhibiting a symptom of the disease of alcoholism. One is still just as liable legally for anything else as he was before passage of the Uniform Act. So it is legal to jail the alcoholic drunk driver even though "ill," and likewise the alcoholic rapist or murderer.

This is true morally as well as legally. The consequences, to the extent they were foreseen and controllable, are still our responsibility. AA Steps 8 and 9 "made a list . . . amends . . ." imply some responsibility. Let us mention some specific instances.

Driving.   One need not be legally drunk to kill somebody with an automobile. Nor must one be an alcoholic. True, many highway deaths involve alcoholics, or at least high blood alcohol levels. But there could be some moral responsibility every time anyone turns the ignition key in a potentially lethal weapon with even small amounts of blood alcohol. Research has shown some impairment at blood alcohol levels below the legal limit. Science and ethics can combine forces here.

Assault.   Alcohol is involved in 60 percent of American homicides, and most homicides among Native Americans. Assault and battery do not always result in death, but we know alcohol is involved in a large percentage of cases. This may diminish responsibility for the act, but also may shift the focus to responsibility for doing something about the drinking problem. One massive brute of a man never touches a drop because he is afraid that if he ever drinks he will kill somebody—and with reason. Few people have this degree of insight.

Sex.   Alcohol is no aphrodisiac. But it can result in illegitimate pregnancy because inhibitions are lowered and jugement is impaired. Again culpability in one or both parties may be minimal.

Harm to Body.   Most viewers of the Dr. Max Schneider film *Medical Aspects of Alcoholism* seem most impressed with the amount of damage alcohol does to the body. When students are asked to list the moral implications of drinking or alcoholism, the most frequent answers involve damage to the body and damage to one's self-respect. This is, of course, usually unforeseen, so responsibility can be discounted; the basic principle of foreknowledge applies. But it is interesting that self-destruction, suicide, is against the law in most jurisdictions.

Family, Employees, or Employers.   The consequences of excessive drinking, again both alcoholic and nonalcoholic, on these others are usually seen as melodrama rather than from the viewpoint of moral responsibility and ethical principles. If the spouse tries to present these consequences objectively, it still often sounds like nagging. When the alcoholic client does state guilt feelings about harm to family and others, it could be more productive if the counselor reflected these feelings in a nondirective way rather than dismissing them too hastily.

Property Destruction.   Not only personal injury, but millions of dollars in damage is done each year through alcohol-related accidents: auto and home, boat, fire, private planes, etc. Passing bad checks might be included here, when the question of amends or restitution is discussed.

A special case that nobody talks about is vandalism. It would be difficult to assess what percentage of the destruction, which might involve whole city blocks, is often due to the fact that many in the mob have been drinking. Who pays? Not the rioters. Should they? How many of them were cold sober at the time? These questions need to be asked.

Liability for Actions of Others.

An interesting recent development is the question of responsibility for the intoxication and subsequent offenses of others than oneself. Regardless of lawsuits, what is the moral responsibility of one who pushes drinks, especially to an alcoholic? This could include not only the host, bartender, or clerk in a liquor store, but also the supplier, manufacturer, and especially the advertiser who makes it so attractive. This responsibility may have a parallel in the multimillion-dollar lawsuits which name as co-defendants the airlines, airplane manufacturers, and others.

Another area of influence on others is the whole question of responsibility for alcohol education: in schools, in the professions (especially medicine), in the public media, in business and industry (promulgation versus burying of plant policy on alcoholism). Irresponsible advertising is condoned by society, and is not just the responsibility of the advertiser.

In this connection, there is the interesting question of what responsibility, if any, we as a nation of consumers and advertisers have for perpetuating the "pill for every ill" mentality. John C. Ford, S.J., in his article "Chemical Comfort and Christian Virtue" (1959) tells of the man lolling in a hammock beside a lake smooth as glass, with not a leaf stirring in the trees, the whole scene one of peace and quiet. He asks, "Honey, would you hand me my tranquilizers?"

Should a pledge be made, usually at confirmation, not to drink until one is twenty-one? Certainly it should not be forced through moral pressure. But if voluntary and with full awareness of the fact that it is not a moral issue unless one intends to so bind oneself, a pledge can be useful.

Next, is there some responsibility in our social agencies for prolonging the abuses of the disease concept? The medical detoxification center becomes just an expensive, if more humane, substitute for the drunk tank, unless the revolving-door alcoholic is gotten into long-term treatment. We know now that forced treatment can work. Maybe the best help we might give a chronic repeater would be to refuse treatment, so that the notion of responsibility for doing something about his *illness* (not his drinking) might eventually penetrate through the alcoholic fog.

Contraction of Habit

Lastly, there is the extremely tricky question of to what extent one might be responsible for contracting or enhancing one's habitual addiction to the drug alcohol. Nobody deliberately and consciously sets out to be an alcoholic. But it is possible that in some subtle and subconscious ways one chooses to neglect facing the danger of addiction? We do know that denial and self-deception are characteristics of the illness. How often we hear at meetings, "I was hooked on alcohol and didn't know it." Is there a parallel to the woman who has a lump on her breast that is sore and growing, but refuses to go to the doctor because "It's not *that* bad yet"? The problem here is that it is in the nature of alcohol to make things seem "not that bad."

No Pat Answers.   Throughout these last sections we have raised more questions than we have given answers. This is not only because answers here are difficult to come by, but also because responsibility cannot be imposed or legislated. It must develop from within the population. Ethics can only indicate principles and try to raise the right questions. The result may be a growing sense of responsibility throughout the alcohol profession, and an awareness that more sensitive counseling is needed in these areas.

Sources

Very little has been written on this topic, except by John C. Ford, S.J. In Royce, *Personality and Mental Health* (rev. ed., 1964, pp. 249–257) the principles are laid down regarding persons with various disorders, but applications to alcohol problems are difficult. We list a few items.

BECKER, ARTHUR H., *Guilt: Curse or Blessing?*

FORD, JOHN C., *Depth Psychology, Morality, and Alcoholism.*

FORD, JOHN C., "Chemical Comfort and Christian Virtue," *American Ecclesiastical Review*, 1959, 141:361–379.

FORD, JOHN C., "Clerical Attitudes on Alcohol—Most of Them Wrong," *The Priest*, April 1955. Reprinted as NCA pamphlet.

GALLAGHER, JOSEPH P., *Pleasure is God's Invention.* Hazelden booklet.

OATES, WAYNE E., *Alcohol In and Out of the Church.* Listed here for completeness. The author respectfully disagrees with some parts.

TIEBOUT, HARRY M., "Surrender Versus Compliance in Therapy with Special Reference to Alcoholism," *Quarterly Journal of Studies on Alcohol*, 1953, 14: 58–68. Reprinted as NCA pamphlet.

CHAPTER 20

Alcohol and the Law

LIKE MANY OF THESE CHAPTERS, this one could be an entire book. We can only point a finger at some of the chief relations between law and the use or misuse of alcohol. Laws differ from state to state and between countries; those actually working in the field must become familiar with statutory law as it applies locally. Moreover, new legal precedents are constantly being set in this rapidly developing field, so today's ruling may be reversed by tomorrow's decision or a change in the law. The prudence of obtaining legal counsel is obvious. On the other hand, both judges and attorneys in presentence investigations or diversion proceedings are turning now to alcoholism professionals for their expertise. Alcohol use may have legal import for both civil and criminal cases. These may include liability from serving drinks to intoxicated persons, job discrimination against alcoholics, traffic violations, legal regulation of liquor sales, and the Uniform Act aimed at diverting the alcoholic from punishment to treatment.

Liability

Courts in a growing number of states, including California, Iowa, New York, and Oregon, have ruled that one can be held liable for death, automobile accidents, and other damages that result if alcoholic beverages are furnished to intoxicated persons under conditions involving a reasonably foreseeable risk of harm to others. This includes not only bars, restaurants, liquor stores, and the company giving an office party, but also the host or hostess in a private home.

Many states have very specific statutes that forbid allowing or furnishing alcoholic beverages to minors, defined as those below eighteen, nineteen or twenty-one years of age, depending on the state. Some states exempt parents serving alcohol to their own children within the home, but others do not. In either case the parent or other adult may be liable for both civil and criminal charges arising from subsequent actions of the minor, including assault and traffic violations.

Discrimination

Section 503 of the Vocational Rehabilitation Act of 1973, amended in 1974, designates the Department of Labor to enforce "affirmative action" regarding employment of handicapped persons by recipients of federal contracts in excess of $2,500, and in its Section 504 names the Department of Health, Education and Welfare (HEW) to administer regulations assuring the handicapped "equal opportunity" in employment, education and services. The secretary of HEW issued regulations in May 1977 that clearly included alcoholics and drug addicts among those so protected against discrimination. On July 5, 1977 the Department of Labor, backed by an intepretation from the U.S. Attorney General, made a similar inclusion. These actions together comprise a historical landmark in the alcoholism field second only to the resolution accepting alcoholism as a disease by the American Medical Association (*JAMA*, October 20, 1956) and by the U.S. Congress in the 1970 Hughes Act (PL 91-616) which established the NIAAA.

The exact force of these regulations will probably be in some dispute for years to come, but the general intent is clear: alcoholism is not a crime nor a moral flaw, but a treatable illness, which should not in itself be reason for discrimination against a person otherwise qualified (see Ford, 1978). Prior status is not grounds for discrimination. The alcoholic is never cured in the sense of return to social drinking, but neither is the amputee cured. The key word is *qualified*, for there is no intent to guarantee jobs for the unqualified or the unemployable. Those whose dependency on alcohol or other drugs interferes with acceptable behavior or normal job performance can be terminated according to the same standards as any other employee. On the other hand, rehabilitation is not a condition for receiving education or services, since many of these are designed precisely to rehabilitate the alcoholic. And the distinction between equal opportunity or nondiscrimination in Section 504 and affirmative action in Section 503 must be observed.

Regulation of Sale

It was noted in Chapter 11 that some researchers advocate prevention of alcoholism by reduction in overall per capita consumption, and we suggested that this lognormal curve theory is not incompatible in practice with a bimodal theory of high-risk population. This is a complex issue. In an effort toward an objective view, we shall simply condense the relevant section in the National Institute on Alcohol Abuse and Alcoholism's (NIAAA) second special report to Congress entitled *Alcohol and Health: New Knowledge* (1974, pp. 154–163).

> Liquor control laws have their roots in antiquity, and the development of variations in the means and methods of control can be traced through various stages of civilization to modern times. Laws and organizations exist in all developed nations and states, and in most underdeveloped nations of the world. In broad terms, their primary goals are the regulation of the manufacture, sale, and consumption of beverage alcohol and its taxation. Most developed countries have national policies on the manufacture and sale of alcoholic beverages, although many countries provide for local variations, especially in retail sales. The United States, on the other hand, has not had a national policy on the manufacture and sale of alcoholic beverages since 1933. There are federal statutes governing the export and import of alcoholic beverages, but each state has full and complete authority over the manufacture, distribution, and sale of alcoholic beverages within its borders.
>
> While broad generalizations should not be hastily formulated from one experiment, the experience with Prohibition clearly suggests that social policies which conflict with widely accepted societal practices and mores are, if not doomed to failure, potentially dysfunctional to societal institutions, including the broad area of law and justice. American experience over the last century and longer suggests that the availability of alcoholic beverages has broad public support. The problem faced by the American system of democracy is how to control the problems associated with the consumption of beverage alcohol without destroying respect for the system that enacts, administers, and adjudicates the controls. It must be recognized also that societal customs that are deeply embedded in and part of accepted behavior patterns are not easily subject to change, cetainly not in the short run, as was attempted through Prohibition.
>
> *Hodgepodge of Laws.* Only recently has attention been focused upon the intricate patchwork quilt of often inconsistent statutes and customs that prevail in the United States. The real effects of different types of regulation are now beginning to be questioned and need to be examined more thoroughly. The 50 States and the District of Columbia, when viewed as a whole, do not present a picture of regulation that is easily described except to say that it is disjointed, full of contradictions, marked by divergent statutory provisions, and lacking in concrete statements of purpose that can be related to functions and activities.
>
> Thirty-two states and the District of Columbia, through regulatory agencies or offices that have different forms and functions, control the manufac-

ture, distribution, and retail sale of alcoholic beverages by *licensing* all segments of the industry. In a few of the license states, municipal governments issue most retail licenses; in others, county governments have complete or partial authority over retail licensing. There is no simple description of retail license procedures. Eighteen states have *monopoly* systems of control which exclude private-sector involvement in the distribution of most alcoholic beverages, especially distilled spirits. As in the license states, there is no uniformity in the regulatory provisions.

Attempts at Control. Licensing, limiting the number of licenses, and monopoly control of off-premise sales are negative controls, as are all or nearly all of the controls established for the industry. Other types of controls include hours of sale, age of purchasers, separation of licenses for on-premise and off-premise sales, prohibitions against "tied house" arrangements, minimum pricing, and limitations on advertising. The negative aspect of the controls arises from the fact that they are aimed at preventing, eliminating, or decreasing intemperance, and restricting licensees from engaging in or allowing on the licensed premises activities that the legislature or the control agency considers undesirable. Although most of the states, in their expressions of legislative purpose, invoke the promotion of temperance, or imply that temperate use of alcoholic beverages is the legislative goal, their statutes which govern the activities of the State Alcohol Beverage Control (ABC) authority do not provide for a positive role to further the goal of temperance. Whether temperance is obtainable by these means is not in fact known.

Juggling Definitions. The legal definition of what constitutes an alcoholic beverage differs among the states, as do the beverages to which the laws apply. In a dozen or more states the terms "alcoholic beverage" and "intoxicating beverage" are not applicable to all classes of beverage alcohol because of legal distinctions in the statutes. For example, beer containing 3.2% alcohol by weight (approximately 4% by volume) in some states is regulated but is not considered an intoxicating beverage. Beer with an alcohol content not exceeding 5% by weight (approximately 6.25% by volume), and wine that contains 21% or less alcohol by volume, are declared to be both nonalcoholic and nonintoxicating in South Carolina.

Prices, Locations, Hours, and Eligibility. One form of control is to regulate prices. Another widespread form of control prohibits the sale of alcoholic beverages within a specified distance of certain public and private institutions. In addition, most states allow local zoning restrictions to prevail in the issuance of most types of new retail licenses. Because of the presumed relation between hours of availability and levels of consumption, all fifty states have some restrictions on times of sale at retail or permit local governments to establish opening and closing hours. But the similarity of the actual restrictions is not great. For example, some jurisdictions prohibit or restrict sales on Sunday, others make distinctions among different classes of licenses, and some leave the question of Sunday sales to local governing bodies or local option. Closing hours vary in some states from municipality to municipality because of local control.

Most states prohibit the sale of beverage alcohol to specified classes of people. Sales to minors are the most obvious example. But there are also restrictions on sales to insane or interdicted persons, persons of ill repute, and intoxicated persons. Enforcement of some of these restrictions is obviously difficult, and data on the level of enforcement are nonexistent. Among the laws commonly held to be important in promoting temperance is the legal age restriction. While a growing number of states recently have lowered to eighteen the minimum age for the purchase of alcoholic beverages, the majority still require a higher age at least for the purchase of distilled spirits and wine.

Retail license quotas are another method of control presumed to affect alcohol consumption and related problems. There are only very limited data on the effect of retail license quotas on alcohol-related problems, or even on consumption. Probably the most extensive study of license limitations was carried out by the Moreland Commission in New York State. The commission found that there was no discernible change in consumption levels or patterns.

Hypothesis Worth Exploring. On the surface it would appear that primary prevention on the basis of the distribution-of-alcohol-consumption theory must include a method of controlling the availability of beverage alcohol to all consumers. In addition, it suggests that it is difficult or impossible to affect the problem drinkers without affecting the drinkers who comprise the vast majority of the median and the mode. While the distribution-of-alcohol-consumption theory itself has some supporting data, knowledge of alcohol consumption patterns is still too meager to allow a conclusion based on a distribution curve. Prohibition is possibly a timeworn omen too often held up as the example of what increased taxation will produce, but it is unavoidable to examine the societal reaction to it when mass control of alcoholic beverages is considered.

If the hypothesis were tested, and if it were demonstrated that the distribution-of-alcohol-consumption theory adequately describes U.S. consumption patterns, and has predictive reliability for levels of alcoholism and alcohol-related mortality and morbidity, and if it can be assumed that the implementation of the pricing or taxing policy suggested by the proponents of the theory will not lead to severe law-enforcement or social problems, such as the growth of an illicit beverage industry similar to what existed in this country during Prohibition, then legislation assigning discretionary taxing policies to ABC agencies might provide a major primary prevention tool. To embark on such an approach without first thoroughly exploring the validity of the theory, and the possible by-products of such a taxing policy, would be premature and even foolhardy. But the exploration of the theory for its predictive capabilities and as a primary prevention tool deserves serious consideration.

Alcohol and Traffic Laws

In Chapter 5 we described briefly the effect of alcohol on driving, the increased impairment at higher levels of blood alcohol content (BAC), and the use of chemical tests of blood alcohol in arrests for driving an automobile while intoxicated (DWI). There research was mentioned that suggests our American laws are too lenient in the level of BAC allowed before a driver is considered to be unsafe. The more stringent laws in other countries seem to reflect more accurately than our own the real dangers of impairment and the consequent risk of accidents, especially fatal accidents. If we include the drinking pedestrian and those drivers who may be slightly impaired even though not legally drunk, the evidence points to alcohol being a causal factor in over half of the automobile fatalities occurring in America each year. Other types of alcohol-related accidents come less directly under the law, but should not be ignored: home, boat, fire, drownings, suicides, and a high percentage of fatal crashes in airplanes other than commercial or military.

Drunk driving, impaired driving, driving while intoxicated, or driving while under the influence of alcohol are variously defined in different jurisdictions. Regardless of these differences, most of the drivers in fatal accidents had a BAC well above the level designated legally as safe, and many had a history of previous alcohol-related offenses. This latter fact points to the need for diversion into some corrective course of action rather than merely imposing a fine or jail sentence. Neither past stringent laws or scare slogans have been scientifically evaluated as to their effectiveness in preventing these problems, but the lack of evidence combined with the above facts suggests that a new approach is called for.

New types of countermeasures have been introduced in Canada and England, in the Scandinavian countries, and in Austria and Czechoslovakia, and some attempt has been made at evaluating the results. The most ambitious program has been the Alcohol Safety Action Program (ASAP) set up in the early 1970s by the U.S. Department of Transportation. Because a substantial proportion of those arrested are problem drinkers or alcoholics, the idea was to utilize the case-finding potential of ASAP not only to prevent further accidents but to get into treatment those who need it. Police surveillance and educational programs were also part of the plan.

Instead of jail, drunk drivers today are being sent by many courts to attend Alcohol Information Schools (AIS), where they learn about the effects of alcohol on driving and other behaviors as well as about alcoholism. This may be enough for some; others discover that they have a drinking problem and go into treatment. The court may give others a choice of jail or treatment, which may include monitored doses of Antabuse, mandatory attendance at AA meetings, or some combination of inpatient or outpatient approaches. Some few states have a *deferred-prosecution* law, whereby the accused can go directly into treatment without entering the criminal justice system at all. A preliminary report from one state (Washington) shows a recidivism rate of only 4 percent out of 2,000 cases handled in this manner from September 1975 to September 1977, but admits that the time period for some was rather short. Judges and attorneys are learning that alcohol education and treatment can save lives more effectively than jail, whereas leniency can actually kill an alcoholic client by failing to stop the progression of a terminal illness.

The Uniform Act

History.   Public intoxication was first made a criminal offense in England by a 1606 statute. This was carried over to the Colonies, and continued in all jurisdictions in the United States until 1966. In the next few years the legal status of public intoxication changed dramatically. In 1966 two different U.S. district courts of appeal (in *Driver* v. *Hinnant* and in *Easter* v. *District of Columbia*) ruled that an alcoholic cannot be jailed for being drunk in public. The two major issues were whether the alcoholic is capable of criminal intent or *mens rea* in such behavior, and whether it is cruel and unusual punishment and therefore unconstitutional to jail a person for exhibiting the symptoms of a disease. In June 1968 the U.S. Supreme Court, in *Powell* v. *Texas*, gave a 5–4 decision, which, although it did not reverse Powell's conviction, confirmed much of the reasoning of the appeals courts. Disagreement among the nine justices centered largely around problems of evidence and whether the practical issue should be left to the states, but a majority accepted the disease concept and the involuntary nature of the alcoholic's public intoxication, according to Attorney General John Mitchell (1971).

Court decisions about whether alcoholism could be used as a defense in other criminal actions continued to be conflicting, but a consensus emerged that alcoholism itself is involuntary. Some civil cases involving labor arbitration and social security benefits, the reports of two crime commissions set up by President Johnson in August 1965, and the welter of criminal court decisions formed a groundswell of legal activity which led to the development of new statutory approaches to the problem of public drunkenness. Thus it was shifted from the judicial to the legislative branch of government. A common thread was the notion that jailing an alcoholic was no solution. The Hughes Act of the 1970 Congress was very broad, but several states addressed the specific issues of being drunk in public between 1967 and 1971. During the same period a joint committee representing the American Medical Association and two sections of the American Bar Association drew up a model law, and the National Institute of Mental Health funded a legislative drafting group at Columbia University to prepare a model act (Grad, 1971).

Finally in August 1971 the National Conference of Commissioners on Uniform State Laws, comprised of representatives of the governors of each state, adopted the *Uniform Alcoholism and Intoxication Treatment Act*. This has been enacted in some form by more than half the states, the state of Washington having been the first. Although varying in how closely they follow the model, the general thrust of these state laws is to take alcoholism out of the drunk tank and the criminal justice system, making the alcoholic not a criminal but a sick person. Similar developments have taken place in many foreign countries in the last decade, as legal sanctions to control intoxication have been found ineffective and public health measures are being adopted to replace criminal law.

Scope.   None of the preceding items in this chapter are touched by the Uniform Act, which only removes the act of being drunk in public from the criminal code and makes alcoholism a matter for treatment instead of punishment. Section 19 of the act explicitly says that it does not apply to such questions as drunk driving or the sale of liquor. The intricate question of using intoxication as a defense in criminal cases is left intact. This is important, because the public has sometimes misunderstood the Uniform Act as allowing one to commit any crime and then use the illness of alcoholism as an excuse. The alcoholic can still be arrested on charges of disorderly conduct, assault, murder, rape, DWI, etc. and the court must decide to what degree responsibility was diminished by alcoholism.

Implementation.   It would be naive to infer that mere passage of laws has solved the problems of alcoholism. For one thing, these laws affect principally the vagrant or homeless, and at most affect perhaps 3 to 5 percent of all alcoholics. Secondly, merely decriminalizing public drunkenness does not create an adequate system of treatment and rehabilitation, nor guarantee its use by those who need it. Some states passed the law but have been woefully negligent in funding adequate treatment facilities to implement it. This may require years of organization, trial and error methods, and the work of many dedicated people. Some thorny attendant problems include the following: applicable definitions, involuntary commitment, confidentiality of records, adequate continuum of care, individualized treatment plans, police and civilian transportation from public places to detoxification or treatment centers, and training of personnel competent in alcoholism. Each of these is provided for in the Uniform Act. None is a simple matter.

The major concern is whether the act is achieving its declared end of getting alcoholics into treatment. Because of our strong tradition of safeguarding human rights, Section 14 on involuntary commitment is so cumbersome that it is almost impossible to enforce. Some argue that by getting alcoholics into emergency care (a term the act prefers to detoxification) it provides the occasion for counselors to motivate into definitive treatment those who would profit from it. But what we know about the success of forced treatment suggests that many more could be rehabilitated if detained longer. Research data on the point is inconclusive, and in any case this population is less likely to have a high success rate than those in occupational programs.

Text and Comments.   As the Uniform Act is adopted by each state legislature in a different form and interpreted differently by the courts in various jurisdictions, we cannot give a final or universal version of the act in practice. The entire model act with comments is printed as Appendix A of the first NIAAA special report to Congress, *Alcohol and Health* (1971). It may be helpful to reproduce salient portions here.

Section 1. *Declaration of Policy.* It is the policy of this state that alcoholics and intoxicated persons may not be subjected to criminal prosecution because of their consumption of alcoholic beverages but rather should be afforded a continuum of treatment in order that they may lead normal lives as productive members of society.

Section 2. *Definitions.* (1) "alcoholic" means a person who habitually lacks self-control as to the use of alcoholic beverages, or uses alcoholic beverages to the extent that his health is substantially impaired or endangered or his social or economic function is substantially disrupted;

(9) "incapacitated by alcohol" means that a person, as a result of the use of alcohol, is unconscious or has his judgment otherwise so impaired that he is incapable of realizing and making a rational decision with respect to his need for treatment;

(10) "incompetent person" means a person who has been adjudged incompetent by the appropriate state court;

(11) "intoxicated person" means a person whose mental or physical functioning is substantially impaired as a result of the use of alcohol;

COMMENT. The term "alcoholic" is defined in two alternative ways for two different purposes. The first alternative is a relatively narrow definition based on lack of self-control regarding the use of alcoholic beverages. Lack of self-control may be manifested either by the inability to abstain from drinking for any significant time period, or by the ability to remain sober between drinking episodes but an inability to refrain from drinking to intoxication whenever drinking an alcoholic beverage. This relatively narrow definition has been the basis for the court decisions holding an alcoholic not criminally responsible for his intoxication.

The second alternative definition adopts the World Health Organization's broad approach that alcoholism can be defined as the use of alcoholic beverages to the extent that health or economic or social functioning are substantially impaired. The purpose of this broad definition is to make as large a group as possible eligible for treatment for alcoholism and related problems. Encouraging early treatment for drinking problems will ultimately lead to prevention. This broad definition of alcoholism is useful in making voluntary treatment available to as large a group as possible, but would be wholly inappropriate to define those alcoholics who justify civil commitment for involuntary treatment.

The act defines "treatment" broadly to include a wide range of types and kinds of services to reflect the fact that there is no single or uniform method of treatment that will be effective for all alcoholics.

Section 5. *Duties of Division of Alcoholism* (of the state department of health or mental health). The division shall (1) develop, encourage, and foster statewide, regional, and local plans and programs for the prevention of alcoholism and treatment of alcoholics and intoxicated persons in cooperation with public and private agencies, organizations, and individuals, and provide technical assistance and consultation services for these purposes;

(15) encourage general hospitals and other appropriate health facilities to admit without discrimination alcoholics and intoxicated persons and to provide them with adequate and appropriate treatment;

(16) encourage all health and disability insurance programs to include alcoholism as a covered illness;

COMMENT. Under PL91-616 each state must prepare a comprehensive alcoholism plan for federal funding. Other laws provide that all pertinent state plans include alcoholism. The provision in Section 5 (15) is particularly important because the 1970 federal act includes a provision under which a general hospital can be denied federal funds under this law for discriminating against alcoholics. Section 5 (16) on all health and disability insurance programs applies to both private and governmental programs. [It is significant that *prevention* and education are mentioned no less than seven times in this section.]

Section 7. *Citizens Advisory Council on Alcoholism.*

COMMENT. The qualifications of the members are defined broadly. It is expected that the govenor would appoint to the council individuals representing a broad range of background and experience, including representatives of citizens groups, voluntary organizations, professional groups, and recovered alcoholics.

Section 8. *Comprehensive Program for Treatment.*

COMMENT. Whether or not the director divides the state into regional units for purposes of administration, it is desirable that all treatment services be community based. Alcoholics and other ill persons are treated more effectively through treatment services in their own communities, located conveniently to population centers so as to be quickly and easily accessible to patients and their families, rather than in large institutional settings.

The act uses the concept of emergency treatment rather than the more popular phrase "detoxification center," as the latter concept tends to stigmatize alcoholics and set them apart from people with other illnesses or problems. These emergency services should be available twenty-four hours a day and be readily accessible to those who need this assistance. In addition to medical services, emergency social services and appropriate diagnostic and referral services should be included.

Section 10. *Acceptance for Treatment; Rules.* (1) If possible a patient shall be treated on a voluntary rather than an involuntary basis.

(3) A person shall not be denied treatment solely because he has withdrawn from treatment against medical advice on a prior occasion or because he has relapsed after earlier treatment.

(4) An individualized treatment plan shall be prepared and maintained on a current basis for each patient.

(5) Provision shall be made for a continuum of coordinated treatment services, so that a person who leaves a facility or a form of treatment will have available and utilize other appropriate treatment.

COMMENT. The possibility of relapse in chronic illness, the need for individualized treatment plan, and the concept of continuum of care are important features of this section.

Section 11. *Voluntary Treatment of Alcoholics.*

COMMENT. Most patients treated under this act will voluntarily seek treatment. The provisions of this section allow the patient to seek treatment in the same manner as he would for any other health problem or illness. The Act encourages voluntary treatment by not requiring the patient to agree to voluntarily commit himself for a specified length of time or to accept any of the other restrictions that apply to involuntarily committed patients.

Section 12. *Treatment and Services for Intoxicated Persons and Persons Incapacitated by Alcohol.* (a) An intoxicated person may come voluntarily to an approved public treatment facility for emergency treatment. A person who appears to be intoxicated in a public place and to be in need of help, if he consents to the proffered help, may be assisted to his home, an approved public treatment facility, an approved private treatment facility, or other health facility by the police or the emergency service patrol.

(b) A person who appears to be incapacitated by alcohol shall be taken into protective custody by the police or the emergency service patrol and forthwith brought to an approved public treatment facility for emergency treatment.

COMMENT. A small minority of intoxicated persons are incapacitated in that they are unconscious or incoherent or similarly so impaired in judgment that they cannot make a rational decision with regard to their need for treatment. Section 12 (b) authorizes the police or emergency service patrol to take such individuals into protective custody and to a public treatment facility for emergency care. This is intended to assure that those most seriously in need of care will get it.

Protective custody under (b) is similar to the way in which the police provide emergency assistance to other ill people, such as those in accidents or those who have sudden heart attacks. It is a civil procedure, and no arrest record or record which implies a criminal charge is to be made. Since the police officer may sometimes have to decide whether a man who refuses help appears to be incapacitated by alcohol or because of some other reason, section 12 (g) protects the policeman should his conclusion, made in good faith, be incorrect.

Section 12 (d) provides that an incapacitated person can be held at a treatment facility without consent or further civil procedures for not longer than forty-eight hours. By the end of forty-eight hours, most persons who have been incapacitated by alcohol will be sufficiently detoxified to be able to make a rational decision about their need for further treatment. To provide for those very few individuals who may still be incapacitated (perhaps even unconscious) at the end of forty-eight hours, Section 13 provides for an emergency commitment procedure based on a written application and a certificate from a physician who is not employed by the division.

Section 15. *Records of Alcoholics and Intoxicated Persons.*

COMMENT. The treatment of privileged information in the courts and disclosure with the consent of the patient are matters of general state law. This section does, however, provide for the use of treatment records for research purposes so long as patients' names and other identifying information are not disclosed.

Section 16. *Emergency Service Patrol.* (a) The division and counties, cities and other municipalities may establish emergency service patrols. A pa-

trol consists of persons trained to give assistance in the streets and in other public places to persons who are intoxicated. Members of an emergency service
patrol shall be capable of providing first aid in emergency situations and shall
transport intoxicated persons to their homes and to and from public treatment
facilities.

COMMENT. The experience of using civilians and plainclothes policemen has
demonstrated the effectiveness of this method. This provision does not require
the establishment of an emergency service patrol, but authorizes such a patrol, should it meet the needs of a particular community. [Boston and Seattle,
among other cities, have used these civilian patrols with considerable success.
The police initially tended to resent them, but now appreciate the cooperation
and admit that the patrol drivers, usually recovered alcoholics who are very
street-wise, make their job easier.]

Sources

In a book entitled *Alcoholism and the Law*, Grad and his coauthors have dealt in
a general way with the legal aspects of alcohol use and of alcoholism. Another
source of general information is the NCALI bibliography, "Selected Publications
on Legal Aspects of Alcohol Use and Abuse." Chapters 13–17, part IV of Ewing
and Rouse's *Drinking: Alcohol in American Society* (1978), pp. 219–238, are well
documented and very relevant.

A good source for the history and legal documentation of cases that led up to
the passage of the Uniform Alcoholism and Intoxication Treatment Act is to be
found in the first NIAAA Special Report to Congress, *Alcohol and Health* (1971),
in Chapter 7 (pp. 85–97), "The Legal Status of Intoxication and Alcoholism." This
report also contains the Uniform Act itself in Appendix A, with a commentary. As
yet little has been published on the experiences attendant upon the implementation of the act. Kurtz and Regier, in their article "Uniform Alcoholism and Intoxication Treatment Act: The Compromising Process of Social Policy Formation"
(1975), speculated on the probable benefits and problems that would result.
Among the few articles to date dealing with actual experience is Daggett and
Rolde's "Decriminalization of Public Drunkenness: The Response of Suburban Police" (1977). With the use of the act there is hope at last that some of the dilemmas
in society's management of the "revolving-door" type of alcoholic will be resolved.
These dilemmas have been described vividly by many writers, among them Pittman and Gordon in *Revolving Door: A Study of the Chronic Police Case Inebriate*,
and Rubington in *Alcohol Problems and Social Control*, chapters 5 and 14.

Medicine in the Public Interest, Inc. (1979) has published an abridged version
of its two-volume study for NIAAA on the effects of various types of governmental
action on the prevalence of problems associated with the use of alcohol (Matlins,
1976). The Addiction Research Foundation of Toronto, Canada, has many publications; for example, a 1975 article by Popham and others, "The Prevention of
Alcoholism: Epidemiological Studies of the Effects of Government Measures," examines in a world context the effects of the taxation of beverage alcohol. Israelstam and Lambert have dealt with legislation concerning the use of motor vehicles
after drinking in *Alcohol, Drugs, and Traffic Safety*. Most of the research on the
effect of lowering the drinking age has dealt with drinking and driving, for exam-

ple, Whitehead, *Alcohol and Young Drivers: Impact and Implications of Lowering the Drinking Age*. Smart and Goodstadt have dealt more broadly with the implications in their article "Effects of Reducing the Legal Alcohol-Purchasing Age on Drinking and Drinking Problems." The NIAAA Second Special Report, *Alcohol and Health: New Knowledge* (1974) has many references on pp. 165–166. See also Sources for Chapter 11 of this book.

For further reading on the subject of Traffic Safety and Alcohol, the following are excellent: Chapter 6 (pp. 97–110), "Alcohol and Highway Traffic Safety," in the NIAAA Second Special Report to Congress, *Alcohol and Health: New Knowledge* (1974); Perrine, *Alcohol and Driving* (1974), especially the section by Driessen and Bryk, and that by Havard.

CHAPTER 21

The New Profession

Since the first Yale Plan Clinic in 1944, recovered alcoholics have been a part of most treatment teams, whether or not they belonged to a profession or had a college degree. Moreover, members of Alcoholics Anonymous were helping thousands of suffering alcoholics to recover through their twelfth step work both before and after alcoholism treatment centers were established. The understanding and empathy these workers gained from their own experience as alcoholics has long been recognized as a valuable contribution to the recovery process.

Human nature being what it is, the picture has not always been one of serene cooperation between degreed professionals and nondegreed workers. Events of the past few decades have occasioned difficulties for both, as rapid developments brought changes for which neither side was prepared. The story is well told in a book edited by George E. Staub and Leona M. Kent (1973), *The Para-Professional in the Treatment of Alcoholism: A New Profession*, which is strongly recommended to all working in the field of alcoholism regardless of background. The growing pains were probably no worse than those occurring in the early stages of any other important achievement, though they may have seemed worse to those going through them at the time.

The chagrin of mental health professionals at the fact that AA was succeeding where traditional psychiatric approaches had failed is understandable. The Krystal-Moore (1963) debate on "Who Is Qualified to Treat the Alcoholic?" found other psychiatrists agreeing with Moore that the recovered alcoholic, degreed or not, has an important role to play (Lemere, 1964). But the psychiatrist, psychologist, or psychiatric social worker with little specialized knowledge or training in alcoholism found it difficult to relate to the alcoholism community, or to abandon traditional methods. Their embarrassment and the threat of competition have both waned, with residual uneasiness making cooperation still an effort for some.

On the other hand, members of AA themselves have come to recognize that mere experience as a recovering alcoholic does not automatically qualify one to work professionally in the treatment field. Not only were the degreed professionals reluctant to accept them but they had problems stemming inherently from their lack of training and limited knowledge.

A New Profession

As a degreed professional who, for many decades, has been very close to AA, I was in an advantageous position to observe all this from both sides, as cochairman of the Washington State committee on norms for the certification of alcoholism workers and later as a member of the NIAAA-Littlejohn Board for the same purpose. Each group began as two mutually suspicious camps: the professional clinging to his degree even though he might not know an alcoholic from an alligator, and the recovered alcoholic smug in his private knowledge and unaware of his lack of other qualifications. And each time it was striking how quickly they dropped their defenses and reached a consensus that *both* were wrong: that both the degreed professional and the recovered alcoholic need training and knowledge that their respective prior experiences did not guarantee them.

A new profession is emerging, based on knowledge and competence rather than on degree. For this reason the term *para-professional* is inappropriate and should be dropped. (George Staub told me that he did not favor the term, and preferred what became his subtitle: *a new profession*.) Moreover, the old dichotomy between degreed professional and recovered alcoholic is disappearing as more and more degreed professionals identify themselves as being also recovered alcoholics. Recovery from alcoholism does not rule out professional training, and vice versa.

Education and Experience

This new profession requires specialized knowledge of alcoholism and training specific to treatment of the illness, regardless of traditional degrees or the experience of recovery. The time is past when mere on-the-job training or attendance at short summer institutes can be considered professional education. Increasingly tied to a degree, certificate programs now tend to require at least one full academic year. This may mean sacrifice for both worker and agency, but one does not become a surgeon without going to medical school. The good of the alcoholic demands competence.

For the professional who happens not to be a recovered alcoholic, other elements of education are necessary or appropriate. All need courses taught by alcohol specialists rather than standard curricula taught by professors, otherwise highly qualified, who have no real expertise in this field. Sporadic introduction of guest lecturers must be complemented by a competent teacher who provides continuity and integration. A mix of recovered alcoholics and nonalcoholic students provides lively exchange in and out of the classroom, wherein both learn from each other. Both have biases that reflect the attitudes of their environment (Kilty, 1975). It is essential to attend meetings of various AA and Al-Anon groups, to get a feel for the variety of styles and people involved (see Grutchfield, 1979). Need for experience in different types of alcoholism facilities is dictated by the fact that the illness is complex and open to many different approaches (see Keller, 1975a). Some trainers have their nonalcoholic students abstain from all alcohol for a month or two, just to heighten sensitivity and develop empathy for how a recovering alcoholic feels. They may give any or no reason for not drinking, except that they are not to say they are in any kind of training or experiment.

Certification

Starting at the grass roots level, a movement has spread through over half the states toward the development of professional standards for alcoholism workers, and means for certifying that one has met these standards. The reasons why this professional status should be given are many, and include:

a) Protection of the client. This is primary. Quality of service requires that we take the means to see that treatment is not bungled.

b) Protection of the worker. If one is to gain recognition and dignity as a professional, compete for third-party (for example, insurance) payment for treatment, be defended in malpractice suits, fit into a career ladder of promotion or have job stability, and be able to move with equal status into another organization, especially when moving to another state, there must be national credentialing with reciprocity between states.

c) Protection of the profession itself. To have confidentiality protected by privilege of communication, to have credibility when testifying in court as an expert witness, to build up a tradition of professional ethics, to gain respect from other professions and agencies, this new profession must have a legally acceptable identity.

The federal government rightly abstains from actual licensing or certification of workers, but has supported the concept of a national clearing-house or coordinating body to facilitate action by the states and to obviate needless duplication of initial effort. The NIAAA funded a twenty-five-person ad hoc board, selected with strong effort at representation from minority groups and nondegreed workers who were recovered alcoholics, as well as from various professions. Several meetings produced a draft which was circulated to two thousand agencies, and the resulting comments embodied in the final report (Littlejohn, 1974) proposed a set of national standards for alcoholism counselors. After many governmental delays and through the efforts of a coalition of national organizations, implementation began in 1980. A delicate balance between rights of individual states and the need for uniformity (both for reciprocity between states and to assure a minimum of high quality) has been a major problem.

Consideration has been given (through a "grandfather clause") of those already working in the field, whether degreed or not, who are truly competent. But it is not to the advantage of either the worker or the client to retain workers who are not suitable. Concern was primarily about counselors, but it should be evident that alcohol information, education, community organization, and other activities also require accurate knowledge and proven ability. Not all alcoholism workers are counselors.

Examination.   Measuring competency by actual examination, rather than by merely evaluating experience and degrees or training records, is an extremely difficult task. There is no perfect way to assess how well a person will function on the job, or even to measure the breadth and correctness of one's knowledge about alcoholism. More difficult or impossible to measure are the most important qualities: the warm empathy, compassionate understanding, communication skills, and generous dedication that create good relations between client and counselor. But a positive attitude suggests that we continue to strive to develop the best measures that human ingenuity can devise, rather than carp at their imperfection. We owe it to the alcoholic client as well as to the professional.

Length of Sobriety.   It is commonly agreed that a certain period of continuous sobriety is necessary before a recovered alcoholic should attempt to work in the field, for many reasons. One is the worker's own protection, lest the stress of dealing with troubled persons precipitate a relapse. It is also for the sake of the clients, who need a model of stable and comfortable sobriety as part of their own recovery. Again, the profession is harmed if a worker starts too soon, either creating a poor impression on members of other professions or risking the bad example of a relapse. Even when not permanent, residual toxicity in the brain may require from six months up to two or three years to disappear entirely. But a major reason often overlooked is that a newly recovering alcoholic is emotionally too close to his or her own case and tends to see all alcoholism in the light of subjective personal experience. It takes time, regardless of intelligence or quality of sobriety, to mature emotionally after recovery to the point where one can diagnose and treat with professional objectivity unspoiled by personal involvement.

There is also common agreement that quality of sobriety cannot be measured in months or years. Some are more ready after a year or two than others are after ten. But a consensus based on the accumulated experience of administrators and trainers throughout the country is confirmed by the AA Guidelines, namely three to five years of sobriety. The two years stipulated in the national norms represent a quasipolitical compromise rather than a majority view of the Littlejohn Board, but at least this sets a minimum. Our experience at Seattle University has led to another criterion: An applicant's inability to see the need for a certain length of sobriety is itself an indication that one is not ready.

The Alcoholism Worker

Staub and Kent (1973) have many excellent chapters discussing the various problems faced by the nondegreed professional in the alcoholism field, especially if also a recovered alcoholic. Some of these problems stem from the attitudes of the degreed professionals, some from personnel boards and other bureaucratic structures outside the alcoholism field, some from punitive attitudes lingering from the old prohibition-temperance movement (Rubington, 1973, pp. 26-27), and some from the disadvantages intrinsic to the very fact of being a recovered alcoholic. The result is often a dead-end job with no hope of advancement. On the part of degreed persons, the following faults have been cited: assuming inferiority and even deterioration in all recovering and recovered alcoholics, fostering a caste system with inequity in salaries and promotion, problems in communication and cooperation, and the unreasonable expectation that every member live up to the ideals of AA in the highest degree.

On the other side, no less a friend of AA than Marty Mann (1973, p. 7) points out that using mere length of sobriety in AA is not a valid criterion of suitability for counseling, as some who have passed the minimum years still retain a tunnel vision that makes them too inflexible to adjust in a cooperative venture. Some are defensive about their lack of a degree. Those whose very real contributions are recognized sometimes become proud and look with disdain on all degrees and professional approaches. Some of these use their new status to promote their own interests in or out of the field, rather than helping sick alcoholics. Some cannot cooperate well with degreed professionals or nonalcoholics because they cannot break out of their inner circle of shared experience.

"Only an alcoholic can help an alcoholic" is still being mouthed by some, in spite of the official disclaimer from AA mentioned earlier. There seems to be little good research on this point, but the truth is probably that a balance of recovered alcoholics and nonalcoholics is the best staffing policy, given the advantages and disadvantages of both. There is always the tendency for the recovered alcoholic to see all alcoholism through the eyes of one's own case history. This impedes correct diagnosis of other types of alcoholics and other kinds of alcoholisms. It blinds one to methods of treatment that might be more appropriate for a given client other than the particular modality through which the counselor achieved sobriety. There is also a tendency for the alcoholic counselor to focus too exclusively on the alcoholic, to the neglect of the spouse and family.

Cooperation but Not Affiliation

Forbidden by its traditions to affiliate with any other cause or group, Alcoholics Anonymous has always cooperated with the medical profession, labor-management programs, the armed services, chaplains, and various institutions. It also cooperates with professional training programs (Norris, 1971). Most gratifying is the trend reported in the periodical surveys of its membership wherein AA reports that an increasingly high percentage of newcomers are being referred to AA by professionals outside the fellowship. This suggests that things have come a long way since the early days of AA, founded soon after the repeal of Prohibition, when recovered alcoholics were looked upon with suspicion and scepticism.

Two Roles.   Some AA members employed in the field experience conflict between their professional role and their membership in AA. This can be due to jealousy or misguided attitudes on the part of other members, who, for example, accuse them of taking money for doing twelfth step work. Aside from the danger of imputing motives to another human being, there is the fact that if all doctors and nurses yielded to the accusation of profiteering off the misfortune of others there would be no hospitals or surgeries. Such misunderstandings led some AA's to reject the term *two hats* when referring to members who pursued the two roles of AA twelfth step work and paid employment in the field. Regardless of the term, the practicalities of delineating the two roles have been worked out with admirable common sense in the *AA Guidelines for Members Employed in the Field* (rev., 1977) and by the Al-Anon Family Groups (with some added insights) in a comparable publication, *Working As, For, or With Professionals* (1976). These two guides, issued by their respective headquarters offices in New York, are a "must" for all members working in the field or those who wish to discuss the matter.

Tradition 8 of AA says "Alcoholics Anonymous should remain forever nonprofessional" but it does not say that members cannot be professionals. Dr. Bob was the first to wear both hats, and his cofounder Bill W. has written extensively about cooperation with the professions and the great contributions that members can make both as professionals and as AA members. Symptomatic of the growing pains this may entail is the fact that for a brief time members employed in the field were excluded from holding office in AA, but this has been reversed in the current *Guidelines* (1977, p. 1, in two paragraphs that do not appear on p. 117 of an older version printed as Chapter X1 "For Those Who Wear Two Hats" in Staub and Kent, 1973). Significantly, this reversal is not an innovation but a return to the original tradition which was temporarily interrupted by that exclusion.

Note that the term *AA counselor* is not used because that would be contrary to the AA tradition of nonaffiliation. A person may happen to be a member of AA and also a counselor, but he or she does not speak for AA and was not hired with that as a credential. The counselor should not act as an AA sponsor for one's own professional client. It is usually felt that AA meetings within an institution should not be organized or run by AA members on staff, to avoid confusion of roles in the minds of both patients and staff. But local circumstances and the group conscience will have to determine this. When those who happen to be psychologists, clergymen, or other professionals attend meetings as members, they go for their own sobriety and spiritual growth—not to counsel others. As long as the two roles are kept distinct, there should be no problems. Some confuse the AA tradition on anonymity (see Chapter 15) and the ethics of confidentiality to be discussed later in this chapter. They are different, but with some overlap.

AA Conference-approved literature, much of it using the writings of Bill W. and all of it reflecting the group conscience of the entire fellowship, contains excellent discussions of these matters, including frank admission of fault on the part of AA members. In addition to the *Guidelines* cited above, see the last section of Sources for this Chapter, and especially pages 7 and 8 of *How AA Members Cooperate with Other Community Efforts to Help Alcoholics*, where members are urged in strong terms to maintain humility with regard to AA and respect for the genuine contributions of other approaches.

In an article on "Pride" in *AA Grapevine* (April 1976, p. 33) Bill W. is quoted as stressing a middle course between the "bog of guilt" on the one hand and pride on the other. A similar middle course appears in the AA leaflet *Understanding Anonymity*, which strikes a nice balance between public exposure and being so anonymous that one fails to help others or spread the message.

Cooperation and Court Programs.   The *AA Guidelines on Cooperating with Court, ASAP, and Similar Programs* (1977) is another publication containing suggestions born of long experience. For more than thirty years AA members have been cooperating, without violating their tradition against affiliation, with courts, correctional facilities, and more recently with safe driving programs such as the Alcohol Safety Action Project (ASAP). This may be in the form of Twelfth Step work, or as part of their duties while employed in the field, or simply by the secretary signing a form which people who have been arrested can bring to the judge as evidence that they have fulfilled their court-ordered attendance at AA meetings.

This latter practice, at first questioned by some members, is now recognized as a valuable means of carrying the AA message to many who would not otherwise have been exposed to it. Granted that eventually one must want sobriety for oneself, most members admit that they were originally forced into AA—if not by a court, then by employer, family, doctor, counselor, or one's own inner suffering. As the *Guidelines* (p. 4) say, "We are not concerned about who or what first sends the alcoholic to us, or how. *Our* responsibility is to show AA as such an attractive way of life that all newcomers who need it soon want it." Various suggestions are made as to how the secretary *after* the meeting may sign a slip or issue an envelope that the individual mails to the court with his own name and address. There is obviously no violation of anonymity here, both because it is not at the level of public media but most importantly because it is the individual offender himself who attests to the court his attendance at a meeting. The secretary merely complies with his request. There is no affiliation of the group with the court (p. 5). The AA General Service Office in New York has also published a four-page leaflet "Information on Alcoholics Anonymous for Anyone Sent to AA, and for Administrators of Court Programs and Other Referring Agencies" (1977) which contains many of these guidelines.

Speaking at Non-AA Meetings is the title of an AA Conference-approved pamphlet for members going out to schools, other institutions, service groups, and the general public. It contains excellent and detailed suggestions as to topics, approach, and available literature. One caution is against giving a "drunkalog" or personal-history talk that a member might give at an AA meeting (p. 6). The audience often finds it hard to identify with this, and may even feel aversion rather than attraction. However, the pamphlet goes on to say that members may find it helpful to relate incidents from their own history to illustrate a point.

AA and Pills. Alcoholics Anonymous members rightly take a strong stand against substituting one addictive drug for another. But overenthusiasm for this realization has trapped some AA members into incautious statements about pills that are not substitute addictions and may be medically necessary for the recovering alcoholic. Thus one sometimes hears horror stories about advice to a heart patient not to take digitalis, a diabetic not to take oral insulin, or an epileptic not to take dilantin. This is not only practicing medicine without a license, it can amount to murder. The same applies to Antabuse, which is not a substitute addiction and may be life-saving for some alcoholics. AA has never approved this kind of advice.

Staff Burn-out Syndrome

The health of the patients will hardly rise above that of the staff. Morale, open communication, and general physical and mental health of all staff members is important to any treatment process. A major problem that workers, and especially administrators, are beginning to face is the high burn-out rate among alcoholism workers. They enter the field with great idealism and high expectations, work for a while with enthusiastic dedication, then leave with disillusionment or broken health.

Many factors may affect staff morale: low percentage of success, negative and pessimistic attitudes toward alcoholics, denial and poor motivation on the part of patients, fragmentation and lack of continuity in treatment services, conflicting objectives of boards and staff (Gottheil, 1975). Other factors might be the slowness of the credentialing process, the impossibility of keeping up with the ever spreading delta of research data, and the uncertainty of federal or state funding.

Other reasons may be more specific to the high turnover rate: unrealistic ideals, emotional immaturity, lack of solid sobriety, frustration at the inequity of salary and career opportunities for nondegreed professionals, bureaucratic structures and endless paperwork which hamper efficient contact with actual clients, boards and administrators who lack understanding, too subjective an involvement with clients which leads to dejection when one of them relapses, and the stress that is inevitable in human services.

Staff burn-out takes many forms. It may manifest itself in psychosomatic illness and various behavioral symptoms. In the context of all the factors enumerated above, the major cause seems to be overcommitment or too-intense dedication. Thinking only of one's work to the neglect of family or other outside interests, spending all one's time and conversation with fellow staff members and patients, may seem very noble and dedicated. But it is a trap that can lead to disaster. Frustration, feelings of not being appreciated, resentment against supervisors, retreat into routine and cheerless performance of duty, use of tranquilizers or sleeping pills, sexual involvement with staff or clients, and other serious consequences can ruin the career of a generous and dedicated worker.

Prevention.   The most obvious preventive measure is that staff take adequate vacations. The administrator should insist that the workers get out of the city or state, or at least forbid them to have any contact with the facility or clients. We agree with the warning of Freudenberger (1975, p. 17) against sending them to marathon encounters, and with his other suggested means of prevention: careful screening, rotation of assignments, sending them away for workshops, physical exercise, limiting client loads, encouraging a hobby or recreation, opportunity to share problems with supervisor or trusted staff member. But there is no substitute for full vacation away from the facility. Probably the second most important item is to accept one's limitations, to realize that no one person can do it all and no one approach is fitting for every client. Dedication does not mean taking full responsibility for the client, nor making oneself available twenty-four hours a day (Valle, 1979a, 1979b).

Professional Ethics

The best corrective for an image of "sick people helping sick people" is a profession with integrity and respect. Knowledge and skill may be acquired by training and experience, but how does a profession gain respect and develop integrity? As a new profession, alcoholism workers have a responsibility to both themselves and their clients to develop a tradition. If one wishes the dignity of being called a professional, he or she must act like one. What are some of the characteristics of a profession?

Service.   Contrary to the myth that professionals are only interested in money rather than in helping sick alcoholics, the very difference between a business and a profession is that a business is frankly aimed at making money whereas a profession is primarily aimed at service. One does not work for a boss, or for dollars, but in a true sense for the client or patient. This implies that in addition to the ability to work under supervision, one must take primary responsibility for one's own functioning.

Education.   A professional is an educated person. A technician can fix your electric toaster, but an electrical engineer knows the principles behind its working. More important, truly educated people know more than just their own field; they have a broad, humanistic knowledge of the history and values related to their subject, which is the origin of the Ph.D. —we speak of a Doctor of *Philosophy* in Chemistry or Psychology or whatever, implying that one knows more than just chemistry or psychology. Alcohol workers must broaden their educational horizons beyond mere technical training. Certainly included is a knowledge of the ethics of counseling. As in many professions, the national norms require continuing education as a condition for recertification.

Self-regulation.   A major characteristic of a profession is that it is supposed to be self-regulating, rather than policed from the outside. Most professions have an ethics committee or conduct review board. Members of the profession take responsibility for the conduct of other members. This is not "tattling" but professional integrity. This includes a confrontation to get a colleague into treatment for alcoholism or other drug misuse, or honesty in recommendations for employment rather than covering up for an incompetent person who may harm clients. This also implies responsibility of a prospective employer to check with previous employers or trainers: it is astounding to have former employees or trainees hired with no such check.

Code of Ethics

It is a mark of a profession to develop its own code of ethics, and many alcoholism counselor associations have done so. The code of ethics developed in the Alcohol Studies Program at Seattle University served as the first draft for several of these groups, and they are all similar. We reproduce here the code adopted by the National Association of Alcoholism Counselors (NAAC).

NAAC Code of Ethics

I do affirm
   That my primary goal is recovery for the client and his family; that I have a total commitment to provide the highest quality care for those who seek my professional services.
   That I shall evidence a genuine interest in all clients and do hereby dedicate myself to the best interest of the client and to helping him to help himself.
   That I shall maintain at all times an objective, nonpossessive, professional relationship with all clients.
   That I shall be willing to recognize when it is in the best interest of the client to release him or refer him to another program or individual.
   That I shall adhere to the rule of confidentiality of all records, material, and knowledge concerning the client.
   That I shall not in any way discriminate between clients or fellow professionals [on the basis of race, color, creed, age, sex, or sexual orientation].

That I shall respect the rights and views of other counselors and professionals.

That I shall maintain respect for institutional policies and management functions within agencies and institutions, but will take the initiative toward improving such policies when it will better serve the interest of the client.

That I have a commitment to assess my own personal strengths, limitations, biases, and effectiveness on a continuing basis; that I shall continuously strive for self-improvement; that I have a personal responsibility for professional growth through further education and training.

That I have an individual responsibility for my own conduct in all areas, including the use of alcohol and all mood altering drugs.

These things I pledge to God, to my client, and to my fellow man.

Comment. Wording may vary in other codes, and discussion could be lengthy. All codes demand acceptance of personal limitations by not attempting services that are beyond one's training or competence. Professional responsibility requires that one always distinguish clearly between any public statements or actions as an individual and as a representative of one's organization. Private and professional roles must be kept cleanly separate, which means not socializing with clients or accepting personal gifts from them while in therapy.

"Helping the client to help himself" discourages fostering, perhaps unconsciously, a client's dependence, which may be flattering to the counselor but stunts the growth of the client. For this reason counselors must be trained in how to handle separation anxiety and terminate the relationship gracefully. All codes forbid exploitation of the client for the counselor's own financial, sexual, or other personal needs. A romantic inclination on the part of either client or therapist really reflects a cry for help from an emotionally confused person, which the inexperienced counselor can mistake for love. Consultation, and usually a switch to another counselor, are necessary to prevent needless hurt for both parties and possible court action.

Confidentiality. The ethics of professional secrecy can bring up a host of complicated issues. The basic principle is that private information divulged by clients in the course of treatment may never be used or repeated in any way that can be identified with the client. This clause allows for generalized statements or research without risking harm to any individual's reputation. One may not make available any information, even the fact that the patient is in an alcoholism facility, without first obtaining their written consent (while rational and sober), unless there is clear and imminent danger of serious harm to them or a third party by not doing so. Professional consultation in a difficult case is allowed, but in that case the consultant is equally bound to secrecy. One may not share private information with a colleague or one's spouse, no matter how trusted.

The new profession has a serious task here. Members of the medical profession occasionally violate their tradition of confidentiality through human weakness, but at least they have a tradition to violate; the alcoholism profession sorely needs to build a tradition to counteract the current laxity which prompted special federal regulations. What you learn as a result of a colleague's carelessness in this regard must still be treated by yourself as confidential. A secretary must be instructed about secrecy of records and correspondence. Volunteers have restricted access to files, but must be informed that even seeing which people come in is private information. Members of AA must understand the differences between their tradition of anonymity and the ethics of confidentiality, and explain this to their non-AA supervisor when appropriate. In both cases the rights of the alcoholic must be protected, as well as the integrity of the entire alcoholism field.

"Privileged communication" refers to the right that evidence be withheld in court. The privilege is that of the client, not of the professional. Nevertheless the law is always tied to a particular profession, and so far there is almost no legislation for alcoholism workers comparable to that for physicians, attorneys, and the clergy. Hence a court may order disclosure of their confidential information or files. There is likewise no provision covering liability for disclosure by other members of a group therapy session, but the group leader is well advised to spell out an explicit obligation of secrecy to all.

The Department of Health, Education and Welfare has issued detailed regulations covering the handling of records by all individuals and programs that receive any form of federal support, direct or indirect, relating to alcohol or drug abuse (see Sources). They are more strict than the usual rules of confidentiality. For instance, the mere fact that a person is or is not a patient in a particular hospital is generally a matter of public knowledge, but may not be revealed if it is an alcohol or drug facility. The usual signed consent for disclosure of information to other agencies or professionals will not suffice; it must specify to whom the disclosure will be made and other details. And the redisclosure of this authorized information to another agency without explicit consent is forbidden. The federal rules allow the courts to authorize disclosure of confidential information for good cause, but this only removes the prohibition and does not in itself require disclosure.

Epilogue

We have said little about advances in alcohol education in the medical and other professions, where there has been much progress since the National Council on Alcoholism Invitational Conference in 1970 (Seixas, 1971). Inclusion of a section on alcoholism in the examination for licensing as a physician serves notice to medical schools that this must be part of the regular curriculum. Attorneys, judges, and correctional workers are becoming aware of alcoholism training needs, as are social workers, psychologists, and others in the helping professions. Nurses have generally been ahead of most others.

All this could mean better understanding and greater cooperation by all concerned. Mutual respect and open-mindedness seem to be replacing the older defensive attitudes among the professions. In spite of human imperfection, the net result will be more help for the object of all this buzz of activity, the alcoholic.

Sources

There is an National Clearinghouse for Alcohol Information (NCALI) bibliography, *Grouped Interest Guide*, No 7-6, Summer 1977 entitled "Education and Training about Alcohol." Especially useful are the books by Staub and Kent (1973) and by S. Valle, *Alcoholism Counseling: Issues for an Emerging Profession* (1979b).

Other material includes

BORRELIZ, M. and P.H. DELEON, "Malpractice: Professional Liability and the Law," *Professional Psychology*, 1978, 9(3):467–477.

CORRIGAN, EILEEN M. and SANDRA C. ANDERSON, "Training for Treatment of Alcoholism in Women," *Social Casework*, 1978, 59:42–50.

CURLEE, JOAN, "How a Therapist Can Use Alcoholics Anonymous," *Annals of the New York Academy of Sciences*, 1974, 233:137–143.

FINKELSTEIN, ANN B. and JOHN J. BOSLEY, *Alcoholism Training in the United States: A Summary Report of Thirty-nine Programs*. National Center for Alcohol Education booklet.

FRUEDENBERGER, HERBERT J., *The Staff Burn-Out Syndrome*. Drug Abuse Council, Washington, D.C., pamphlet.

GOTTHEIL, EDWARD, "Poor Morale in Treatment Personnel," *Alcohol Health and Research World*, Spring 1975, 20–25.

GRUTCHFIELD, LEE, "What AA Meetings Taught a Non-AA Counselor," *Alcohol Health and Research World*, Spring 1979, 3(3):15–17. Reprinted from *AA Grapevine*, December 1977.

KELLER, MARK, "Multidisciplinary Perspectives on Alcoholism and the Need for Integration: An Historical and Prospective Note," *Journal of Studies on Alcohol*, 1975, 36:133–147.

KILTY, KEITH M., "Attitudes Toward Alcohol and Alcoholism Among Professionals and Nonprofessionals," *Journal of Studies on Alcohol*, 1975, 36:327–347.

KRIMMEL, HERMAN, *Alcoholism: Challenge for Social Work Education*.

KRYSTAL, H. and R.A. MOORE, "Who is Qualified to Treat the Alcoholic? A Discussion," *Quarterly Journal of Studies on Alcohol*, 1963, 42:705–720.

LEMERE, FREDERICK, "Who is Qualified to Treat the Alcoholic? Comment on the Krystal-Moore Discussion," *Quarterly Journal of Studies on Alcohol*, 1964, 25:558–560.

LITTLEJOHN ASSOCIATES, *Proposed National Standard for Alcoholism Counselors: Final Report.*

MANN, MARTY, "Attitude: Key to Successful Treatment,"in Staub, George and Leona Kent (eds.), *The Para-Professional in the Treatment of Alcoholism: A New Profession*, pp. 3–8.

NORRIS, JOHN, "What AA Can Offer Professional Schools and What It Cannot," *Annals of the New York Academy of Sciences*, 1971, 178:61–65.

PACE, NICHOLAS, *How the Professionals and AA Should Cooperate with Each Other.* NCA, paper.

SEIXAS, FRANK A. (ed.), "Professional Training in Alcoholism," *Annals of the New York Academy of Sciences*, 1971, vol. 178 (entire).

STAUB, GEORGE and LEONA KENT (eds.), *The Para-Professional in the Treatment of Alcoholism: A New Profession.*

VALLE, STEPHEN K., "Burnout: Occupational Hazard for Counselors," *Alcohol Health and Research World*, Spring, 1979, 3(3):10–14.

WEINBERG, JON R., *Quick Test of Professionals' Understanding of Alcoholism.* Hazelden pamphlet.

For Physicians

The National Institute on Alcohol Abuse and Alcoholism in 1978 produced a very comprehensive set of items called *Medical Education in Drug and Alcohol Abuse: A Catalog of Sources.* The staff of the National Clearinghouse for Alcohol Information and Kristi Brown give ample references in "Alcoholism Education for Physicians and Medical Students: An Overview," *Alcohol Health and Research World*, Spring 1979, 3(3):2–9. See also Jon R. Weinberg and R. Morse, "Understanding Alcoholism: A Test for Use in Medical Education," *Journal of Medical Education*, 1975, 50:978–979.

Ethics, Confidentiality

BLUME, SHEILA B., *Confidentiality of Medical Records in Alcohol-Related Problems.* NCA pamphlet.

GAZDA, GEORGE M., *Group Counseling: A Developmental Approach.* 2nd ed., 1978. Chapter 10, "Guidelines for Ethical Practice in Group Counseling and Related Group Work" reports survey of twenty professional associations who shared codes of ethics; Chapter 12 is "Controversial Issues in Small Group Work—With an Emphasis on Encounter Groups."

GILL, JAMES J., FRANCIS J. BRACELAND et al., "Ethics and Psychiatry," *Psychiatric Annals*, February 1979, 9(2):entire issue.

HARE-MUSTIN, RACHEL T. et al., "Rights of Clients, Responsibilities of Therapists," *American Psychologist*, 1979, 34:3–16. Ample references.

MOORE, BETTYE ANN et al., *The Confidentiality of Alcohol and Drug Abuse Patient Records: A Self-Paced Programmed Instructional Course.*

U.S. DEPARTMENT OF HEALTH, EDUCATION AND WELFARE, "Confidentiality of Alcohol and Drug Abuse Records," *Federal Register*, July 1, 1975, 40(127), Part IV:27802-27821. Also Title 42 of Code of Federal Regulations (42CFR) Part 2, 16 pp.

Alcoholics Anonymous

AA Grapevine, October 1963 and September 1974 issues.
AA Guidelines for Members Employed in the Field.
Alcoholics Anonymous and the Medical Profession.
Alcoholics Anonymous Comes of Age.
How AA Members Cooperate with Other Community Efforts to Help Alcoholics.
If You Are a Professional, AA Wants to Work with You.
Let's Be Friendly with Our Friends.
Three Talks to Medical Societies, by Bill W.

Appendix: Sources for Literature on Alcoholism

Much valuable material is available in pamphlet form rather than in hardback books. Merely for information, we list the addresses where material can be obtained. The asterisk indicates a source of some free materials.

Addiction Research Foundation
33 Russell Street
Toronto, Ontario, Canada M5S 2S1

Al-Anon Family Group Headquarters
(Al-Anon and Alateen)
Box 182, Madison Square Station
New York, NY 10159

Alcohol and Drug Problems Association of
   North America (ADPA)
1101 15th Street, N.W., Suite 204
Washington, DC 20005

Alcoholics Anonymous World Services, Inc.
Box 459 Grand Central Station
New York, NY 10163

Association of Halfway House Alcoholism
   Programs of North America, Inc.
   (AHHAP)
786 East 7th Street
St. Paul, MN 55106

The Association of Labor-Management Administrators and Consultants on Alcoholism (ALMACA)
1800 North Kent Street
Arlington, VA 22209

CompCare Publications
Box 27777
Minneapolis, MN 55427

Cottage Program International
P.O. Box 25152
Salt Lake City, UT 84125

DO IT NOW Foundation
Institute for Chemical Survival
P.O. Box 5115
Phoenix, AZ 85010

Education Service—DISCUS
Distilled Spirits Council of the United
States
1300 Pennsylvania Building
Washington, DC 20004

Harmony Program
Drug Education Center
685 A Street
Hayward, CA 94541

Hazelden Foundation
Box 176
Center City, MN 55012

Johnson Institute
10700 Olson Memorial Highway
Minneapolis, MN 55411

*Kemper Insurance Companies
Communications and Public Affairs
Dept., D-1
Long Grove, IL 60049

Mitchell Press Limited
P.O. Box 6000
Vancouver, British Columbia,
Canada V6B 4B9

National Center for Alcohol Education
(NCAE)
1601 North Kent Street
Arlington, VA 22209

*National Clearinghouse for Alcohol Infor-
mation (NCALI)
Box 2345
Rockville, MD 20852

National Clergy Council on Alcoholism
3112 Seventh St., N.E.
Washington, DC 20017

National Council on Alcoholism (NCA)
Publications Division
733 Third Avenue
New York, New York 10017

National Institute on Alcohol Abuse and Al-
coholism (NIAAA)
P.O. Box 2045
Rockville, MD 20852

National Institute on Drug Abuse (NIDA)
11400 Rockville Pike
Rockville, MD 20852

*Operation Threshold
U.S. Jaycees
Box 7
Tulsa, OK 74102

Public Affairs Committee, Inc.
381 Park Avenue South
New York, NY 10016

Recovered Alcoholic Clergy Association
(RACA)
P.O. Box 95
Albion, IL 62806

Rutgers Center of Alcohol Studies
Publications Division
P.O. Box 969
Piscataway, NJ 08854

Christopher D. Smithers Foundation
P.O. Box 67
Oyster Bay Road
Mill Neck, New York 11765

Utah Alcoholism Foundation
2880 South Main Street, Suite 210
Salt Lake City, UT 84115

Winston Products for Education
P.O. Box 12219
San Diego, CA 92112

Wisconsin Clearinghouse
1954 East Washington Ave.
Madison, WI 53704

Women For Sobriety, Inc.
P.O. Box 618
Quakertown, PA 18951

General Bibliography

The *Quarterly Journal of Studies on Alcohol* is abbreviated as QJSA; in 1975 it became a monthly, the *Journal of Studies on Alcohol* (JSA). See the Appendix for NCA, NCALI, etc.

ABLES, BILLIE S., "A Note on the Treatment of Adolescents Who Use Drugs," *Journal of Psychedelic Drugs*, 1977, 9:127–131.

ABLON, JOAN, "Family Structure and Behavior in Alcoholism: A Review of the Literature," in Kissin, B. and H. Begleiter (eds.), *The Biology of Alcoholism*. Plenum, New York, 1976, vol. 4, pp.205–242.

ABLON, JOAN, "Perspectives on Al-Anon Family Groups," in Estes, Nada J. and M. Edith Heinemann (eds.), *Alcoholism: Development, Consequences, and Interventions*. Mosby, St. Louis, 1977, pp. 274–282.

ACKERMAN, ROBERT J., *Children of Alcoholics: A Guidebook for Educators, Therapists, and Parents*. Learning Publications, Holmes Beach, Florida, 1978.

ADAMS, K.M. et al., *Polydrug Abuse: The Results of a National Collaborative Study*. Academic Press, San Francisco, 1978.

ADAMS, RUTH and FRANK MURRAY, *Megavitamin Therapy*. Larchmont Books, New York, 1973.

AGERIOU, M., "The Jellinek Estimation Formula Revisited," QJSA, 1974, 35: 1053–1057.

AL-ANON, *Al-Anon Faces Alcoholism*. Al-Anon Family Group Headquarters, Inc., New York, rev. ed., 1975.

AL-ANON, *Alateen: Hope for the Children of Alcoholics*. Al-Anon Family Group Headquarters, New York, 1973.

AL-ANON, *Dilemma of the Alcoholic Marriage*. Al-Anon Family Group Headquarters, New York, 4th ed., 1977.

AL-ANON, *Living with an Alcoholic*. Al-Anon Family Group Headquarters, New York, rev. ed., 1978.

AL-ANON, *One Day at a Time in Al-Anon*. Al-Anon Family Group Headquarters, New York, rev. ed., 1978.

AL-ANON, *Twelve Steps and Twelve Traditions for Al-Anon*. Al-Anon Family Group Headquarters, New York, n.d.

AL-ANON, *Twelve Steps and Twelve Traditions for Alateen*. Al-Anon Family Group Headquarters, New York, n.d.

AL-ANON, *Working As, For, or With Professionals.* Al-Anon Family Group Headquarters, New York, 1976. [Pamphlet]

Alcohol and Nutrition. NIAAA Research Monograph No. 2. U.S. Government Printing Office, Washington, D.C., 1979.

Alcohol Health and Research World, special issue on women and alcohol, Fall 1978, 3(1).

Alcoholics Anonymous, *Alcoholics Anonymous Come of Age: A Brief History of AA.* Alcoholics Anonymous World Services, New York, 1957.

Alcoholics Anonymous, *AA Guidelines for Members Employed in the Alcoholism Field.* Alcoholics Anonymous World Services, New York, rev. ed., 1977.

Alcoholics Anonymous, *AA Guidelines on Cooperating with Court, ASAP, and Similar Programs.* Alcoholics Anonymous World Services, New York, 1977.

Alcoholics Anonymous, *Alcoholics Anonymous: The Story of How Many Thousands of Men and Women Have Recovered from Alcoholism.* Alcoholics Anonymous World Services, New York, 3rd ed., 1976.

Alcoholics Anonymous, *AA Way of Life (As Bill Sees It).* Alcoholics Anonymous World Services, New York, 1967.

Alcoholics Anonymous, *Came to Believe.* Alcoholics Anonymous World Services, New York, 1973.

Alcoholics Anonymous, *How AA Members Cooperate with Other Community Efforts to Help Alcoholics.* Alcoholics Anonymous World Services, New York n.d. [Pamphlet]

Alcoholics Anonymous, *Living Sober.* Alcoholics Anonymous World Services, New York, 1975.

Alcoholics Anonymous, *Speaking at Non-AA Meetings.* Alcoholics Anonymous World Services, New York, 1974. [Pamphlet]

Alcoholics Anonymous, *Twelve Steps and Twelve Traditions.* Alcoholics Anonymous World Services, New York, 1953.

Alcoholics Anonymous, *Understanding Anonymity.* Alcoholics Anonymous World Services, New York, n.d. [Pamphlet]

[*AA Grapevine*] "Search for Spiritual Experience," *AA Grapevine,* April 1978, pp. 2–16.

ALEXANDER, JACK, "Alcoholics Anonymous: Freed Slaves of Drink, Now They Free Others," *Saturday Evening Post,* March 1, 1941, 213:9–11+.

ALIBRANDI, TOM, *The Young Alcoholics.* CompCare Corp., Minneapolis, 1977.

ALLEY, SAM and JUDITH BLANTON (eds.), *Paraprofessionals in Mental Health: An Annotated Bibliography 1966 to 1977.* Section on Alcohol. Social Action Research Center, Berkeley, California, 1978, pp. 224–230.

American Psychiatric Association, "Megavitamin and Orthomolecular Therapy in Psychiatry," *Nutrition Review,* 1974, 32(suppl.): 44–47.

An Assessment of the Needs of and Resources for Children of Alcoholic Parents. Final Report, 1979, PB-241-119A/S. National Technical Information Service, Springfield, VA 22161.

ANDERSON, DANIEL J., *A History of Our Confused Attitudes Towad Beverage Alcohol.* Hazelden Books, Center City, MN, 1967.

ANDERSON, DANIEL J., *The Joys and Sorrows of Sobriety*. Hazelden Books, Center City, MN, 1977.

ANDERSON, DANIEL J., MARY LEE KAMMEIER and HELEN HOLMES, *Applied Research: Impact on Decision Making*. Hazelden Books, Center City, MN, 1978.

Anonymous, "Where Good Drinkers Go," *Collier's*, September 1939, 104:14–15.

ARCHIBALD, H. DAVID, *Toward Saturation—In Search of Control*. Addiction Research Foundation, Toronto, 1975. [Reprint from *Addictions*, Fall 1975]

ARMOR, DAVID J., *Alcoholism and Treatment*. Rand Corporation, Santa Monica, CA, 1976.

ASBURY, HERBERT, *The Great Illusion: An Informal History of Prohibition*. Doubleday, New York, 1950.

ASHLEY, MARY JANE et al., "Skid Row Alcoholism: A Distinct Socio-Medical Entity," *Archives of Internal Medicine*, 1976, 136:272–278.

ASHLEY, MARY JANE et al., " 'Mixed' (Drug Abusing) and 'Pure' Alcoholics: A Socio-Medical Comparison," *British Journal of Addiction*, 1978, 73:19–34.

Association of Halfway House Alcoholism Programs, *Standards for Halfway House Alcoholism Programs*. Association of Halfway House Alcoholism Programs, St. Paul, MN, 1974.

BACON, SELDEN D., "The Process of Addiction to Alcohol: Social Aspects," QJSA, 1973, 34:1–27.

BACON, SELDEN D., "Concepts," in Filstead, William, Jean Rossi and Mark Keller (eds.), *Alcohol and Alcohol Problems: New Thinking and New Directions*. Ballinger Publishing Company, Cambridge, MA, 1976, pp. 57–134.

BACON, SELDEN D., "On the Prevention of Alcohol Problems and Alcoholism," JSA, 1978, 39:1125–1147.

BADRI, M.B., *Islam and Alcoholism*. National Council on Alcoholism, New York, 1978.

BAEKELAND, FREDERICK, LAWRENCE LUNDWALL and BENJAMIN KISSIN, "Methods for the Treatment of Chronic Alcoholism: A Critical Appraisal," in Gibbins, R.J. and others (eds.), *Research Advances in Alcohol and Drug Problems*. Wiley, New York, 1975, vol. 2, pp. 247–327.

BAHR, H.M., *Skid Row: An Introduction to Disaffiliation*. Oxford University Press, New York, 1973.

BAILEY, MARGARET B., "Al-Anon Family Groups as an Aid to Wives of Alcoholics," *Social Work*, 1965, 10:68–74.

BAILEY, MARGARET B., P. HABERMAN and H. ALKSNE, "Outcomes of Alcoholic Marriages: Endurance, Termination or Recovery," QJSA, 1962, 23:610–623. [NCA reprint]

BAKER, JOAN K., "Alcoholism and the American Indian," in Estes, Nada J. and Edith Heinemann (eds.), *Alcoholism: Development, Consequences, and Interventions*. Mosby, St. Louis, 1977, pp. 194–203.

BAKER, STEWART L., THEODORE LOREI and HARRY A. McKNIGHT, *Veterans Administration's Comparison Study: Alcoholism and Drug Abuse—Combined and Conventional Treatment Settings*. National Alcoholism Forum, San Diego, 1977.

BARD, BERNARD, "The Shameful Truth and Consequences of School Drug Programs," *Parents' Magazine*, 1974, 49(9):40–52.

BARKER, JOHN MARSHALL, *The Saloon Problem and Social Reform*. Arno Press, New York, 1970.

BARNES, GRACE M., "The Development of Adolescent Drinking Behavior: An Evaluative Review of the Impact of the Socialization Process within the Family," *Adolescence*, 1977, 12:571–591.

BEAN, MARGARET, "Alcoholics Anonymous: Principles and Methods," *Psychiatric Annals*, 1975, vol. 5, nos. 2 and 3.

BEARD, J.D. and D.H. KNOTT, "Fluid and Electrolyte Balance During Acute Withdrawal in Chronic Alcoholic Patients," *Journal of the American Medical Association*, 1969, 204:133–137.

BEAUCHAMP, DAN E., *Beyond Alcoholism: Alcohol and Public Health Policy*. Temple University Press, Philadelphia, 1980.

BECKER, ARTHUR H., *Guilt: Curse or Blessing?* Augsburg, Minneapolis, 1977.

BECKER, CHARLES E., R.L. ROE and R.A. SCOTT, *Alcohol as a Drug: A Curriculum on Pharmacology, Neurology and Toxicology*. William and Wilkins, Baltimore, 1974.

BECKMAN, L.J., "Women Alcoholics: A Review of Social and Psychological Studies," QJSA, 1975, 36:797–824.

BEGLEITER, HENRI (ed.) *Biological Effects of Alcohol*. Plenum, New York, 1980.

BELL, ROBERT G., *Escape from Addiction*. McGraw-Hill, New York, 1970.

BELLWOOD, LESTER R., "Grief Work in Alcoholism Treatment," *Alcohol Health and Research World*, Spring 1975, pp. 8–11.

BENNETT, A.E., *Alcoholism and the Brain*. Stratton Intercontinental Medical Book Corp., New York, 1977.

BENNION, LYNN J. and TING-KAI LI, "Alcohol Metabolism in American Indians and Whites: Lack of Racial Differences in Metabolic Rate and Liver Alcohol Dehydrogenase," *New England Journal of Medicine*, 1976, 294:9–13.

BERNE, ERIC, *Transactional Analysis in Psychotherapy*. Grove Press, New York, 1961.

BERNE ERIC, *Games People Play*. Grove Press, New York, 1967.

BERRY, RALPH E. JR., "Estimating the Economic Costs of Alcohol Abuse," *New England Journal of Medicine*, 1976, 295:620–621.

BERRY, RALPH E. and JAMES P. BOLAND, *The Economic Cost of Alcohol Abuse*. The Free Press, New York, 1977.

BICKERTON, YVONNE J. and ROBERTA V. SANDERS, "Ethnic Preferences in Alcoholism Treatment: The Case of Hawaii," *Annals of the New York Academy of Sciences*, 1976, 273:653–658.

BILLINGS, JOHN S. et al., *The Liquor Problem*. Houghton-Mifflin, Boston, 1903.

BIRNBAUM, I.M. and E.S. PARKER (eds.), *Alcohol and Human Memory*. Lawrence Erlbaum Associates, Hillsdale, NJ, 1977.

BISSELL, LECLAIR and ROBERT W. JONES, "The Alcoholic Physician: A Survey," *American Journal of Psychiatry*, 1976, 133:1142–1146.

BISSONETTE, RAYMOND, "Bartender as a Mental Health Service Gatekeeper: A Role Analysis," *Community Mental Health Journal*, 1977, 13:92–99.

BLACK, CLAUDIA, "Innocent Bystanders at Risk: The Children of Alcoholics," *Alcoholism: The National Magazine*, January/February, 1981, 1(3):22–26.

BLANE, HOWARD T., *The Personality of the Alcoholic*. Harper, New York, 1968.

BLANE, HOWARD T., "Education and Prevention of Alcoholism," in Kissin, B. and H. Begleiter (eds.), *The Biology of Alcoholism*, Plenum Press, New York, 1975, vol. 4, pp. 519–578.

BLANE, HOWARD T. and LINDA E. HEWITT, *Alcohol and Youth: An Analysis of the Literature, 1960–1975*. National Institute on Alcohol Abuse and Alcoholism, Rockville, MD., 1977. [U.S. Department of Commerce, National Technical Information Service, PB-268 698]

BLOCK, MARVIN A., "Don't Place Alcohol on a Pedestal," *Journal of the American Medical Association*, 1976, 253:2103.

BLUM, E.M. and R.H. BLUM, *Alcoholism: Modern Psychological Approaches to Treatment*. Jossey-Bass, San Francisco, rev. ed., 1974.

BLUMBERG, LEONARD, "The Ideology of a Therapeutic Social Movement: Alcoholics Anonymous," JSA, 1977, 38:2122–2143.

BLUMBERG, LEONARD U., THOMAS E. SHIPLEY, and STEPHEN F. BARSKY, *Liquor and Poverty: Skid Row as a Human Condition*. Rutgers Center of Alcohol Studies, New Brunswick, NJ, 1978. [Monograph 13]

BLUME, SHEILA B., *Confidentiality of Medical Records in Alcohol-Related Problems*. National Council on Alcoholism, New York, n.d. [Pamphlet]

BLUME, SHEILA B., "Iatrogenic Alcoholism," QJSA, 1973, 34:1348–1352.

BOOZ ALLEN and HAMILTON, Inc., *Final Report on the Needs of and Resources for Children of Alcoholic Parents*. National Institute on Alcohol Abuse and Alcoholism, Rockville, MD. 1974a.

BOOZ-ALLEN and HAMILTON, Inc., *Model Benefit Costs in Alcohol Treatment Programs*. 2 vols., Booz-Allen and Hamilton, Washington, DC, 1974b.

"Booze and the Writer," *Writer's Digest*, , 1978, 58:25–33.

BORKENSTEIN, R.F., R.F. CROWTHER, R.P. SHUMATE, W.B. ZILL, and R. ZYLAM, *The Role of the Drinking Driver in Traffic Accidents*. Indiana University, Department of Police Administration, Bloomington, 1964.

BORRELIZ, M. and P.H. DELEON, "Malpractice: Professional Liability and the Law," *Professional Psychology*, 1978, 9(3):467–477.

BORTHWICK, H.H., *Summary of Cost-Benefit Study Results for Navy Alcoholism Rehabilitation Programs*. USN Bureau of Navy Personnel, Washington, DC, July 1, 1977, Technical Report No. 346.

BOSWELL, B. and S. WRIGHT, *The Cottage Meeting Program*. Utah Alcoholism Foundation, Salt Lake City, 1976.

BOURNE, P.G. "Alcoholism in the Urban Negro Population," in Bourne, P.G. and R. Fox (eds.), *Alcoholism: Progress in Research and Treatment*. Academic Press, New York, 1973, pp. 211–226.

BOURNE, P.G. and R. FOX (eds.), *Alcoholism: Progress in Research and Treatment*. Academic Press, New York, 1973.

BOWEN, MURRAY, "Alcoholism as Viewed Through Family Systems Theory and Family Psychotherapy," *Annals of the New York Academy of Sciences*, 1974, 233:115–222.

BRECHER, EDWARD (ed.), *Licit and Illicit Drugs*. Little, Brown and Co. for *Consumer Reports*, Boston, 1972.

BREED, WARREN, "Study Criticizes Portrayal of Drinking on TV," *NIAAA Information and Feature Service*, Washington, DC, May 31, 1978, p. 2.

BRISOLARA, ASHTON, *The Alcoholic Employee*. Human Sciences Press, New York, 1979.

BRUEL, L., "Fight Against Chronic Alcoholism. Intravenous Injections of 30% Alcohol," *Écho Médical du Nord*, 1939, 10:497–501.

BRUEL, L. and R. LECOQ, "La prevention des accidents operatoires chez les ethyliques," *Concours Médical*, 1947, 69:2172–2175.

BRUNSWICK, ANN F. and CAROL TARICA, "Drinking and Health: A Study of Urban Black Adolescents," *Addictive Diseases*, 1974, 1:21–42.

BURCH, GEORGE F. and THOMAS D. GILES, "Alcoholic Cardiomyopathy: Concept of the Disease and Its Treatment," *American Journal of Medicine*, 1971, 50:141–145.

BURGENER, V.E., *Alcohol and Highway Safety Curriculum Workshops for K-12*. U.S. Department of Transportation, Washington, DC, 1974. [Report No. DOT HS-149]

BUSSE, S., C.T. MALLOY, and C.E. WEISE, *Disulfiram in the Treatment of Alcoholism: A Bibliography*. Addiction Research Foundation, Toronto, Canada, 1979.

BUTZ, ROGER H., "Intoxication and Withdrawal," in Estes, Nada J. and M. Edith Heinemann (eds.), *Alcoholism: Development, Consequences, and Interventions*. Mosby, St. Louis, 1977, pp. 79–85.

C., BILL, "The Growth and Effectiveness of Alcoholics Anonymous in a Southwestern City," *QJSA*, 1965, 26:279–284.

CADDY, G.R., "Abstinence and Controlled Drinking," in Newman, J. (ed.), *Time for Change in Alcoholism Treatment: Traditional and Emerging Concepts*. University of Pittsburgh Press, 1979.

CAHALAN, DON, "Drinking Practices and Problems: Research Perspectives in Remedial Measures," *Public Affairs Report*, 1973, 14(2):1–6.

CAHALAN, DON and ROBIN ROOM, *Problem Drinking Among American Men*. Rutgers Center of Alcohol Studies, New Brunswick, NJ, 1974. [Monograph No. 7]

CAHALAN, DON, I.H. CISSIN, and H.M. CROSSLEY, *American Drinking Practices: A National Study of Drinking Behavior and Attitudes*. Rutgers Center of Alcohol Studies, New Brunswick, NJ, 1969. [Monograph No. 6]

CAHN, SIDNEY, *The Treatment of Alcoholics*. Oxford University Press, New York, 1970.

CAIN, ARTHUR H., *The "Cured" Alcoholic*. John Day, New York, 1964.

CAMPBELL, DONALD T., "On the Conflicts between Biological and Social Evolution and between Psychology and Moral Tradition," *American Psychologist*, 1975, 30:1103–1126.

CAPPELL, HOWARD and C.P. HERMAN, "Alcohol and Tension Reduction," *QJSA*, 1972, 33:33–64.

CARLEN, P.L. et al., "Reversible Cerebral Atrophy in Recently Abstinent Chronic Alcoholics Measured by Computed Tomography Scans," *Science*, June 2, 1978, 200:1076–1078.

CARROLL, J. F. and T.E. MALLOY, "Combined Treatment of Alcohol- and Drug-Dependent Persons: A Literature Review and Evaluation," *American Journal of Drug and Alcohol Abuse*, 1977, 4:343–364.

CARROLL, J.F., T. E. MALLOY, and F. McKENDRICK, "Alcohol Abuse by Drug-Dependent Persons: A Literature Review and Evaluation," *American Journal of Drug and Alcohol Abuse*, 1977, 4:293–316.

CARROLL, J.F., T.E. MALLOY, and F. McKENDRICK, "Drug Abuse by Alcoholics and Problem Drinkers: A Literature Review and Evaluation," *American Journal of Drug and Alcohol Abuse*, 1977, 4:317–342.

CARTWRIGHT, A.K. et al., "Trends in the Epidemiology of Alcoholism," *Psychological Medicine*, 1978, 8:1–4.

CATANZARO, RONALD J. (ed.), *Alcoholism: The Total Treatment Approach*. Charles C. Thomas, Springfield, IL, rev. ed., 1972.

CHERRINGTON, ERNEST, *The Evolution of Prohibition in the United States of America*. American Issue Press, Westerville, Ohio, 1920.

CHIDSEY, D.B., *On and Off the Wagon: A Sober Analysis of the Temperance Movement from the Pilgrims through Prohibition*. Cowles, New York, 1969.

CHODORKOFF, B., H. KRYSTAL, J. NUNN, and R. WITTENBERG, "Employment Characteristics of Hospitalized Alcoholics," *QJSA*, 1961, 22:106–110.

CHRISTMAS, JUNE J., "Alcoholism Services for Minorities: Training Issues and Concerns," *Alcohol Health and Research World*, 1978, 2(Spring):20–27.

CHRISTOPHER D. SMITHERS FOUNDATION, *Understanding Alcoholism*, Smithers Foundation, New York, 1968.

CHRISTOPHER D. SMITHERS FOUNDATION, *Preventing Alcoholism*, Smithers Foundation, New York, 1975.

CLARK, NORMAN H., *Deliver Us from Evil: An Interpretation of American Prohibition*. Norton, New York, 1976.

CLARREN, STERLING K. and DAVID W. SMITH, "The Fetal Alcohol Syndrome," *New England Journal of Medicine*, 1978, 298:1063–1067.

CLINEBELL, HOWARD J., "Philosophical-Religious Factors in the Etiology and Treatment of Alcoholism," *QJSA*, 1963, 24:473–488.

CLINEBELL, HOWARD J., *Understanding and Counseling the Alcoholic through Religion and Psychology*. Abington Press, New York, rev. ed., 1968.

COAKLEY, JUDY F. and SANDIE JOHNSON, *Alcohol Abuse and Alcoholism in the United States: Selected Recent Prevalence Estimates* [Working Paper #1]. National Institute on Alcohol Abuse and Alcoholism, Washington, DC, March 27, 1978.

COFFEY, THOMAS M., *The Long Thirst: Prohibition in America*. Norton, New York, 1975.

COHEN, P.C. and M.S. KRAUSE, *Casework with Wives of Alcoholics*. Family Service Association of America, New York, 1971.

COLE, JONATHAN O. (ed.), *Clinical Research in Alcoholism*. American Psychiatric Association, Washington, DC, 1968.

COLEMAN, J.H. and W.E. EVANS, "Drug Interaction with Alcohol," *Alcohol Health and Research World*, Winter 1975/76, pp. 16–19.

CONLEY, PAUL and ANDREW SORENSEN, *The Staggering Steeple: The Story of Alcoholism and the Churches*. Pilgrim Press, Philadelphia, 1971.

CORK, R. MARGARET, *The Forgotten Children*. Addiction Research Foundation, Toronto, 1969.

CORK, R. MARGARET, *Alcoholism and the Family*. Addiction Research Foundation, Toronto, 1971.

CORRECTIONAL ASSOCIATION OF NEW YORK, *Alcohol and Alcoholism: A Police Handbook*. Correctional Association of New York, New York, 1965.

CORRIGAN, EILEEN M., *Alcoholic Women in Treatment*. Oxford University Press, New York, 1980.

CORRIGAN, EILEEN M., "Linking the Problem Drinker with Treatment," *Social Case Work*, 1972, 7:54–56.

CORRIGAN, EILEEN M., and SANDRA C. ANDERSON, "Training for Treatment of Alcoholism in Women," *Social Casework*, 1978, 59:42–50.

COSTELLO, C.G., "An Evaluation of Aversion and LSD Therapy in the Treatment of Alcoholism," *Canadian Psychiatric Association Journal*, 1969, 14:31–42.

COSTELLO, R.M., "Alcoholism Treatment and Evaluation: In Search of Methods," *International Journal of Medicine*, 1975, 10:251–276.

COUDERT, JO, *The Alcoholic in Your Life*. Stein and Day, New York, 1972.

COURVILLE, C.H., *The Effects of Alcohol on the Nervous System of Man*. San Lucas Press, Los Angeles, 1955.

CRAMER, PATRICE A., *An Educational Strategy to Impact the Children of Alcoholic Parents: A Feasibility Study*. National Center for Alcohol Education, Arlington, VA, 1977.

CRANCER, ALFRED et al., "Comparison of the Effects of Marihuana and Alcohol on Simulated Driving Performance," *Science*, 1969, 164:851–854.

CRUZ-COKE, R. and A. VARDA, "Genetic Factors in Alcoholism," in Popham, R.E. (ed.), *Alcohol and Alcoholism*. University of Toronto Press, Toronto, 1970, pp. 284–289.

CURLEE, JOAN, "Combined Use of Alcoholics Anonymous and Outpatient Psychotherapy," *Bulletin of the Menninger Clinic*, 1971, 35:368–371. [NCA reprint]

CURLEE, JOAN, "How a Therapist Can Use Alcoholics Anonymous," *Annals of the New York Academy of Sciences*, 1974, 233:137–144.

CURLEE-SALISBURY, JOAN, "Perspectives on Alcoholics Anonymous," in Estes, Nada J. and M. Edith Heinemann (eds.), *Alcoholism: Development, Consequences, and Interventions*. Mosby, St. Louis, 1977, pp. 266–273.

CURLEE-SALISBURY, JOAN, *When the Woman You Love Is An Alcoholic*. Abbey Press, St. Meinrad, IN, 1978.

DAGGETT, L.R. and E.J. ROLDE, "Decriminalization of Public Drunkenness: The Response of Suburban Police," *Archives of General Psychiatry*, 1977, 34:937–941.

DAVIDSON, W.S., "Studies of Aversive Conditioning for Alcoholics: A Critical Review of Theory and Research Methodology," *Psychological Bulletin*, 1974, 81:571–581.

DAVIES, D.L., "Normal Drinking in Recovered Alcohol Addicts," *QJSA*, 1962, 23:94–104.

DAVIES, D.L., "Normal Drinking in Recovered Alcohol Addicts: Response," *QJSA*, 1963, 24:330–332.

[DAVIES, D.L.] Notes and Comments. "Normal Drinking in Recovered Alcohol Addicts: Comment on the Article by D.L. Davies," *QJSA*, 1963, 24:109–121, 321–332, 727–735.

DAVIS, V.E. et al., "Alcohol, Amines, and Alkaloids: A Possible Biochemical Basis for Alcohol Addiction," *Science*, 1970, 167:1005–1007.

DAWKINS, M.P., *Alcohol and the Black Community: Exploratory Studies of Selected Issues*. Century Twenty One Publishing, Saratoga, CA, 1980.

DELEHANTY, EDWARD J., *The Therapeutic Value of the Twelve Steps of AA*. Utah Alcoholism Foundation, Salt Lake City, n.d. [Hazelden pamphlet]

DE LINT, JAN, "The Prevention of Alcoholism," *Preventive Medicine*, 1974, 3:24–35.

DE LINT, JAN, "Current Trends in the Prevalence of Excessive Alcohol Use and Alcohol-Related Health Damage," *British Journal of Addiction*, 1975, 70:3–13.

DE LINT, JAN and W. SCHMIDT, "Consumption Averages and Alcoholism Prevalence: A Brief Review of Epidemiological Investigations," *British Journal of Addiction*, 1971a, 66:97–107.

DE LINT, JAN and W. SCHMIDT, "The Epidemiology of Alcoholism," in Israel, Y. and J. Mardones (eds.), *Biological Basis of Alcoholism*. Wiley, New York, 1971b, pp. 423–442.

DITMAN, KEITH S., "Review and Evaluation of Current Drug Therapies in Alcoholism," *International Journal of Psychiatry*, 1967, 3:248–266.

DOE, FATHER JOHN (RALPH PFAU), *Sobriety and Beyond*. Guild, 1955. Also his *Sobriety Without End*. [Hazelden reprints]

DOHERTY, JAMES, "Disulfiram (Antabuse): Chemical Commitment to Abstinence," *Alcohol Health and Research World*, Spring 1976, 2–9.

DONIGAN, ROBERT L., *Chemical Tests and the Law*. Northwestern University Press, Evanston, IL, 1966.

DORRIS, ROBERT and DOYLE LINDLEY, *Counseling on Alcoholism*. Glencoe, Beverly Hills, 1968.

DOUGLASS, RICHARD L., "The Consequences of Lower Legal Drinking Ages on Alcohol-Related Crash Involvement of Young People," *Report on Alcohol*, Fall 1976, 19:13–19.

DOWSLING, JANET and ANNE MACLENNAN (eds.), *The Chemically Dependent Woman*. Addiction Research Foundation, Toronto, 1978.

DRIESSEN, G.J. and J.A. BRYK, "Alcohol Countermeasures: Solid Rock and Shifting Sand," in Perrine, M.W. (ed.), *Alcohol, Drugs and Driving*. National Highway Traffic Safety Administration, 1974. [Technical Report DOT HS-801-096]

DUFFY, J.C., "Alcohol Consumption, Alcoholism and Excessive Drinking—Errors in Estimates from Consumption Figures," *International Journal of Epidemiology*, 1977, 6:375–379.

DUNN, ROBERT B., JAMES W. SMITH et al., "A Comprehensive Intensive Treatment Program for Alcoholism," *Southwestern Medicine*, 1971, 52:102–104.

EDWARDS, G., "Epidemiology Applied to Alcoholism: A Review and Examination of Purposes," *QJSA*, 1973, 34:28–56.

EDWARDS, G. and M. GRANT (eds.), *Alcoholism: New Knowledge and New Responses*. University Park Press, Baltimore, MD, 1976.

EDWARDS, G., M.M. GROSS, M. KELLER, J. MOSER, and R. ROOM (eds.), *Alcohol-Related Disabilities*. World Health Organization, Geneva, 1977. [No. 32]

EDWARDS, PATRICIA, CHERYL HARVEY, and P.D. WHITEHEAD, "Wives of Alcoholics: A Critical Review and Analysis," *QJSA*, 1973, 34:112–132.

EFRON, V., MARK KELLER and C. GURIOLI, *Statistics on Consumption of Alcohol and on Alcoholism*. Rutgers Center for Alcohol Studies, New Brunswick, NJ, 1974.

EIDELBERG, EDUARDO, "Acute Effects of Ethanol and Opiates on the Nervous System," in Gibbins, Robert J. et al. (eds.), *Research Advances in Alcohol and Drug Problems*. Wiley, New York, 1975, vol. 2, pp. 147–176.

EL-GUEBALY, N. and D. OFFORD, "The Offspring of Alcoholics: A Critical Review," *American Journal of Psychiatry*, 1977, 134:357–365.

EMRICK, CHAD D., "The Rand Report," *JSA*, 1977, 38:152–163.

ERIKSSON, K., "Behavioral and Physiological Differences among Rat Strains Specially Selected for Their Alcohol Consumption," *Annals of the New York Academy of Sciences*, 1972, 197:32–41.

ESTES, NADA J., "Counseling the Wife of an Alcoholic Spouse," in Estes, Nada J. and M. Edith Heinemann (eds.), *Alcoholism: Development, Consequences, and Interventions*. Mosby, St. Louis, 1977, pp. 259–265.

ESTES, NADA J. and JOAN M. BAKER, "Spouses of Alcoholic Women," in Estes, Nada J. and M. Edith Heinemann (eds.), *Alcoholism: Development, Consequences, and Interventions*. Mosby, St. Louis, 1977, pp. 186–193.

ESTES, NADA J. and M. EDITH HEINEMANN (eds.), *Alcoholism: Development, Consequences, and Interventions*. C.V. Mosby, St. Louis, MO, 1977.

EVERETT, MICHAEL W., JACK O. WADDELL, and DWIGHT R. HEATH (eds.), *Cross-Cultural Approaches to the Study of Alcohol: An Interdisciplinary Perspective*. Mouton, The Hague, 1976.

EWING, JOHN A., *Psychiatric News*, September 17, 1975, 10, no. 18.

EWING, JOHN A. and BEATRICE A. ROUSE, "Alcohol Sensitivity and Ethnic Background," *American Journal of Psychiatry*, 1974, 131:206–210.

EWING, JOHN A. and BEATRICE A. ROUSE (eds.), *Drinking: Alcohol in American Society*. Nelson-Hall, Chicago, 1977.

EWING, JOHN A. and BEATRICE A. ROUSE, "Failure of an Experimental Treatment Program to Inculcate Controlled Drinking in Alcoholics," *British Journal of Addiction*, 1976, 71:123–134.

FAJARDO, ROQUE, *Helping Your Alcoholic before He or She Hits Bottom*. Crown Publishers, New York, 1976.

FARMER, RAE H., "Functional Changes during Early Weeks of Abstinence, Measured by the Bender-Gestalt," *QJSA*, 1973, 34:786–796.

FAVAZZA, A.R. and B. CANNELL, "Screening for Alcoholism among College Students," *American Journal of Psychiatry*, 1977, 34:1414–1416.

FAVAZZA, A. and J. PIRES, "The Michigan Alcoholism Screening Test: Application in a General Military Hospital," *QJSA*, 1974, 35:925–929.

FENSTER, L. FREDERICK, "Alcohol and Disorders of the Gastrointestinal System," in Estes, Nada J. and M. Edith Heinemann (eds.), *Alcoholism: Development, Consequences, and Interventions*. Mosby, St. Louis, 1977, pp. 102–108.

FILSTEAD, WILLIAM, JEAN ROSSI, and MARK KELLER (eds.), *Alcohol and Alcohol Problems: New Thinking and New Directions*. Ballinger Publishing Company, Cambridge, MA, 1976.

FICHTER, JOSEPH H., "Priests and Alcohol," *Homiletic and Pastoral Review*, 1976, August-September:10–21. [Reprinted in: *Military Chaplain's Review*, 1977, Winter:39–50. (Department of the Army, PAM 165-112)]

FICHTER, JOSEPH H., "Spirituality, Religiosity, and Alcoholism," *America*, 1977a, 136:458–461.

FICHTER, JOSEPH H., "Alcohol and Addiction: Priests and Prelates," *America*, 1977b, 137:258–260.

FINCH, JOHN R., *Psychiatric and Legal Aspects of Automobile Fatalities*. Charles C. Thomas, Springfield, 1970.

FINKELSTEIN, ANN B. and JOHN J. BOSLEY, *Alcoholism Training in the United States: A Summary Report of Thirty-nine Programs*. National Center for Alcohol Education, Arlington, VA, 1974.

FINLAY, DONALD G., "Effect of Role Network Pressure on an Alcoholic's Approach to Treatment," *Social Casework*, 1966, 11:71–77.

FINN, PETER, *Alcohol: You Can Help Your Kids Cope. A Guide for the Elementary School Teacher*. National Council on Alcoholism, New York, 1975.

FINN, PETER and JUDITH PLATT, *Alcohol and Traffic Safety (Elementary School)*. United States Government Printing Office, Washington, DC, 1972 [Pamphlet]

FLAHERTY, J.A., "The Psychodynamics of the 'Dry Drunk'," *American Journal of Psychiatry*, 1955, 112:460–464.

FLEMING, ALICE, *Alcohol: The Delightful Poison*. Delacorte Press, New York, 1975.

FORD, JOHN C., *Depth Psychology, Morality, and Alcoholism*. Weston College, Weston, MA, 1951.

FORD, JOHN C., "Clerical Attitudes on Alcohol—Most of Them Wrong," *The Priest*, April 1955. [NCA reprint]

FORD, JOHN C., "Chemical Comfort and Christian Virtue," *American Ecclesiastical Review*, 1959, 141:361–379.

FORD, MICHAEL, "NCA Fights Efforts to Diminish Rehabilitation Act Safeguards," *Labor-Management Alcoholism Journal*, 1978, 8(2):57–61.

FORNEY, ROBERT and FRANCIS W. HUGHES, *Combined Effects of Alcohol and Other Drugs*. Charles C. Thomas, Springfield, IL, 1968.

FORREST, GARY G., *The Diagnosis and Treatment of Alcoholism*. Charles C. Thomas, Springfield, IL, 2nd ed., 1978.

FORSANDER, O. and K. ERIKSSON (eds.), *Biological Aspects of Alcohol Consumption*. Swets and Zeitlinger, Helsinki, 1972.

FORT, JOEL, *Alcohol: Our Biggest Drug Problem*. McGraw-Hill, New York, 1973.

FOX, RUTH, "Antabuse as an Adjunct to Psychotherapy in Alcoholism," *New York State Journal of Medicine*, 1958, 58:1540–1544. [NCA reprint]

FOX, RUTH, "Children in the Alcoholic Family," in Bier, W.C. (ed.), *Problems in Addiction: Alcohol and Drug Addiction*. Fordham University Press, New York, 1962, pp. 71–96.

FOX, RUTH, "Disulfiram (Antabuse) as an Adjunct in the Treatment of Alcoholism," in Fox, Ruth (ed.), *Alcoholism: Behavioral Research, Therapeutic Approaches*. Springer, New York, 1967a, pp. 242–255.

FOX, RUTH, "A Multidisciplinary Approach to the Treatment of Alcoholism," *American Journal of Psychiatry*, 1967b, 123:769–778.

FOX, RUTH, "Treating the Alcoholic's Family," in Catanzaro, R.J. (ed.), *Alcoholism: The Total Treatment Approach*. Charles C. Thomas, Springfield, IL, 1968, pp. 105–115.

FOX, RUTH, *The Effects of Alcoholism on Children*. National Council on Alcoholism, New York, 1972. [Pamphlet]

FOX, RUTH, "Disulfiram," in Bourne, Peter and Ruth Fox (eds.), *Alcoholism: Progress in Research and Treatment*. Academic Press, New York, 1973, pp. 236–239.

FOX, VERNELLE, *Day Hospital as a Treatment Modality for Alcoholism*. National Clearinghouse for Alcohol Information, Rockville, MD, 1974. [Pamphlet]

FRANKLIN, R.A., "One Hundred Doctors at *The Retreat*: A Contribution to the Subject of Mental Disorders in the Medical Profession," *British Journal of Psychiatry*, 1977, 113:11–14.

FRANKS, H.M. et al., "The Interaction of Alcohol and Tetrahydrocannabinol in Man: Effects on Psychomotor Skills Related to Driving," in Israelstam, S. and S. Lambert (eds.), *Alcohol, Drugs, and Traffic Safety*. Addiction Research Foundation, Toronto, 1975, pp. 461–466.

FREUDENBERGER, HERBERT J., *The Staff Burn-Out Syndrome*. Drug Abuse Council, Washington, DC, 1975.

FREUND, G., "Chronic Central Nervous System Toxicity of Alcohol," *Annual Review of Pharmacology*, 1973, 13:217–227.

FUNKHOUSER, M.N., "Identifying Alcohol Problems among Elderly Hospital Patients," *Alcohol Health and Research World*, Winter 1977/78, pp. 27–34.

FURNAS, J.C., *The Life and Times of the Late Demon Rum*. Putnam, New York, 1965.

FUTTERMAN, S., "Personality Trends in Wives of Alcoholics," *Journal of Psychiatric Social Work*, 1953, 23:37–41.

GAZDA, GEORGE M., *Group Counseling: A Developmental Approach*. Allyn and Bacon, Boston, 2nd ed., 1978.

GELLMAN, I.P., *The Sober Alcoholic: An Organizational Analysis of Alcoholics Anonymous*. College and University Press, New Haven, 1964.

GERMAN, WILLIAM P.Z. JR., *An Analytical Survey of the Rand Report on Alcoholism and Treatment*. Fundamental Research Organization, 2365 N. Oakland St., Arlington VA 22207, 1978.

GIBBINS, R.J. et al. (eds.), *Research Advances in Alcohol and Drug Problems*. Wiley, New York, 5 vols., 1974–1978.

GIBBS, LEONARD and JOHN FLANAGAN, "Prognostic Indicators of Alcoholism Treatment Outcome," *International Journal of the Addictions*, 1977, 12:1097–1141.

GILL, JAMES J., FRANCIS J. BRACELAND et al., "Ethics and Psychiatry," *Psychiatric Annals*, February 1979, vol. 9, no. 2.

GITLOW, S.E. (ed.), *Alcoholism: A Practical Treatment Guide*. Grune and Stratton, New York, 1980.

GLASER, FREDERICK B. et al., *A Systems Approach to Alcohol Treatment*. Addiction Research Foundation, Toronto, 1978.

GLATT, MAX M., "Group Therapy in Alcoholism," *British Journal of Addiction*, 1957/58, 54:133–148.

GLATT, MAX M., *The Alcoholic and the Help He Needs*. Taplinger, New York, 1974a.

GLATT, MAX M., *A Guide to Addiction and Its Treatment*. Halstead Press, New York, 1974b.

GLATT, MAX M., *Alcoholism: A Social Disease*. St. Paul's, London, 1975a.

GLATT, MAX M., "The Alcoholisms. The Disease Concept—Newer Developments," *Nursing Times*, 1975b, 71:856–858.

GLATT, MAX M., "Alcoholism Disease Concept and Loss of Control Revisited," *British Journal of Addiction*, 1976, 71:135–144.

GLATT, MAX M., "Characteristics and Prognoses of Alcoholic Doctors," *British Medical Journal*, 1977, 1:507.

GLOBETTI, GERALD, "An Appraisal of Drug Education Programs," in Gibbins, R.J. (ed.), *Research Advances in Alcohol and Drug Problems*. Wiley, New York, 1975, vol. 2, pp. 93–122.

GLOBETTI, GERALD, "Teenage Drinking," in Estes, Nada J. and M. Edith Heinemann (eds.), *Alcoholism: Development, Consequences, and Interventions*. Mosby, St. Louis, 1977, pp. 162–173.

GOLDMAN, M.S. et al., "Recoverability of Sensory and Motor Functioning Following Chronic Alcohol Abuse," in Seixas, Frank A. (ed.), *Currents in Alcoholism*. Grune and Stratton, New York, vol. 3, pp. 493–504.

GOMBERG, EDITH S., "Women with Alcohol Problems," in Estes, Nada J. and M. Edith Heinemann (eds.), *Alcoholism: Development, Consequences, and Interventions*. Mosby, St. Louis, 1977, pp. 174–185.

GONZALES, G.M., *A Model for Developing a Campus Alcohol Abuse Prevention Program*. SAAETP, Inc., 4875 Powers Ferry Rd. N.W., Atlanta, GA 30327, 1977.

GOODWIN, D.W., "Is Alcoholism Hereditary? A Review and Critique," *Archives of General Psychiatry*, 1971, 25:545–549.

GOODWIN, D.W., "Drinking Problems in Adopted and Nonadopted Sons of Alcoholics," *Arch. Gen. Psychiat.*, 1974, 31:164–169.

GOODWIN, D.W., *Is Alcoholism Hereditary?* Oxford University Press, New York, 1976.

GOODWIN, D.W., "The Alcoholic Blackout and How to Prevent It," in Birnbaum, I.M. and E.S. Parker (eds.), *Alcohol and Memory.* Lawrence Erlbaum Associates, Hillsdale, NJ, 1977, pp. 177–183.

GOODWIN, D.W., "Hereditary Factors in Alcoholism," *Hospital Practice*, 1978a, 13:121–130.

GOODWIN, D.W., "The Genetics of Alcoholism: A State of the Art Review," *Alcohol Health and Research World*, Spring 1978b, 2:2–12.

GOODWIN, D.W. and C. K. ERICKSON (eds.), *Alcoholism and Affective Disorders: Clinical, Genetic, and Biochemical Studies.* SP Medical and Scientific Books, New York, 1979.

GOODWIN, D.W., F. SCHULSINGER, L. HERMANESEN, S.B. GUZE, and G. WINOKUR, "Alcohol Problems in Adoptees Reared Apart from Alcoholic Biological Parents," *Archives of General Psychiatry*, 1973, 28:238–243.

GORDON, GARY, KURT ALTMAN, A.L. SOUTHREN, E. RUBIN, and C.S. LIEBER, "Effects of Alcohol Administration on Sex-Hormone Metabolism in Normal Men," *New England Journal of Medicine*, 1976, 295:793–797.

GOTTHEIL, EDWARD, "Poor Morale in Treatment Personnel," *Alcohol Health and Research World*, Spring 1975, pp. 20–25.

GRAD, F.P. et al., *Alcoholism and the Law.* Oceana Publications, Dobbs Ferry, NY, 1971.

GRATEFUL MEMBERS, *The Twelve Steps for Everyone . . . Who Really Wants Them.* CompCare Publications, Minneapolis, 1977. [Pamphlet]

GREEN, R.C., G.J. CARROLL, and W.D. BUXTON (eds.), *The Care and Management of the Sick and Incompetent Physician.* Charles C. Thomas, Springfield, IL, 1978.

GREENBLATT, M. and M.A. SCHUCKIT (eds.), *Alcoholism Problems in Women and Children.* Grune and Stratton, New York, 1976.

GRIMMETT, JOHN O., *Barriers Against Recovery.* Hazelden Books, Center City, MN, n.d. [Pamphlet]

GROSS, M.M. (ed.), *Alcohol Intoxication and Withdrawal: Experimental Studies I.* Plenum, New York, 1973. (*Advances in Experimental Medicine and Biology*, vol. 35, 1972.) Experimental Studies II, 1975.

GROSS, M.M., "Psychobiological Contributions to the Alcohol Dependence Syndrome: A Selective Review of Recent Research," in Edwards, G., M.M. Gross, M. Keller, J. Moser, and R. Room (eds.), *Alcohol-Related Disabilities.* World Health Organization, Geneva, 1977, (No. 32) pp. 107–131.

GROUPÉ, VINCENT (ed.), *Alcoholism Rehabilitation: Methods and Experiences of Private Rehabilitation Centers.* National Institute on Alcohol Abuse and Alcoholism and Rutgers Center of Alcohol Studies, New Brunswick, NJ, 1978.

GRUTCHFIELD, LEE, "What AA Meetings Taught a Non-AA Counselor," *Alcohol Health and Research World*, Spring 1979, 3(3):15–17. [Reprinted from *AA Grapevine*, December 1977]

GUSFIELD, JOSEPH R., *Symbolic Crusade: Status Politics and the American Temperance Movement*. University of Illinois Press, Urbana, IL, 1963.

GUSFIELD, JOSEPH R., "The Prevention of Drinking Problems," in Filstead, William, Jean Rossi and Mark Keller (eds.), *Alcohol and Alcohol Problems: New Thinking and New Directions*. Ballinger Publishing Co., Cambridge, MA, 1976, pp. 267–291.

GUST, DODIE, *Up, Down and Sideways on Wet and Dry Booze*. CompCare Publications, Minneapolis, 1977.

HABERMAN, PAUL W. and MICHAEL M. BADEN, *Alcohol, Other Drugs and Violent Death*. Oxford University Press, New York, 1978.

HAGGARD, H.W. and E.M. JELLINEK, *Alcohol Explored*. Doubleday, New York, 1942.

HANNA, JOEL M., "Metabolic Responses of Chinese, Japanese and Europeans to Alcohol," *Alcoholism: Clinical and Experimental Research*, 1978, 2:89–92.

HARE-MUSTIN, RACHEL T. et al., "Rights of Clients, Responsibilities of Therapists," *American Psychologist*, 1979, 34:3–16.

HARPER, FREDERICK D. (ed.), *Alcohol Abuse and Black America*. Douglass Publications, Alexandria, VA, 1976.

HARPER, FREDERICK D., "Alcohol Use among North American Blacks," in Israel, Y. et al. (eds.), *Research Advances in Alcohol and Drug Problems*. Plenum, New York, vols. 4–5, 1978. Vol. 4, pp. 349–361.

HARPER, FREDERICK D. and MARVIN P. DAWKINS, "Alcohol and Blacks: Survey of the Periodical Literature," *British Journal of Addiction*, 1976, 71:327–334.

HARTLEY, D. et al., "Deterioration Effects in Encounter Groups," *American Psychologist*, 1976, 31:247–255.

HARTMAN, B.J., "Approaches to the Treatment of Alcoholism," *Journal of the National Medical Association*, 1976, 68(2):101–103.

HAVARD, J.D., "Drinking Driver and the Law: Legal Countermeasures in the Prevention of Alcohol-Related Road Traffic Accidents," in Gibbins, Robert J. and Yedy Israel (eds.), *Research Advances in Alcohol and Drug Problems*. Wiley, New York, 1975, Vol. 2, pp. 123–145.

HAZELDEN FOUNDATION, *Chemical Dependence: Psychological vs. Physiological*. Hazelden Books, Center City, MN, 1974. [Pamphlet]

HEATH, DWIGHT B., "A Critical Review of Ethnographic Studies of Alcohol Use," in Gibbins, R.J. (ed.), *Research Advances in Alcohol and Drug Problems*. Wiley, New York, 1975, vol. 2, pp. 1–92.

HEATH, DWIGHT B., "Anthropological Perspectives on Alcohol: An Historical Review," in Everett, M. et al. (eds.), *Cross-Cultural Approaches to the Study of Alcohol: An Interdisciplinary Perspective*. Mouton, The Hague, 1976.

HEILMAN, RICHARD O., *Dynamics of Drug Dependency*. Hazelden Books, Center City, MN, 1973.

HEINEMANN, M. EDITH and KATHLEEN SMITH-DIJULIO, "Assessment and Care of the Chronically Ill Alcoholic Person," in Estes, Nada J. and M. Edith Heinemann (eds.), *Alcoholism: Development, Consequences, and Interventions.* Mosby, St. Louis, 1977, pp. 239–248.

HEYMAN, MARGARET, "Employer-Sponsored Programs for Problem Drinkers," *Social Casework*, 1971, 52:547–552.

HIGHWAY SAFETY RESEARCH INSTITUTE, *HIT LAB Reports.* University of Michigan, Ann Arbor, 1970.

HINDMAN, MARGARET, "Rational Emotive Therapy in Alcoholism Treatment," *Alcohol Health and Research World*, Spring 1976, 13–17.

HINDMAN, MARGARET, "Child Abuse and Neglect: The Alcohol Connection," *Alcohol Health and Research World*, Spring 1977, 2–7.

HOFF, EBBE CURTIS, *Alcoholism: The Hidden Addiction.* Seabury Press, New York, 1974.

HOFSTADTER, R., *Age of Reform: From Bryan to F.D.R.* Alfred A. Knopf, New York, 1960.

HOMILLER, JONICA D., *Women and Alcohol: A Guide for State and Local Decision Makers.* Alcohol and Drug Problems Association of North America, Washington, DC, 1977.

HORNIK, EDITH LYNN, *You and Your Alcoholic Parent.* Association Press, New York, 1974.

HORNIK, EDITH LYNN, *The Drinking Woman.* Association Press, New York, 1978.

HOUGHLAND, JAMES G. JR. and SAMUEL A. MUELLER, "Organizational 'Goal Submergence': The Methodist Church and the Failure of the Temperance Movement," *Sociology and Social Research*, 1974, 58:408–416.

HUBERTY, C. and D.J. HUBERTY, "Treating the Parents of Adolescent Drug Abusers," *Contemporary Drug Problems*, 1976, 5:573–592.

HUGHES, J.M., "Adolescent Children of Alcoholic Parents and the Relationship of Alateen to These Children," *Journal of Consulting and Clinical Psychology*, 1977, 45:946–947.

IBER, FRANK L., "The Effect of Fructose on Alcohol Metabolism," *Archives of Internal Medicine*, 1977, 137:1121.

ISRAEL, Y. and J. MARDONES (eds.), *Biological Basis of Alcoholism.* Wiley, New York, 1971.

ISRAEL, Y. et al. (eds.), *Research Advances in Alcohol and Drug Problems.* Plenum, New York, 1978, vols. 4–5.

ISRAELSTAM, S. and S. LAMBERT (eds.), *Alcohol, Drugs, and Traffic Safety.* Addiction Research Foundation, Toronto, Canada, 1975.

ISSELBACHER, KURT, "Metabolic and Hepatic Effects of Alcohol," *New England Journal of Medicine*, 1977, 296:612–617.

JACKSON, JOAN K., "The Adjustment of the Family to the Crisis of Alcoholism," *QJSA*, 1954, 15:562–586. [NCA reprint]

JACKSON, JOAN K., "Types of Drinking Patterns of Male Alcoholics," *QJSA*, 1958, 19:269–302.

JACKSON, JOAN K. and RALPH G. CONNOR, "The Skid-Road Alcoholic," *QJSA*, 1953a, 14:468–486.

JACKSON, JOAN K. and RALPH G. CONNOR, "The Attitudes of Parents of Alcoholics, Moderate Drinkers, and Nondrinkers Toward Alcohol," *QJSA*, 1953b, 14:569–613.

JACKSON, THOMAS R. and JAMES W. SMITH, "A Comparison of Two Aversion Treatment Methods for Alcoholism," *JSA*, 1978, 39:187–191.

JACOBSON, GEORGE R., *The Alcoholisms: Detection, Assessment and Diagnosis*. Human Sciences Press, New York, 1976a.

JACOBSON, GEORGE R., "The Mortimer-Filkins Test: Court Procedures for Identifying Problem Drinkers," *Alcohol Health and Research World*, Summer 1976b, 22–26.

JAMES, I. PIERCE, "Blood Alcohol Levels Following Successful Suicide," *QJSA*, 1966, 27:23–29.

JELLINEK, E.M., "Phases of Alcohol Addiction," *QJSA*, 1952, 13:673–684.

JELLINEK, E.M., "Estimating the Prevalence of Alcoholism: Modified Values in the Jellinek Formula and an Alternative Approach," *QJSA*, 1959, 20:261–269.

JELLINEK, E.M., *The Disease Concept of Alcoholism*. College and University Press, New Haven, CT, 1960.

JELLINEK, E.M. and M. KELLER, "Rates of Alcoholism in the United States of America, 1940–1948," *QJSA*, 1952, 13:49–59.

JESSOR, R. and S. JESSOR, "Adolescent Development and the Onset of Drinking," *JSA*, 1975, 36:27–51.

JESSOR, R. and S. JESSOR, *Problem Behavior and Psychosocial Development: A Longitudinal Study of Youth*. Academic Press, New York, 1977.

JESSOR, R., M. COLLINS and S. JESSOR, "On Becoming a Drinker: Social-Psychological Aspects of an Adolescent Tradition," *Annals of the New York Academy of Sciences*, 1972, 197:199–213.

JOHN, HARRISON W., "The Church and Alcoholism: A Growing Involvement," *Alcohol Health and Research World*, Summer 1977, 2–10.

JOHN, HARRISON W., "Alcohol and the Impaired Physician," *Alcohol Health and Research World*, Winter 1978, 2–8.

JOHNSON, VERNON, *I'll Quit Tomorrow*. Harper and Row, New York, 1973.

JOHNSTON, HENRY ALAN, *What Rights Are Left*. Macmillan, New York, 1930.

JONES, K.J., "Sectarian Characteristics of Alcoholics Anonymous," *Sociology*, 1970, 4:181–195.

JONES, K.L., D.W. SMITH, C.N. ULLELAND, and A.P. STREISSGUTH, "Pattern of Malformation in Offspring of Chronic Alcoholic Mothers," *Lancet*, 1973, 1:1267–1271.

JONES, R.E., "A Study of 100 Physician Psychiatric Inpatients," *American Journal of Psychiatry*, 1977, 134:1119–1123.

JONES, R.W. and A.R. HELRICH, "Treatment of Alcoholism by Physicians in Private Practice, A National Survey," *QJSA*, 1972, 33:117–131.

KAIJ, H.L., "Definitions of Alcoholism and Genetic Research, *Annals of the New York Academy of Sciences*, 1972, 97:110–113.

KAIJ, H.L. and J. DOCK, "Grandsons of Alcoholics," *Archives of General Psychiatry*, 1975, 32:1379–1381.

KALANT, H., "Absorption, Diffusion, Distribution, and Elimination of Ethanol: Effects on Biological Membranes," in Kissin, B. and H. Begleiter (eds.), *The Biology of Alcoholism*. Plenum, New York, 1971, vol. 1, pp. 1–62.

KALANT, ORIANA (ed.), *Alcohol and Drug Problems in Women*. Vol. 5, *Research Advances in Alcohol and Drug Problems*. Plenum, New York, 1978.

KEEHN, J.D., "Neuroticism and Extraversion: Chronic Alcoholic's Report on Effects of Drinking," *Psychological Reports*, 1970, 27:767–770.

KELLER, JOHN E., *Ministering to Alcoholics*. Augsburg Publishing, Minneapolis, 1966.

KELLER, MARK, "The Definition of Alcoholism," *QJSA*, 1960, 21:125–134.

KELLER, MARK, "Alcohol in Health and Disease: Some Historical Perspectives," *Annals of the New York Academy of Sciences*, 1966, 133:820–827.

KELLER, MARK, *Some Views on the Nature of Addiction*. Rutgers Center of Alcohol Studies, New Brunswick, NJ, 1969.

KELLER, MARK, "The Great Jewish Drink Mystery," *British Journal of Addiction*, 1970, 64:287–296.

KELLER, MARK, "On the Loss-of-Control Phenomenon in Alcoholism," *British Journal of Addiction*, 1972, 67:153–166.

KELLER, MARK, "Multidisciplinary Perspectives on Alcoholism and the Need for Integration: An Historical and Prospective Note," *JSA*, 1975a, 36:133–147.

KELLER, MARK, "Problems of Epidemiology in Alcohol Problems," *JSA*, 1975b, 36:1442–1451.

KELLER, MARK, "Problems with Alcohol: An Historical Perspective," in Filstead, William, Jean Rossi, and Mark Keller (eds.), *Alcohol and Alcohol Problems: New Thinking and New Directions*. Ballinger, Cambridge, MA, 1976a, pp. 5–28.

KELLER, MARK, "Disease Concept of Alcoholism Revisited," *JSA*, 1976b, 37:1694–1717.

KELLER, MARK, "A Lexicon of Disablements Related to Alcohol Consumption," in Edwards, G., M.M. Gross, M. Keller, J. Moser and R. Room (eds.), *Alcohol-Related Disabilities*, World Health Organization, Geneva, 1977, (No. 32) pp. 23–60.

KELLER, MARK and C. GURIOLI, *Statistics on Consumption of Alcohol and on Alcoholism. 1976 Edition*. Journal of Studies on Alcohol, Rutgers University, New Brunswick, NJ, 1976.

KELLER, MARK and V. EFRON, "The Rate of Alcoholism in the USA, 1954–1956," *QJSA*, 1958, 19:316–319.

KELLER, MARTIN H., "Reports of Antabuse Depression Debunked," *The Journal* (ARF), July 1976, 5(7):8.

KELLERMAN, JOSEPH L., *Alcoholism: A Guide for the Clergy*. National Council on Alcoholism, New York, 1963.

KELLERMAN, JOSEPH L., *Guide for the Family of the Alcoholic*. Al-Anon Family Group Headquarters, New York, 1965.

KELLERMAN, JOSEPH L., *Alcoholism: A Merry-Go-Round Named Denial*. Hazelden Books, Center City, MN, 1973.

KELLERMAN, JOSEPH L., "AA—A Family Affair," *Addictions*, 1974a, 21(1):19–33.

KELLERMAN, JOSEPH L., "Pastoral Care in Alcoholism," *Annals of the New York Academy of Sciences*, 1974b, 233:144–147.

KELLERMAN, JOSEPH L., *Al-Anon: A Message of Hope*. Hazelden Books, Center City, MN, 1976.

KELLERMAN, JOSEPH L., *Grief: A Basic Reaction to Alcoholism*. Hazelden Books, Center City, MN, 1977.

KELSO, DENNIS (ed.), *Descriptive Analysis of the Impact of Alcoholism and Alcohol Abuse in Alaska*. State Office of Alcoholism, Juneau, Alaska, 1977. (5 vols.)

KENDIS, JOSEPH B., "The Effect of Attitudes in the Therapy of the Alcoholic," *British Journal of Addiction*, 1967, 62:307–315.

KENNEDY, RAYMOND J.H., *Steps to Sobriety*. Joseph Wagner Publications, New York, 1966.

KILTY, KEITH N., "Attitudes Toward Alcohol and Alcoholism among Professionals and Nonprofessionals," *JSA*, 1975, 36:327–347.

KIMBALL, BONNIE-JEAN, *The Alcoholic Woman's Mad, Mad World of Denial and Mind Games*. Hazelden Books, Center City, Minn., 1978.

KINNEY, JEAN and GWEN LEATON, *Loosening the Grip*. Mosby, St. Louis, 1978.

KISSIN, B. and H. BEGLEITER (eds.), *The Biology of Alcoholism*. Plenum, New York, 1971–1977. (5 vols.)

KNOTT, DAVID H. and JAMES D. BEARD, "Acute Withdrawal from Alcohol," *Postgraduate Medicine*, 1967, 42:A-109–115.

KOBLER, J., *Ardent Spirits: The Rise and Fall of Prohibition*. Putnam, New York, 1973.

KRIMMEL, H., *Alcoholism: Challenge for Social Work Education*. Council on Social Work Education, New York, 1971.

KRYSTAL, H. and R.A. MOORE, "Who is Qualified to Treat the Alcoholic? A Discussion," *QJSA*, 1963, 24:705–720.

KURTZ, ERNEST, *Not-God: A History of Alcoholics Anonymous*. Hazelden, Center City, MN, 1979.

KURTZ, NORMAN R. and MARILYN REGIER, "Uniform Alcoholism and Intoxication Treatment Act: The Compromising Process of Social Policy Formation," *JSA*, 1975, 36:1421–1441.

LANDESMAN-DWYER, S., L.S. KELLER and A.P. STREISSGUTH, "Naturalistic Observations of Newborns: Effects of Maternal Alcohol Intake," *Alcoholism: Clinical and Experimental Research*, 1978, 2:171–177.

LARKIN, E.J., *The Treatment of Alcoholism: Theory, Practice, Evaluation*. Addiction Research Foundation, Toronto, rev. ed., 1976.

LARKINS, JOHN R., *Alcohol and the Negro: Explosive Issues*. Record Pub. Co., Zebulon, N.C., 1965.

LEACH, BARRY, "Does Alcoholics Anonymous Really Work?" in Bourne, P.G. and R. Fox (eds.), *Alcoholism: Progress in Research and Treatment.* Academic Press, New York, 1973, pp. 245–284.

LEACH, B. and J.L. NORRIS, "Factors in the Development of Alcoholics Anonymous (AA)," in Kissin, B. and H. Begleiter (eds.), *The Biology of Alcoholism*, Plenum, New York, 1971–1977. (5 vols.) Vol. 5, pp. 441–453.

LEDERMANN, S., *Alcool, alcoolisme, alcoolization; donnés scientifiques de caracterè physiologique, économique et social*, (Institut National d'Etudes Démographiques, Travaux et Documents, Cahier no. 29). Presses Universitaires, Paris, 1956.

LEE, H., *How Dry We Were: Prohibition Revisited.* Prentice-Hall, Englewood Cliffs, NJ, 1963.

LEE, JOHN PARK, "Alcoholics Anonymous as a Community Resource," *Social Work*, 1960, 5:20–26. [NCA reprint]

LEE, JOHN PARK, *The Church's Ministry to the Alcoholic.* National Council on Alcoholism, New York, 1968.

LELAND, JOY, *Firewater Myths: North American Indian Drinking and Alcohol Addiction.* Rutgers University, Center of Alcohol Studies (Monograph 11), New Brunswick, NJ, 1976.

LEMERE, FREDERICK, "What Causes Alcoholism?" *Journal of Clinical and Experimental Psychopathology*, 1956, 17:202–206.

LEMERE, FREDERICK, "Who is Qualified to Treat the Alcoholic? Comment on the Krystal-Moore Discussion," *QJSA*, 1964, 25:558–560.

LEMERE, FREDERICK et al., "Motivation in the Treatment of Alcoholism," *QJSA*, 1958, 19:428–431.

LEMERE, FREDERICK and JAMES W. SMITH, "Alcohol-Induced Sexual Impotence," *American Journal of Psychiatry*, 1973, 130:212–213.

LEMERE, FREDERICK and WALTER L. VOEGTLIN, "Heredity as an Etiological Factor in Chronic Alcoholism," *Northwest Medicine*, 1943, 42:110–114.

LEMERT, EDWIN M., "The Occurrence and Sequence of Events in the Adjustment of Families to Alcoholism," *QJSA*, 1960, 21:679–697.

LEMERT, EDWIN M., "Alcohol, Values, and Social Control," in Pittman, David J. and Charles R. Snyder (eds.), *Society, Culture and Drinking Patterns.* Wiley, New York, 1962, pp. 553–571.

LEMERT, EDWIN M., "Secular Use of Kava in Tonga," *QJSA*, 1967, 28:328–341.

LEMOINE, P., H. HARAOUSSEAU, J.-P. BORTEYRU and J.-C. MENUET, "Les enfants de parents alcooliques. Anomalies observées. A propos de 127 cas." *Ouest Médical*, 1968, 25:477–482.

LESTER, DAVID, "Self-Selection of Alcohol by Animals, Human Variation, and the Etiology of Alcoholism," *QJSA*, 1966, 27:395–438.

LEVY, JERROLD E. and STEPHEN J. KUNITZ, *Indian Drinking: Navajo Practices and Anglo-American Theories.* Wiley, New York, 1974.

LEVY, RICHARD et al., "Intravenous Fructose Treatment of Acute Alcohol Intoxication," *Archives of Internal Medicine*, 1977, 137:1175–1177.

LIEBER, CHARLES S., "Metabolism of Ethanol and Alcoholism: Racial and Acquired Factors," *Annals of Internal Medicine*, 1972, 76:326–327.

LIEBER, CHARLES S., "The Metabolism of Alcohol," *Scientific American*, 1976, 234:25–33.

LIEBER, CHARLES S. (ed.), *Metabolic Aspects of Alcoholism*. University Park Press, Baltimore, 1977.

LINCOLN COUNCIL ON ALCOHOLISM AND DRUGS, *Parishioner's Assistance Program*. Lincoln Council on Alcoholism and Drugs, Lincoln, Nebraska, 1976.

LINDBECK, VERA L., "The Woman Alcoholic: A Review of the Literature," *The International Journal of Addictions*, 1972, 7:567–580.

LINDWORSKY, JOHANNES, S.J., *The Training of the Will*. Bruce, Milwaukee, 1928.

LISANSKY, E.S., "Etiology of Alcoholism," *Journal of Consulting and Clinical Psychology*, 1968, 32:18–20.

LISANSKY, EPHRAIM T., "Alcoholism—The Avoided Diagnosis," *The Bulletin of the American College of Physicians*, 1974, 15:18–24.

LITMAN, GLORIA K., "Behavioral Modification Techniques in the Treatment of Alcoholism: A Review and Critique," in Gibbins, R.J. et al. (ed.), *Research Advances in Alcohol and Drug Problems*. Wiley, New York, 1976, vol. 3, pp. 359–399.

LITTLEJOHN ASSOCIATES, *Proposed National Standard for Alcoholism Counselors: Final Report*. Roy Littlejohn Associates, Inc., Washington, DC, 1974.

LOLLI, G., E. SERRIANI, G.M. GOLDER and P. LUZZATTO-FEGIZ, *Alcohol in Italian Culture: Food and Wine in Relation to Sobriety among Italians and Italian Americans*. Yale Center of Alcohol Studies, New Haven, CT, 1958. [Monograph No. 3]

LONG, J.R., I.E. HEWITT, and H.T. BLANE, "Alcohol Abuse in the Armed Services: A Review. I. Policies and Programs," *Military Medicine*, 1976, 141:844–850; "II. Problem Areas and Recommendations," *Military Medicine*, 1977, 142:116–128.

LOWENFELS, ALBERT B., *The Alcoholic Patient in Surgery*. William and Wilkins, Baltimore, 1971.

LUCE, BRYAN R. and STUART O. SCHWEITZER, "Smoking and Alcohol Abuse: A Comparison of Their Economic Consequences," *New England Journal of Medicine*, 1978, 298:569–571.

LUDWIG, A.A. and L. STARK, "Alcohol Craving—Subjective and Situational Aspects," *QJSA*, 1974, 35:899–905.

LUKS, ALLAN et al., *The Rights of Alcoholics and Their Families*. National Council on Alcoholism, New York, 1976.

LUM, DOMAN, "The Church and the Prevention of Alcoholism," *Journal of Religion and Health*, 1970, 9:138–161.

LUNDQUIST, FRANK, "Medical Consequences of Alcoholism," *Annals of the New York Academy of Sciences*, 1975, 252:11–20.

LURIE, NANCY O., "The World's Oldest On-Going Protest Demonstration: North American Indian Drinking Patterns," *Pacific Historical Review*, 1971, 40:311–332.

MacAndrew, Craig, *Drunken Comportment: A Social Explanation*. Aldine, Chicago, 1969.

Madden, J.S. et al. (eds.), *Alcoholism and Drug Dependence: A Multidisciplinary Approach*. Plenum, New York, 1977.

Maddox, G.L. (ed.), *The Domesticated Drug: Drinking among Collegians*. College and University Press, New Haven, CT, 1970.

Maddox, G.L. and B.C. McCall, *Drinking among Teenagers: A Sociological Interpretation of Alcohol Use by High-School Students*. Rutgers Center of Alcohol Studies, New Brunswick, NJ, 1964.

Maddox, G.L. and J.R. Williams, "Drinking Behavior in Negro Collegians: Patterns, Problems and Correlations with Social Factors," *QJSA*, 1968, 29:117–129.

Madsen, William, "The Alcoholic Agrongado," *American Anthropologist*, 1964, 66:355–361.

Madsen, William, *The American Alcoholic: The Nature-Nurture Controversy in Alcoholic Research and Therapy*. Charles C. Thomas, Springfield, IL, 1973.

Madsen, William, "AA: Birds of a Feather," in Madsen, William, *The American Alcoholic: The Nature-Nurture Controversy in Alcoholic Research and Therapy*. Charles C. Thomas, Springfield, IL, 1973, pp. 154–197.

Maguire, Patricia, *The Liberated Woman*. Hazelden Books, Center City, MN, 1977.

Mail, Patricia D. and David R. McDonald, "Native Americans and Alcohol: A Preliminary Annotated Bibliography," *Behavior Science Research*, 1977, 3:169–196.

Maisto, S.A., "The Constructs of Craving for Alcohol and Loss of Control in Drinking: Help or Hindrance to Research," *Addictive Behaviors*, 1977: 2:207–217.

Majchrowicz, E. and E.P. Noble (eds.), *Biochemistry and Pharmacology of Ethanol*. Plenum, New York, 1979.

Malfetti, James L. et al., *Instructor's Manual for DWI Mini-Course for High School Driver Education Program*. American Automobile Association, Chicago, 1976.

Malzberg, B., *The Alcoholic Psychoses*. United Publishing Service, New Haven, CT, 1960.

Mandel, W. and H.M. Ginsburg, "Youthful Alcohol Use, Abuse and Alcoholism," in Kissin, B. and H. Begleiter (eds.), *The Biology of Alcoholism*. Plenum Press, New York, 1976, vol. 4, pp. 167–204.

Mann, Marty, *Marty Mann Answers Your Questions about Drinking and Alcoholism*. Holt, Rinehart and Winston, New York, 1970.

Mann, Marty, *New Primer on Alcoholism*. Holt, Rinehart and Winston, New York, 1972.

Mann, Marty, "Attitude: Key to Successful Treatment," in Staub, George and Leona Kent (eds.), *The Para-Professional in the Treatment of Alcoholism: A New Profession*. Charles C. Thomas, Springfield, IL, 1973, pp. 3–8.

Mannello, Timothy A., "Primary Prevention Education: A Primer," *National Center for Alcohol Education Quarterly Report*, January 1976, 1–12.

MARDEN, PARKER G., *A Procedure for Estimating the Potential Clientele of Alcoholism Service Programs.* National Institute on Alcohol Abuse and Alcoholism, Rockville, MD, 1974.

MARDONES, J., "Evidence of Genetic Factors in the Appetite for Alcohol and Alcoholism," *Annals of the New York Academy of Sciences,* 1972, 197:138–142.

MARKEY, MORRIS, "Alcoholics and God," *Liberty,* September 30, 1939, 16:6–7.

MARLATT, G. ALAN and PETER E. NATHAN (eds.), *Behavioral Approaches to Alcoholism.* Rutgers Center of Alcohol Studies, New Brunswick, NJ, 1978.

MARSHALL, MAC (ed.), *Beliefs, Behaviors, and Alcoholic Beverages: A Cross-Cultural Survey.* University of Michigan Press, Ann Arbor, 1979.

MARTINI, G.A. and C. BODE (eds.), *Metabolic Changes Induced by Alcohol.* Springer-Verlag, New York, 1971.

MASSERMAN, JULES, "Experimental Neuroses," *Scientific American,* 1950, 182:38–43.

MATLINS, STUART M., *A Study of the Actual Effects of Alcoholic Beverage Control Laws.* National Institute on Alcohol Abuse and Alcoholism, Rockville, MD, 1976. PB-262-641 and -642. (2 vols.)

MAXWELL, MILTON A., "Alcoholics Anonymous: An Intepretation," in Pittman, David J. and Charles R. Snyder (eds.), *Society, Culture, and Drinking Patterns.* John Wiley and Sons, New York, 1962, pp. 577–585.

MAXWELL, RUTH, *The Booze Battle.* Praeger, New York, 1976. [Ballantine Books paperback, 1977]

McCABE, THOMAS R., *Victims No More.* Hazelden Books, Center City, MN, 1978.

McCARTHY, RAYMOND G. (ed.), *Drinking and Intoxication: Selected Readings in Social Attitudes and Controls.* The Free Press, Glencoe, IL, 1959.

McCLELLAND, DAVID C., "Managing Motivation to Expand Human Freedom," *American Psychologist,* 1978, 33:201–210.

McCLELLAND, DAVID C., et al. (eds.), *The Drinking Man.* The Free Press, New York, 1972.

McF., M., "Reality Can Be Uncomfortable," *AA Grapevine,* 1976, 33(6):53–65.

McKINSEY, JOHN P., *Handling the Alcoholic Man: A Guide for Pastors.* Tane Press, Dallas, 1974.

McLACHLAN, JOHN F.C., "Therapy Strategies, Personality Orientation and Recovery from Alcoholism," *Canadian Psychiatric Association Journal,* 1974, 19:25–30.

MEDICAL SOCIETY OF THE STATE OF NEW YORK, "Special Report," *New York State Journal of Medicine,* 1975, 75:420–423.

MEDICINE IN THE PUBLIC INTEREST, *The Effects of Alcohol Beverage Control Laws.* U.S. Government Printing Office, Washington, DC, 1979.

MELLO, N.K., "Behavioral Studies in Alcoholism," in Kissin, B. and H. Begleiter (eds.), *The Biology of Alcoholism.* Wiley, New York, 1972, vol. 2, pp., 219–291.

MELLO, N.K., "A Review of Methods to Induce Alcohol Addiction in Animals," *Pharmacology, Biochemistry and Behavior,* 1973, 1:89–101.

MELLO, N.K., "Some Issues in Research on the Biology of Alcoholism," in Filstead,

William, Jean Rossi, and Mark Keller (eds.), *Alcohol and Alcohol Problems: New Thinking and New Directions.* Ballinger, Cambridge, MA, 1976, pp. 167–191.

MELLO, N.K. and J.H. MENDELSON (eds.), *Recent Advances in Studies of Alcoholism: An Interdisciplinary Symposium, Washington, DC, June 25–27, 1970.* National Institute on Alcohol Abuse and Alcoholism, Rockville, MD, 1971.

MENDELSON, J.H. and N.K. MELLO (eds.), *Diagnosis and Treatment of Alcoholism.* McGraw-Hill, New York, 1978.

MENNINGER, KARL, *Whatever Became of Sin?* Hawthorn Books, New York, 1973.

MERTZ, CHARLES, *The Dry Decade.* Doubleday, New York, 1931.

MEYER, LEWIS, *Off the Sauce.* Macmillan, New York, 1976.

MILAM, JAMES R., *The Emergent Comprehensive Concept of Alcoholism.* Alcenas, Box 286, Kirkland, WA 98033, rev. ed., 1974.

MILES, SAMUEL A., *Learning about Alcohol: A Source Book for Teachers.* American Association for Health, Physical Education, and Recreation, National Education Association, Washington, DC, 1974.

MILGRAM, GAIL G., *Alcohol Education Materials: An Annotated Bibliography.* Rutgers Center of Alcohol Studies, New Brunswick, NJ, 1975.

[MILITARY CHAPLAIN'S REVIEW] "Alcohol Abuse," *Military Chaplain's Review,* Winter 1977. Entire Issue. [Department of the Army, PAM 165-112]

MILLER, GARY E., "On the Nature of Addiction," *Inventory,* 1970, 20(2):7–16.

MILLER, GARY E. and NEIL AGNEW, " The Ledermann Model of Alcohol Consumption," *QJSA,* 1974, 35:877–898.

MILLER, PETER M. and MARIE A. MASTRIA, *Alternatives to Alcohol Abuse: A Social Learning Model.* Research Press, Champaign, IL, 1977.

MILLER, W.R., "Alcoholism Scales and Objective Assessment Methods: A Critical Review," *Psychological Bulletin,* 1976, 83:649–674.

MILNER, G., *Drugs and Driving: A Survey of the Relationship of Adverse Drug Reactions, and Drug-Alcohol Interaction to Driving Safety.* Swetz and Zeitlinger, Basel/Sydney, 1972.

MITCHELL, JOHN N., "Alcoholism—To Heal, and Not to Punish," *117 Congressional Record* 21499, December 11, 1971. [Appendix B, NIAAA, *Alcohol and Health,* 1971]

MOORE, BETTYE ANN et al., *The Confidentiality of Alcohol and Drug Abuse Patient Records: A Self-Paced Programmed Instructional Course.* National Drug Abuse Center for Training and Resource Development, Arlington, VA, 1976.

MULFORD, H.A., "Drinking and Deviant Drinking, USA," *QJSA,* 1964, 25:634–650.

MYERS, ROBERT D. and C.L. MELCHIOR, "Alcohol Drinking: Abnormal Intake Caused by Tetrahydropapaveroline in Brain," *Science,* 1977, 196:554–556.

NATIONAL CLEARINGHOUSE FOR ALCOHOL INFORMATION, *The Whole College Catalogue about Drinking: A Guide to Alcohol Abuse Prevention.* National Clearinghouse for Alcohol Information, Rockville, MD, 1976.

NATIONAL CLEARINGHOUSE FOR MENTAL HEALTH INFORMATION, *Alcoholism Treatment and Rehabilitation: Selected Abstracts.* National Clearinghouse for Mental Health Information, Rockville, MD, 1972.

NATIONAL CLERGY COUNCIL ON ALCOHOLISM, *The Blue Book.* NCCA, Washington, DC. Annually since 1949.

NATIONAL CLERGY COUNCIL ON ALCOHOLISM, *Alcoholism: A Source Book for the Priest.* NCCA, Washington, DC, 1960.

NATIONAL COUNCIL ON ALCOHOLISM, *What Can Be Done About Alcoholism?* National Council on Alcoholism, New York, 1959.

NATIONAL COUNCIL ON ALCOHOLISM, *A Joint Labor-Management Approach to Alcoholism Recovery Programs.* National Council on Alcoholism, New York, 1976.

NATIONAL COUNCIL ON ALCOHOLISM, *The Lollipop Program: Alcohol Education for Young Children of Alcoholics.* National Council on Alcoholism, New York, 1978.

NATIONAL COUNCIL ON ALCOHOLISM and AMERICAN MEDICAL SOCIETY ON ALCOHOLISM, Committee on Definitions, "Definition of Alcoholism," *Annals of Internal Medicine,* 1976, 85:764.

NATIONAL COUNCIL ON ALCOHOLISM, Criteria Committee, "Criteria for the Diagnosis of Alcoholism," *Annals of Internal Medicine,* 1972, 77:249–258; and *The American Journal of Psychiatry,* 1972, 129:127–135.

NATIONAL PARENT-TEACHERS ASSOCIATION, *Alcohol Education Project (8 Model Programs).* National Parent-Teachers Association, Chicago, 1978.

NCALI STAFF and KRISTI BROWN, "Alcoholism Education for Physicians and Medical Students: An Overview," *Alcohol Health and Research World,* Spring 1979, 3(3):2–9.

NEGRETE, J.C., "Cultural Influences on Social Performance of Alcoholics: A Comparative Study," *QJSA,* 1973, 34:905–916.

NELLIS, MURIEL, *Final Report on Drugs, Alcohol and Womens' Health.* National Institute of Drug Abuse, Rockville, MD, 1978.

NOBLE, ERNEST P., *Biochemical Pharmacology of Alcohol.* Plenum, New York, 1977.

NOBLE, ERNEST P., *Role of Halfway Houses in the Rehabilitation of Alcoholics.* National Clearinghouse for Alcohol Information, Rockville, MD, 1977.

NORRIS, JOHN L., "Alcoholics Anonymous," in Whitney, E.D. (ed.), *World Dialogue on Alcohol and Drug Dependence.* Beacon Press, Boston, MA, 1970, pp. 155–172.

NORRIS, JOHN L., "What AA Can Offer Professional Schools and What It Cannot," *Annals of the New York Academy of Sciences,* 1971, 178:61–65.

NORRIS, JOHN L., "Alcoholic Anonymous and Other Self-Help Groups," in Tarter, R. and A Sugerman (eds.), *Alcoholism: Interdisciplinary Approaches to an Enduring Problem.* Addison-Wesley, Reading, MA, 1976, pp. 735–776.

OATES, WAYNE E., *Alcohol In and Out of the Church.* Broadman Press, Nashville, 1966.

O'BRIANT, ROBERT G. and H.L. LENNARD, *Recovery from Alcoholism: A Social Treatment Model.* Charles C. Thomas, Springfield, IL, 1973.

ODEGARD, PETER H., *Pressure Politics: The Story of the Anti-Saloon League.* Columbia University Press, New York,, 1966.

OGBORNE, ALAN, "Evaluating Halfway Houses," *Addictions,* 1976, 23:53–65.

O'Gorman, Patricia, *Defining Adolescent Alcohol Use: Implications Toward a Definition of Adolescent Alcoholism.* National Council on Alcoholism, New York, 1977.

O'Gorman, Patricia, *Aspects of Youthful Drinking.* National Council on Alcoholism, New York, 1978. [Pamphlet]

O'Gorman, Patricia and Peter Finn, *Teaching About Alcohol: Concepts, Methods, and Classroom Activities.* Allyn and Bacon, Boston, 1981.

"Older Problem Drinkers," *Alcohol Health Research World,* Spring 1975, pp. 12–17.

Olds, J., "Differentiation of Reward Systems in Brain by Self-Stimulation Technics," in Ramey, E.R. and D.S. O'Doherty (eds.), *Electrical Studies on Unanesthetized Brain.* Hoebler, New York, 1960, pp. 17–51.

O'Leary, Michael R., Damaris J. Rohsenow, and Edward J. Schau, "Defensive Style and Treatment Outcome among Men Alcoholics," *JSA,* 1977, 38:1036–1040.

Ontario Medical Association, *Diagnosis and Treatment of Alcoholism for Primary Care Physicians.* Addiction Research Foundation, Toronto, 1978.

Orford, Jim, "Alcoholism and Marriage: The Argument Against Specialism," *JSA,* 1975, 36:1537–1563.

Orford, Jim, "Impact of Alcoholism on Family and Home," in Edwards, G. and M. Grant (eds.), *Alcoholism: New Knowledge and New Responses.* University Park Press, Baltimore, 1976, pp. 234–243.

Orford, Jim, "The Future of Alcoholism: A Commentary on the Rand Report," [editorial] *Psychological Medicine,* 1978, 8:5–8.

Orford, Jim and Griffith Edwards, *Alcoholism: A Comparison of Treatment and Advice, with a Study of the Influence of Marriage.* Oxford University Press, New York, 1978.

Paine, H.S., "Attitudes and Patterns of Alcohol Use among Mexican Americans: Implications for Service Delivery," *JSA,* 1977, 38:544–553.

Paolino, Thomas J. and Barbara S. McCrady, *The Alcoholic Marriage: Alternative Perspectives.* Grune and Stratton, New York, 1977.

Partanen, J., "On the Relevance of Twin Studies," *Annals of the New York Academy of Sciences* 1972, 197:114–116.

Partanen, J., K. Bruun, and T. Markkanen, *Inheritance of Drinking Behavior.* Rutgers Center of Alcohol Studies, New Brunswick, NJ, 1966.

Partington, John T. and F. Gordon Johnson, "Personality Types among Alcoholics," *QJSA,* 1969, 30:21–34.

Pastor Paul, *The 13th American.* David C. Cook, Elgin, IL, 1973.

Pattison, E.M., "A Critique of Alcoholism Treatment Concepts, with Special Reference to Abstinence," *QJSA,* 1966, 27:49–71.

Pattison, E.M., "Differential Diagnosis of Alcoholism," *Postgraduate Medicine,* 1967, 41:A-127–132.

Pattison, E.M., "Abstinence Criteria: A Critique of Abstinence Criteria in the Treatment of Alcoholism," *International Journal of Social Psychiatry,* 1968, 14:268–276.

PATTISON, E.M., "Population Variation among Alcoholism Treatment Facilities," *International Journal of the Addictions*, 1973, 8:199–229.

PATTISON, E.M., M.B. SOBELL and L.C. SOBELL (eds.), *Emerging Concepts of Alcohol Dependence*. Springer, New York, 1977.

PEELE, STANTON, "Addiction Not a Biochemical Phenomenon," *U.S. Journal of Drug and Alcohol Dependence*, June 1977, p. 4.

PEELE, STANTON and ARCHIE BRODSKY, *Love and Addiction*. Taplinger, New York, 1975.

PENNINGTON, R.C. and M.H. KNISELY, "Experiments Aimed at Separating the Mechanical Circulatory Effects of Ethanol from Specific Chemical Effects," *Annals of the New York Academy of Sciences*, 1973, 215:356–365.

PERRINE, M.W. (ed.), *Alcohol, Drugs and Driving*. National Highway Traffic Safety Administration, Washington, DC, 1974. [Technical report DOT HS-801-096]

PFAU, FATHER RALPH, *Prodigal Shepherd*. Lippincott, Philadelphia, 1958. [Hazelden reprint]

PHILLIPS, J.B., *Your God Is Too Small*. Macmillan, New York, 1954.

PIROLA, R.C., *Drug Metabolism and Alcohol: A Survey of Alcohol-Drug Reactions — Mechanisms, Clinical Aspects, Experimental Studies*. University Park Press, Baltimore, 1978.

PITTMAN, DAVID J. and C.W. GORDON, *Revolving Door: A Study of the Chronic Police Case Inebriate*. Free Press, Glencoe, IL, 1968.

PITTMAN, DAVID J. and CHARLES R. SNYDER (eds.), *Society, Culture, and Drinking Patterns*. Wiley, New York, 1962.

PLAUT, THOMAS F.A., *Alcoholic Problems: A Report to the Nation by the Cooperative Commission on the Study of Alcoholism*. Oxford University Press, New York, 1967.

POLACSEK, E. (ed.), *Interaction of Alcohol and Other Drugs: A Bibliography*. Addiction Research Foundation, Toronto, 1972. Supplement, 1973.

POLEY, WAYNE et al., *Alcoholism: A Treatment Manual*. Gardner Press, New York, 1979.

POLICH, J.M. et al., *The Course of Alcoholism: Four Years after Treatment*. Rand Corporation, Santa Monica, 1980.

POPHAM, ROBERT E., "The Relevance of Basic Research," *Addictions*, 1968, 15:21–25.

POPHAM, ROBERT E. (ed.), *Alcohol and Alcoholism*. University of Toronto Press, Toronto, Canada, 1970.

POPHAM, ROBERT. E., WOLFGANG SCHMIDT and JAN DE LINT, "Prevention of Alcoholism: Epidemiological Studies of the Effects of Government Control Measures," *British Journal of Addiction*, 1975, 70:125–144.

POPHAM, ROBERT E., WOLFGANG SCHMIDT and JAN DE LINT, "The Effects of Legal Restraint on Drinking," in Kissin, B. and H. Begleiter (eds.), *The Biology of Alcoholism*. Plenum, New York, vol. 4, 1976, pp. 579–625.

PORTER, THOMAS L. et al., *Alcohol Abuse Training Relevant to Minority Populations*. Alcoholism Research Information Center, Arlington, VA, 1977, pp. 51–58.

PRASCH, WILLIAM J., *How to Beat the Blues.* Daughters of St. Paul, Boston, 1977.

PRICE, G.M., "A Study of the Wives of Twenty Alcoholics," *QJSA*, 1945, 5:620–627.

[QUARTERLY JOURNAL OF STUDIES ON ALCOHOL] "Studies of Drinking and Driving," *QJSA*, supplement no. 4, 1968.

RACHAL, J.V., J.R. WILLIAMS, M.L. BREHM, B. CAVANAUGH, R.P. MOORE, and W.C. ECKERMAN, *A National Study of Adolescent Drinking Behavior, Attitudes and Correlates: Final Report.* Research Triangle Institute, Center for the Study of Social Behavior, Research Triangle Park, NC, 1975.

"RACIAL DIFFERENCES IN ALCOHOL METABOLISM: FACTS AND THEIR INTEPRETATIONS—A SEMINAR," *Alcoholism: Clinical and Experimental Research*, 1978, 2:59–92.

RADA, RICHARD T., "Alcoholism and Forcible Rape," *American Journal of Psychiatry*, 1975, 132:444–446.

RANKIN, JAMES G. (ed.), *Alcohol, Drugs and Brain Damage.* Addiction Research Foundation, Toronto, 1973.

RAPOPORT, LYDIA, "Crisis Intervention as a Mode of Treatment," in Roberts, Robert W. and Robert H. Nee (eds.), *Theories of Social Casework.* University of Chicago Press, Chicago, 1970, pp. 265–311.

RATHBONE-McCUAN, ELOISE and J. BLAND, "Treatment Typology for the Elderly Alcohol Abuser," *Journal of the American Geriatrics Society*, 1975, 23:553–557.

REDDY, BETTY and ORVILLE H. McELFRESH, "Detachment and Recovery from Alcoholism," *Alcohol Health and Research World*, Spring 1978, 2:28–33.

REED, T. EDWARD, "Racial Comparisons of Alcohol Metabolism: Background, Problems, and Results," *Alcoholism: Clinical and Experimental Research*, 1978, 2:83–87.

RIMMER, J., "Psychiatric Illness in Husbands of Alcoholics," *QJSA*, 1974, 35:281–283.

RIMMER, J., T. REICH, and G. WINOKUR, "Alcoholism vs. Diagnosis and Clinical Variation among Alcoholics," *QJSA*, 1972, 33:658–666.

RIPLEY, H.S. and JOAN K. JACKSON, "Therapeutic Factors in Alcoholics Anonymous," *American Journal of Psychiatry*, 1959, 116:44–50.

RITSON, BRUCE and C. HASSAL, *Management of Alcoholism.* William and Wilkins, Baltimore, 1970.

ROACH, MARY K. and WILLIAM M. McISAAC (eds.), *Biological Aspects of Alcohol.* University of Texas Press, Austin, 1971.

ROBE, LUCY B., *Just So Its Healthy.* CompCare Publications, Minneapolis, 1977.

ROBE, LUCY B., "Rich Alcoholics: How Dollars Buy Denial," *Addictions*, 1977, 24(2):43–57.

ROBE, LUCY B., "Jewish Alcoholics Coming out of the Woodwork," *U.S. Journal of Drug and Alcohol Dependence*, March 1978.

ROBERTS, CLAY and CAROL MOONEY, *Here's Looking at You. Teacher's Manual for K-12 Alcohol Education.* Educational Service District 121, Seattle, WA, 1976.

ROBINS, L.N. and S.B. GUZE, "Drinking Practices and Problems in Urban Ghetto Populations," in Mello, N.K. and J.H. Mendelson (eds.), *Recent Advances in Studies of Alcoholism: An Interdisciplinary Symposium, Washington, DC,*

June 25–27, 1970. National Institute of Alcohol Abuse and Alcoholism, Rockville, MD, 1971, pp. 825–842.

Roe, A., "The Adult Adjustment of Children of Alcoholic Parents Raised in Foster Homes," *QJSA*, 1944, 5:378–393.

Roebuck, J.G. and R. Kessler, *The Etiology of Alcoholism*. Charles C. Thomas, Springfield, IL, 1972.

Rohan, W.P. et al., "MMPI Changes in Alcoholics during Hospitalization," *QJSA*, 1969, 30:389–401.

Roman, Paul M., "The Emphasis on Alcoholism in Employee Assistance Programming," *Labor-Management Alcoholism Journal*, 1979, 8(5):186–191.

Rosenberg, Chaim M. and Joseph Liftik, "Use of Coercion in the Outpatient Treatment of Alcoholism," *JSA*, 1976, 37:58–65.

Rossi, Jean and William J. Filstead, " 'Treating' the Treatment Issues: Some General Observations about the Treatment of Alcoholism," in Filstead, William J., Jean Rossi, and Mark Keller (eds.), *Alcohol and Alcohol Problems: New Thinking and New Directions*. Ballinger, Cambridge, MA, 1976, pp. 193–227.

Royce, James E., S.J., *Personality and Mental Health*. Bruce, Benziger and Glencoe, Beverly Hills, rev. ed. 1964.

Rubington, Earl, *Alcohol Problems and Social Control*. Charles E. Merrill, Columbus, Ohio, 1973.

Rubington, Earl, "Top and Bottom: How Police Administrators and Public Inebriates View Decriminalization," *Journal of Drug Issues*, 1975, 5:412–423.

Rudolph, Margaret, *Therapeutic Intervention: Counseling in Post-Treatment Programs*. Association of Halfway House Alcoholism Programs, St. Paul, MN, 1978 [Pamphlet]

Ruprecht, A.L., "Day-Care Facilities in the Treatment of Alcoholics," *QJSA*, 1961, 22:461–470.

Russell, Robert D., "What Shall We Teach the Young about Drinking?" Rutgers Popular Pamphlets on Alcohol Problems, no. 5, 1970.

Ryback, Ralph S., "The Continuum and Specificity of the Effects of Alcohol on Memory," *QJSA*, 1971, 32:995–1016.

S., L., "That Thirteenth Step," *A.A. Grapevine*, 1978, 34(9):13–15.

Sadoun, R., L. Giorgio, and M. Silverman, *Drinking in French Culture*. Rutgers Center of Alcohol Studies, New Brunswick, N.J., 1965. [Monograph No. 5]

Sandmaier, Marian, *Alcohol Programs for Women: Issues, Strategies and Resources*. National Clearinghouse for Alcohol Information, Rockville, Md., 1978.

Sandmaier, Marian, *The Invisible Alcoholics: Women and Alcohol Abuse in America*. McGraw-Hill, New York, 1979.

Sardesai, Vishwarath M. (ed.), *Biochemical and Clinical Aspects of Alcohol Metabolism*. Charles C. Thomas, Springfield, IL, 1969.

Sauer, Joan, *The Neglected Majority*. De Paul Rehabilitation Hospital, Milwaukee, 1976.

Sauter, A.M. et al., "Reevaluation of the Disulfiram-Alcohol Reaction in Man," *JSA*, 1977, 38:1680–1695.

SCHACTER, STANLEY, "Studies of the Interaction of Psychological and Pharmacological Determinants of Smoking," *Journal of Experimental Psychology: General*, 1977, 106(1):3–40. ["Behavior," *Time* Magazine, February 21, 1977]

SCHMIDT, W.G. and J. DE LINT, "Estimating the Prevalence of Alcoholism from Alcohol Consumption and Mortality Data," *QJSA*, 1970, 31:957–964.

SCHMIDT, W.G. and R.E. POPHAM, "Heavy Alcohol Consumption and Physical Health Problems: A Review of the Epidemiological Evidence," *Drug and Alcohol Dependence*, 1975–1976, 1:27–50.

SCHMIDT, W.G. and R.E. POPHAM, "The Single Distribution Theory of Alcohol Consumption. A Rejoinder to the Critique of Parker and Harman," *JSA*, 1978, 39:400–419.

SCHMIDT, W.G., R.G. SMART, and M.K. MOSS, *Social Class and the Treatment of Alcoholism*. University of Toronto Press, Toronto, 1968.

SCHNEIDER, KARL A., *Alcoholism and Addiction: A Study Program for Adults and Youth*. Fortress Press, Philadelphia, 1976.

SCHRAMM, CARL J., *Alcoholism and Its Treatment in Industry*. Johns Hopkins University Press, Baltimore, 1978.

SCHUCKIT, MARC A., "Sexual Disturbance in the Woman Alcoholic," *Medical Aspects of Human Sexuality*, 1971, 6:44–65.

SCHUCKIT, MARC A., "Family History and Half-Sibling Research in Alcoholism," *Annals of the New York Academy of Sciences*, 1972a, 197:121–125.

SCHUCKIT, MARC A., "The Alcoholic Woman: A Literature Review," *Psychiatry in Medicine*, 1972b, 3:37–43.

SCHUCKIT, MARC A., "Alcohol and Alcoholism: An Introduction for the Health Care Specialist," *Journal of Emergency Services*, 1976a, 8:26–34.

SCHUCKIT, MARC A., "Family History as a Predictor of Alcoholism in the U.S. Navy," *JSA*, 1976b, 37:1678–1685.

SCHUCKIT, MARC A., "Geriatric Alcoholism and Drug Abuse," *Gerontologist*, 1977, 17:168–174.

SCHUCKIT, MARC A., "Alcoholism: A Symposium with CME Credit Quiz," *Postgraduate Medicine*, 1978a, 64(6):76–158.

SCHUCKIT, MARC A., "The Identification and Management of Alcoholic and Depressive Problems," *Drug Abuse and Alcoholism Review*, 1978b, 1(4):1–8.

SCHUCKIT, MARC A., "Ethanol Ingestion: Differences in Blood Acetaldehyde Concentrations in Relatives of Alcoholics and Controls," *Science*, January 5, 1979, 203:54–55.

SCHUCKIT, MARC A., D.W. GOODWIN, and G. WINOKUR, "A Study of Alcoholism in Half-Siblings," *American Journal of Psychiatry*, 1972, 128:1132–1136.

SCHUCKIT, MARC A. and ERIC K. GUNDERSON, "Alcoholism in Navy and Marine Corps Women: A First Look," *Military Medicine*, 1975, 40:268–271.

SCHUCKIT, MARC A. and PATRICIA L. MILLER, "Alcoholism in Elderly Men: A Survey of a General Medical Ward," *Annals of the New York Academy of Sciences*, 1976, 273:558–570.

SCHUCKIT, MARC A., ELIZABETH MORRISSEY, NANCY LEWIS, and WILLIAM BUCK, "Adolescent Problem Drinkers," in Seixas, Frank A. (ed.), *Currents in Alcoholism*.

Grune and Stratton, New York, 1977, vol. 2, pp. 325–355.

SCOTT, BOB et al., "Flare-up: Stress Time in Recovery from Alcoholism" *The Osteopathic Physician*, February 1969.

SCOTT, EDWARD M., *Struggles in an Alcoholic Family*. Charles C. Thomas, Springfield, IL, 1970.

SEDLACEK, DAVID, "Evaluation of Residential Alcoholism Treatment Programs," *Alcohol Health and Research World*, Summer 1975, 24–26.

SEELEY, J.R., "The WHO Definition of Alcoholism," *QJSA*, 1959, 20:352–356.

SEIXAS, FRANK A. (ed.), "Professional Training on Alcoholism" *Annals of the New York Academy of Sciences*, 1971, p. 178.

SEIXAS, FRANK A. (ed.), "Alcoholism and the Central Nervous System," *Annals of the New York Academy of Sciences*, 1973, 215:1–389.

SEIXAS, FRANK A., "Alcohol and Its Drug Interactions," *Annals of Internal Medicine*, 1975, 83:86–92.

SEIXAS, FRANK A., "The Physician with Alcoholism," *Journal of the Medical Association of Georgia*, 1976, 65:82–83.

SEIXAS, FRANK A., "The Course of Alcoholism," in Estes, Nada J. and M. Edith Heinemann (eds.), *Alcoholism: Development, Consequences, and Interventions*. Mosby, St. Louis, 1977, pp. 59–66.

SEIXAS, FRANK A. (ed.), *Currents in Alcoholism*. Grune and Stratton, New York, 7 vols., 1977–1980.

SEIXAS, FRANK A. and others (eds.), "Work in Progress in Alcoholism," *Annals of the New York Academy of Sciences*, 1970–1976. Titles include: "Professional Training in Alcoholism," 1971, n. 178; "Nature and Nurture in Alcoholism," 1072, n. 197; "Alcoholism and the Central Nervous System," 1973, n. 215; "The Person with Alcoholism," 1974, n. 233; "Medical Consequences of Alcoholism," 1974, n. 252.

SEIXAS, JUDITH, "Children from Alcoholic Families," in Estes, Nada J. and M. Edith Heinemann (eds.), *Alcoholism: Development, Consequences and Interventions*. Mosby, St. Louis, 1977, pp. 153–161.

SEIXAS, JUDITH, *Living with a Parent Who Drinks Too Much*. Greenwillow Books, New York, 1979.

SELYE, HANS, *The Stress of Life*. McGraw-Hill, New York, 1956.

SELZER, M.L., "Normal Drinking in Recovered Alcohol Addicts: Comment on the Article by D.L. Davies," *QJSA*, 1963, 24:113–114.

SELZER, M.L., "The Michigan Alcoholism Screening Test: The Quest for a New Diagnostic Instrument," *American Journal of Psychiatry*, 1971, 127:1653–1658.

SHIPP, THOMAS J., *Helping the Alcoholic and His Family*. Prentice-Hall, New York, 1963.

SILVER, RICHARD, *Reaching Out to the Alcoholic and the Family*. Hazelden Books, Center City, MN, 1977. [Pamphlet]

SINCLAIR, ANDREW. *Prohibition: The Era of Excess*. Little, Brown, Boston, 1962.

SMALL, JACQUELYN and SIDNEY WOLF, "Beyond Abstinence," *Alcohol Health and Research World*, 1978, 2(4):32–36.

SMART, REGINALD G., "Future Time Perspectives in Alcoholics and Social Drinkers," *Journal of Abnormal Psychology*, 1968, 73:81–83.

SMART, REGINALD G., "Spontaneous Recovery in Alcoholics: A Review and Analysis of the Available Research," *Drug and Alcohol Dependence*, 1975/1976, 1:277–285.

SMART, REGINALD G., *The New Drinkers: Teenage Use and Abuse of Alcohol*. Addiction Research Foundation, Toronto, 1976.

SMART, REGINALD G., "Young Alcoholics in Treatment: Their Characteristics and Recovery Rates at Follow-Up," *Alcoholism: Clinical and Experimental Research*, 1979, 3:19–23.

SMART, REGINALD G. et al., "A Controlled Study of Lysergide in the Treatment of Alcoholism: I. The Effects on Drinking Behavior," *QJSA*, 1966, 27:469–482.

SMART, REGINALD G. et al., *Lysergic Acid Diethylamide (LSD) in the Treatment of Alcoholism*. University of Toronto Press, Toronto, 1967.

SMART, REGINALD G. and M. GOODSTADT, "Effects of Reducing the Legal Alcohol-Purchasing Age on Drinking and Drinking Problems," *JSA*, 1977, 38:1313–1323.

SMITH, DAVID W., "Fetal Alcohol Syndrome: A Tragic and Preventable Disorder," in Estes, Nada J. and M. Edith Heinemann (eds.), *Alcoholism: Development, Consequences and Interventions*. Mosby, St. Louis, 1977, pp. 144–149.

SMITH, JAMES W., "Neurological Disorders in Alcoholism," in Estes, Nada J. and M. Edith Heinemann (eds.), *Alcoholism: Development, Consequences and Interventions*. Mosby, St. Louis, 1977a, pp. 109–128.

SMITH, JAMES W., "Alcohol and Disorders of the Heart and Skeletal Muscles," in Estes, Nada J. and M. Edith Heinemann (eds.), *Alcoholism: Development, Consequences, and Interventions*. Mosby, St. Louis, 1977b, pp. 136–143.

SMITH, JAMES W., "Rehabilitation for Alcoholics," *Postgraduate Medicine*, December 1978, 64(6):143–152.

SMITH, JAMES W., "Abstinence-Oriented Alcoholism Treatment Approaches," in Ferguson, J. (ed.), *Advances in Behavioral Medicine*. Spectrum Publications, NJ, 1979.

SMITH, JAMES W. and G.A. BRINTON, "Color Vision Defects in Alcoholism" *QJSA*, 1971, 32:41–44.

SMITH, JAMES W., F. LEMERE, and R.B. DUNN, "Pentothal Interviews in the Treatment of Alcoholism," *Psychosomatics*, 1971, 12:330–331.

SMITH, JAMES W., F. LEMERE, and R.B. DUNN, "Impotence in Alcoholism," *Northwest Medicine*, 1974, 71:523–524.

SMITH, REVEREND SUSANNE, *Working the Steps*. Hazelden Books, Center City, MN, 1977.

SMITH-DiJULIO, KATHLEEN, M. EDITH HEINEMANN, and LARENE OGDEN, "Diagnosis and Care of the Alcoholic Patient During Acute Episodes," in Estes, Nada J. and M. Edith Heinemann (eds.), *Alcoholism: Development, Consequences, and Interventions*. Mosby, St. Louis, 1977, pp. 228–238.

SMITHERS, CHRISTOPHER D. FOUNDATION, *Understanding Alcoholism. Smithers Foundation, New York, 1968*.

SMITHERS, CHRISTOPHER D. FOUNDATION, *Preventing Alcoholism*. Smithers Foundation, New York, 1975.

SNYDER, CHARLES R., *Alcohol and the Jews: A Cultural Study of Drinking and Sobriety*. The Free Press and Yale Center of Alcohol Studies, New Haven, CT, 1958.

SOBELL, M. and L. SOBELL, "Alternatives to Abstinence: Time to Acknowledge Reality," *Addictions*, 1974, 21:2–29.

SOBELL, M. and L. SOBELL, *Behavioral Treatment of Alcohol Problems: Individualized Therapy and Controlled Drinking*. Plenum, New York, 1978.

SORENSEN, ANDREW A., *Alcoholic Priests: A Sociological Study*. Seabury, New York, 1976.

SORENSON, DARRELL, *Employee Assistance Program, The Art of Preserving Human Resources*. National Publishing, Omaha, NB, 1978.

SPICER, JERRY, "Assessing Client Outcome: The Role of Client Self-Selection and Motivation," *Addictions*, 1977, 5:16–17.

SPRADLEY, JAMES P., *You Owe Yourself a Drunk*. Little, Brown, Boston, 1970.

STAUB, GEORGE and LEONA KENT (eds.), *The Para-Professional in the Treatment of Alcoholism: A New Profession*. Charles C. Thomas, Springfield, IL, 1973.

STEINDLER, E.M., "Help for the Alcoholic Physician: A Seminar," *Alcoholism: Clinical and Experimental Research*, 1977, 1:129–130.

STEINER, CLAUDE M., *Games Alcoholics Play: The Analysis of Life Scripts*. Grove Press, NY, 1972.

STEINGLASS, P., "Experimenting with Family Treatment Approaches to Alcoholism, 1950–1975. A Review," *Family Process*, 1976, 15:97–123.

STEWART, DAVID, *Thirst for Freedom*. Hazelden Books, Center City, MN, 1960.

STIVERS, RICHARD, *A Hair of the Dog: Irish Drinking and American Stereotype*. Pennsylvania State University Press, University Park, 1976.

STRACHAN, J. GEORGE, *Alcoholism: Treatable Illness*. Mitchell Press, Vancouver, BC, 1968.

STRACHAN, J. GEORGE, *Practical Alcoholism Programming*. Mitchell Press, Vancouver, BC, 1971.

STRAUS, ROBERT, "Alcohol and Society," *Psychiatric Annals*, 1973, 3(10):9–103.

STREISSGUTH, A.P., "Psychologic Handicaps in Children with Fetal Alcohol Syndrome," *Annals of the New York Academy of Sciences*, 1976, 273:140–145.

STREISSGUTH, A.P., "Maternal Alcoholism and the Outcome of Pregnancy," in M. Greenblatt (ed.), *Alcohol Problems in Women and Children*. Grune and Stratton, New York, 1976, pp. 251–277.

STREISSGUTH, A.P., C.S. HERMAN, and D.W. SMITH, "Intelligence, Behavior, and Dysmorphogenesis in the Fetal Alcohol Syndrome: A Report on 20 Patients," *Journal of Pediatrics*, 1978, 92:363–367.

SUDDUTH, WILLIAM V., "The Role of Bacteria and Enterotoxemia in Physical Addiction to Alcohol," *Journal of the International Academy of Preventive Medicine*, 1977, 4(2):23–46.

TABOR, JONATHAN, "My Trials as a Nondrinking Alcoholic," *Saturday Evening Post*,

October 24, 1959, 232:36 ff. [Reprinted in *Reader's Digest*, November, 1960, 77:78–82]

TARTER, R. and A. SUGERMAN (eds.), *Alcoholism: Interdisciplinary Approaches to an Enduring Problem*. Addison-Wesley, Reading, MA, 1976.

TASK FORCE ELEVEN, *Report on Alcohol and Drug Abuse*. U.S. Government Printing Office, Washington, DC, 1976.

TAYLOR, G. AIKEN, *A Sober Faith: Religion and Alcoholics Anonymous*. Macmillan, New York, 1953.

TAYLOR, R.L., *Vessel of Wrath: The Life and Times of Carry Nation*. New American Library, New York, 1966.

TERRIS, M., "Breaking the Barriers to Prevention," *Bulletin of the New York Academy of Medicine*, 1975, 51:242–257.

TEWARI, S. and E.P. NOBLE, "Ethanol and Brain Protein Synthesis," *Brain Research*, 1971, 26:469–474.

THOMAS, SAM D. and WARREN C. LOWE, "Acute Treatment as Motivation for Rehabilitation," *Alcohol Health and Research World*, Spring 1978, 2:38–40.

THOMSEN, ROBERT, *Bill W*. Harper and Row, New York, 1975.

TIEBOUT, HARRY M., *Conversion as a Psychological Phenomenon*. National Council on Alcoholism, New York, 1944. [Pamphlet]

TIEBOUT, HARRY M. "Therapeutic Mechanisms of Alcoholics Anonymous," *American Journal of Psychiatry*, 1944, 100:468–473.

TIEBOUT, HARRY M., "The Syndrome of Alcohol Addiction," *QJSA*, 1945, 5:535–546.

TIEBOUT, HARRY M., "The Act of Surrender in the Therapeutic Process with Special Reference to Alcoholism," *QJSA*, 1949, 10:48–58. [NCA reprint]

TIEBOUT, HARRY M., "The Role of Psychiatry in the Field of Alcoholism," *QJSA*, 1951, 12:52–57. [NCA reprint]

TIEBOUT, HARRY M., "Surrender Versus Compliance in Therapy with Special Reference to Alcoholism," *QJSA*, 1953, 14:58–68. [NCA reprint]

TIEBOUT, HARRY M., "The Ego Factors in Surrender in Alcoholism," *QJSA*, 1954, 15:610–621. [NCA reprint]

TIEBOUT, HARRY M., "Direct Treatment of a Symptom," in Hoch, P.H. and J. Zubin (eds.), *Problems of Addiction and Habituation*. Grune and Stratton, New York, 1958, pp. 17–26. [NCA reprint]

TIEBOUT, HARRY M., "Alcoholics Anonymous: An Experiment of Nature," *QJSA*, 1961, 22:52–68. [NCA reprint]

TIEBOUT, HARRY M., "Intervention in Psychotherapy," *American Journal of Psychoanalysis*, 1962, 22:74–80. [NCA reprint]

TIEBOUT, HARRY M., *Alcoholism: Its Nature and Treatment*. National Council on Alcoholism, New York, n.d.

TONG, J.E. et al., "Alcohol, Visual Discrimination and Heart Rate," *QJSA*, 1974, 35:1003–1022.

TRICE, HARRISON M., "A Study of the Process of Affiliation with Alcoholics Anonymous," *QJSA*, 1957, 18:39–54.

TRICE, HARRISON M., "The Affiliation Motive and Readiness to Join Alcoholics Anonymous," *QJSA*, 1959, 20:313–320.

TRICE, HARRISON M. and PAUL M. ROMAN, "Delabeling, Relabeling, and Alcoholics Anonymous," *Social Problems*, 1969–1970, 17:538–546.

TRICE, HARRISON M. and PAUL ROMAN, *Spirits and Demons at Work: Alcohol and Other Drugs on the Job*. Publications Division, New York State School of Industrial and Labor Relations, Ithaca, NY, 2nd ed., 1979.

TUYNS, ALBERT J., "Alcohol and Cancer," *Alcohol Health and Research World*, Summer 1978, 2(4):20–31.

UDELL, GILMAN G. (ed.), *Liquor Laws*. U.S. Government Printing Office, Washington, DC, 1968.

ULLMAN, A., "The First Drinking Experience of Normal and Addictive Drinkers," *QJSA*, 1953, 14:181–191.

UNGER, ROBERT A., "The Treatment of Adolescent Alcoholism," *Social Casework*, 1978, 59:27–35.

UNITED STATES AIR FORCE, Ad Hoc Task Group on Alcohol Abuse, *Final Report*. U.S. Air Force, Washington, DC, October 13, 1976.

UNITED STATES DEPARTMENT OF HEALTH, EDUCATION and WELFARE, "Confidentiality of Alcohol and Drug Abuse Records," *Federal Register*, July 1, 1975, 40(127), Part IV:27802-27821. Title 42 of Code of Federal Registration, (42CFR) Part 2, 16 pp.

UNITED STATES DEPARTMENT OF HEALTH, EDUCATION and WELFARE, NIAAA, *Alcohol and Health*: First Special Report to the United States Congress. U.S. Government Printing Office, Washington, DC, 1971.

UNITED STATES DEPARTMENT OF HEALTH, EDUCATION and WELFARE, NIAAA, *Alcohol and Health: New Knowledge*: Second Special Report to the United States Congress. U.S. Government Printing Office, Washington, DC, 1974.

UNITED STATES DEPARTMENT OF HEALTH, EDUCATION and WELFARE, NIAAA, *Alcohol and Health*: Third Special Report to the United States Congress. U.S. Government Printing Office, Washington, DC, 1978.

UNITED STATES DEPARTMENT OF HEALTH, EDUCATION and WELFARE, NIAAA, *Alcohol and Health*: Fourth Special Report to the United States Congress. U.S. Government Printing Office, Washington, DC, 1981.

UNITED STATES DEPARTMENT OF HEALTH, EDUCATION and WELFARE, NIAAA, *Medical Profiles*. U.S. Government Printing Office, Washington, DC, 1976.

UNITED STATES DEPARTMENT OF HEALTH, EDUCATION and WELFARE, National Institute of Mental Health, *Utilization of Mental Health Facilities by Persons Diagnosed with Alcohol Disorders*. (Mental Health Statistics, B-4; DHEW Publ. No. HSM73-9114) U.S. Government Printing Office, Washington, DC, 1973.

UNITED STATES GENERAL ACCOUNTING OFFICE, Comptroller General of the United States, *Alcohol Abuse is More Prevalent in the Military than Drug Abuse*. U.S. General Accounting Office, Washington, DC, April 8, 1976. MWD 76-99.

UNITED STATES GENERAL ACCOUNTING OFFICE, *Comptroller General's Report to Special Subcommittee on Alcoholism and Narcotics, Committee on Labor and Public Welfare, United States Senate: Substantial Cost Savings from Estab-*

lishment of Alcoholism Program for Federal Civilian Employees. U.S. Government Printing Office, Washington, DC, 1970.

UNITED STATES INDIAN HEALTH SERVICE, *Alcoholism: A High Priority Health Problem*. U.S. Government Printing Office DHEW Publ. 73-12002, Washington, DC, 1972.

UNITED STATES NATIONAL COMMISSION ON MARIHUANA and DRUG ABUSE, *Drug Abuse in America: Problem in Perspective*. U.S. Government Printing Office, Washington, DC, 1973.

UNITED STATES NAVY, Navy Alcohol Safety Action Program (NASAP), *Crisis Intervention*. USN Bureau of Navy Personnel, Washington, DC, July 1976.

UNITED STATES NAVY, Navy Alcoholism Prevention Program, *The Chaplain's Role*. USN Bureau of Naval Personnel, Washington, DC, n.d.

VALLE, STEPHEN K., "Burnout: Occupational Hazard for Counselors," *Alcohol Health and Research World*, Spring 1979a, 3(3):10–14.

VALLE, STEPHEN K., *Alcoholism Counseling: Issues for an Emerging Profession*. Charles C. Thomas, Springfield, IL, 1979b.

VALLES, JORGE, *How to Live with an Alcoholic*. Essandess Special Editions, Simon and Schuster, New York, 1965.

VALLES, JORGE, *From Social Drinking to Alcoholism*. TANE Press, Dallas, Texas, 1969.

VALLIANT, GEORGE, "Alcoholism Not a Symptom of Neurotic or Psychotic Disorders," *Alcoholism and Alcohol Education*, May 1977, 11–12.

VAN THIEL, DAVID H. et al., "Alcohol-Induced Testicular Atrophy: An Experimental Model for Hypogonadism Occurring in Chronic Alcoholic Men," *Gastroenterology*, 1975, 69:326–332.

VAN THIEL, DAVID H. and ROGER LESTER, "Sex and Alcohol: A Second Peek," *New England Journal of Medicine*, 1976, 295:835–836.

VERDERY, E.A., *Pastoral Counseling and the Alcoholic*. National Council on Alcoholism, New York, 1969. [Pamphlet]

VIAMONTES, J.A., "Review of Drug Effectiveness in the Treatment of Alcoholism," *American Journal of Psychiatry*, 1972, 128:1570–1571.

VICTOR, MAURICE et al., *The Wernicke-Korsakoff Syndrome*. F.A. Davis, Philadelphia, 1972.

VON WARTBURG, P.J., "Alcohol Dehydrogenase Distribution in Tissues of Different Species," in Popham, R.E. (ed.), *Alcohol and Alcoholism*. University of Toronto Press, Toronto, 1970, pp. 13–21.

WALLACE, JOHN, "Alcoholism from the Inside Out: A Phenomenological Analysis," in Estes, Nada J. and M. Edith Heinemann (eds.), *Alcoholism: Development, Consequences and Interventions*. Mosby, St. Louis, 1977, pp. 3–14.

WALLGREN, H. and H. BARRY (eds.), *Actions of Alcohol*. American Elsevier, New York, 2 vols., 1970.

WARNER, R.H. and H.L. ROSETT, "The Effect of Drinking on Offspring: An Historical Survey of the American and British Literature," *JSA*, 1975, 36:1395–1420.

WEBB, W.R. and I.U. DEGERLI, "Ethyl Alcohol and the Cardiovascular System: Effects on Coronary Blood Flow," *Journal of the American Medical Association*, March 29, 1965, 191(13):1055–1058.

WECHSLER, H., E.H. KASEY, D. THUM, and H.W. DEMONE, "Alcohol Level and Home Accidents," *Public Health Reports*, 1969, 84:1043–1050.

WEIL, ANDREW, *The Natural Mind*. Houghton Mifflin, Boston, 1972.

WEINBERG, JON R., *Sex and Recovery*. Recovery Press, Minneapolis, 1977a. [Pamphlet]

WEINBERG, JON R., "Counseling the Person with Alcohol Problems," in Estes, Nada J. and M. Edith Heinemann (eds.), *Alcoholism: Development, Consequences and Interventions*. Mosby, St. Louis, 1977b, pp. 249–258.

WEINBERG, JON R. and R. MORSE, "Understanding Alcoholism: A Test for Use in Medical Education," *Journal of Medical Education*, 1975, 50:978–979.

WEINER, HANNAH B., "Psychosomatic Treatment for the Alcoholic," in Fox, Ruth (ed.), *Alcoholism: Behavioral Research, Therapeutic Approaches*. Springer, New York, 1967, pp. 218–233.

WEISMAN, J., *Stations of the Lost: Treatment of Skid Road Alcoholics*. Prentice-Hall, Englewood Cliffs, NJ, 1970.

WESTERMEYER, JOSEPH, "The Drunken Indian: Myths and Realities," *Psychiatric Annals*, 1974, 4(11):29–36.

WESTERMEYER, JOSEPH, *Primer on Chemical Dependency: A Clinical Guide to Alcohol and Drug Problems*. Williams and Wilkins, Baltimore, 1976.

WHALEN, THELMA, "Wives of Alcoholics: Four Types Observed in a Family Service Agency," *QJSA*, 1953, 14:632–641.

WHEALON, JOHN F., "Church's Reply to the Alcoholic Plea," *The Blue Book: Proceedings, 28th National Clergy Conference on Alcoholism*. National Clergy Council on Alcoholism, Chicago, 1976, pp. 1–7.

WHELAN, ELIZABETH, *Preventing Cancer*. W.W. Norton, New York, 1978, Chapter 5.

WHITE, W.F., "Personality and Cognitive Learning among Alcoholics with Different Intervals of Sobriety," *Psychological Reports*, 1965, 16:1125–1140.

WHITE, W.F. and P.T.L. PORTER, "Self-Concept Reports among Hospitalized Alcoholics during Early Periods of Sobriety," *Journal of Consulting Psychology*, 1966, 13:352–355.

WHITEHEAD, PAUL C., "Effects of Liberalizing Alcohol Control Measures," *Addictive Behaviors*, 1976, 1:197–202.

WHITEHEAD, PAUL C., *Alcohol and Young Drivers: Impact and Implications of Lowering the Drinking Age*. Research Bureau, Department of National Health and Welfare, Ottawa, Canada, 1977.

WILKINSON, R., *The Prevention of Drinking Problems*. Oxford University Press, New York, 1970.

WILLIAMS, RICHARD L. and GENE H. MOFFATT, *Occupational Alcoholism Programs*. Charles C. Thomas, Springfield, IL, 1975.

WILLIAMS, ROGER J., *Alcoholism: The Nutritional Approach*. University of Texas Press, Austin, 1959.

WILLIAMS, ROGER J., *Biochemical Individuality: The Basis for the Genetotrophic Concept.* University of Texas Press, Austin, 1969.

WILLOUGHBY, ALAN, *The Alcohol Troubled Person: Known and Unknown.* Nelson-Hall, Chicago, 1979.

WILSNACK, S.C., "Effects of Social Drinking on Women's Fantasy," *Journal of Personality*, 1974, 42:43–61.

WINE INSTITUTE, *Code of Advertising Standards.* The Trade Association of California Winegrowers, San Francisco, April 1978.

WINKLER, ALLAN M., "Lyman Beecher and the Temperance Crusade," *QJSA*, 1972, 33:939–957.

WINOKUR, G., T. REICH, J. RIMMER, and F.N. PITTS, "Alcoholism III. Diagnosis and Familial Psychiatric Illness in 259 Alcoholic Probands," *Arch. Gen. Psychiat.*, 1970, 23:104–111.

WOLF, IRVING and M.E. CHAFETZ, "Social Factors in the Diagnosis of Alcoholism. II. Attitudes of Physicians," *QJSA*, 1965, 26:72–79.

WRICH, JAMES T., *The Employee Assistance Program.* Hazelden Books, Center City, MN, n.d.

YOUCHA, GERALDINE, *A Dangerous Pleasure: Alcohol from the Woman's Perspective.* Hawthorn, New York, 1979.

"Young People and Alcohol: Drinking Practices, Drinking Problems, Initiatives in Prevention and Treatment," *Alcohol Health and Research World*, Summer 1975, 2–10.

ZELHART, PAUL F. and BRYCE SCHURR, "People Who Drive While Impaired: Issues in Treating the Drinking Driver," in Estes, Nada J. and M. Edith Heinemann (eds.), *Alcoholism: Development, Consequences and Interventions.* Mosby, St. Louis, 1977, pp. 204–218.

ZIMBERG, SHELDON, JOHN WALLACE, and SHEILA BLUME (eds.), *Practical Approaches to Alcoholism Psychotherapy.* Plenum, New York, 1978.

ZINBERG, N.E., "Alcoholics Anonymous and the Treatment and Prevention of Alcoholism," *Alcoholism: Clinical and Experimental Research*, 1977, 1:91–102.

ZUSKA, JOSEPH J., "Alcohol: The Violent Connection," *Newsletter of the California Society for the Treatment of Alcoholism and Other Drug Dependencies*, 1975, 2(2).

Index